THE JAPANESE POWER ELITE

The Japanese Power Elite

Albrecht Rothacher

St. Martin's Press

© Albrecht Rothacher 1993

First published in Great Britain 1993 by
THE MACMILLAN PRESS LTD
Houndmills, Basingstoke, Hampshire RG21 2XS
and London
Companies and representatives
throughout the world

A catalogue record for this book is available
from the British Library.

ISBN 0–333–58463–5 ✓

Printed in Great Britain by
Ipswich Book Co Ltd
Ipswich, Suffolk

First published in the United States of America 1993 by
Scholarly and Reference Division,
ST. MARTIN'S PRESS, INC.,
175 Fifth Avenue,
New York, N.Y. 10010

ISBN 0–312–10291–7

Library of Congress Cataloging-in-Publication Data
Rothacher, Albrecht.
The Japanese power elite / Albrecht Rothacher.
p.   cm.
Includes bibliographical references and index.
ISBN 0–312–10291–7
1. Elite (Social sciences)—Japan.   I. Title.
HN730.Z9E45   1993
305.5'2'0952—dc20   93–14245
                                        CIP

For Nora, Jan-Ulrich and Hanna

Contents

List of Figures

List of Tables

Preface

This book reflects a dual origin: it is based partly on straightforward academic research, and equally it is the product of my personal experience as a diplomat in Tokyo during 1987–91.

After a lengthy period of gestation, it was finally the publication Karel Van Wolferen's *The Enigma of Japanese Power*, and its public discussion, which motivated this study. At the time many prominent foreign and Japanese experts argued that Japan's power structure was in fact so diffused as to be 'empty' at its centre (symbolised appropriately by the Emperor's lack of power). This made Japan appear as a pre-programmed anonymous system devoid of any sense of individual or collective responsibility and moral code. It is then only a small step to dehumanise such a country and to argue that it is run by faceless, industriously conditioned creatures like ants, as was once prominently opined during 1991.

I have always strongly believed in and argued for an opposite concept: that Japan's power structure is not *substantially* different from other Western capitalist democracies. At any given time, any observer of Japan's political scene should be able to name Japan's five or six most powerful men, who are in a position to affect the country's historical course. Certainly, in most presidential or prime ministerial democracies, such as the USA, the UK, France, Germany, Spain or Canada, the name of the ultimate powerholder is known to every schoolchild. In countries enjoying traditions of cabinet government with complex and fragile coalition arrangements (Italy, Belgium, the Netherlands, Denmark, Israel and so on), the allocation of ultimate power and responsibility is more diffuse, but a limited group of key power players can clearly be identified. In my view, Japan belongs to this second group of countries.

Two approaches are possible to prove this assertion: (a) to undertake analyses of decision-making on issues of major national importance, or (b) to examine the membership and the interactions of the most senior strata of Japan's society. It is this latter approach which I have chosen to prove my case. Almost through default by other potentially competing societal actors, it is a triumvirate, led by the LDP's faction leaders, comprising the LDP's parliamentary party, the senior bureaucracy of the core ministries, and the business leaders of the *keiretsu* conglomerates, which ultimately act as the power centre of Japan's political economy.

I have tried as far as possible to make the men, their careers, perceptions, ideas and experiences explicit in my portrait of the Japanese mighty and rich. They are at the apex of a very human – from a legalistic point of view, perhaps too human – society, not the leading character-masks of a system called Japan Inc. As a staff member of the Delegation of the Commission of the European Communities, a mission with diplomatic status in Tokyo, I was able to meet and to see in action more members of the Japanese socio-political elite than is probably possible for most Japanese. As a humble note-taker I was present during formal talks and courtesy calls when, during 1988–91, visiting EC Commissioners (such as Vice President Andriessen and Commissioners Papandreou and Cardoso e Cunha) or my ambassadors in Tokyo, Andries Van Agt and Jean-Pierre Leng, called on ministers, whose ministry files I covered (that is, Agriculture, Health and Welfare, Labour, Education, and Transport). There were repeated opportunities to visit the party headquarters of LDP and JSP, which included a meeting in which President Delors and Vice President Andriessen talked with the top three LDP executives in May 1991. There were also ample opportunities to meet with individual MPs – either in their offices, at receptions or incidentally at political lectures or party congresses.

Most of my contacts with senior business leaders have been in the context of visits of Commissioners, other senior Brussels officials and Euro MPs to *Keidanren*, *Nikkeiren* and to the Japan Chamber of Commerce, or through direct working relationships with managers, notably of the Japa-nese food-processing and drinks industry. I was in regular working contact with Japanese ministries (Foreign, Agriculture, Health and Welfare, La-bour, Transport, and Finance in particular). My natural partners in terms of hierarchy and of age were deputy division chiefs (*kachohosa*) and younger division chiefs (*kacho*), most of whom I learned to respect as intelligent and resourceful partners and occasional opponents, who nearly always managed to deflect successfully the Community's *démarches* on the sixty-odd trade issues within the areas of my responsibility. Yet there was usually a meeting of minds in shared habits of workaholism and a passion for technical dossiers.

My understanding of the inner workings, the power and the constraints of the Japanese bureaucracy was helped by an internship of five months spent in Hokkaido's Prefectural Government (*docho*) in Sapporo and in MITI during the summer of 1988. I remain most grateful for these invalu-able experiences and the warm hospitality and wealth of documentation received in both these hardworking institutions. My special thanks go to Governor Takahiro Yokomichi and to my friends at Docho's International Relations Department and to MITI's Deputy Director General Kazuo Seiki, and to Directors Tsugio Ide and Harumi Takahashi in particular. At the time, my hosts at MITI and at Docho consistently encouraged me to write about my bureaucratic experiences in Japan. Somewhat belatedly, this experience is now reflected in this book.

In addition to this real-life exposure, when dealing with one's subject of inquiry, a trade officer has two valuable advantages compared with those of an academic researcher. The first is that a lot of good, well-researched information (produced both in-house and outside) and good rare raw data just cross one's desk, ready for filing and evaluation. This saves a lot of library time and rechewing others' secondary research. The second advantage is that one can test various hypotheses about Japanese decision-making on plenty of minor and not-so-minor trade issues.

As effective means for external political intervention one can alternatively try technical-level talks (hypothesis: junior officials decide); senior-level interventions (hypothesis: senior officials decide); *démarches* at ministerial level (hypothesis: ministers decide); interventions at various other ministries (hypothesis: ministries decide on a collegiate basis); at the senior competent LDP levels (hypothesis: the *zoku* chiefs decide); with the Prime Minister (hypothesis: the PM will decree a solution); try to mobilise domestic Japanese economic interests affected (hypothesis: business pressure will do the job); use press leaks (hypothesis: public pressure will sway the issue); or raise the problem at international conferences (hypothesis: Japan, fearing international isolation/condemnation, will finally give in). In fact, I have experienced 'sensitive' dossiers – the Japan Harbour Management Fund which charged extortionate fees for foreign shipping lines, or the 'Nagoya Connection' of fraudulent pork imports from Taiwan which damaged European and North American legitimate trading interests, for instance – on which most of the above options were taken and were systematically falsified. Yet in some rare instances technical talks were helpful, with Japanese middle-level officers essentially deciding on import facilitation (market access for mineral water, for instance). In others, *zoku* intervention did the trick (on import derestrictions for flower bulbs, for example). On major issues (the reform of liquor taxation during 1987–9) a sustained campaign intensively covering all levels had to be maintained for a successful compromise outcome. Overall, however, Japan was able to say 'no' forcefully at all levels of its foreign trade decision-making mechanism – and to get away with it.

The major drawback which one encounters as a player in practical trade diplomacy is an acute lack of time to pursue off-duty research. This lack of time has severely curtailed my ability to deal intensively with Japanese language sources, which I had to limit to the essentials (newspaper articles, handbooks, statistics and so on). Yet I was privileged to learn a lot from the research of our Delegation's Japanese staff and from their patient guidance in occasionally fairly enigmatic intercultural encounters with the senior hierarchy of Japan's political economy. Hajime Takahashi, Susumu Yamamoto, Kyoko Tanaka and Junko Shimizu deserve a special mention here. From my European colleagues I benefited from long discussions of all aspects of Japan's political economy.

I am also indebted to Professor Rei Shiratori's Japan Political Studies Seminar Series, at which mostly senior and middle-ranking LDP MPs would explain and discuss their policy views and their analysis of Japan's current political scene to an audience of foreign diplomats and journalists in Tokyo.

Last but not least, my thanks go to my secretaries, Ms Yoko Sugiki and Ms Belen Sainz, for their unfailingly painstaking efforts to put my piles of scribble into a readable manuscript.

It goes without saying that this book in its entirety reflects my personal views and in no sense expresses the official position of my employer, the Commission of the European Communities.

Tokyo   ALBRECHT ROTHACHER

List of Abbreviations

ANA	All-Nippon Airways
BOJ	Bank of Japan
DA	Defence Agency
DKB	Daiichi Kangyo Bank
DSP	Democratic Socialist Party
EPA	Economic Planning Agency
FEER	*Far Eastern Economic Review*
FTC	Fair Trade Commission
GOJ	Government of Japan
IBJ	Industrial Bank of Japan
IHI	Ishikawajima Harima Heavy Industries
JAL	Japan Airlines
JCP	Japan Communist Party
JETRO	Japan External Trade Office
JFTC	Japan Foreign Trade Council
JICA	Japan International Co-operation Agency
JNR	(*later* JR) Japan (National) Railways
JSP	Japan Socialist Party; *later* Japan Social-democratic Party
JT	Japan Tobacco
KAL	Korean Airlines
KDD	Kokusai Denshin Denwa (International Telegraph and Telephone)
LDP	Liberal Democratic Party
LIPC	Livestock Industry Promotion Council
MAFF	Ministry of Agriculture, Forestry and Fisheries
MCA	Management and Co-ordination Agency
MFA	Ministry of Foreign Affairs
MHI	Mitsubishi Heavy Industries
MHW	Ministry of Health and Welfare
MITI	Ministry of International Trade and Industry
MOC	Ministry of Construction
MOE	Ministry of Education
MOF	Ministry of Finance
MOL	Ministry of Labour
MOT	Ministry of Transport
MP	Member of Parliament

MPT	Ministry of Post and Telecommunication
NEC	Nippon Electric Corporation (Nippon Denki)
NHK	Nihon Hoso Kyokai (Japan Broadcasting Corporation)
NLC	New Liberal Club
NPA	National Personnel Authority
NTAA	National Tax Administration Agency
ODA	Official Development Aid
PM	Prime Minister
PMO	Prime Minister's Office
PRC	Policy Research Council (of the LDP)
SCAP	Supreme Commander for the Allied Powers
SDF	Self-Defence Forces
SII	Strategic Impediments Initiative
SME	Small and Medium Enterprises
STA	Science and Technology Agency

Japanese Expressions Used

amakudari	retired ministry officials in secondary private-sector careers ('descendants from heaven')
bucho	director (general) of department
chonaikai	neighbourhood association
Domei	private-sector trade-union federation (absorbed in *Rengo* in 1987)
Gaimusho	Ministry of Foreign Affairs
gakubatsu	clique based on same school/university attendance
gikan	technical official (specialist career)
gyoseishido	administrative guidance
hancho	section chief
hanko	personal seal/stamp
Hokudai	University of Hokkaido
ie	household/family
jiban	constituency, political stronghold
jicho	deputy director general
jikan	vice-minister
jimujikan	administrative vice-minister
jimukan	administrative official (generalist career)
jomu	managing director
juku	private 'cram' school
juyaku	senior company directors
kaban	cash ('bag')
Kabuto-cho	(district of) Tokyo Stock Exchange
kacho	head of division ('director')
kachohosa	deputy division chief
kaicho	chairman of the board
kakaricho	section chief
kanban	name recognition ('signboard')
kanbocho	director general of minister's secretariat
kanji	Chinese characters
Kansai	metropolitan area around Kyoto/Osaka/Kobe
kantei	Prime Minister's residence
Kanto	metropolitan area around Tokyo/Yokohama
Kasumigaseki	(Tokyo district of) central ministries and agencies
keibatsu	matrimonial links

Keidanren	Federation of Economic Organisations
keiretsu	business conglomerates
Keizai Doyukai	Japan Committee for Economic Development
kigyo keiretsu	vertically structured (manufacturing company centred) business conglomerate
kisha club	working organisation of journalists (accredited to a ministry, a party, an LDP faction, and so on)
koenkai	local supporters' association
Komeito	Clean Government Party (affiliate of *soka gakkei* sect)
komon	senior adviser
kuromaku	influential backstage operator ('unseen wirepuller')
kyodobatsu	clique based on shared local origin
kyokucho	director general
Kyudai	University of Kyushu
machi	small town
Minseito	Democratic Party (until 1955)
Nagatacho	(Tokyo district of) Parliament and most party headquarters
Naimusho	Ministry of the Interior (dissolved after Second World War)
nemawashi	informal approval-seeking procedure ('digging around the roots of a tree' – before transplanting)
Nikkeiren	Japan Federation of Employers' Association
nisei	second generation (of politicians)
Nissho	Japan Chamber of Commerce and Industry
nokyo	agricultural co-operative
omiai	meeting with a view to (arranged) marriage
oyabun–kobun	leader–follower
Rengo	Trade Union Federation (as from 1987)
ringi-sei	circulation of document for formal 'seen and approved' procedure
ringi-sho	document in circulation for formal approval
ryokan	Japanese-style inn
ryotei	Japanese-style high-class restaurant
sansei	third generation (of politicians)
seiyukai	Liberal Party ('Society of Political Friends')
senmu	managing director
sensei	honorific suffix ('teacher') for, amongst others, LDP Dietmen
shachokai	Presidents' Club

Shaminren	Social Democratic Federation
shi	city
shicho	city mayor
Shitamachi	Tokyo's 'Lower City'
sogo shosha	general trading company
Sohyo	Federation of (Public-Sector) Trade Unions (absorbed in *Rengo* in 1989)
Soka gakkei	Buddhist sect
soikaiya	corporate blackmailers
somukacho	director of general affairs division
somukachohosa	(most senior) deputy division director
Todai	University of Tokyo
torishimari yaku	corporate director
yakuza	gangster, crime syndicate
yubenkai	debating club of Waseda University
zaibatsu	prewar business conglomerates owned by family holdings
zaikai	business elite ('financial circles')
zaitech	financial engineering
zoku	senior policy specialists among LDP Dietmen ('tribe')

1 Society and Power in Japan

As in any other society, power and social influence are distributed unequally in contemporary Japan. As Japanese society appears more rigidly
stratified than other comparable Western societies,[1] the observation of
inequitable access to and exercise of social, political and economic power
should come as no surprise.

Three major groups – the leading representatives of the Liberal Democratic Party, the senior bureaucrats of the major ministries and the business
executives of the giant *keiretsu* companies active in the major national
economic federations – form a closely related and cohesive power elite.
This elite, which comprises some 2000 individuals altogether, with some
400 elderly men at its core, makes all the *major* political and economic
decisions affecting the course of Japan's society and economy and, increasingly, the economic lives of other people as well. The Japanese power elite
decides how most of Japan's public and corporate budgets will be spent.
It determines the focus of national research and development; the direction
and quality of development aid; Japan's environmental conditions; labour
and welfare standards; the basics of the educational system; the thrust of
export efforts; the shape of the military; the levels of taxation and of interest
rates; and, by implication, the framework of the conditions of life and work
for Japan's 123 million inhabitants.

Japan's power elite is not a cohesive monolith. Rather, it is noted for
its fractious nature: there are hostile factions within the LDP, unending
feuds between the central ministries and intense competition between the
keiretsu conglomerates. The complementarity of functions between government party, ministries and business elite also provides checks and balances:
the political elite, which is clearly in the driver's seat on issues of national
politics and pork-barrel policies, commands the loyalty and the co-operation of the public administration but remains utterly dependent on financial
contributions from the corporate sector.

The administrative elite, which has always had to accept and to live with
its political masters, remains strong on issues of low politics which require
high technical and legal expertise, and it enjoys wide discretion in using
effectively its licensing, supervisory and administrative guidance powers
vis-à-vis the private sector.

The corporate elite, which has to acquiesce to the 'guidance', tax audits
and controls emanating from the public sector, at the same time enjoys its

1

more or less voluntary pay-master status to the political establishment for which, as long as it is done effectively, it can exact rewards. The corporate elite, through its control of the four major business federations and through direct management functions, shapes the world's second largest economy and directly or indirectly affects the working lives of most of Japan's 47 million private-sector employees.

There are other influential social groups as well: organised labour, farmers' co-operatives, religious sects, professional associations, veterans groups, and so on. Yet their influence remains limited to their respective domains and they neither claim nor exercise the overall societal influence of the three component groups of the power elite.

Japan's power elite is best visualised as a multi-tiered pyramid (see Figure 1.1). A national power elite can be defined as group of men who enjoy relatively the largest command over the resources of a country and who are able to make – if not to initiate – most of the key political and economic decisions affecting the life of a nation. In this political-economy

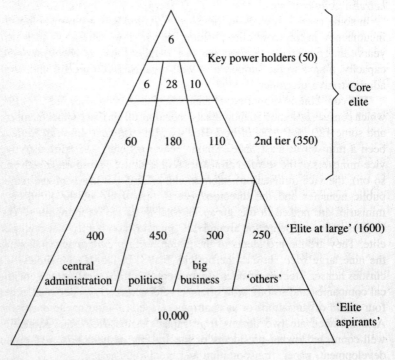

Figure 1.1 Membership of the power pyramid

definition, then, most members of the core elite are likely to be power-holders in the political estabilshment. In Japan, it is the leaders of the LDP who control the ministries, who allocate the public budget and who decide on legislation, on macro-economic and high-politics matters.

Japan's core elite consists of about 50 men, including at its top the leaders of the LDP's four major factions and one or two major power-brokers, such as Kakuei Tanaka in the 1980s and Shin Kanemaru today, who do not hold any formal office. The other members of this core group are senior faction members, elder statesmen, the Prime Minister, three or four senior cabinet ministers, the three party executives and the *zoku* chiefs controlling key ministries. On the administrative side are the President of the Bank of Japan, the administrative vice-ministers of the three key ministries (Finance, MITI and Foreign), the deputy chief cabinet secretary, the head of the National Police Agency and the director general of MOF's Budget Bureau. Representing organised big business (*zaikai*) are about ten members of the core elite: the presidents of the four main economic federations (*Keidanren, Nikkeiren*, the Japan Chamber of Commerce and *Keizai Doyukai*), and the chairmen of the presidents' councils of the six largest *keiretsu* conglomerates.

In some cases – such as in the case of administrative power-holders – incumbency in this core elite position is very short (often less than two years), and power is exercised less in a *personal* than in an *institutional* capacity, thanks to the support of a well-organised, resourceful and loyal administrative machinery.

The core elite is supported by and replenished from a second-tier elite, which consists of some 350 individuals, including all current cabinet members and some 120 LDP MPs of both Houses with sufficient seniority to have been a minister at least once. Among senior officials, the administrative vice-ministers of the sectoral ministries (Agriculture, Transport, Health and so on), the vice-ministers of international affairs, the heads of the major public agencies and the directors/general (*kyokucho*) of the three core ministries are ranked in this group. In total these are 60 individuals. The business elite accounts for around 110 men in the country's second-tier elite. They are the presidents of the major *keiretsu* enterprises (including the nine large *sogo shosha*, the big city banks, insurance companies, securities houses, steel companies, car-makers, electronics producers, chemical companies and so on), who often serve concurrently as deputies in the four *zaikai* organisations or as chairmen of sectoral industry associations. Also included are two dozens from Japan's 'super-rich': the politically well-connected owner-presidents of the leading construction, real-estate development, paper, transportation and media businesses.

The third tier of Japan's mighty could be termed the 'power elite at large'. Their political members are junior LDP Members of Parliament (240), the 47 prefectural governors, the mayors of Japan's 11 metropolises (with above one million inhabitants), leading opposition party MPs and a few leading trade unionists. There are also 400 on the administrative side: the bureau and department chiefs in the central ministries and major agencies, the ambassadors to Japan's major partner countries, the heads of large public and semi-public organisations, the vice-governors, supreme court judges, as well as the senior division heads in the central ministries. The business leaders, being part of the 'power elite at large', are some 500 chairmen or senior vice-presidents of the *keiretsu* core companies, presidents of the medium-ranking companies listed in the first section of the Tokyo Stock Exchange, and owner-presidents of medium-sized firms with political ambitions and/or connections.

Among the power elite at large there is also an influential group of 'others', not affiliated with the administration, the political system or big business, exercising power at the national policy level: the publishers, chief editors and senior opinion leaders of the main newspapers and TV stations, the presidents of major universities and economic research institutes and other publicly influential academics in the social sciences and humanities, the heads of sectoral national business associations, such as agricultural co-operatives, the Japanese Medical Association, the associations of dentists, retailers, taxi-drivers, nurses, war veterans, major Buddhist sects, and the rest. Finally, there are super-rich individuals (to the extent that they are publicly involved), but also a handful of characters of lesser repute: the infamous *kuromaku* ('unseen wirepullers') and the chiefs of major crime syndicates.

Out of a power elite consisting of some 2000 individuals, the residual pluralist category of 'others' accounts for some 250 people (or 12 per cent), who usually never have a chance to rise to the polito-economic core elite. Hence our presentation has largely (except for the gangsters) ignored this colourful element of societal pluralism. But the reader should remain aware that societal power and influence in Japan also exists outside politics, the central administration and big business – albeit to a much smaller degree.

The top of the societal pyramid finds its sociological extension through the various strata of Japan's onion-shaped social hierarchy. Yet we are not interested in further layers of social hierarchy (which do exist very evidently), but in a specific sub-elite of largely upper- or upper-middle-class 'elite aspirants', which may number some 10,000 individuals. At the political level, these are the sons of MPs, sitting MPs of the centrist opposition parties, prefectural assemblymen, town mayors and other local power figures. In the central administration these are the ambitious deputy division chiefs (*kachohosa*) and the young division heads (*kacho*) who have one or two decades to go prior to their executive promotions. This also applies to the middle/senior-middle management of the main *keiretsu* companies, and, *mutatis mutandis*, to the heirs apparent of Japan's great business fortunes. The 'aspirant elite' fulfils an important role: though still excluded from positions of genuine politico-economic power, its members anticipate their future role requirements (which most of them eventually never attain), work hard at it (putting in 70 hours a week, plus lessons in golf) and serve as a pool to replenish Japan's gerontocratic power elite at some later date.

The power elite is never static. The positions of individuals may change rapidly. The changes in institutional power and influence are slower but still of perceptible dynamism (such as the secular decline of administrative power since the bureaucratisation of the LDP's perennial rule in the 1960s and the deregulations of the 1970s, and the rise of new money made in services and real estates over old money generated in manufacturing and commodity trading). While individual climbs take most of a life-span (and often depend on sacrifices made by preceding socially ascending generations as well), falls can be rapid. Kakuei Tanaka was Japan's most powerful individual throughout most of the 1970s and 1980s, yet today neither he nor any member of his family or his few remaining followers figure anywhere among the power elite pyramid's current inhabitants. While most of the subsequent chapters focus on social climbing and elite incumbency, the phenomenon of falls from public grace and power is equally frequent. The air is thin for the 0.001 per cent of Japan's population who enjoy power elite status. Loss of this status is usually by death, incapacitation through ill health, lost elections, often involuntary retirement or because of scandal. In fact, this aspect of elite downward mobility appears to be a very popular spectator sport, and seems to hold some emotional compensation for many of those 99.99 per cent of Japan's population who can never entertain hopes of 'aspirant status' to their national elite.

More-prudent, lucky and/or resilient operators in the power elite, and who are advanced in years, have dynastic ambitions. This may reflect a wish to achieve immortality by procreation. Given the frequency and relative success of nepotist practices – notably in LDP politics, but also (though to a lesser extent) in the field of big business, especially but not exclusively in family-owned enterprises – Japan's contemporary power elite in large measure appears to be a new aristocracy in the making. Elite recruitment by merit and achievement is therefore restricted because of recruitment by right of birth. The current and future power elite will hence be short of both talent and legitimacy in a country which, by and large, is socially mobile, with achievement based on merit.

Although Japan's current semi-aristocratic power elite seems to have weathered its periodic crises of legitimacy (which arise because of its innate tendency to view the country and its resources as its self-service shop), its hold on power has always been defended successfully, though requiring occasionally public humiliations and symbolic human sacrifices. But in the long run – and it may be a very long run of some 15–20 years – the tendency of the elite towards ossification may, in a Japanese *perestroika*, overcome the power elite of the next generation and trigger a wholesome change of regime. This, however, requires not only that the current elite and its successors continue past policies and mistakes (which is easy) but that an alternative elite offers plausibly more attractive options for the country's administration, for its public policies and for running its economy. So far, such an alternative has not become public knowledge in Japan, and, almost by default, Japan's power elite is allowed to continue its generally benevolent, if somewhat self-serving and frequently corrupt, rule of Japan's political economy.

Part I
The Political Elite

2 The Liberal Democratic Party: Structure and Factions

INTRODUCTION

In 1898 the first party-based cabinet was established. Since then conservative parties have ruled Japan almost uninterruptedly, the longest break being the quasi-military dictatorship of 1940–5.

Since the merger of the Liberal Party (*Jiyuto*) with the Democratic Party (*Minshuto*) in 1955 created the Liberal Democratic Party (LDP – *Jiyuminshuto*, or *Jiminto* for short), the party has governed Japan for 'half an eternity', in the minds of contemporary Japanese. The LDP is without doubt the democratic world's most successful conservative power-holder. This success has not been free of crises: there was a prolonged structural crisis during the 1970s and a shorter-lived legitimacy crisis in the late 1980s which threatened the continuation of the LDP's rule, and this is likely to be repeated.

From 1960 until 1976 the LDP's electoral share declined with each election (see Table 2.1). During the Lower House elections of 1976 the party, receiving only 41.8 per cent of the votes, scored its lowest-ever result. In the 1960s the Socialists and other opposition parties, after successfully fighting local and prefectural elections, gained key local power bastions and government experience in the metropolises of the industrialised Pacific belt – particularly in Kanto (Tokyo, Yokohama) and Kansai (Osaka, Kyoto). At the time, the LDP appeared worn out and discredited due to an accumulation of scandals at national level (amongst which Lockheed was only the most prominent) and more numerously at local level, where LDP politicians had shown a disconcerting tendency to become lucratively involved in real-estate speculation, with benefits accruing with little risk and effort due to public projects and infrastructural investments.

Further in the late 1960s massive environmental pollution, including poisoning by mercury (Minamata), cadmium (Itai Itai) and arsenic, occurred, due to the negligence of the public authorities. These scandals were also blamed on the ruling LDP, which was alleged to have acted in collusion with ruthless big business.

9

Table 2.1   The results of the Lower House elections, 1955–90
(% of popular vote)

Election	LDP	NLC	Indep.*	DSP	Komeito	JSP	JCP	Others
1955	63.2	–	3.3	–	–	29.2	2.0	2.3
1958	57.8	–	6.0	–	–	32.9	2.6	0.7
1960	57.6	–	2.8	8.8	–	27.6	2.9	0.4
1963	54.7	–	4.8	7.4	–	29.0	4.0	0.2
1967	48.8	–	5.6	7.4	5.4	27.9	4.8	0.2
1969	47.6	–	5.3	7.7	10.9	21.4	6.8	0.2
1972	46.9	–	5.1	7.0	8.5	21.9	10.5	0.3
1976	41.8	4.2	5.7	6.3	10.9	20.7	10.4	0.1
1979	44.6	3.0	4.9	6.8	9.8	19.7	10.4	0.8
1980	47.9	3.0	3.5	6.6	9.0	19.3	9.8	0.9
1983	45.8	2.4	4.9	7.3	10.1	19.5	9.3	0.8
1986	49.4	1.8	5.8	6.4	9.4	17.2	8.8	1.0
1990	46.1	–	7.3	4.8	8.0	24.4	8.0	1.4

*   The majority are unendorsed conservative candidates who, if elected, re-join
the LDP.

With its close links with, if not outright financial dependency on, big
business, the party appeared incapable of resolving the pressing environmental problems that resulted from Japan's rapid and unconstrained economic growth during the previous two decades and of carrying out neglected
public social infrastructural investments (parks, libraries, nurseries, sewage
systems, and so on), the lack of which, due to rapid and massive urban
migration, severely taxed the quality of life in Japan's metropolitan centres.

Yet, at the end of the 1970s there were signs that change was imminent.
In 1978 Socialist-led coalitions lost the governorships in their strongholds
Okinawa and Kyoto to the LDP. In 1979 the JSP-held positions of governors of Osaka and Tokyo fell, as did the mayoralty of Yokohama. In 1980
the LDP regained 48 per cent of the popular vote and a comfortable
majority in the Lower House, which it managed to defend comfortably
during most of the 1980s.

During the 1970s and most of the 1980s it was JSP which, as the major
opposition party, appeared unable to shed its doctrinaire Marxist image and
free itself from its organisational dependency on Japan's unpopular public-
sector unions. The party then, in its turn, appeared as the candidate of
perennial decline, destined for irrelevance as an eternal opposition party
without feasible policy alternatives. The LDP, in contrast, demonstrated

that it had coped successfully with the challenges brought about by the oil crises of 1974 and 1979 and with the economic restructuring required by the yen's appreciation since that time. The government also, if belatedly, addressed some of Japan's most urgent environmental and welfare concerns.

When the Recruit scandal unfolded in 1989, it revealed wide-spread corruption and corruptibility at all levels of Japan's political establishment – including again the Prime Minister, most faction leaders, their lieutenants (plus token opposition politicians), as well as top level bureaucrats, business leaders and newspaper editors) – the JSP experienced a short-lived renaissance in fielding, in co-operation with *Rengo*, Japan's newly unified trade-union federation, a new crop of non-union, often female and youngish professionals during the Upper House elections of 1989. Most JSP and *Rengo* candidates actually won. The LDP in consequence lost its majority in the Upper House for the first time (not even purchasing some mini-parties' MPs would later restore the party's majority). The introduction of a highly unpopular sales tax and the liberalisation of beef and orange imports antagonised the LDP's rural Nokyo clientele. This coincided with the peak of Japan's speculative asset inflation of real-estate properties and share prices, and threatened to divide Japan's middle class into haves and have-nots. These cleavages in the meantime have only partially been resolved by some inevitable corrective fissures in the bubble of paper wealth. The Socialists, however, unable to agree on either tactics or substantial policies with their similarly incompetent fellow opposition parties, managed more effectively to dispel any notion of governmental respectability in only seven months. In the Lower House elections of February 1990, the vindicated LDP strode home (after showing sufficient public repentance by temporarily withdrawing most of the Recruit-tainted leadership), commencing yet another cycle in its semi-eternal rule.

As is evident in Table 2.1, there is a certain periodicity in Japan's party structure: between 1955 and 1967 a 'one-and-a-half party' system, which between 1969 and 1989 turned in a more plural system, only to re-establish the old 'one-and-a-half' pattern in 1990. This reversal was caused less by the beneficiaries' strategic brilliance than by what appeared to be a windfall profit from the minor parties' misfortune. The NLC decided in 1986 to disband, with most MPs (including party leaders Yohei Kono and Toshio Yamaguchi) returning to the LDP's fold. The DSP, with the merger of S*ohyo* and (the former) *Domei* to form *Shin-Rengo* in 1989, lost most of the organisational efficiency of its blue-collar union support. *Komeito*, the self-proclaimed 'Clean Government Party', was rocked by scandals and revelations about the business and political conduct of the *Komeito* guiding

Soka gakkai sect and their absolutist leader Daisaku Ikeda (whom Kakuei Tanaka once called 'a *sutra*-chanting Hitler'). The totalitarian JCP remains discredited by its Stalinist structures and its past policies (varying endorsements of now very unappealing Chinese, Soviet, East European and North Korean models of socialist comradeship). Some largely cyclical inter-party variations in voter preferences apart, there appears to be a persistent left-wing (socialist/communist) vs. right/centrist cleavage among Japanese voters, with the first commanding only one-third of national votes, and the second accounting for two-thirds of the votes which are given to the LDP and to the centrist nominal opposition/tacit coalition parties (DSP, *Komeito*, ex-NLC). This confirms Norman MacRae's observation that the Japanese are after all a conservative nation.[1] Perhaps this has not always been so.

Enjoying some of the lowest corporate and individual tax rates in the developed world, Japan in 40 years of conservative regimes has developed from a war-devastated semi-developed country into the world's second largest and financially most potent industrial nation. Subsequent to the first oil shock of 1974, Japan's economy was systematically restructured. Heavy industrialisation was successively reduced, energy-saving policies introduced, and the worst excesses of uninhibited and uncontrolled growth of the 1960s curbed and remedied through often strict environmental legislation and emission controls.

Still, most Japanese (some 90 per cent) continue to believe that they are part of a 'middle class'. Looking at individual educational levels, nominal incomes and savings, possession of consumer products and social values shared, this certainly appears justified. Other indicators, such as quality of housing, the lack of leisure facilities, of balanced regional development, the illiberality of its primary and secondary education, the strictness of working conditions, and the evident lack of public political participation, belie the notion of a liberal, middle-class society. The country, then, rather resembles a uniformed, almost fully functionalised work camp. 'Middle class' in this military analogy means that most respondents would see themselves as being of junior officer rank; and how content they are to be no longer privates.

Yet in the early 1970s most sociological literature on Japan commonly assumed that the inevitable advent of modernisation would liberalise Japan's society and break the mould of the LDP's dominance. At the time, a vote for the LDP correlated with rural/small town residence, basic educational levels, low political information, traditional values, female gender, old age, and an agricultural, retailing or artisanal occupation. In contrast, socialist voting was typical of people with a university education, metropolitan residence, relatively young age, high political knowledge, male gender, and an occupation in medium to large companies or public organisations. All this seemed to indicate that the JSP was the party of Japan's urban future, while the conservatives remained representatives of a rural/feudalist past whose demise was only a question of time.

With the LDP's comeback in the metropolises in the late 1970s and the spread of post-industrial forms of employment and of social identification since then – evident, for instance, in drastically declining levels of unionisation (down to 26 per cent in 1989, compared to 35 per cent in 1970) – these assumptions proved mistaken. JSP and DSP remained strong only in Japan's rust belt – the more strongly unionised cities of the Kansai, the Nagoya area and in Northern Kyushu, as well as in the industrial towns of Japan's neglected periphery. The LDP, however, apart from serving its traditional big- and small-business clientele faithfully, to most educated and informed Japanese today remains, more by default, the only perceptible option as a party of government. The socialists are welcome only as the recipients of protest votes.

THE ORIGINS

The rudimentary beginnings of Japan's political parties were in the 1880s. The founders were landowners and former samurai who looked for entrepreneurial ventures, journalism and politics as dignified outlets for their energies and leadership talents rendered obsolete by the Meiji Restauration which had stripped the latter of their feudal privileges. With the first elections to the National Diet in 1890 their loose political associations consolidated into two conservative groupings, the Progressive Party and the Liberal Party. Briefly united, both in 1898 formed the first party-based cabinet under the Meiji Constitution. However, after six months both parties split again and created the dual conservative party system which characterised Japan's political scene until 1955. It is still felt in contemporary faction struggles, which often follow the inherited fault lines both at the national and at the grassroots levels. After the First World War former central government officials began increasingly to dominate the Liberal Party (*Seiyukai*), thus setting a precedent for the postwar years. The party was considered more intellectual and urban than the Progressive Party (*Minseito*), in which local politicians and journalists were more prevalent. *Minseito* also had a rather stronger rural electoral base.

Japan's big business groups (*Zaibatsu*) generously sponsored both parties, particularly so during the time of the '*Taisho* democracy' (1912–26).

Mitsui promoted the Liberals (*Seiyukai*), with Mitsubishi supporting the Progressives (*Minseito*).

Intra-party factions were initially cliques of shared regional origin. Kyushu politicians grouped against those from Kanto. A further differential was the mutual dislike between former civil servants and the full-time politicians who had begun their careers in local politics. Family bonds and financial support handed out by the faction chiefs provided for additional faction and party coherence.

In the 1930s Liberals and Progressives differed strongly in their attitude to the military: the Liberal Party (*Seiyukai*) supported its political ascent, whereas the Progressive Party (*Minseito*) initially opposed the war policies of the Konoe Cabinet.

All Japanese parties – including the Socialists – were merged forcibly in 1940 to form the 'Imperial Rule Assistance Association', which although never resembling the totalitarian pattern of the European fascist parties, none the less served to support the Japanese war effort without reservations.

THE POSTWAR PERIOD (1945–55)

Soon after the war ended in November 1945 conservative parties were reconstituted. The new Progressive Party recruited 270 current members of parliament, predictably mostly previous *Minseito* MPs, who had earlier been active in the Imperial Rule Assistance Association. In the new/old Liberal Party founded by Ichiro Hatayama, later to become PM, 46 MPs were organised, previously *Seiyukai* members for the most part. Hatoyama received most of the cash required for the reconstruction of his party from Yoshio Kodama, whom the allied occupation authorities for some time put in jail as a suspected war criminal. Kodama through dubious channels was still able to command the caches of diamonds and platinum which he had confiscated in occupied China for the use of the naval Aviation Corps. Thanks in part to these means Hatoyama won the first postwar election in May 1946. Shortly after his victory, however, he fell victim to one of MacArthur's numerous purges. A total of 210,000 Japanese wartime officials, managers and politicians were ultimately banned by the Supreme Commander for the Allied Powers from exercising public functions on account of their alleged misbehaviour during the war. Among the newly elected MPs, 20 Liberal and 250 Progressive MPs were purged, a loss from which the Progressive Party never recovered.

Hatoyama's deputy in the Liberal Party, Shigeru Yoshida, previously Japan's ambassador in London, was now elected Japan's first postwar prime minister. According to the Hatoyama camp, Yoshida had promised to relinquish the prime minister's position immediately after Hatoyama's eventual rehabilitation. However, when Hatoyama, together with all other SCAP-afflicted wartime politicians, was depurged in 1951, Yoshida did not make any moves to implement his alleged 'promise'. Instead, he had in the meantime built up his power base in the rejuvenated Liberal Party by systematically recruiting talented politically inclined elite-track officials of the Ministry of Finance and other economic ministries into the LDP's parliamentary party.

The 'mainstream' prime ministers, Hayato Ikeda and Takeo Fukuda, had been recruited by Yoshida from MOF. Eisaku Sato he picked from MOT. Ikeda later recruited Masayoshi Ohira and Kiichi Miyazama from MOF in the 1950s. Successors to the old Yoshida school of elite bureaucrats – his faction split into the Ikeda and Sato factions in 1956–7 – today effectively only control the Miyazawa faction which passed on from Ikeda to Miyazawa via Ohira and Suzuki). The ex-bureaucrats' grip over the Sato faction was lost when Kakuei Tanaka took over in 1971. (Today this faction is jointly managed by Noburo Takeshita and Shin Kanemaru).

A third conservative party, the Co-operative Party, was founded in 1945 by Takeo Miki. It merged in 1950 with the remains of the Progressive Party. The new party was a curious amalgam of professional politicians, some of whom, such as Miki, were considered at times to be slightly on the political left with a touch of social democratic ideas. Within the Progressive Party there were also some small centrist factions, and others who criticised the US-orientated Yoshida government from a traditionalist/nationalist right-wing angle, which included at the time Yasuhiro Nakasone.

The Peace Treaty of San Francisco in 1951 brought back the prewar politicians, who were rehabilitated immediately once Japan regained her sovereignty. After the Lower House elections of 1952 they won one-third of the Progressive and the Liberal Parties' seats. As expected, an extensive power struggle soon erupted between Yoshida and Hatoyama and their followers. This also concerned issues of political substance.

Yoshida's principle orientation was one of close co-operation with the US occupation authorities while attempting to reconstruct Japan's international standing and the Japanese economy on pro-business lines with a heavy dose of government interventionism. In 1951 the US–Japan Security Agreement provided for unilateral US guarantees against external aggression and undefined US guarantees against external aggression and undefined internal security threats within Japan. A firm commitment to a close alliance with the US and a 'developmental state' interventionism aimed at forceful economic growth remained the ideological mainstay of the 'Yoshida school' after Yoshida's forcible resignation later in 1954. By then the factions of Hatoyama and of Nobusuke Kishi (who had been Minister of Commerce and Industry in Tojo's war cabinet) had left the ruling Liberal Party. They merged with the Progressive Party to form the Democratic Party which, after Yoshida's fall, managed to have Hatoyama elected as head of a minority government. Hatoyama attempted to pursue a more independent foreign policy and began to negotiate in Moscow on a Peace Treaty with the Soviet Union. After the failure of these talks – the Soviets were only willing to return two minor islands (Shikotan and the Habomais) of the 'Northern territories' of the Southern Kurile islands, off the coast of Hokkaido, which were being reclaimed by Japan – Hatoyama was overthrown by Kishi.

THE LDP'S UNIFICATION

The year 1955 marked a new era in Japan's postwar history. There had always been plans for a merger of Japan's conservative parties. They were actively supported by big business which hoped that a unified party would contribute to the political stability of Japan and would help to revise the 'impractical' reforms imposed by MacArthur's past regime. Foremost on their agenda was the anti-trust legislation which had resulted not only in the dissolution of the *zaibatsu*, the expropriation of the owner families, but also in the disaggregation of many *zaibatsu* member-companies themselves, such as the trading houses, Japan's major steel, brewing and paper companies and so on.

When Hatoyama became prime minister in November 1954, his faction began to support the merger fully. The Kishi and Fujiyama factions followed suit. Early in 1955 the previously separate right-wing and left-wing Socialists amalgamated (only to separate again in 1961). This made the JSP the strongest opposition party and for the first time an effective alternative to the quarrelling and split government parties. This prospect persuaded Yoshida and mellowed the resistance of the reformist Miki and Matsumura factions.

With Ichiro Hatoyama as the first party president, the LDP was founded in November 1955. The fault lines between the factions of the 'Yoshida' school – long considered the LDP's dominant stream – and of the previous Democratic Party as a sidestream however, are still visible today (see Figure 2.1). As a programme the party's new constitution (of 15 November 1955) declared:

The Liberal Democratic Party is a progressive, national political party, faithful to the principle of parliamentary government derived from a true democratic basis; a party which strives for elimination of the pro-communistic forces, exerts itself in the construction of a welfare state through innovations in politics and wishes to contribute to world peace.

THE FACTIONS

Until the mid-1950s the factions had been relatively loose groupings for discussion and mutual support. With the consolidation of the political scene after 1955 the factions became progressively formalised, hierarchical and disciplined. Factional secretariats were set up. Weekly meetings with regular attendance were scheduled. Mutually exclusive membership lists of LDP Diet members in hierarchial order were issued. Decision-making influence shifted perceptibly from the individual MPs to their factional leaderships, who collectively acquired a firm hold over the LDP's policies and the cabinet's agenda. Today, factions are strongly hierarchial and their members subject to strict discipline which is enforced by the faction chief and his secretary general.

The rank of a faction member is determined by several factors:

(a) the number of re-elections (determining the overall seniority and standing of an MP);
(b) the length of adherence to the faction;
(c) the quality and loyalty of services rendered to the faction;
(d) political performance, including mastery of political files, his leadership record, the MP's standing in his electoral district (which reflects also his ability to raise funds and to deliver public projects and other public services to the constituency); and finally
(e) his personality (his ability to get along well with fellow MPs, to do favours for more junior MPs without antagonising the seniors).

Once a faction member has obtained sufficient seniority, with repeated ministerial experience, and has procured sufficient funding sources of his own (which presupposes that Japanese business also views him as a sensible investment) and is thus able to secure his own sub-factional following, he will be defined as one of the LDP's potential 'new leaders' by the Japanese media and be treated as one of the lieutenants to the faction's boss, whom the latter will view with particular attention – and suspicion. Once a succession is ripe – either because the faction leader's prime ministerial aspirations have become fulfilled, or because he has been incapacitated by illness, shortage of funds or other signs of leadership incompetence – the lieutenants and their followers will start intensive manoeuvres and fight intricate battles for succession.

At such times the risk of factional schism and disintegration is high, since factional loyalty has so far for most members been exclusively to the boss, to whom they owe a great deal for their political career, for funding, for campaign support and ministerial assignments on a personal basis. A new faction chief has to work hard to reconstruct this loyalty and to receive the collaboration of fellow lieutenants. In the 1960s factions would split frequently over succession issues. Today faction members are more hesitant about risking their seniority and their funding. During most factional successions during the last two decades there were no major splits. A few discontented 'lone wolves' exist within the LDP's parliamentary party – and lost their political influence because they, as senior MPs, were unwilling to serve under a new, younger faction chief and obey his instructions.

When in 1987 Noboru Takeshita, with Shin Kanemaru's support after lengthy preparation and careful groundwork *against* the explicit will of Kakuei Tanaka (who had been incapacitated by a stroke in February 1985) assumed the helm of Tanaka's faction, only a handful of faithful elderly Tanaka loyalists rebelled. Under the leadership of Susumu Nikaido they seceded and, starved of funding and influence, disappeared into political oblivion. Today the Nikaido group comprises only four MPs.

Figure 2.1 shows the factional development successions since 1955. It indicates a relatively strong continuity and stability among the factions which originated in the previous Liberal Party of Shigeru Yoshida with its strong intake of elite bureaucrats. In contrast, the faction of 'politicians' originating in the Democratic Party demonstrate a much more varied story of schisms, regroupings and disappearance of factions. The Kono faction during the height of the Lockheed Scandal even formed its own political party which, as the 'New Liberal Club' initially had some electoral success. After the Lockheed Scandal had subsided the NLC, however, showed itself only too willing to support the LDP in parliament. It even entered into a coalition with the LDP during 1983–6, whereupon the party's fortunes faded. Having been reduced to six MPs in 1986, the NLC decided to disband and to rejoin the LDP. Yohei Kono today is a leading light in the Miyazawa faction (which he joined together with Takeo Nishioka). Toshio Yamaguchi, who had been Minister of Labour in the LDP/NLC cabinet, joined what is today the Watanabe faction, where he serves a secretary general of the faction.

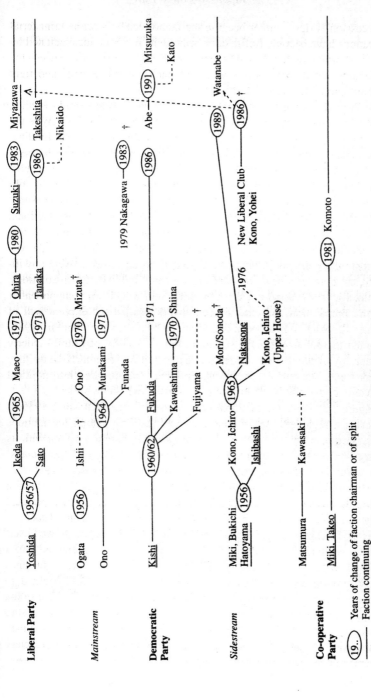

Figure 2.1 Development of the factions, 1955–91

The factions which showed the strongest growth over the years (see Table 2.2) – the Nakasone/Watanabe faction and the Kishi/Fukuda/Abe/Mitsuzuka faction – are a pretty heterogeneous lot, since many disbanded factions and independent MPs were absorbed, with relatively strong centrapetal tendencies as a result.

Sometimes it is argued that factions, with their membership of between 40 and 100, satisfy the psychological and communication needs of their members, which otherwise could not be fulfilled in the 400-strong crowd of LDP MPs in both chambers. More important for the existence and the current structure of the factions is Japan's system of multiple-seat constituencies (three, four or five seats), in which the LDP is obliged to run several candidates if it wants to retain its majority in the Lower House. These LDP candidates compete mostly against each other for the same conservatively inclined voters (as hardly any committed opposition party adherent will vote for them anyway). In this competitive situation an overall party organisation has obvious difficulties in operating as an effective election machine: the candidates need to rely on mutually independent local and national organisations for finance and support. This is where, at the national level, the faction steps in, supplying cash, endorsements, logistics, as well as career opportunities and presentable pork-barrel achievements for the local MP struggling for his political survival. Only in very rare cases (such as when their support base is clearly localised and distinct) do MPs from the same electoral district belong to the same faction. Usually, however, the antagonism between them is intense. The most prominent rivalry of this sort – which has usually turned into personal animosity as well – has been between Takeo Fukuda and Yasuhiro Nakasone in their shared Gunma 3 district. With 129 electoral districts in Japan there is also a clear limit to

Table 2.2　Factional strength (membership among MPs of Lower and Upper House)

Dec. 1982		Feb. 1988		June 1991	
Tanaka	105	Takeshita	120		106
Suzuki	87	Miyazawa	88		82
Nakasone	49		89	Watanabe	70
Fukuda	72	Abe	89	Mitsuzuka	89
Komoto	43		30		33
ex-Nakagawa	11				
		Nikaido	14		3
Unaffiliated	56		22		10

growth for the maximum expansion of a faction (to which Tanaka's 'Army Corps' during its heyday had come fairly close).

The upkeep of a faction is a costly enterprise. A faction chief is expected to contribute the lion's share to the costs of his MPs' election campaigns and to the maintenance of their secretariat and constituency support organisation (*koenkai*). These every-pressing financial needs (some faction chiefs are deeply in debt) are the root cause of the 'structural corruption' in Japanese politics. While the mainstream factions (Miyazawa, Takeshita, Mitsuzuka) are regularly payrolled without much ado by *Keidanren* and the established business associations (banks, security houses, electricity companies, car industry, steel industry and so on) and some, in addition, can rely on close links with the construction industry (the Takeshita faction, through Shin Kanemaru, like Tanaka before him), the less-well-connected sidestream factions (Nakasone/Watanabe and Komoto and as demonstrated by Ichiro Nakagawa during his failed attempt to become party president in 1982), have to struggle hard and often feel forced to resort to imaginative new ways of securing finance (such as accepting donations and bargain-priced Recruit Cosmos shares from Mr Ezoe during 1984–6).

Changes in the strength of a faction are determined by

(a) the number of faction members returned in an election (which may in turn depend on the faction's campaign budget);
(b) the successful election of newcomers endorsed by the party and financed by the faction;
(c) the recruitment of independent MPs;
(d) the poaching of MPs from other factions.

The larger a faction is and the more coherently it acts (which is often difficult in rapid-growth factions composed of semi-independent and recently recruited 'barons'), the stronger is its standing with big business (and hence its funding capacity) and its ability to place followers in ministerial and other coveted slots. Large factions can claim three to four cabinet seats, plus one of the four executive party posts. Next to the LDP presidency, these are: the party's secretary general, the chairman of the General Council, and the chairman of the Policy Research Council (PRC). Medium-sized factions, such as Komoto's, can command at most two cabinet positions. A small faction such as Mr Nikaido's group will get one at most or none.

Faction leaders propose name lists of their men for the previously negotiated cabinet positions to the prime minister, who has often little choice or veto power (depending on his party standing of course; with PM Kaifu, for instance, the latter was relatively small) but must accept and accommodate the faction chiefs' preferences. The same modus applies to the occupation of senior party and parliamentary posts, as well as to the appointments for (relatively unimportant) positions of parliamentary vice-minister for middle-ranking MPs.

A ministerial assignment, then, may reflect a politician's interests and expertise, but it does not need to be so. Most attractive are the three classical ministries, MOF, MITI and Foreign Affairs (MFA), and the position of Chief Cabinet Secretary, whose successful (that is problem-free) management is seen as a necessary qualification for those with prime ministerial ambitions. More down-to-earth attractions lie in the ministries with large discretionary budgets and decision-making: Construction, Transportation, Agriculture and Defence. They offer an MP the possibility to prove his usefulness to his faction and open up new avenues for his own financially secured future.

The factional scene is in a constant state of flux. As factional ties are of personal/financial nature they are inherently unstable. Since factions form the core of the LDP's power structure, which appears as the most significant single element in Japan's power equation, the latter is strongly affected by the twists and turns of factional politics. Media interest is consequently intense for the latest news and gossip emanating from the factions. Rumours about the ill-health of a faction leader can trigger violent presuccession manoeuvres among his lieutenants. This will lead to intense positioning moves by fellow faction leaders, as old alliances risk being negated. Ultimately the prime minister and his cabinet may appear in jeopardy.

The influence of a faction leader declines when his revenues, which reflect his estimated power, begin to shrink. Reduced revenues have a cumulative effect: financial means are now missing to maintain his followers who have to keep up their expensive secretariat and *koenkai* operations. As they in turn have to augment their own sources of finance they will become targets of recruitment efforts by competing factions (provided that the constituency situation and earlier friendly relations allow for a switch). Such power erosions can be triggered by a variety of mishaps, such as sickness or scandals affecting the chief, fights between lieutenants, tactical misjudgements or a lost factional war: the faction will be bypassed when strategic ministerial posts are distributed and forfeits part of its finance and ability to deliver. Reduced material resources may result in the faction losing a string of important seats and MPs in a Lower House election. Its lieutenants may become insubordinate and begin preparations to defect or to overthrow the stricken chief. The decline is often upstoppable. The faction chief will publicly be labelled a man of the past in whose friendship it is obviously no longer worthwhile to invest. He will be dumped unceremoniously, as was Kakuei Tanaka in 1987, who only two years earlier had been the most powerful man of Japan; or be driven into suicide, like Nakagawa after losing the LDP presidential election in December 1982.

Once factional wars have been settled, and when sufficient annoyance has been caused to the general public and the media (whose editorial writers untiringly denounce these 'feudalist' and corrupting elements in Japanese politics), the faction leaders usually solemnly pledge to disband their factions, and ceremonially close their factional headquarters. In new PR material the LDP will be presented as a modern, faction-free party. Inevitably, however, the factions re-emerge with a new name ('Political Studies Group' and so on) but under old management.

While factions have no clear programme (although the Nakasone/Watanabe and the Abe/Mitsuzuka factions host a few prominent right-wingers and hawks, and the Komoto faction a dwindling band of left-wingers and doves), there were in the past a few suprafactional groupings with programmatic overtones. There was the now-defunct 'progressive' Asian African Study Group led by Aiichiro Fujiyama, Kenzo Matsumura, Toshio Kimura and Tokuma Utsunomiya (who, as the only survivor, is today an independent Upper House MP). The AA Group in the 1960s asked for diplomatic relations and a peace treaty with Beijing. It wanted Japan's foreign policy shift towards the non-aligned Third World and struggled for progressive domestic policy issues.

Equally defunct today is the right-wing *Seirenkai*, which advocated the revision of Japan's constitution and stronger rearmament policies. Leading members were Masayuki Fujio (whom Nakasone later fired as Education Minister), Ichiro Nakagawa, Michio Watanabe (successor to Nakasone's faction leadership) and Eiichi Nakao (later MITI minister). There are also occasional suprafactional young Turks' rebellions – most recently against PM's Takeshita, Uno and the implicated factional chieftains in the wake of the Recruit scandal in summer 1989. For lack of clear leadership and financial backing, these revolts usually die down as mere media events of no substantial consequence.

In each Diet there are a handful of 'lone wolves' who belong to neither faction. They are either remnants of extinct factions, or MPs who have been expelled (or resigned in repentance) for disciplinary reasons, or are former top politicians who lost in a succession struggle and no longer wish to serve under a victorious rival. Often they have their own independent financial means or their prominence guarantees a safe seat without too many worries and expenses for re-election.

In the Japanese political scene the factions operate as the most effective system of checks and balances against the accumulation of power by any individual politician. Once a prime minister (like Tanaka or Nakasone) or a back-stage operator (like Kanemaru or Gotoda) appears too powerful, other faction leaders will align against him and make sure that an equilibrium of sorts (assuring their own political survival) is re-established. The LDP's rule is hence far from being the exercise of power by monolithic one-party rule (a mistaken impression which the totalitarian conduct of the party congresses and the conformist party literature attempts to convey), but is, rather, a coalition system of intensely competing factions. The system is costly and noisy, but it is better than its alternative: the authoritarian dictate of what is a fairly reactionary party. Factional politics and warfare also make for an entertaining spectator sport for the *cognoscenti*, both foreign and domestic.

PARTY INSTITUTIONS AND DECISION-MAKING

The LDP's most important nominal (and sometimes real) figure is the party president, who concurrently, since the beginnings of the party, also serves as the prime minister of Japan. As prime minister he has the right to select his cabinet. As party president he can choose the LDP's three top executive officers. Between 1955 and 1977 the party president had been elected by the LDP's parliamentary party and by one or two delegates from each prefectural chapter. As some of the prefectural delegates became inordinately rich in the process, in 1977 the rules were democratised in order to allow a ballot of all LDP members (which in the heat of the battle included names taken from telephone directories and members' pets), with the parliamentary party then deciding among the three front-runners. After it transpired that the rules of 1977 were being utilised most effectively by Tanaka's formidable political machine, they were modified again in 1981: selection is by the LDP's Diet members only. Each candidate must document the support of at least 50 MPs. Only in the (very unlikely) event of more than three admitted candidates would a membership ballot be held.

With his command over the cabinet and the party, the prime minister, in theory at least, should be the most powerful individual in Japan. However, since his status essentially depends on the cohesion of his precarious factional alliance, he will usually forgo his personal political convictions (should he have any), in the interests of factional peace and power maintenance. Important decisions, even at this senior level, will only be reached as cumbersome and time-consuming negotiations, with the results of which the major factions, interests groups and ministries concerned should then be able to agree.

The LDP's Secretary General is the party's second most important man. He is in charge of the party's organisation, election management, Diet business and fund-raising. He is the party's spokesman and appoints key party personnel. Being responsible for the party's local and national election strategies, he is in charge of candidate selection. For Lower House elections this involves painful choices and the right feel for what is possible in each electoral district: too many endorsed candidates will dilute the LDP's vote and risk the seats of incumbents (who are strongly opposed to new candidates). Too few endorsements mean wasted votes and the LDP's parliamentary majority put at risk. Sometimes the job means dissuading an incompetent or superannuated incumbent from seeking re-election (witness Ichiro Ozawa's work on Governor Suzuki in the Tokyo governatorial election of 1991). Picking the wrong candidates, upsetting factional balances or – worst of all – losing elections will be blamed on the Secretary General. Still, a job well done will boost his party standing enormously. That he is in charge of the party's treasury (with few questions asked) helps to smooth his task.

The LDP's General Council is the party's formal policy decision body acting as a proxy for a full party convention. Its 30 members (all of them senior Diet members) meet twice a week to approve all important cabinet and Diet projects and other political business. Its chairman is one of the party's top three executives.

Prior to being submitted to the General Council, draft bills and other policy decisions are discussed by the party's Policy Research Council (PRC) after they had been approved by the PRC's appropriate specialist divisions. There are 17 permanent divisions (corresponding to each ministry and the major agencies) and some 75 more specific and often *ad hoc* research commissions and special committees (covering subjects ranging from public pensions to problems of the silk and silk yarn industries). In the PRC's permanent divisions the policy specialists (*zoku*) of the LDP's parliamentary party are active in monitoring 'their' ministry's or agency's policies and draft legislation. Former (and future) ministers attend the deliberations and request the presence of the Ministry's vice-minister, and order director generals and division chiefs to give explanations and to receive instructions. On issues of political importance, decisions may actually originate in the PRC division. Its members also receive pertinent input from their interest groups, and will, wherever possible, wish to appear receptive and helpful. The ministry is then given orders to work out the details and the legal fine print. (A good vice-minister may of course try to steer the politicians' decisions gently.) On more technical issues, the ministry may originate the project and, after legal clearance by the Cabinet Legislation Bureau, may submit the draft for routine acceptance by the PRC. The PRC division chief then will undertake to ensure the passage of the draft bill through the diet's proceedings (see Figure 2.2). Once a PRC division has approved a policy decision, it will be put before the PRC's Policy Deliberation Commission – which is headed by the PRC chairman – and to the General Council, usually as a matter for routine approval.

LDP decision-making does not always need to take place in the austere surroundings of the LDP headquarters in Nagatacho. The most effective consultation and compromise-seeking often happens in the tea-houses of Akasaka or on exclusive golf courses in Karuizawa or Hakone.

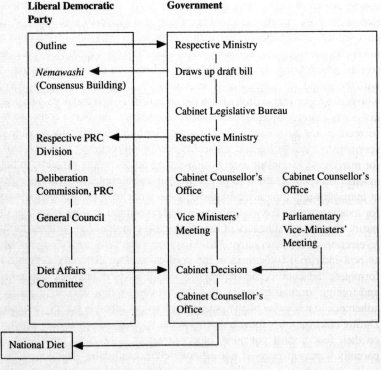

Figure 2.2   The flow of draft legislation[2]

THE PARTY BASIS

Paradoxically, the LDP, although declaring large membership figures (1988:5.8 million members), is a party without real activist members (as normally understood in the rest of the world). Even the local and prefectural party organisation often has a mere formal existence. What really exists are networks of personal ties (*koenkai*) between Diet MPs and their followers among local notables, businessmen, power-brokers and politicians. All conservative politicians maintain their own political grassroots support groups covering individual households, clans, clubs, agricultural co-operatives, companies, guilds, business associations, neighbourhood groups (*chonaikai*), temples, and entire neigbourhoods and hamlets (*jiban*). This expensive support organisation is bankrolled by the MP (who may control his *koenkai* in part directly or indirectly through intermediary local politicians), for whom these people will vote at elections, and who, if need be (as between 1977 and 1981) will mobilise these followers to vote for his faction chief (in return for a sizeable contribution covering expenses incurred at each level) or to collect signatures for world peace and against rice imports. Normally the *koenkai* (which also maintain youth and women's sections) busy themselves with non-political activities (excursions to hot springs or to Tokyo, and with parties, sports events, local festivities and so on), which bring welcome relief to the boredom of rural life in Japan, with the added advantage that all expenses are paid for by the great *sensei* who raises money so skilfully from the fat cats in Tokyo and does not forget his needy country cousins back home. In addition, the MP's constituency secretaries are busy winning and keeping loyalties by offering a range of services: to mediate job and university admission requests; to match-make for marriages; to consult local businesses on public works projects; to help in other business matters; to promote local associations; to distribute gifts at marriages and funerals; and above all to work with the MP as lobbyists for local causes in Tokyo. Only dedicated constituency work – and not the purity and rhetorical beauty of his ideological convictions – will secure the re-election of a conservative MP. His voters are fully aware of this and, as post-industrial consumers in the political service economy, are able to formulate the appropriate requests. Some ill-advised Japanese academics and foreign journalists have called the *koenkai* system 'feudalist'. In fact, adherence to a *koenkai* or any political activity in Japan is purely voluntary. During election time, some households put up only one candidate's picture on their fence; most put none, others however – the most intelligent apparently – put up many if not *all* competing candidates' posters on their walls, ranging from Communists to assorted Liberal Democrats. Not that it looks pretty, but it may be useful to hedge one's bets. Besides, some LDP campaigners have an ingrained habit of leaving behind a money-filled envelope during their housecalls. This cash will help to buy some *sake* to toast the *sensei*'s good health, even should he lose his election – and his secretaries' their jobs.

The average Japanese, like any modern man, enjoys a plurality of roles which, if he wishes, he can skilfully play so as to retain a free choice (ultimately, of course, the vote is completely secret). As a post office worker, Mr Tanaka is member of the postal workers union, whose prefectural chapter has endorsed the Socialist candidate. As a part-time farmer he is a member of the local agricultural co-op which has endorsed the LDP candidate of the X faction. At the same time he is the treasurer of the municipal orchid-growers association, to which the LDP candidate of Y faction is a regular, if somewhat lacklustre contributor. His wife, a fervent reborn Buddhist, professes noisily that only the Komeito candidate can rescue Japan from political corruption. With these cross-pressures in place and election day approaching, Tanaka-*san* is pretty relaxed: good weather means rod-fishing, bad weather means playing at the *pachinko* parlour. In any case, most of the helpful *sensei* will be re-elected anyway. Of course, Mr Tanaka will not mind becoming an LDP member, provided that his membership fees are paid by someone else. There are no qualifications for membership, other than Japanese nationality. On the other hand, as a party member in a party dominated in its decision-making by the party president, the faction chiefs and the MPs, there are no formal participatory rights for the ordinary member either.

Haruhiro Fukui estimated that there were only 50,000 true card-carrying fee-paying LDP members among the 120 million Japanese.[3] Most of them are local or prefectural politicians. In fact, in 1986 the LDP claimed that 44 of the 47 governors, 595 of the 652 mayors, 1907 of the 2899 prefectural assemblymen, 14,056 of the 21,151 city councillors and 41,363 of the 45,466 town and village councillors had been elected with LDP endorsement. Most are content with their roles as local and regional politicians. They have shown little inclination to participate on matters of substance in national politics. This task is left to the MPs and to their faction chiefs.

Let us look at the LDP's party conventions, which, according to the statutes, are the 'supreme organ of the party'. This supreme organ of the party meets twice annually in the crowded and decrepit Hibiya Hall in Central Tokyo. The convention begin at 10.00 a.m. prompt and finishes at 12.30 equally promptly to allow for what is the most important part for the prefectural delegate: attendance at the reception in the prime ministerial residence in order to be photographed in group pictures together with the

PM, other LDP VIPs, or alone on the august stairs which are used for cabinet pictures.

For the rest, during the convention all LDP chieftains will be assembled on stage. The prime minister, the secretary general and other dignitaries will read out prepared speeches (distributed in advance, so that foreign diplomatic participants can check their *kanji* knowledge). The sponsors of the party congress are read out, and some of the party faithful (essentially when they have just lost an election) are honoured. Hymns are sung, followed by standing ovations. There is no trace of any substantial discussion. Although with fairly totalitarian features, the event resembles a somewhat predictable and only mildly interesting stage play. It reminds one of a tame Japanese stockholders' meeting rather than of a Nuremberg rally. In the 1960s, when personnel matters where discussed, passions could run so high as to result in physical violence between rival factions. Today, old age and careful stage management prevent such entertainments.

For a local politician, factional ties mean essentially to have a link to his Dietman, and to the Dietman's faction in Tokyo – including the faction's ministers, policy experts (*zoku*) and budget-procuring specialists. His primary hope is to get public projects allocated to his corporate sponsors and to his district (thus demonstrating his usefulness over that of his competitors): bridges, roads, school buildings, railways stations, dams, ports and so on, as well as mobilising public subsidies for a range of other worthy causes.

Living on the periphery in Japan, people feel excluded from actual decision-making. Regional politicians also feel their constituents' keen sense of having been left out by the economic and cultural miracles performed in the metropolises. The LDP's 'machine politics' offers a welcome opportunity for them to redress the record. The *koenkai* is seen as an instrument to remedy the unfairness of excessive political and economic centralism by insisting on a reverse flow of selective, often fairly symbolic, privileges to the regions. Whatever its shortfalls, this appears for many living on the Japanese periphery as the only effective mechanism for power participation and as partial redress for the unequal regional distribution of income and wealth in Japan.

FINANCES

The party's financial needs are easily calculated. With some 320 candidates per Lower House election, campaign costs are around 400 million yen on average per candidate. This totals some 130 billion yen of fund-raising needs per election year. Upper House elections have fewer candidates, who in turn run cheaper campaigns (as they usually do not maintain extensive *koenkai* organisations, and in the single prefectural election districts will not compete with fellow LDP candidates). The funds have to raised by the party, by the factions and by the candidate himself. Public monies (a free railway pass, two secretaries paid from public funds, an office expense allowance, and (limited) free advertising space and free TV broadcasts on NHK (in a standard set format, of equal length accorded to all candidates, including the loony fringe) are only a drop in the ocean.

As membership fees and the sale of LDP T-shirts and LDP ash-trays are no real source of income, the main party funding comes from industry and business associations. This task is largely organised by *Keidanren*, the federation of big business, which through a subsidiary organisation (*Kokumin Seiji Kyokai*), assesses contributions from each member business association and each individual enterprise according to pre-fixed ratios. The total amount to be collected is negotiated between the head of *Keidanren* and the LDP's secretary general, who sometimes (like Mr Ozawa in early 1990) had to threaten corporate tax hikes if *Keidanren* did not comply with the LDP's ever-increasing funding requests. During LDP factional wars and declining party fortunes industry is often hesitant to obey, and urges more prudent and economical ways of doing politics. Table 2.3 shows the amounts raised by the *Kokumin Kyokai* for the benefit of the LDP in 1987 (a non-election year). As an additional funding request, to avert defeat in the Lower House elections of February 1990, LDP Secretary General Ozawa requested a supplementary contribution of ¥15 billion, which he raised *directly* from the various industry associations. The car industry he advised successfully: 'Between the shouldering of a tax burden of several hundred billion yen through the revival of the commodity tax and the contribution of 5 billion yen to the LDP, I want you to consider carefully which is the wiser policy.'[4] He also collected ¥4 billion from the electronics industry, and ¥3 billion from the banking and construction associations.

Table 2.3   *Keidanren's political fundraising, 1987 (million yen)*

Banks	1432
Construction/real estate	428
Car industry	403
Electronics/telecommunications	385
Steel and other metal	362
Trading houses	347
Securities	303

In total he raised ¥14 billion directly, on top of the ¥6 billion collected by *Keidanren* conventionally. The money was spent as follows: ¥6 billion were given to endorsed candidates (that is, ¥20 million per person); ¥5 billion were spent for the party's campaign activities; ¥2 billion were handed to the factions, and the rest to candidates in severely contested districts at Mr Ozawa's discretion. Corporate Japan considers these contributions as a sort of special taxation, which it pays without much enthusiasm but with a sense of inevitability, in order to secure political goodwill and influence in Nagatacho. Some of the smaller centrist parties (the DSP notably) also receive business contributions, which are, however, more of a token nature.

In addition to the central party organisation, represented by the secretary general, the factions and their leaders also request financing, which after all forms the lifeline of their factional cohesion. While some companies maintain close ties to a particular faction (be it due to personal friendship, family ties or special business interests shared between the faction leader and a corporate chieftain), most of big business will spread its cash fairly evenly among the factions – with some preference for the mainstream in power – with some preference for the mainstream in power – in order to avoid antagonising any LDP bigwig.

For fundraising, mutual friendship and consultation with big business, all faction chiefs maintain a series of exclusive associations. Past examples included: New Study Association for Political Economy (Fukuda), Study Association for Fiscal Problems (Ohira), Research Federation for Financial Questions (Tanaka), Research Circle for the Socio-economy (Tanaka), Policy Consultancy Society (Miki), Study Association for Modernity Questions (Miki), Study Circle for Modern Politics (Nakasone), in which the invited corporate executives and owners can engage in earnest study and research for an appropriate fee, which increases with the degree of exclusivity. The meetings take place in the discrete atmosphere of Ginza or Akasaka geisha restaurants, with presumably less political philosophy but concrete economic and political issues on the agenda, before the usual drinking and merriment begins, to enhance human relations and mutual understanding.

The *Mainichi* in January 1989[5] gave a detailed account of how, during a meeting of company presidents organised by Nakasone as the *Sanno Keizai Kenkyukai*, money was collected. The meeting was held on the evening of 11 June 1986 at *Fukuden ryotei* (a traditional Japanese high-class restaurant located between the New Otani and the Akasaka Prince Hotel in Tokyo). After a brief speech by Nakasone the corporate presidents present pledged amounts between ¥5 and 10 million to support Nakasone. Hiromasu Ezoe stood out by donating ¥50 million. the group was essentially made up of owner-presidents of middle-class companies, who, like Ezoe, might have hoped that their association with Nakasone would allow them to enhance their standing in the world of organised business (*zaikai*).

Finally, individual MPs have to secure some financing of their own, particularly if their constituency situation requires additional outlays. Most expensive are rural districts in which past election results have been close or if a new challenger is seen to emerge. Some politicians are closely linked to certain businesses, be it for family reasons or for their policy speciality. An MP following road transport and covering MOT affairs will obviously receive special attention from the Japanese trucking and road haulage industry.

Analysing the financial dependency of LDP leaders, their permanent contacts and frequent family bonds with big business (*zaikai*), had led some observers to the hasty conclusion that it was Japan's economic elite that determined all economic policies and finally also decided who would become prime minister. This overlooks the fact that big business is rarely unified, that most of its pay cheques are unconditional, and that, finance apart, the LDP also depends on voters' approval and hence needs the support of large social strata and of other organised interests (agriculture, retail trade, small businesses, religious groups, medical doctors, civil servants and so on), who will deliver the votes. Still, *zaikai* ability to target and to promote a certain respectable mainstream in the LDP and to contact the LDP faction chiefs at almost any time on any subject of interest, gives it a key role in Japan's political economy.

FACTIONAL WARS (1972–80)

The last 20 years of LDP history indicate two distinct periods: an eight-year span of intensive 'mainstream'–'sidestream' conflicts, which ultimately contributed to the premature death of an incumbent prime minister, Masayoshi Ohira in 1980, followed by a period of relative *détente* in which the 'mainstream'–'sidestream' distinction became more blurred, enabling Yasuhiro Nakasone, a sidestream representative, to remain safely in power for almost five full years (1982–7).

The conflicts of 1872–80 started when Takeo Fukuda, the inheritor of the Kishi faction, was promised the prime ministership by then PM Eisaku Sato (1964–72). Fukuda had been a faithful ally during Sato's long rule. However, Sato soon lost his factional chairmanship to Kakuei Tanaka, a self-made construction entrepreneur from Niigata, who went on to challenge Fukuda for the party presidency, thus starting the 'Kaku–Fuku War' for the votes of the 435 LDP MPs and the 47 prefectural delegates who were to elect the party president. Reportedly up to 10 billion yen changed hands and Fukuda, a former MOF elite-track official lacking Tanaka's unscrupulous resourcefulness, was duly defeated. Preferred beneficiaries of Tanaka's attention were the chiefs of the smaller factions, the independent MPs and the prefectural delegates. Fukuda remained resentful and unforgiving. During his tenure (1972–4) Tanaka enriched his companies and himself openly through the purchase and resale of land which had in the meantime benefited from significant appreciation due to public development projects. Public revulsion encouraged Ohira and Fukuda to force Tanaka's resignation in November 1974. With each blocking the other for succession, a mediator (and friend of Tanaka), Etsusaburo Shiina, was selected from the venerable party elders. Shiina then picked Takeo Miki, the chief of a small sidestream faction, whom he erroneously believed he would be able to control easily. With the unveiling of the Lockheed Scandal, in which the bribing of Tanaka and some of his friends with some ¥2 billion had become apparent, Miki used the public uproar and allowed Tanaka to be arrested in July 1976. Later, the transport minister Tomisaburo Hashimoto and his parliamentary vice-minister Takayuki Sato, both members of the Tanaka faction, were put behind bars.

Miki promised a thorough public investigation, also covering the 'grey' officials – including Nakasone, Nikaido and so on, who were equally suspected of having received Lockheed cash. The elimination of political rivals by unleashing the public prosecutor was going too far for Ohira and Fukuda. With Shiina's mediation they allied themselves with Tanaka and Nakasone, forcing Miki to block all investigations that were underway. When the LDP in November 1976 suffered a predictable defeat with only 41.8 per cent of the votes received in the Lower House elections, to the LDP establishment the culprit was obvious: Miki had to go.

Between the two successor candidates, Ohira and Fukuda, a secret deal was worked out. For a two-year term Fukuda would rule as prime minister, to be followed by Ohira. When Fukuda, his term being up in 1978, eventually proved unwilling to resign, Ohira with the able help of Tanaka forced him out. Reflecting the experience of the Kaku–Fuku war of 1972 with its massive corruption of party delegates, in 1977 the selection procedure for party president was 'democratised'. All party members became eligible to preselect their president. The first election as to be held in 1978. Until 1977 the number of nominal party members had oscillated around 450,000, corresponding to the number of LDP politicians holding seats in local parliaments and their family members. In 1978 party membership tripled. With Fukuda relying on the prestige of his office – he had just signed a

Peace and Friendship Treaty with the People's Republic of China – the Ohira and Tanaka factions mobilised their MPs' *koenkai* in the prefectures. Koenkai members' annual party membership fees (¥1500 at the time) were reimbursed from factional coffers. Some recruiters simply copied the pages of telephone directories and later filled out their ballots. The Ohira faction alone reportedly spent ¥2 billion for its recruitment drive. On average, each of the local politicians received a compensation of some ¥400,000 through his local MP and *koenkai* chief for his trouble and the support of his faction. Finally, in November 1978 Ohira's and Tanaka's efforts paid off. Ohira received 551,000 votes (42 per cent), Fukuda 473,000 (36 per cent), Nakasone 198,000 (15 per cent) and Komoto 89,000 (9 per cent). Faced with this humiliating defeat, Fukuda resigned and forsook the run-off ballot among MPs which was to have taken place subsequent to the membership's poll.

With the prospect of a renewed poll in 1980, particularly the smaller factions, such as Komoto's, continued their membership drive, which in 1979 doubled to 3.1 million. Then the mainstream factions decided to change the rules again: membership polls would only be held if there were more than three candidates who had the endorsement of at least 50 MPs. This eliminated unilateral candidacies of the smaller faction chiefs (such as Komoto) and made future polls very unlikely. In 1981 the LDP's membership had consequently shrunk back to some 400,000.

With his victory in 1978 Ohira, in setting up his cabinet, attempted to reconcile his former rivals Fukuda, Komoto and Nakasone, on whose support his parliamentary majority depended. Ohira offered four cabinet posts to Fukuda's and to his own faction, three to Tanaka's faction, and two each to the Miki/Komoto and the Nakasone factions. Three factionless MPs received fairly unimportant state minister posts. This compromise his men's ministerial wishes to his own exercise of influence in a Ohira cabinet dependent on his co-operation and good will. It was already a bad omen that no leading Fukuda men were willing to serve under Ohira.

Throughout 1979 the Fukuda and Nakasone factions (in which right-wingers are more prominent) pushed Ohira to legislate on various symbolic nationalist causes (such as making the use of the imperial calender (*gengo*) compulsory; making official visits to the Yasukuni shrine; revising history textbooks, embellishing Japanese performance during the first half of the century) and so on. This created new conflicts with the centrist opposition parties (Komeito, DSP, NLC) with which Ohira tended to co-operate. Ohira felt encouraged to call early elections in October 1979 by the LDP's victory in the elections for metropolitan governor in Osaka and Tokyo (ending the reign of Minobe (1967–79), who had been a popular socialist governor, proving the JSP's ability to govern at the time) as well as by the July 1979

Tokyo summit's PR fallout. Confidently he increased the number of LDP-endorsed candidates (particularly of his own and of Tanaka's faction) and hinted at increased indirect taxation to balance the government's budget. This proved unpopular and the LDP's tally unexpectedly fell by 3 per cent to 44.6 per cent and one seat was lost overall.

The LDP sidestream factions made Ohira responsible for the 'loss' of this election. Their opposition was embittered by the fact that Ohira had managed to increase his faction by 17 new Lower House members, and Tanaka's by four, while Fukuda, Nakasone and Miki all saw their factional strength reduced. With Ohira refusing to resign, the sidestream factions took the unprecedented step of nominating Fukuda against Ohira as candidate for prime minister in the Lower House. Again Tanaka's resourcefulness carried the day. Through a series of backdoor deals he secured the votes of some 30 independent or factionless MPs, of nine renegades from the LDP sidestream and the support of the NLC. With other opposition parties voting for their own hopeless chairmen, Ohira was safely re-elected. Still the bitterness of the defeated Fukuda camp remained.

Early in 1980 two minor scandals broke. A senior MP in the Tanaka faction, Koichi Hamada, a one-time gangster with continuing underworld links, had lost US$2.5 million mysteriously had his debts paid. At the same time it became known that KDD, the public telecommunications monopoly, had stashed away high undeclared profits, most of which had apparently been used to finance its senior managers' extensive night life in Tokyo and overseas. Part, however, was used for political donations, which prevented audits and checks by the MPT and the diet Commission in charge.

In May 1980 the Socialists, supported by fellow opposition parties, submitted a motion of no-confidence, against the Ohira cabinet. Shortly before the vote and the Fukuda and Miki factions requested Ohira to condemn formally all forms of political corruption and vote-purchasing. This would have been tantamount to a public condemnation of his most reliable ally and friend, Tanaka, whose political practices included these activities. When Ohira refused, the Miki, Fukuda and Nakagawa factions decided to abstain from the vote. To the consternation of the Socialists, the no-confidence motion was passed and new elections were called.

At the start of the campaign, however, Ohira collapsed with a heart attack and died soon after. Instantly all LDP factions were united in praise of the dead man. Media and public opinion were touched by Ohira's ultimate sacrifice, and the opposition parties were unable to capitalise on the LDP's previous disunity and past sins. Enjoying a landslide victory (47.9 per cent of the votes, resulting in an absolute Lower House majority), Zenko Suzuki, a reticent fisheries expert and Ohira's right-hand man, was selected as his factional successor (since two powerful lieutenants, Kiichi Miyazawa and Rokusuke Tanaka, had blocked each other) and elected prime minister. Nobusuke Kishi had dissuaded Fukuda from running again this time. This also enhanced the future standing of Shintaro Abe, his son-in-law and Fukuda's likely successor as faction chief. Again Tanaka's faction did not put up a candidate of its own, but vetoed the bid of Komoto, Miki's successor. Suzuki, apparently surprised by his selection as prime minister, declared universal harmony as the motto of his tenure. While this remained his only audible political utterance, he succeeded in integrating all major LDP big-wigs into his cabinet, thus bringing almost a decade of internecine strife virtually to an end.

FACTIONAL FRICTIONS (1980–91)

Compared to the cyclical factional warfare of previous decades, the intraparty power games of the 1980s were relatively placid and less intense. This relative tranquillity allowed Yasuhiro Nakasone to rule energetically for a good part of the decade. There were no major factional splits (if one ignores the slightly messy Tanaka–Takeshita succession in 1987 and the Abe–Mitsuzuka transition in 1991) with only the Recruit Scandal of 1989 upsetting the LDP's increasingly bureaucratised power structure.

Following the LDP landslide victory of June 1980 in the wake of Ohira's death, the three main factions of Suzuki (succeeding to Ohira), Fukuda and Tanaka speedily agreed on Zenko Suzuki as prime minister. Suzuki, a fisheries expert from Iwate, was a low-key confidant of Ohira, a smooth operator with few enemies and little overt ambition. The factions had been formally dissolved in July, but after the summer break were quickly re-organised, under new names but with their old structure, in September 1980.

Although Suzuki's inability to lead soon became patently obvious, his reign continued undisturbed for two years due to the factions' disagreement on a more suitable successor. The mainstream factions were split between competing crown princes: Miyazawa and Rokusuke Tanaka in the Suzuki faction, Nikaido, Takeshita and Ganri Yamashita in the Tanaka faction, with Abe's rule still insufficiently consolidated in the Fukuda faction. At the same time the mainstream factions were still unwilling to back any of the rival sidestream chiefs: Yasuhiro Nakasone, Toshio Komoto or Ichiro Nakagawa.

With Suzuki doing little perceptible to reduce Japan's spiralling public budget deficit or to implement administrative reform (of which Nakasone, as head of the Administrative Management Agency, and Shin Kanemaru, as chairman of the relevant Lower House special committee, were in charge), public and intraparty criticism mounted. Prior to the party president's re-election date of November 1982, Suzuki suddenly resigned, unnerved by the criticism.

The chieftains of the Tanaka and the Suzuki factions then decided to support Nakasone in his election bid (both factions being unable to agree on candidates of their own) and he won easily in consequence. Among the losing candidates Komoto did reasonably well – after spending a great deal of cash from his shipping company, Sanko Steamship. But Shintaro Abe, the heir apparent to the Fukuda faction, and Ichiro Nakagawa, the Hokkaido based founder of his own right-wing and agricultural interests-based faction, suffered crushing defeats. Nakagawa, five weeks later, hanged himself in a bout of depression in a Sapporo hotel.

Nakasone, in power by the grace of Tanaka and Suzuki, in November 1982 pledged to cut Japan's budget deficits by reducing public spending and by privatising Japan's national railways and other public enterprises. Nakasone reacted to his campaign pledges in a strangely un-Japanese way: he attempted to keep his campaign promises. In real terms his 1983 fiscal budget was cut by 3 per cent (with only defence spending going up by a nominal 6.5 per cent). At the subsequent round of local elections in April 1983, the LDP lost the two governorships of Hokkaido and Fukuoka to the Socialists (the two successful contenders were reconfirmed for the third time in April 1991).

Nakasone was safe from mainstream challengers due to the fact that Kiichi Miyazawa was considered too aloof and intellectual to be a good political boss even of the aristo-bureaucratic Ohira/Suzuki faction and only after the local elections of April 1983 was he able to secure his succession as factional head to Suzuki – against the opposition of Ohira loyalists, Rokusuke Tanaka and Masayoshi Ito.

Nakasone's key backer, Kakuei Tanaka, who obtained six cabinet seats and the position of LDP Secretary General in the first Nakasone cabinet for his men, with his conviction for bribery in the Lockheed case in October 1983, was unable to run for the party presidency himself, but at same time he vetoed the candidacy of anybody from his faction. (If successful this would have created an effective successor as faction chief and would have cost Tanaka the control of his 119-member faction, of which Susumu Nikaido was only very nominally in charge.) When Tanaka remained defiant and unrepenting in public statements and challenged his four-year prison term, the opposition parties began to boycott the Diet, and Nakasone was forced to call new elections to the Lower House in December 1983.

Unexpectedly, the LDP lost two percentage points of votes cast (down to 45.8 percent) and 34 seats in Parliament. While his party lost, Kakuei Tanaka was himself re-elected in Niigata 3 (a rural district around Nagaoka City) with 221,000 votes – the best result ever for a Japanese politician. Ever since Tanaka's days as prime minister Niigata benefited handsomely: for each yen paid in taxes, Niigata received three yen back in subsidies or public works. Of the Tokyo cash flow, one-third was placed with Tanaka-affiliated companies.[6]

Ironically, Tanaka's personal victory and the LDP's loss strengthened Nakasone's hand. He had to search for allies among Tanaka's intraparty enemies (Fukuda) and to co-opt the eight NLC and eight independent MPs into the LDP's parliamentary party (thus re-establishing the LDP's absolute majority). Most of them made it a precondition for their support that Nakasone should distance himself from Tanaka. Nakasone was hence able to utilise the public revulsion over Tanaka by replacing two of Tanaka's henchmen in key positions – Nikaido, the Secretary General and Gotoda, the Chief Cabinet Secretary – by Rokusuke Tanaka (Suzuki/Miyazawa faction) and by Takao Fujinami, his own loyalist, respectively. Subsequently, during 1984 Nakasone managed to score a success in the smooth Diet passage of the administration reform bills, was praised for his fiscal frugality, as well as for his foreign policy management in getting along well with the Reagan administration, and for becoming an articulate and responsive representative of Japan at world summits. His approval ratings were reasonably high at around 40 per cent.

With the passage of time Kakuei Tanaka's influence recovered, also aided by the terminal illness of Rokusuke Tanaka, whose tasks as LDP secretary general were gradually taken over again by Susumu Nikaido, formally the LDP's vice-president, during the summer of 1984. Nakasone continued to enjoy Tanaka's conditional backing and could weather the opposition of party elders such as Takeo Fukuda and Zenko Suzuki, whom Nakasone managed to antagonise by publicly denigrating Suzuki's record in office. After their vetoes, Shintaro Abe and Kiichi Miyazawa opted out of the unlikely race to challenge Nakasone for his second term in office as party president, the reselection for which was due in October 1984. Instead, they attempted to persuade Nikaido to break away with his followers from Tanaka's faction and be elected prime minister with the help of their two factions – a deal which included coalition arrangements with Komeito and Minshato (DSP). Although tempted, Nikaido ultimately bowed to Tanaka's orders and did not run. The same applied to Noboru Takeshita, who with the support of Shin Kanemaru (the new secretary general) – linked through marriage (*keibatsu*) ties of their children – ventured a possible candidacy, but also withdrew on Tanaka's instructions. Nakasone finally had an unchallenged re-election, courtesy of Kakuei Tanaka, who as 'shogun in the shadows' and commander of the *Tanaka Gundan* (Tanaka Army Corps) continued to enjoy his role as the LDP's kingmaker and hence Japan's most single powerful man until well into 1985.

His hint that Nikaido would ultimately be selected as his successor prompted Shin Kanemaru, the LDP's secretary general and a construction kingpin in his own right, to support his protégé Takeshita in forming his own 'study group', the *Soseikai*, within the Tanaka faction early in 1985. In spite of a vigorous Tanaka campaign to squash this intra-faction strategy (paying his men twice the sum of Takeshita's welcoming money of ¥3 million to stay away), Takeshita and Kanemaru succeeded in recruiting some 88 (out of 120 Tanaka faction members) – especially the younger and middle-ranking – into their new sub-faction. Their challenge could survive and blossom, as Tanaka at the end of February 1985 was felled by a stroke, an affliction from which he would never recover. Nikaido suggested that this had been caused by the strain produced by Takeshita's infidelity.

For Nakasone the demise of his principal backer obviously had worrying implications. Still, his personal popularity (which persisted, since he did not attempt to implement his own right-wing convictions: constitutional revision, doubled defence spending and more patriotism taught in the schools) helped him to remain in power until the advent of a new general election (which Nakasone set as a double – Upper and Lower House – election for July 1986). Nakasone designed the election to be referendum about his own policies – and to everybody's surprise won with a landslide. With 49.5 per cent of total votes and 300 seats he won a handsome absolute majority in the Lower House – with the LDP holding more than four times the number of seats of the Socialists (down to 85).

In the election both the Tanaka and Nakasone factions did well, controlling between them almost half the LDP's parliamentary party in both Houses. Altogether the LDP had benefited from high voter turnout (71 per cent), as well as from Nakasone's enhanced credibility – as compared with 'classical' politicians, he seemed to say what he meant. He had promised domestic demand-led growth in the context of rising recession fears due to *endaka* (the 40 per cent appreciation of the yen since September 1985) and no new taxes. In spite of Nakasone's electoral triumph, with the tacit support of Abe, Miyazawa still requested that he should step down. Yet even after the eclipse of Tanaka, Nakasone could still rely on Takeshita/ Kanemaru's continued support: both controlled only some two-thirds of the Tanaka faction, with the remainder still sticking to Tanaka loyalist Nikaido and to a neutral group around Hajime Tamura. Hence they required more time for power consolidation. Nakasone thus could obtain a dispensation 'for the time being' (which was later defined to mean 'one more year' – until October 1987) from party rules which would have limited him to only two two-year terms as party president (and by implication as prime minister).

With a programme of privatising JNR, pursuing educational reform, import liberalisation, and increasing the revenue share of indirect taxation, Nakasone introduced his new team with his rivals Miyazawa (MOF), Takeshita (Secretary General) and Abe (chairman Executive Council) firmly integrated in key cabinet and party positions. Tadashi Kuranari, one of his loyal retainers, became foreign minister. In September 1986, 49 days after the inauguration of his cabinet, Nakasone had to sack his education minister, Masayoki Fujio (Abe faction), who tried to undermine Nakasone's right-wing credentials by deliberate provocation (saying the annexation of Korea in 1910 was based on 'mutual agreement', discounting the Nanking Massacre; challenging the legitimacy of the Tokyo War Crimes tribunal, and so on.

After overcoming considerable union resistance, Nakasone had the break-up and privatisation of J(N)R largely wrapped up by January 1987. Then as an additional agenda for his term of office he introduced educational and tax reform. For the latter he reneged on his campaign pledge and reverted to Ohira's ill-fated plans for an indirect (value added) sales tax of some 5 per cent, long advocated by MOF to solidify Japan's tax structure and to set the basis for a more equitable and balanced tax system. Nakasone also advocated the abolition of tax exemption for the popular '*Maruyu*' system of savings for small investors. In return he promised to cut income taxes, with the net effect being fiscally neutral. His proposals triggered a storm of protest, particular among the consumers' and retailers' organisations. This reinvigorated the opposition parties, which unexpectedly won two Upper House seats by elections in Iwate and Tokyo and a round of local elections in April 1987. Also LDP MPs were markedly unenthusiastic about the tax reforms, and began to talk about Nakasone's days being numbered (in fact, in January 1987 he was suspected of having introduced the new agenda in order to prolong his term of office beyond October 1987). Finally, by May 1987 Nakasone had to drop his tax proposals in order to secure the opposition parties' co-operation to pass the annual budget.

Increasingly, as his rivals for succession, Nikaido, Takeshita, Miyazawa and Abe, geared up their preparations, Nakasone was seen as not actively seeking an extension of his mandate, which had been agreed earlier by the three major rival faction chiefs to run out by 30 October 1987. The voluntary acceptance of this resignation date allowed him a 'second-best' option: to appear strong when resigning and to play the role of kingmaker within the LDP.

Nikaido was to announce his – politically ultimately suicidal – candidacy first, although his command of the Tanaka loyalists within the faction, of which he had nominally remained chairman, had withered to 16 MPs. His announcement was followed by Takeshita's, who could count on the support of nearly all the 120 MPs of the Tanaka faction who had attended Takeshita's 2 billion yen fund-raising party at the end of May 1987. With two competing candidacies (Nikaido stubbornly refusing to yield to various mediation efforts to abandon his hopeless bid) – and a small neutral camp around Hajime Tamura, ex-MITI minister, in between – Tanaka's fabulous Army Corps had finally split. The entire summer of 1987 was spent in intense plots and factional scheming that centred around the four declared candidates and Nakasone, involving them and their principal backers and lieutenants. Most observers saw Takeshita and Abe as agreeing among themselves to successive presidential terms, possibly supported by Komoto, whose faction had become too weak to compete again and who owed Kanemaru a favour, because he had helped out when Komoto's Sanko Steamship Co. went bankrupt in 1985.[7]

Miyazawa, the favourite of the business and bureaucratic community, remained isolated, but was later supported by Nikaido, after the latter's belated withdrawal. All four were vying for Nakasone's favour. Nakasone in turn was said to harbour hopes that the four might block each other, so as to able to continue against all the odds. With Nakasone remaining aloof and silent as to whom he preferred as his successor (Nakasone said 'he must have a sense of history, a philosophy on history, as did de Gaulle, Churchill and Mao Zedong. He must be aware of Japan's status in the world'[8]) and with Nikaido, for lack of support, finally having withdrawn, the three remaining contenders, who for months had showered Nakasone with praise and were all pledged to continue his policies, finally agreed to submit to Nakasone's ultimate arbitration. Nakasone played his cards close to his chest, and hence was able to maximise the price for his support (which should translate into considerable post-election influence and standing). Yet with the benefit of hindsight, his decision in favour of Takeshita, the candidate who was most likely to win a contested election on the strength of votes and cash, appeared perfectly plausible (though the candidate had the least foreign exposure to conform to Nakasone's august ideal of a world leading philosopher-statesman). Already when appointing Takeshita LDP secretary general in September 1986, Nakasone had lent decisive support for Takeshita's eventual bid to take over most of the Tanaka faction. When setting up his cabinet in November 1987, PM Takeshita was seen to heed Nakasone's wishes: Sosuke Uno, a faithful Nakasone man with few apparent ambitions of his own, was made foreign minister. Nakasone's faction also got hold of two most lucrative ministries: MOC and MPT.

As his single priority Takeshita defined the left-over business of his predecessor: tax reform. As a more attractive slogan for his tenure he chose *furusato* (hometown), which was intended to mean a certain measure of decentralisation and local autonomy, but in real political life was before long to stand for (public) cash gifts to local constituencies.

While in the process of preparing the legislative agenda to introduce a consumption tax of 3 per cent, and accepting US requests for the eventual liberalisation of beef and orange imports, during the early summer of 1988 the Recruit Scandal broke. It gradually became known that a great number of Japanese politicians (including Takeshita, Nakasone, Abe and Miyazawa), senior businessmen, newspaper editors and bureaucrats had purchased bargain-priced pre-listed shares of Recruit Cosmos, a real-estate company managed by Hiromasa Ezoe, which they were able to resell at huge profits when the shares were listed at the Tokyo Stock Exchange. The 159 beneficiaries did return the favour in the form of general goodwill or in more-or-less identifiable benefits to Ezoe. With new details being revealed daily by the excited media, this scandal was to dominate Japan's political scene until the Lower House elections of January 1990. It was to lead to Takeshita's downfall, it interrupted the careers of some of the best and brightest LDP junior leaders and eclipsed the influence of Nakasone and his immediate followers.

However, by the end of November 1988 Takeshita finally had his tax reform approved by the Diet (with Komeito and DSP voting against the package, but not boycotting the session as the Socialists and Communists did), having appeared to sit out problems during most of his first year in office. Later in December he reshuffled his cabinet, appointing a senior Miyazawa man, Tatsuo Maruyama, as minister of finance, a position from which Miyazawa himself had had to resign earlier, due to his implausible versions of how his personal seal had been used by an unidentifiable secretary to purchase Recruit shares without his knowledge. Takeshita also kept Michio Watanabe, Nakasone's ever-more-active challenger to factional succession, in the position of chairman to the Policy Research Council (from where Watanabe continued his demolition job on Takao Fujinami, who was equally Recruit-damaged and Nakasone's preferred heir). Takeshita also kept Sosuke Uno in place, although Nakasone rather wanted to exchange him for a more effective henchman. Even before Recruit had tainted

Nakasone's reputation, his influence on Takeshita had been less than expected from a traditional 'kingmaker'.

One year after the power transition, Nakasone's influence was perceptibly on the wane. Since Miyazawa had also knocked himself out of the reckoning, it appeared as if Shintaro Abe's star – then the LDP's reappointed secretary general – was on the rise, if only be default.

In the meantime, continuing relevations about additional Recruit largesse received not only by Takeshita and his peers but also by almost all prominent middle-ranking LDP politicians, brought down the cabinet's approval rating to a new historical low of 3.9 per cent in April 1989. Already, in February 1989 the Takeshita faction had to withdraw its Recruit-tainted candidate, Kazuo Aichi, from the governatorial race in Sendai, for fear of losing in the LDP's heartland in Tohoku.

In early May 1989, Takeshita (after the relevation of a hitherto unsuspected ¥50 million Recruit loan to one of Takeshita's secretaries, coming on top of a list of Recruit donations which Takeshita had already declared exhaustive earlier) announced his intention to resign once the budget had become effective. The budgetary deliberations were boycotted by the Socialists, who requested that Nakasone testify before the Diet under oath (as they were confident that his previous assertions of innocence were untrue), which he refused. With Takeshita's announced resignation likely to take effect in late May, there was little reason left for him to continue to protect Nakasone. Yet there was no obvious successor in sight: one who was both untainted by Recruit and willing to serve as the fall-guy for the LDP's likely losses at the Upper House elections in July, when Recruit, together with highly unpopular sales tax and the beef and orange import liberalisation, would dominate the campaign.

Masayoshi Ito (Miyazawa faction), as undisputedly honest senior LDP statesman, refused to play their role that was offered to him unless he had a clear and unconditional mandate for political reform and a free hand in choosing his cabinet and senior party appointees without factional interference. When such a mandate was not forthcoming from the factional chieftains, who had already begun to squabble about the spoils of power of a post-Takeshita regime, Ito rejected the prime ministerial slot.

After Ito's refusal, Takeshita and Nakasone selected Sosuke Uno, who had the proven advantage of being more malleable. He had an apparently clean record, having received no funding from Recruit (with no factional power base of his own his financial needs – and attraction – were much reduced), and enjoyed a distinguished ministerial record (Defence, MITI,

MFA and so on). In spite of the misgivings of some party elders (Kanemaru, Suzuki and Fukuda among them), Mr Uno, 'a man without enemies and without friends', was voted in on 3 June 1989.

It was clear from the outset that PM Uno's tenure would remain limited until public fury over the Recruit Scandal had blown over. Uno, in fact, had hardly been able to unveil his – almost imperceptible – political agenda, when the news over his less-than-romantic involvement with an untraditional *geisha* broke. (It was first brought out by a weekly – the *Mainichi Sunday* – and then magnified by the US media, so that other Japanese papers could no longer ignore the story.) Apparently he had been too miserly to pay her the customary consolation money when he broke off their engagement, so she decided to give pres briefings about his alleged abusive and adulterous conduct. Uno implausibly claimed that he had never known the lady, but he offered his immediate resignation. His party elders, however, ordered him to soldier on. Dutifully Uno put on a brave face at the Paris Summit and shouldered the LDP's subsequent crushing Upper House defeat. On 23 July 1989 the LDP managed to obtain only 27.3 per cent of the national vote, thus losing their majority in the Chamber, with the Socialists (JSP) rising to first place with 35.1 per cent of the votes. *Rengo*, the newly merged trade union federation, also succeeded in having 11 of its 12 mostly single-constituency candidates elected against LDP incumbents.

Uno immediately resigned. Undeterred, the faction chiefs searched for a new untainted fall-guy who would lead the country until the next general (Lower House) election, due in early 1990, when, after anticipated vote losses, he would take 'responsibility' and, with the party thus 'cleansed', would make way for Shintaro Abe. Toshiki Kaifu, a low-key and reasonably 'clean' lieutenant in the Komoto faction and a leading education *zoku* member with not much of a personal following, was selected. In a pro forma election, with the support of the Takeshita, Abe, Komoto and Watanabe/Nakasone factions among LDP MPs and prefectural representatives, Kaifu was voted into office against candidates Yoshiro Hayashi (a former MHW minister, then of the Nikaido faction and supported by the Miyazawa faction) and Shintaro Ishihara (a novelist, ex-MOT minister and semi-independent right-winger in the Abe faction). Kaifu was designed to be yet another seat-warmer and 'remote-control PM' before he actually took office. He neither smoked nor drank, and was considered sufficiently fearful of his wife as not to engage in extramarital affairs, nor was he politically attractive enough to risk being offered donations of dubious origin.

While the faction chiefs determined his cabinet, the cabinet's agenda was obvious from the outset: foremost, to produce a face-saving modification of the hated sales tax and then to proceed to electoral reform, which it was hoped would lead to a voting system which would breed less corruption without endangering the LDP's re-election prospects. Under the circumstances, in the public mind Kaifu performed better than expected. Supported by opposition party disunity (and a lot of bullying of big business by Ichiro Ozawa, LDP secretary general, for additional campaign funds), the LDP on 18 February 1990 won 46.1 per cent of votes (down only 3.3 per cent compared to Nakasone's Lower House election of 1987) and a majority of 275 of the 512 seats of the Lower House. This represented a net loss of only 25 seats, mostly affecting the Nakasone/Watanabe and Nikaido factions. The other factions' totals remained almost unchanged. The initial losses were almost made up by 11 independent MPs joining the LDP. All villians of the Recruit drama, including Nakasone, were safely re-elected. Among the VIPs, only Sadanori Yamanaka, the tough chairman of the LDP's Tax Council which had finalised the 3 per cent sales tax proposal, failed to hold on to his seat. The seats which the Socialists won were largely at the expense of the smaller opposition parties with which the party had earlier promised to 'co-operate'.

Shintaro Abe, who had already undertaken coalition soundings with the DSP and with Komeito in the event that the LDP lost its Lower House majority and Kaifu had to take his 'responsibility', was visibly disappointed with Kaifu's success. He could hardly be dumped now by the LDP. While still unable to select his own men, Kaifu was at least strong enough to exclude most Recruit-tainted figures from cabinet and senior party positions, who had been proposed by the hostile Abe and Watanabe factions.

With the sales tax gradually fading from the political agenda, external pressures in the form of the US Strategic Impediments Initiative (SII) emerged. This initiative was safely embraced and smothered by a larger public works budget (happily received by the construction *zoku*) and by a few cosmetic reforms. Kaifu now declared that he would stake his 'political life' on 'political reform'. Political reform, according to the report of April 1990 by the prime ministerial advisory panel charged with the task, would imply replacing the costly and corruption-breeding multi-seat constituency system by a suitable mixture of 60 per cent of Lower House seats allocated to single-seat constituencies and 40 per cent awarded by proportional representation. With suitably gerrymandered local constituencies this system would almost a guarantee most local- (*jiban*) based LDP MP's automatic re-election (at much-reduced costs), while probably reducing the factions' influence and decreasing the number of seats principally of the smaller democratic opposition parties (whose co-operation is also a very costly undertaking) and of the Communists, who have only nuisance value (mainly to the Socialists). Political reform was – and still is – clearly defined as a long-term issue affecting all Dietmen's – and the LDP factions' – core interests, and faces the opposition parties' embittered resistance. Hence some faction leaders, and Shintaro Abe in particular, battling with terminal cancer (to which he succumbed in May 1991), were unhappy with Kaifu volunteering to shoulder this long-term task. Most analysts believe that for its implication a transition period of five to ten years is necessary.

With Kaifu's public approval ratings running high at 60 per cent during 1990 and 1991, it was increasingly thought likely that he could serve his two-year term in full until October 1991. This was, however, due less to Kaifu's performance and strengths than to the result of his potential successors' misfortune and disunity. Abe, the nominal front-runner, was terminally ill, and four 'crown princes' (Yoshiro Mori, Hiroshi Mitsuzuka, Mutsuki Kato and Masajiro Shiokawa) were jockeying for succession in the faction. (Mitsuzuka in alliance with Mori, made it in June 1991.) Miyazawa plotted actively for the Kaifu succession by courting successively Kanemaru, Watanabe and Takeshita, while his faction was being torn apart in a duel of crown princes between Yohei Kono and Koichi Kato.

Watanabe, who also made his aspirations public, was similarly unable to settle the deep-seated division between his own followers and Nakasone loyalists in his newly inherited faction. In the Takeshita faction, Kanemaru, the LDP's ultimate strongman, fell out with his earlier protégé Takeshita (who in alliance with Hashimoto harboured overt ambitions for a return to power), while Kanemaru favoured his new protégé Ozawa, who was more of his *alter ego* as a bullying construction man, as LDP secretary general. However, even these power figures were reduced to size when a Kanemaru-backed candidate for governor lost on his home turf of Yamanashi, and when Ozawa's intended replacement for Shinichi Suzuki, Tokyo's superannuated governor, failed in the face of stubborn resistance from the octogenarian, who benefited from an upsurge in public support caused by the widespread revulsion against Ozawa's tactics. Ozawa subsequently resigned as secretary general in April 1991 to be replaced by the more consensus-seeking Keizo Obuchi, also a senior Takeshita faction member. Ryotaro Hashimoto (a protégé of Takashita, and minister of finance) stumbled in August 1991 when, in the context of Japan's securities scandals, it became known that his secretary had introduced credit-seekers to a Fuji Bank manager, who awarded bank loans on the basis of falsified collaterals.

The 1980s were a decade of reduced factional warfare – which none the less finished the careers of quite a number of hopefuls who took the wrong side at the wrong moment. The decade saw the demise of Tanaka's 'Army Corps'; the relative marginalisation of the former Yoshida/Ikeda/Ohira mainstream under the often unlucky management of Kiichi Miyazawa; the disappearance of Nakagawa as head of a 'pure' right-wing faction; the rise and fall of Nakasone; the rise and the (temporary) fall of a whole generation of talented second-generation leaders tainted by Recruit money; and the emergence and survival of a most unlikely political non-leader, Toshiki Kaifu, for a full prime ministerial term from 1989 to 1991, until Miyazawa's decade-long persistence finally paid off. These and all Japan's postwar prime ministers, are listed in Table 2.4.

Table 2.4   Japan's postwar prime ministers

Beginning of term	Name	Professional background	University
May 1946	Shigeru Yoshida	Bureaucrat (MFA)	Todai
May 1947	Tetsu Katayama	Politician (JSP)	Todai
March 1948	Hitoshi Ashida	Politician	Todai
October 1948	Shigeru Yoshida	Bureaucrat (MFA)	Todai
December 1954	Ichiro Hatoyama	Politician	Todai
December 1956	Tanzan Ishibashi	Politician	Waseda
February 1957	Nobusuke Kishi	Bureaucrat (MITI)	Todai
July 1960	Hayato Ikeda	Bureaucrat (MOF)	Kyodai
November 1964	Eisaku Sato	Bureaucrat (MOT)	Todai
July 1972	Kakuei Tanaka	Politician (Construction industry)	—
December 1974	Takeo Miki	Politician	Meiji
December 1976	Takeo Fukuda	Bureaucrat (MOF)	Todai
December 1978	Masayoshi Ohira	Bureaucrat (MOF)	Hitotsubashi
July 1980	Zenko Suzuki	Politician (Fisheries interests)	Tokyo University of Fisheries
November 1982	Yasuhiro Nakasone	Politician (briefly Police Agency)	Todai
November 1987	Noboru Takeshita	Politician (briefly school teacher, construction industry interests)	Waseda
June 1989	Sosuke Uno	Politician (*sake* interests)	Kobe University of Commerce
August 1989	Toshiki Kaifu	Politician	Waseda
October 1991	Kiichi Miyazawa	Bureaucrat (MOF)	Todai

3 Political Careers

RECRUITMENT

How does one become a LDP Member of Parliament? Gerald Curtis[1] followed in 1967 the campaign of Bunsei Sato, a first-time candidate and local politician, in the electoral district (Oita 2) around Beppu, a spa in Oita prefecture. The candidacy of Sato, previously a member of Oita's prefectural assembly, first had to be approved by the leaders of the prefectural party and then be endorsed by the LDP's national election committee, in which all faction chiefs are represented. At both levels, Sato had to overcome the bitter opposition of two senior-ranking LDP MPs who already (together with a Socialist) represented Oita 2 in the Diet. Both feared (rightly) that Sato would displace one of them and not the Socialist incumbent of the third Diet seat. At the prefectural level Sato was approved due to the vigorous backing of two locally powerful politicians who saw in him their political heir and representative in Tokyo. They also facilitated his adoption as a factional candidate by Isamu Murakami (whose faction has since been dissolved and absorbed into Nakasone's), who had to push for Sato's party endorsement against the resistance of the faction chiefs of his two local rivals. The endorsement was achieved in a complex compromise which had relatively little to do with Sato or with the situation in Oita 2.

Without factional support a candidate in this situation could not have received party endorsement. He would have had to run as an independent, with increased risk of failure due to subsequent funding and local support problems. Only in the – fairly unlikely – event of a successful election would this independent MP rejoin the LDP after his victory. Sometimes faction-supported candidates also run as 'independents' after failing to receive official party endorsement.

As Japan's restrictive election law restrains most contemporary standard campaign activities (canvassing, advertising, rallies and so on) considerably, Sato's main task was to enlarge and to activate his too-narrowly-based *koenkai* by winning over fellow local politicians and persuading them to switch the electoral support of their own political machines to his benefit (and to the disadvantage of the two incumbents). Making the right choice in this three-way battle was essential – that is, guessing the winning horse – if the local politician wished to continue to have direct access to Nagatacho, Tokyo's political centre, and through Nagatacho to Kasumigaseki, Tokyo's ministry district. In return for promises of support and delivery of votes Sato would generously reimburse their campaign and *koenkai-related* expenditure. Most of the money was, in fact, not spent to buy votes, but to pay wages to the campaign staff, to organise social events with free meals, to rent rooms and to hire cars.

Sato received the necessary capital from party headquarters, from his future faction chief, from the two local chieftains who were his principal backers and through direct contributions from businessmen from Beppu. For total campaign outlays for newcomers at Lower House elections it was estimated during the 1970s that '500 million yen will win, 300 will lose'. Today the estimates for winning stand at ¥700 million.

In his hometown Beppu Sato activated his local *koenkai* which he had built up during his days as a prefectural politician. This *koenkai* was based on the chairmen of the neighbourhood associations (*chonaikai*), the hotel owners' association, the dentists' association, the bamboo-growers' co-operative, some sports and veterans clubs, Buddhist sects, his school and university mates, relatives, and some underworld figures as well. In order to win the election it was, however, decisive for Sato to expand his urban home base into the rural hinterland which so far had been committed to his competitors. With the help of his backers and his campaign staff some of this support, however, could be persuaded that Sato would be a more suitable, dynamic and helpful character to represent the larger Beppu area energetically in Tokyo. On election day his labours proved successful and Sato entered Parliament as a low-ranking freshman (one of the previous incumbents, a meritorious former cabinet member, lost – thus ending his career in politics). Sato subsequently worked his way up the parliamentary party. Having reached the right seniority, he was duly appointed as a one-term cabinet minister (Minister of Posts and Telecommunication). Ironically, he lost his seat to a young LDP upstart, as he himself had been 23 years earlier, in the February 1990 election. Sato, however, still maintains an office in Tokyo and plans a comeback.

HEREDITARY POLITICS

With the difficulties of securing a sufficient electoral support base (*jiban*), the party and factional endorsement, the enormous amounts of cash (*kaban*) and the name recognition (*kanban*) required for the high-risk first election, self-made politicians like Bunsei Sato have increasingly become rare among freshmen LDP MPs. As in medical practice and the Buddhist priesthood, LDP politics has become a lucrative family trade, with successors taking advantage of past investments and the popular Japanese perceptions of family identity. By 1986, 115 (38 per cent) of the LDP's Lower House MPs were second-generation (*nisei*) politicians. Among new freshman MPs their share already stood at over 60 per cent. While in other countries the Bushes, Kennedys, Churchills, de Gaulles and Adenauers also founded political dynasties, Japan's LDP has certainly achieved new dimensions of political nepotism. In 1990 its world record of second-generation MPs was further improved to 117 (or 41 per cent). Of its MPs, 13 are already third-generation politicians (*sansei*) and two, the younger Hatoyamas, represent the fourth generation (*yonsei*). Four LDP MPs, in fact, are descended from the old nobility, their grandfathers having been members of the prewar House of Peers (MM. Shinichiro Shimojo, Osamu Takatori, Takeshi Maeda and Yoshiro Hayashi, a leading knight of the Miyazawa faction).

Japan's most famous dynasty is the Hatoyamas. Brothers Kunio and Yukio are both youngish, Lower House MPs and members of the Takeshita faction. Kunio Hatoyama was appointed Minister of Education in the Miyazawa cabinet in November 1991. Father Iichiro, after being foreign minister in the Fukuda cabinet, has now retired to the Upper House. Grandfather Ichiro Hatoyama was prime minister (1954–6), and a great-grandfather was Speaker of the prewar Lower House. Ichiro Hatoyama's great opponent, Shigeru Yoshida, is also represented in the Lower House by a grandson, Mr Taro Aso, who is predictably in the Miyazawa faction, the true descendant of the Yoshida school. Mr Aso is also, suitably, a son-in-law of former PM Zenko Suzuki and a brother-in-law of Prince Tomohito, a cousin of the Emperor.

Zenko Suzuki in 1990 left his Iwate constituency to his son Shinichi (Miyazawa faction), who, like his father, had become a fisheries expert affiliated with the fisheries co-ops. Former PM Takeo Fukuda, like Suzuki, has his son-in-law Mr Michio Ochi in the Diet, his own son Yasuo having inherited his father's famous (and expensive) Gunma 3 constituency in 1990. Takeo Fukuda's younger brother Hiroichi Fukuda is a member of the Upper House. All of the Fukudas remain faithful members of the Abe/Mitsuzuka faction. The late Shintaro Abe's father had been an MP himself, his father-in-law Mr Nobusuke Kishi (prime minister during 1957–60) having been most helpful in propelling his son-in-law into prominence.

Other prime ministerial sons are Lower House MP Shinji Sato and Upper House MP Hirofumi Nakasone. Prime ministerial in-laws are ex-defence minister Yukihiko Ikeda and Masayoshi Ohira's son-in-law Hajime Morita. Among prominent retired postwar PMs so far, only Kakuei Tanaka has been unsuccessful in assisting his own clan into political prominence. With his own local support organisation, the *Etsuzankai*, deciding to disband in 1990 rather than support his daughter, his (adopted) son-in-law Naoki Tanaka in the same year lost his first re-election bid in Fukushima 3.

Sometimes cross-breeding by political fathers and political mothers produces remarkable political talents. Mr Takeo Nishioka, a former chairman of the LDP's General Council, is the son of a former governor of Nagano Prefecture and Lower House MP. His mother had been an Upper House MP. Mr Taro Nakayama, the foreign minister under PM Kaifu, and his brother Masaaki, MP and former minister of posts and telecommunications, are sons of members of parliament; their mother was an Upper House member, having been minister of health and welfare. The current PM Kiichi Miyazawa was also born to a prewar Dietman; his mother was the daughter of a minister of railways.

Sometimes arranged marriage bonds (K*eibatsu*) are made with the elite of the business community. Nakasone's daughter is married to the heir-apparent of Kajima Corporation, Japan's largest building firm. Takeshita's youngest daughter has married the son of Takenaka Kommuten, which ranks among the top five of Japan's construction companies, while his oldest daughter is married to the son of Shin Kanemaru, a former deputy prime minister and the doyen of the LDP's construction *zoku*. Ohira's second son has married the daughter of the president of Oji Paper Co., one of his father's first major benefactors.

By comparison, among current opposition party MPs only 13 had fathers who served in parliament, and only one (Hideo Den of Shaminren) had a grandfather who had been a prewar minister of trade and agriculture.

Among LDP *nisei* or *sansei* MPs one might suspect that a priviledged upbringing would have reduced their motivation for educational performance and achievement. Looking at their educational record this can be disproved: 29 have studied at Keio, 27 at Todai (of which eight however are adopted sons and/or sons-in-law) and 14 at Waseda University. Only a small percentage dropped out or went to schools or universities of lesser standing. Subjects studied were essentially law (55), followed by economics (23), engineering (8) and political economy (7).

While political passions and charisma may have lessened in the second or third generation, still senior *nisei* politicians such as Kiichi Miyazawa, Ichiro Ozawa, Tsutomu Hata, Yohei Kono, Toshio Yamaguchi, Kosuke Hori and so on, are intelligent and skilful politicians in their own right. Others appear to be less-worthy sons of their high achieving fathers.

The rise of hereditary politics in general has corresponded to the relative decline of elite bureaucratic recruitment to the LDP's parliamentary ranks (although there are some initial bureaucratic careers by a few *nisei* politicians, such as Yoshiro Hayashi in MITI and Koichi Kato in MFA – up

to *kacho* level usually – and some adoptions and/or *keibatsu* of elite bureaucrats with politicians' daughters, as with Hajime Morita and Yukihiko
Ikeda, both of MOF). The LDP's seniority system, which today requires
some four or five re-elections (that is, some 20 years in the Diet) in order
to be considered for a first cabinet post, has worked against senior bureaucrats choosing a political secondary career, and has benefited the young
sons of established politicians who were able – unlike any of their peers
– to enter parliament on strength of inherited *jiban*, *kaban* and *kanban*, and
to rise in the LDP's parliamentary pecking order with first ministerial
appointments in their mid-fifties (at an age when elite bureaucrats begin
to retire). They are thus able to accumulate top political experience to
qualify eventually for prime ministerial election some 15 years later. The
current system has narrowed the already small pool for Japan's top leadership to such an extent that if extrapolated for only a few generations, it
would result in the refeudalisation of political power in Japan, with the
country being run by a handful of very powerful, rich and mutually related
clans.

THE LOCAL POWER BASE

Building up a supporters' association (*koenkai*) that will form the core of
the local electoral base (*jiban*) – it is often locally distinct from the home
bases of competing LDP politicians in the same electoral district – is a
young MP's foremost task. Yukio Hatoyama, a freshman MP in 1986,
during his first term alone put 38 secretaries (that is, political assistants)
to work in his new constituency in Hokkaido 4 in which the Tokyo-based
Hatoyamas so far had no connections. The result can be a formidable
election machine. Kakuei Tanaka's *Etsuzankai* had 320 branches in Niigata
3 with nearly 100,000 members. In his last re-election in 1986 the *Etsuzankai*,
unperturbed by Tanaka's previous bribery conviction and his incapacitation
by a stroke, delivered 179,000 votes, far in excess of the 70,000 votes
arithmetically needed to obtain re-election. Maintenance costs for this
political machine were estimated at between ¥500 million and ¥1 billion
per annum.[2] As Tanaka's family was unable to secure these funds, on top
of the succession squabbles, the *Etsuzankai* fell apart in late 1989 after
Tanaka's announced retirement. Its prime members (local mayors, assemblymen, construction companies) were then raided and gobbled up by
erstwhile rivals and hopeful newcomers.

Takao Fujinami, former chief cabinet secretary and Nakasone's factional
heir-apparent until the Recruit Scandal cut down both of them, similar to

Tanaka earlier, had to leave the party in disgrace. Still, Fujinami's 45,000 member-strong *koenkai* in rural Ise remained loyal. 'Personal relations are everything in Japan. When a person is having problems you must help him', one follower was quoted as saying.[3] Fujinami, who had promised a new bridge, a grand exposition, an expressway and tourism development during his campaign speeches, was safely re-elected in February 1990, his *koenkai* delivering 20,000 votes on top of their own.

Asahiko Mihara, a second-term *nisei* MP from Fukuoka, has to defend his home turf against the encroachments of Taro Aso, Yoshida's grandson, who shares the same electoral district. As a result, his political agenda is equally dominated by local politics and his schedule filled with local appearances.[4] Mihara's time is mostly spent in lobbying in Tokyo on his constituents' behalf: to petition ministries for local businessmen and to steer public works projects towards his electoral district. These lobbying efforts, sometimes take the form of calling at senior bureaucrats' offices, but more frequently he invites them to high-class restaurants in Akasaka or to bars in the Ginza (and sends the bills for these treats to the companies seeking favours).

Lobbying of a particular sort is that practised with private universities' admission officers to obtain special entrance examinations or a waiver thereof for children whose parents offer a sizeable donation to the university through the Dietman's good offices. (While the donations are usually accepted, some of the academically deficient candidates sometimes still fail to gain admission.)

Michio Watanabe, a former minister of MOF, MITI and MAFF and an incumbent faction chief, in a speech to the Tokyo Foreign Correspondents Club in December 1988 explained at great length and detail the financial needs of LDP Dietmen. Most had 10 to 15 secretaries, costing around ¥10 million per month in wages. Most secretaries were employed full-time to do constituency work; that is, to visit hospitals, attend funerals and marriage ceremonies. Each such visit cost ¥10,000 in flowers and ¥20,000 in cash gifts. There was a funeral every day and four or five marriages on good, auspicious days. Schools asked for donations for monuments and pianos, and so did all shrines, temples and local festival associations. On a normal year there were invitations to 200–300 *bonenkai* (year-end) parties and to 300–350 *shonenkai* (New Year) parties – 200 of which were to be attended (with ¥10,000–20,000 in gifts to be brought to each). If Dietmen failed to donate or to attend, they would lose their re-election. Probably the electorate got the political system it deserved, Watanabe concluded.

Mihara explained to the *FEER* that he would also have to donate at shrine openings and to winning baseball and rugby teams. He visited his constituency at least four times a month in order to stay in touch ('to weed the rice paddies').[5] The airline costs to visit outlying prefectures accumulated (Japan's three airlines, however, have 25, 50 and 100 per cent discount tickets available for air-transportation-linked MPs).

Hyosuke Kujiraoka, a former Environment Agency chief and senior Komoto faction member, counts the number of year-end and New Year parties to be attended by either himself or his secretaries at 30 a day, totalling 600 during the season. According to him the expected contributions per event vary between ¥3000 and ¥10,000.[6]

Wining, dining and entertaining supporters outside election time is also a must, particularly when local politicians make their trips to Tokyo. A *Mainichi* reporter thus joined the journey to Tokyo of some *koenkai* members of Shin Sakurai, a third-term MP from Niigata 3 who had carved his support group out of Tanaka's disintegrating empire.[7] Three buses with some 150 supporters led by a town assembly member went for a trip sponsored by Sakurai. During their journey drinks were distributed, the *koenkai* singing happily. In Tokyo they were received by Sakurai's secretary who gave them a guided tour of the Diet building, in the dining room of which they finally were greeted by the *sensei* in person, who declared himself terribly busy but none the less shared lunch with the group.

Souvenir photographs were taken, and over beers on the ride back Mr Sakurai's fans appeared duly impressed by their encounter with the great man.

MPS' FINANCES

The only thing on which all LDP MPs will instantly agree is that their official income is clearly insufficient for their political needs. Still, salary and allowances appear to be fairly generous not only when compared to Japanese wage levels but also by international standards (see Table 3.1). In addition an MP is given a small apartment and a smallish office in one of the Members' square office-buildings located behind the Diet building.

Figures on additional income and expenditure vary a lot between LDP politicians (on the revenue side depending on the strength of business connections, perceived influence and past merits, and on the expenditure side on constituency situation and factional status). Figures are notoriously difficult to verify, since public disclosure requirements allow a great variety of loopholes to be extensively utilised, and most surveys need to rely on voluntary information which has only been forthcoming so far from relatively junior Dietmen with little to hide. This seems to apply to the 'Utopia

Table 3.1 Allowances of a Diet member[8]

	per month(¥)	per year(¥)
Monthly salary	1,091,000	13,092,000
Term-end salary		5,182,250
Allowances for documents, communication and transportation	750,000	9,000,000
JR free pass or airline ticket coupon	65,000	780,000
Allowances for legislative activities	650,000	7,800,000
Salary for two secretaries	671,770	8,061,240
Total	3,227,770	43,915,490

Study Group' of LDP MPs ready to publish their finances in full, which was set up in 1986. Their spending averaged ¥116 million in 1987 (a non-election year) with total revenues standing at ¥126 million per MP. Fifteen per cent of income came from the state allowances detailed in Table 3.1. Political donations accounted for 43 per cent, 16 per cent from fund-raising parties, and 8 per cent from factions and party headquarters. Most of the donations were made from a large number of constituency-based businesses that contributed monthly dues of ¥5000–10,000 to the Diet members' *koenkai*. Only more senior MPs have access to large donations from the major national business groups and their associations.

Spending is mostly on constituency activities (38 per cent), followed by personal expenses (34 per cent), travel and communications (17 per cent) and office expenditure (10 per cent).

The Utopia Group members employ on average 3.7 secretaries in Nagatacho (mostly to attend political committee meetings in place of the *sensei*) and 12.5 secretaries in the constituency, where their main task is to follow local politics, to animate the *koenkai*, to show the *sensei's* face and to distribute his cash-stuffed envelopes at the above-mentioned variety of social occasions: funerals (¥10,000), weddings (¥20,000), local festivals and sports events (¥200,000).

A survey of *Asahi Shimbun*[9] describes types of corporate help that result in significant cost savings: company employees work as the Dietman's assistants while remaining on the corporate payroll; cars are often supplied – sometimes with a driver – for the MP's use free of charge; the three major domestic airlines' system of 'preferential boarding tickets' has already been mentioned. Offices and private apartments are sometimes rented (or sold) at only nominal prices by a generous developer friend. (One of the beneficiaries of the latter system has been PM Kaifu, with the bargain-price purchase of an expensive apartment in Chiyoda-ku's exclusive Sanban-cho district in central Tokyo.)

With increasing seniority and sectoral importance, donations increase. One MP is quoted by the *Asahi* as having observed that the number of his regular corporate contributions jumped to between 40 and 50 as soon as he was appointed parliamentary vice-minister at MOT.[10] An individual politician's major sales pitch *vis-à-vis* potential corporate donors is his ability to supply introductions and to offer lobbying of the central ministries on their behalf. A politician's name-card bearing a reference for a company to bureaucrats is estimated to be worth ¥300,000. Most LDP MPs will actively solicit the business community for funds, taking advantage of their positioning in Japan's uniquely structured power triangle: while they hold sway over the bureaucracy, the bureaucracy in turn is feared for its discretionary license-allocation and controlling powers by the business sector. The politicians, of course, remain dependent on corporate Japan for funding.

Given the decisive importance of revenue for making and unmaking political careers, many LDP MPs are correspondingly creative – and sometimes ruthless – in their fund-raising (while remaining considerably more discreet on their revenue work than on their spending needs, which they can blame on greedy voters and local politicians). The *Mainichi* in a fifteen-part survey[11] which a medium-ranking LDP MP, Tsuneo Suzuki, later considered very accurate,[12] pointed out the diversity in sourcing efforts:

(a) *The sale of 'party tickets'*, priced at ¥20,000 each and sold aggressively in sets of ten to corporate sponsors, whose executives however often hardly bother to attend these crowded events held in Tokyo hotels. (Sales of these tickets netted a reported total income of ¥9.5 billion in 1987, until the Recruit Scandal in 1989 enforced a temporary ban on this sort of low-cost fund-raising.) For the time being, 'parties' have been replaced by more sombre but hardly less lucrative 'policy seminars' in which the *sensei* expounds his priceless political philosophy before an audience of hapless junior corporate salarymen. There is even a secondary market for unsold tickets in which shady dealers pretend to talk for the MP's secretaries, and receive a 50 per cent commission on the tickets' selling price when successful.[13] In order to improve the sales record, bureaucrats from typical clientele ministries (Finance, Transport, Construction, MITI and so on) were reported to have pushed individual companies and the associations of 'their' industries to purchase specific quantities of tickets benefiting 'their' LDP politicians (that is, sitting on the competent Diet committee or being part of their ministry's *zoku*). Apparently, this type of bureaucratic pressure – given only indirectly or by phone – is illegal under Japan's Civil Service Law.[14]

An incumbent construction minister, 80-year-old Kosei Amano, on 20 April 1987 held a fund-raising party (with the pretext of celebrating his becoming the oldest cabinet minister in Japan's postwar history). Conveniently, the party was scheduled during Diet deliberations of a ¥5 trillion supplementary budget which focused on public works. Priced at ¥20,000 each, 10,440 tickets were sold, grossing ¥208.8 million. Costs for the event (rent, food, drinks) were only ¥8.5 million, creating an impressive profit rate of some 2500 per cent. Amano, who stressed that none of this money was spent for private purposes, thus gave ultimate proof of his political skills.

(b) *Stock speculation.* Dietmen, through their financial secretary, attempt to capitalise on their political standing by entrusting their funds to major securities firms (or sometimes to professional speculators of lesser repute), with instructions to multiply the principal and to compensate in case of losses incurred. Occasionally their secretaries have to do the *zaitech* (financial wizardry) speculation by themselves. Sometimes, in order to reduce risks, they avail themselves of bargain-priced pre-flotation issues of stocks (such as those offered by Ezoe in the case of his Recruit Cosmos company). At other times they deal with the help of insider information, as did Toshiyuki Imamura, a former Environment Agency minister and member of the Watanabe faction (subsequently indicted and condemned for tax evasion), who made ¥2.8 billion profit by purchasing stocks of companies staked by corporate raider Mitsuhiro Kotani to whom he later sold at a huge risk-free profit margin.[15]

A very particular feature are 'political stocks' of a company in which a senior politician is said to have either a significant stake or to whose president he has strong personal links. An upturn in his political fortunes will also cause a rise in the company's share prices (as they are expected to benefit from the former, so he will profit from the latter)

The *Mainichi* has listed the following political stocks:[16]

Takeshita: Aoki (construction), Fukuda Construction, Kyowa Hakko Kogyo (chemicals, drugs, food, alcohol), and Yamanouchi Pharmaceuticals;

Nakasone: Mochida Pharmaceuticals, Kobori Juken (construction), and Minebea (bearings and machine parts);

Abe: Maeda Construction, Nisshin Food Products, and Ube Industries (cement, chemicals);

Miyazawa: Kitagawa Iron Works, Fujita (construction) and Kureha Chemical Industry.

While most LDP MPs are more opportunistic beneficiaries of bullish stock market moves and suitably delegate their financial management, a handful of MPs are professional speculators (operating in the name of their support group in order to remain income-tax exempt). The late Kazuo Tamaki, a minister of the Management and Co-ordination Agency, who died in 1987, and Eitaro Itoyama, a three-term MP (until he lost his seat in 1990), owner-president of a tour-operating company and a nephew to Ryoichi Sasagawa, acquired fame for their large-scale successful gambling at Kabuto-cho, Japan's Wall Street.

(c) *Land speculation*, an art which has been brought to unsurpassed perfection by Kakuei Tanaka: to have dummy companies or straw men buy land which is destined for public development ('new towns', new industrial parks, *Shinkansen* stations and so on) or which will appreciate, due to being in the vicinity of such developments.

(d) *Rewards for services rendered.* This covers a wide range of activities in which a Dietman can prove his usefulness: lobbying for the award of public contracts (especially of construction projects) to certain companies (which will result in sizeable subsequent campaign contributions); working with bureaucrats to allocate licences to transportation companies, to private universities; lobbying for permits for new drugs, shopping centres, and so on. A prominent field of action is to arrange backdoor admissions to medical schools and to prestigious private universities. Sometimes Dietmen have admission 'quotas' which they sell to the candidates' parents at prices of up to ¥20 million. More frequently their secretaries will work on behalf of candidates who fear they will fail the formal entry tests: be it by transmitting an official 'donation' to the university or by bribing professors or admission clerks outright. For their Dietmen (or for themselves) they will charge a commission of some 30 per cent.

In the age of post-materialism many affluent and successful Japanese strive for symbols of public recognition, as expressed in government awards and medals. A Dietman can be helpful by putting forward convincingly an aspirant's merits to the award-giving authorities – for a fee. In the cultural sector, it has become customary for artists desiring to receive the order of Cultural Merit or the Academy of Arts Award to express their appreciation to helpful politicians by presenting them with one of their paintings or other art works which the beneficiary will easily mutate into cash. (As gifts of paintings are also frequently used by corporations as contributions in lieu of cash, it is done to top up real-estate transfer payments in a non-taxable way.)

(e) *Goodwill contributions*. Lucrative business arrangements that want to avoid public scrutiny, controls, crackdowns or other unwanted attention; horse-racing and motorboat-racing associations (the latter controlled by Mr Ryoichi Sasagawa) give generously, as does Nikkokyo, the national stevedores federation (controlled by Mr Shiro Takashima). These donations, of course, are sensibly given primarily to those MPs active in the *zoku* of the supervisory ministry (horse-racing – Agriculture; motorboat racing and stevedoring – Transportation). *Pachinko*-parlour operators are equally underworld-controlled and notorious for tax evasion. During 1984–8 the Diet deliberated a draft bill that would have closed down a few tax loopholes for the industry. During the height of the Recruit Scandal in August 1979 LDP sources let it be known that the JSP and her chairwoman, Takako Doi, had received sizeable contributions from the National Pinball Parlours Association (*Zenyuren*), which may have included North Korean money (most *pachinko* establishments are in Korean hands), a country dear to the hearts of the JSP's left wing. Soon, however, it transpired that DSP and Komeito had also received some ¥2.75 million each, and that PM Kaifu and seven of his cabinet members had been awarded ¥5 million from the *pachinko* industry. Its Kansai-based ministers Toida (Health and Welfare) and Nakayama (Foreign) alone had received ¥1.8 and ¥1.1 million each.[17] The 'scandal' was subsequently hushed up.

(f) *Silent partners in business*. Wherever public or private businesses enjoy lucrative monopoly profit operations – be it in telecommunications (KDD, NTT) or in beef imports (the LIPC until April 1991) – related (*zoku*) LDP MPs take their share. Also for illegal business transactions, protection from the law can be bought with political commissions, as in the case of the 'Nagoya connection', when pork imports from Taiwan undercut the minimum import price. For the protection of this lucrative business Nagoya-based government and opposition party politicians were said to have been paid.[18]

With most politicians being hard-pressed for cash, as was proved during the Recruit relevations, ethical standards are not particularly high: when offered contributions almost all had accepted. Mr Tsuneo Suzuki, a second-term LDP MP (Takeshita faction, formerly with the NLC) and a self-styled 'left winger' among the LDP's 'reformists', with the declared motto of 'honesty is the best policy', admitted that it was 'difficult' to prevent 'dirty money' flowing into one's coffers. While he refused some contributions, he still needed cash. There were plenty of temptations as one climbed the political ladder.[19]

An *Asahi* survey of 1989[20] calculated the sources of the average LDP Dietman's annual income as follows (note that there is some variation from the Utopia Group's breakdown): corporate contributions: 39 per cent; revenue from parties: 17 per cent; individual contributions: 15 per cent; Diet allowances: 12 per cent; faction: 9 per cent; and debts: 8 per cent. It is not clear whether corporate contributions in kind (leasing cars, apartments, offices and so on at nominal fees, putting secretaries and campaign workers on corporate payrolls, donating paintings, airline tickets and the rest) are included in the above statistics, in which directly identifiable corporate donations – which include party tickets – already account for 56 per cent alone.

Getting rich is probably not a primary motive for becoming involved in politics. Still, successful LDP politicians don't appear to become poor in the process. Faction chiefs usually own luxury residences in the centre of Tokyo and summer residences in Karuizawa or other resorts, as well as stately homes in their constituencies – none of which they could afford on their Dietman's stipend alone. As mentioned above, they often also own sizeable shares in corporate Japan as well as in local businesses. At the annual cabinet reshuffles the personal finances of new ministers are regularly made public. Although real estate is only appraised at (strongly deflated) nominal values, the figures generally reveal a healthy prosperity as befits the owners/managers of medium-sized family businesses in Japan's service sector with on average 13 employees and ¥200 million annual turnover.

CAREERS

The road of a freshman LDP Dietman to prime ministership is a long and winding one, with political corpses strewn by the wayside. Perhaps one or two in a freshman class of 50 have the prospect of filling Japan's highest elective office after being re-elected some ten times to the Lower House. Prospects of becoming a minister at least once during one's political career are more realistic after surviving some six election campaigns. Cabinets are reshuffled every nine months or so – mainly to readjust factional balances but also to reward faithful backbenchers and to satisfy the ambitions of restless young Turks, to whom most of the 21 cabinet-level positions (except the three key ministries – Finance, Foreign, and Trade and Industry – and the Chief Cabinet Secretary) will be available.

In Japanese politics, as in other social sectors, seniority counts. The principal indication of an MP's rank is his number of elections to the Lower House (previous elections to the Upper House hardly count). The seniority criterion also applies within the egalitarian, progressive opposition parties.

A first-term MP has to start low down the pecking order in the factions and in the parliamentary party. This also applies to the sons of famous fathers and to previous senior bureaucrats. As their record of political and pork-barrel achievements is of necessity short, they feel vulnerable in their constituencies to possible challengers. Hence they need to spend a lot of time, energy and cash back home, while lacking the clout of old timers for fund-raising and effective bureaucratic lobbying. A first-timer will therefore be most grateful for a helping hand from a faction chief or one of his lieutenants, and will not forget the favours received in such a humble and vulnerable position. A first-term MP will attempt to sit on Diet committees and LDP PRC committees of constituency interest. He will try to develop and demonstrate a recognised specialist policy expertise to his party and faction seniors, to possible corporate sponsors and to his constituency – a speciality which, if continued during subsequent terms, should ultimately lead to his membership in the LDP's respective *zoku* and to his first ministerial appointment. However, a freshman will consider himself lucky if he gains a seat in the Diet's finance committee, sits on a decent PRC subcommittee and becomes a deputy director in the LDP headquarters youth bureau. He will have to do a lot of bowing and dining to have more farm-roads paved and fishery harbours rebuilt in his home district.

DIET COMMITTEES

Being entitled to fill 336 committee seats (1988) in the 18 standing committees of the Lower House, the LDP's then 302 MPs all had a fair chance to get a seat on at least one committee. As indicated in Table 3.2, the freshmen MPs' presence is most numerous in the committees for Social and Labour Affairs, and for Finance and proportionally strongest in the exciting committee for Rules and Administration. Among the other committees, Budget and Construction are clearly off-limits (not even a first-term former MOC administrative vice-minister was admitted), as is Discipline, in which elder statesman and faction chiefs watch and judge over the follies of youth. It is a safe bet to assume that the importance and prestige of a standing committee is inversely related to the number of freshmen MPs in its midst.

Most junior MPs serve as ordinary committee members, filling backbench positions. A handful of freshman MPs (particularly those who had already achieved a distinguished career in regional politics (governorship, speaker of prefectural assembly and so on) or in the national administration are given a more elevated 'director' status in their respective committees, which is normally reserved for second- or third-term MPs. The chairmanship of most Lower House committees is limited to fifth-term MPs (and to some high-flying fourth-termers). The sole exceptions are Budget and

Table 3.2 Diet standing committees, Lower House, 1988

	LDP freshmen on the committee	LDP seats on the committee	Total seats on the committee
Cabinet	4	18	30
Local administration	5	18	30
Justicial affairs	1	17	30
Foreign affairs	3	18	30
Finance	8	24	40
Education	5	17	30
Social and labour affairs	10	24	40
Agriculture	1	24	40
Commerce and industry	3	24	40
Transport	2	18	30
Construction	0	18	30
Communications	4	19	30
Science and technology	2	14	25
Environment	3	14	25
Budget	0	30	50
Audit	3	13	25
Rules and Administration	7	15	25
Discipline	0	11	20

Discipline, which are chaired by ex-ministers of more senior standing. Most ministers after a cabinet reshuffle will continue to serve as ordinary members in one or other committee (Budget being a clear favourite).

LDP BUREAUCRACY

A second source of political management experience considered indispensable prior to a ministerial appointment is provided by the LDP's central party functions (see Figure 3.1).

The party's four most senior positions (the presidency, the secretary general and the chairmanships of the PRC and the General Council) are obviously filled by political heavyweights with all major factions being represented. Two more positions (chairman of the National Organisation Committee and the chief of the National Campaign HQ) are headed by relatively senior figures (ex-ministers, of at least seven parliament terms with strong standing in their factions). The LDP HQ has a fairly fuzzy

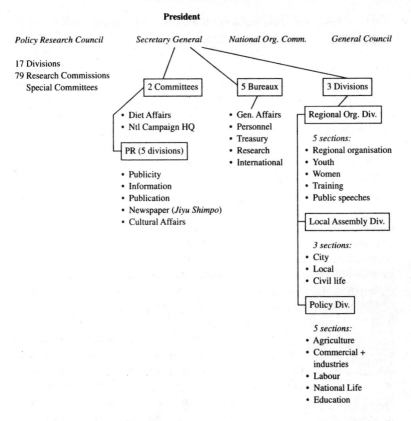

President

Policy Research Council   *Secretary General*   *National Org. Comm.*   *General Council*

17 Divisions
79 Research Commissions
Special Committees

| 2 Committees |
| 5 Bureaux |
| 3 Divisions |

- Diet Affairs
- Ntl Campaign HQ

| PR (5 divisions) |

- Publicity
- Information
- Publication
- Newspaper (*Jiyu Shimpo*)
- Cultural Affairs

- Gen. Affairs
- Personnel
- Treasury
- Research
- International

| Regional Org. Div. |

5 sections:
- Regional organisation
- Youth
- Women
- Training
- Public speeches

| Local Assembly Div. |

3 sections:
- City
- Local
- Civil life

| Policy Div. |

5 sections:
- Agriculture
- Commercial +
  industries
- Labour
- National Life
- Education

Figure 3.1 LDP central organisation

structure of five bureaux (General Affairs, Personnel, Treasury, Research, International), most of which are headed by middle-ranking fifth-term MPs shortly before their ministerial appointments. There are also eight divisions (Publicity, Information, Publications, Newspaper, Culture, Regional Organisation, Local Assemblies, and Policy), which are run largely by fourth-term MPs. Some of the divisions are subdivided into sections (13 in total) which are run by junior MPs in their second or third term. These middle-level positions in the party apparatus give these MPs a certain sense of importance, and may enlarge their policy management experience. But, most importantly, they give these middle-ranking Dietmen decent titles (*kacho, bucho, kyokucho* in the ruling party) which, while they await ministerial posts, they can demonstrate to their constituency faithfuls as symbols of achievement in Tokyo.

Within the party structure it is the divisions and many subcommittees of the Policy Research Council (*Seichokai*) which offer an MP scope for genuine policy training and opportunities for substantial input and for showing policy competence before his peers. While the PRC divisions roughly follow the ministries' structure and follow their agendas, and are headed typically by a fourth-term MP (who has already served his customary two terms as parliamentary vice-minister), the multitude of subcommittees affiliated to each division is more puzzling. While some are hardly operational, esoteric in substance and mainly serve to lend a title to its chairman, others – 'research commissions' (*seichochosakai*) – are headed by an experienced ex-minister of the policy area and contain a number of senior-ranking policy specialists in the field. In fact, these 'research commissions' are homes of the *zoku* – where the real policy decisions affecting a ministry are made. On agricultural policies, for instance, the Research Commission on Comprehensive Agriculture (*sogo nosei chosakai*), formerly headed by Tsutomu Hata – a two-term former minister and the recognised head of the *norinzoku* (all incumbent MAFF ministers will listen to his advice on any significant policy issue) – is most influential. Other prominent *zoku* chiefs are Shin Kanemaru (construction), Ryotaro Hashimoto (health and welfare), and Yoshiro Mori (education).

During their third term Lower House MPs are appointed to the position of parliamentary vice-minister – normally at two different ministries/agencies. The post is almost exclusively ceremonial: reading out prepared ministry answers during Diet sessions and receiving visitors for whom the minister cannot find time. Still, the vice-ministership is a must on the way to ministerial rank. It offers a more dignified ambiance than the Dietmen's normal working offices, and proves to the folks back home that after some ten years on the job their man in Tokyo is finally working his way up.

BECOMING A MINISTER

Among the 180 MPs (from both Houses) who became ministers during the 1980s – a figure probably also indicative of a world record in the share of ex-ministers in any parliamentary party – 47 became ministers during their sixth term in the Lower House, 24 were lucky during their fifth term (mostly being members of the Tanaka/Takeshita camp), four were exceptionally fast in securing their ministership during their fourth term (sometimes because they served in the Upper House earlier), and two, Gotoda and T. Kosaka – the first exercised considerable political powers as former head of the Police Agency, and the second as a business tycoon prominent in *zaikai* prior to entering parliament – became ministers during their second terms. On the slow track, 17 MPs made it during their seventh terms, three became ministers for the first time during their eighth term, and four only in their ninth term. On the slow side were those who changed factions frequently (and who were now with the Fukuda/Abe or Komoto factions), who had been with the NLC, or who were either extremely 'quiet' or an embarrassment to the ruling party, because of their personality, temperament or extremist (usually right-wing) political views.

Upper House members receive their first (and only) ministerial appointment usually (in 15 cases) during their third six-year term. The second term (eight cases) could be considered fast-track, and the fourth term (seven cases) a sure sign of a late achiever. As with their slow-track Lower House colleagues, inconspicuous backbenchers and those perceived as not quite up to ministerial standards will be appointed to head second-rate agencies (National Land, Environment, Science and Technology, and Hokkaido/ Okinawa Development) where their ability to inflict damage is very limited.

During the 1980s only one Upper House MP, Iichiro Hatoyama, was appointed a minister (Foreign Ministry) in his first term. Not only was he the son of a former prime minister, he also, on account of his own strength and talents, had earlier risen to the rank of administrative vice-minister in MOF. Regularly re-elected since, with the largest number of votes in the national constituency, it was only his evident lack of interest in party and factional politics which precluded the continuation of this brilliant political career start.

Any Upper House member wishing to obtain a second ministership or to rise to a more senior position within the parliamentary party must at the earliest possible occasion switch to the Lower House, where in terms of seniority some (but not full) credit is given for his time in the Upper House. While in the 1980s 133 first ministerial appointments were made, 37 MPs were made minister for a second time (usually in their eighth term), 13 lucky MPs for a third time (mostly in their ninth term) and a very small number of senior Dietmen for a fourth time.

When ministerial slots are filled, some attempt is made by the prime minister and the faction chiefs to match candidates' expertise with the competent ministries. More often than not, factional balancing interests override the individuals' expertise and policy interests. Table 3.3 is a sample in alphabetical order of ministerial appointments made in the 1980s of MPs who claim a particular policy expertise. Less than one-third proved to be appropriate matchings.

If we look at the 20 cabinet positions filled in the third Kaifu cabinet, which was considered typical for factional balance and for seniority re-

Table 3.3   Ministerial appointments and fields of policy expertise

	Expertise	Ministry/Agency
Fumio Abe	Fisheries	Hokkaido/Okinawa
Kazuo Aichi	Foreign affairs	Environment
Hideyuki Aizawa	Budget	Economic Planning (EPA)
Kosei Amano	Construction	Construction (MOC)
Masahisa Aoki	Education	Environment
Takami Eto	Agriculture	Transport (MOT)
Takao Fujimoto	Environment/science	Okinawa/MHW
Takao Fujinami	Education	Labour (MOL)
Joji Fukushima	Political reform	Labour (MOL)
Tsutomu Hata	Agriculture	Agriculture (MAFF)
Takiichiro Hatomura	Fisheries	Labour (MOL)
Kosuke Hori	Agriculture	Education (MOE)
Mitsuo Horiuchi	Labour	Labour (MOL)
Toshio Horiuchi	Education	Environment
Kichizo Hosoda	Transport	Transport (MOT)

wards: 15 slots were filled by first-time ministers (during their fifth or sixth term of LH or their second or third Upper House term), four by second-timers (Justice, Foreign, MITI, Chief Cabinet Secretary) – Sato, Nakayama, Nakao and Sakamoto. One by a third-timer (Finance) – Mr Hashimoto. The second group were in their eighth to tenth Lower House terms – with the exception of Nakayama, who had started with three Upper House terms, followed by two in the Lower House, giving him the requisite years of parliamentary experience for this senior job. Factional balance was maintained with six posts going to Takeshita, five to Abe, four each to Miyazawa and Abe, one to Komoto, and none to the Nikaido group and other independents. The three top-ranking ministries (Finance, Foreign, MITI) went evenly between the Takeshita, Abe and Watanabe factions, with the Chief Cabinet Secretary's post going to a Komoto loyalist. Big public spending positions (Transport, Construction, Agriculture and Posts/Telecom) were distributed between the Takeshita, Abe, Miyazawa and Watanabe camps. In sum, the Miyazawa faction, which had opposed Kaifu in vain, was somewhat short-changed, with the allied Takeshita/Kanemaru, Abe and Watanabe factions appearing quite satisfied with this temporary arrangement. In terms of regional balance, 12 ministers came from rural prefectures (two alone from Akita and Ehime), with only four representing metropolitan Japan (Osaka: 2, Tokyo: 2) in their electoral districts.

Apart from this rural bias, on a North–South continuum (Hokkaido being an exception, as its volatile voters rarely permit an MP to reach the necessary seniority) the distribution seems even. The only distinction of this unremarkable, if somewhat typical, cabinet are the first cabinet terms of three new generation members with prominent names: Yukihiko Ikeda and Kazuo Aichi, previously adopted sons-in-law of Japan's former PM and Foreign Minister respectively, and Michio Ochi, son-in-law to PM Fukuda. All of them, however, were dutifully now in their sixth term. There are no dispensations from serving time for lucky matches!

The core cabinet positions (Finance, MITI and Foreign) are usually reserved for senior-ranking MPs who have already had two ministerial appointments. Also the Chief Cabinet Secretary as a rule has already had some previous cabinet experience. Designated high-flyers who enjoy the special protection of a major faction chief may receive dispensation from the standard seniority rules. Being groomed for an eventual prime ministerial post, they rapidly accumulate the 'right' ministerial experience (Construction/Transport for pork-barrels; Home Affairs to control and advance the party machine in local politics; Finance, MITI and Foreign to gain from increased media coverage and to achieve the necessary statesmanlike image and world perspective). Appointments to the three most senior party positions allow proper control of the party's central functions and of the parliamentary party. A politician of this senior standing has already outgrown the narrow confines of his sectoral *zoku*. Having proven his mastery of sectoral policy details in the past (including fund-raising and the ability to deliver), when bidding for more senior assignments he must show his statesmenlike credentials, which should include a command of general economic and fiscal policy and a certain, sometimes painfully acquired, international exposure. While career advancement was rapid and seemingly effortless for those MPs favoured as loyal henchmen and preferred successors to senior faction chiefs (like Nikaido to Tanaka, and Fujinami to Nakasone), their fall from grace and into political oblivion was swift if they failed to build up their own independent power base, once their beloved leader lost power and influence.

HIERARCHIES IN THE PARLIAMENTARY PARTY

For a successful MP it is essential to remain allied to the right people at the right time; to avoid changing factions and falling out with the faction chief or one of his likely successors; and during the first two decades (six terms) in national politics, to set up an immaculate political record (which includes being safely re-elected at each election); to stay clear of major scandals; to have mastered a lucrative political file (*zoku*); and to be on good personal terms with most of one's fellow and junior MPs – transcending one's own faction and stretching into the opposition camp; and to have served once or twice in a presentable ministry and finally to have created during that period a favourable impression on the ministry officials, the media and the general public. To become a more universal and powerful politician, an ex-minister will start to consolidate his role within his faction. Toshio Yamaguchi, ex-MOL minister, once said he preferred his position of secretary general in the Nakasone/Watanabe faction to a second ministerial appointment.[21]

Alternatively, an MP has to head a PRC committee of genuine importance and preside over visible policy changes (so that his name will remain associated with the implementation of the particular policy reform). National name recognition and a recognised ability to deliver should facilitate fund-raising, transcending the needs of his own constituency, and begin to allow the collection of funds to be distributed to 'friends' among junior faction members. This marks the beginning of the build-up of a personal power base in Parliament. Suspiciously watched by the faction chief and fellow senior faction colleagues, the setting up of one's own 'study group' is a high-risk exercise which can backfire if continued funding proves to be too difficult (indicating that few businessmen believe in investing in his political future and friendship).

With a sizable intra-factional study group (of 20 to 30 core members and a fringe of sympathisers) an MP rises to senior status within his faction. He can lay legitimate claim to a senior ministry and to top party posts for himself (as he is now publicly traded as a 'neo-new leader' of sorts and a potential successor at the faction's helm). But by the same token he has to work hard so that his faithful study group followers also receive their due share of political positions, constituency business and non-monetary rewards (the usual cash flow notwithstanding).

With factional succession, the mainstream factions' practice of 'amicable' transition to the strongest sub-faction leader has spread over the last 20 years to the previously more fractious sidestream factions. But Nagatacho is littered with political corpses – longstanding MPs who at some point were allied with the wrong (losing) side during some internal battle, and who in consequence lost most of their political influence (and independent funding). The groups of Susumu Nikaido and of Mitsuki Kato, who lost succession battles against Takashita/Kanemaru and Mitsuzuka/Mori in their respective factions, are recent examples to illustrate this point.

About 50 per cent of the LDP's 250 Lower House MPs have had ministerial experience. Some 50 MPs have been ministers twice, 20 of them even more frequently. This structure gives only a rough idea of the stratification of power and influence in the parliamentary party, yet some multi-ministerial talents are clearly 'have-beens' due to age, lost power battles, or simply a reduced liking for the rough and tumble of interfactional plotting and horsetrading.

It would be more sensible to rank the actual faction chiefs at the top of Japan's political hierarchy. Added to these are the semi-retired senior statesmen, who, like Kanemaru, are still in control of major decisions, although no longer holding formal senior positions. This upper crust is followed by a string of key lieutenants (three to five in each of the four major factions) and other senior power-brokers either within the parliamentary party or, like Fukuda and Suzuki, recently retired. A third tier is made up of MPs who cut a smart figure as ministers, show good potential for the future, but are still a decade away (which will weed out quite a few of their number) from having a fair shot at positions of genuine power.

Loss of a seat in Parliament normally means an immediate (if re-elected later only temporary) loss of most power and influence. An MP, having lost his seat, may either resign himself to an involuntary and premature end to his political career or devote all his resources during the next years to preserving and rebuilding his *koenkai* constituency organisation. Graceful voluntary retirement and handing over the constituency in good order to one's preferred successor (preferably a son) is obviously a more attractive option than losing elections or death in office. The only problem is to choose and to accept the right timing. During the 1990 election, voluntary retirement ages of LDP MPs who decided not to run again was between 78 and 85 years. Successor-sons were then fairly middle-aged already when they were able to begin their Lower House career (and would need to dedicate at least some 20 to 30 years before being able to go after the senior slots from which some of their fathers had just retired).

A first-term Lower House MP has a 50 per cent probability of political survival into this third term, whence a period of fewer re-election worries begins. With their eighth term concluded (and after some 24 years of parliamentary life), the number of MPs of the same seniority begins to shrink again. Advanced age reduces their numbers, while for some of the survivors, physical vitality often declines while they close in on the most powerful positions attainable in Japanese society.

For those who have a choice, the consequence of the seniority system is clear: to anticipate the lifetime requirements of a political career and to begin a parliamentary life as early as possible. For the bureaucratic elite recruits this means opting out of the ministries as a youthful *kacho* at the age of 40 (and to risk unemployment and a truncated career if the election falls through), instead of going through a full bureaucratic career until

Table 3.4 *Parliamentary seniority by factions (1990): number of successful elections of faction members*

Number of elections	LDP Parliamentary Party (total)	Factions					
		Takeshita	Abe	Watanabe	Miyazawa	Komoto	Nikaido and factionless
(a) Lower House							
18	1			1			
17	2			1			1
16	2			1		1	
15	1						1
14							
13	3	2	1				
12	5	2		1	1	1	
11	5		1	1	1	1	1
10	11	4	2	1	1	2	1
9	15	2	2	3	5	2	1
8	28	8	4	10	4	2	
7	20	3	3	4	7	1	2
6	25	6	7	5	5	1	1
5	28	9	4	3	10	1	1
4	22	4	4	4	8	2	
3	23	7	5	4	4	2	1
2	45	15	10	9	7	4	
1	41	8	20	5	5	1	2
(b) Upper House							
5	2		2				
4	11	2	4	1	2	1	1
3	23	7	2	7	3	2	2
2	37	13	6	3	8	3	4
1	39	13	11	8	5	1	1

retiring as director general or administrative vice-minister at 56. For those who expect to inherit a seat in parliament (often with mixed feelings), it implies a waiting game familiar to all prospective legatees.

For the Upper House, where MPs serve full terms of six years – two terms already mean some seniority in age – those, such as Kiichi Miyazawa in 1967, wishing to pursue a more senior political career have to change to the Lower House. Those staying on opt for a quiet ministerial posting with subsequent *de facto* political retirement.

BACKGROUNDS

The ever-increasing role of hereditary politics in the LDP undertaken as a quasi-family business has already been discussed. Yet it often comes in combination with one or more of the other typical preparatory political pre-career occupations:

the administrative elite track;
political journalism;
political secretary/assistant to a Dietman;
mayorality or prefectural assembly membership;
a senior business career.

The contemporary prerequisite to most if not all of the above pre-careers is a decent university degree. Self-made careers of people such as Kakuei Tanaka, who with barely middle school education have worked their way up in postwar Japan on the strength of individual performance, ruthlessness and acumen, and have built their own personal power base and economic fortunes from scratch, are getting distinctly rare. For once, the bureaucratisation of LDP politics today requires a proper degree. It has additional uses: the alumni network will supply votes, useful contacts, and access to donations. Lower House LDP Dietmen, analysed by alma mater, attended Todai (85 in total or 28 per cent), followed by Waseka (42, corresponding to 14 per cent) Keio (35, or 12 per cent), Chuo (25), Nihon (14), Hitotsubashi (7), Kyodai, Gakushuin and Meiji (6 each), Tohoku (5), Hokudai, Kyudai, Rikkyo, Takushoku and the Tokyo University of Agriculture (3 each). Twenty-three MPs attended other, mostly regional, universities. Five went through military academies, four to technical and five to agricultural colleges. Two MPs finally graduated from US universities (Nikaido from UCLA and Ishii from Stanford). Only a small number of MPs never ventured into tertiary education: eight have high school education, five went to middle school, and two terminated after primary school.

In all, LDP MPs went to better universities than their opposition colleagues. Also by any international standard they are an extremely well-educated lot. If only their performance and policies would show this. This observation also applies to Waseda University's debating club (*yubenkai*) which plays a prominent role in the CVs of some of the graduates in this 'politicians and journalists'-breeding private elite institution. The club was attended by Noburo Takeshita, Toshiki Kaifu, Yoshiro Mori, Takeo Nishioka, Kozo Watanabe, Keizo Obuchi and Hiroshi Mitsuzuka. The rhetorical performance of some of these politically successful alumni, however, does not appear to be matched by the club's fame for developing debating skills.

Seventy-two Lower House and 30 Upper House LDP MPs had earlier served in Japan's central administration.

By comparison, only three ex-central bureaucrats currently represent opposition parties in the Diet: two sit for Komeito (one each from MITI and from MFA) in the Lower House, and one (a former Naimusho and subsequent MHW official) for the DSP in the Upper House.

In terms of rank, among Lower House LDP members, five were former administrative vice-ministers, 12 were former directors general (*kyokucho*), one a former department director general (*bucho*), 20 were formerly division directors (*kacho*), and 27 were of a more junior rank, such as counsellor, *kachohosa*, *kakaricho* and so on, (and thus not necessarily 'elite track' class I officers).

Ten former officials mentioned that they had last served as administrative secretaries (assistants) to their ministers, who had recruited them subsequently into active politics. In addition, 12 MPs report that they have earlier served as personal (political) secretaries to ministers (sometimes to their own fathers): they have not been career officials but have filled some of the few temporary slots open for political appointees in Japan's civil service.

Table 3.5   Ministry of origin of bureaucrat LDP MPs

	Lower House	Upper House
MOF	27	3
MITI	13	–
MAFF	10	8
Prewar *Naimusho*	6	6
MOC	6	7
Home Affairs (MHA)	5	5
MOL	2	2
MHW	1	2
MOT	1	1
Police Agency	2	3
Foreign Affairs (MFA)	2	1
Defence Agency	1	2
MPT	1	3
EPA	1	1
MOE		1
Management & Co-ordination Agency		1
Total	72	30

Journalism was the previous career of 19 LDP MPs in the Lower House and two in the Upper House. By medium of origin: six are from the conservative *Yomiuri Shimbun*, four from impartial *NHK*, three from centrist *Mainichi* (including most prominently the late Shintaro Abe), two from the right wing *Sankei Shimbun*, and the rest from other, mostly regional papers, TV stations and newsagencies. Forty opposition MPs nominally are journalists – a slightly misleading figure: all four JCP 'journalists' are with *Akahata*, the in-house Red Flag paper, and the 19 Komeito 'journalists' report for equally closely affiliated sectarian Buddhist papers. The five JSP journalist parliamentarians all work for TV stations.

By comparison with the ex-bureaucrats who mostly hailed from Todai Law, the LDP ex-journalists graduated from Waseda's economics and political science departments (11), followed by Keio and Todai (three each), and Tohoku University (two). Typically a journalist is befriended and recruited by a senior politician whom he is covering (as happened to Abe, himself the son of a prewar Dietmember, when following in the footsteps of Nobusuke Kishi, whose oldest daughter he subsequently married). Sometimes their step into national politics is preluded by a period in a prefectural assembly, thus testing the waters of electoral politics.

The political career is obviously facilitated when the local print and electronic news media are already family property (which must have helped Mr Nishioka in Nagasaki (*Nagasaki Shimbun*) and Upper House MP Hirai in Kagawa (*Shikoku Shimbun*), and the Kosaka brothers (*Shimane Mainichi Shimbun*) in Nagano.

Sixty-six MPs list 'secretary' to Dietman/Minister/Prime Minister/faction chief as a major previous occupation (and sometimes, as in case of ex-PM Kaifu, as his only one. Kaifu was then serving faction chief Takeo Miki). Often they assisted their own fathers. As sons of sitting MPs even more frequently they served the faction head or another senior-ranking faction member in a political apprenticeship and as an investment in human networking.

In ten cases the former political secretary became a prefectural assemblyman (and in one case a city mayor) before venturing back into national politics.

As earlier careers, fourteen MPs and ex-secretaries list a private-sector occupation as 'salarymen' (they were often seconded to serve as Dietmen while remaining on the corporate payroll – sometimes their employer may also have lent a helping hand to get their political careers started).

Eighty-six LDP Lower House members and 29 LDP Upper House men originated in local and prefectural politics. Prominent examples are Noboru Takeshita, Sosuke Uno and Michio Watanabe.

Table 3.6 *'Local politicians' in the Diet*

Former political position	LDP		Opposition parties	
	Lower House	Upper House	Lower House	Upper House
Prefectural assemblyman	66	17	55	10
Prefectural assemblyman & mayor	5	4	1	4
City mayor (*machi* + *shi*)	9	3	6	1
City assemblyman	4	2	11	5
Governor	2[1]	3[2]		

Notes

[1] The ex-governors of Yamanashi and Saga prefectures.

[2] The ex-governors of Okayama, Kyoto and Hiroshima prefectures.

As major sources of recruitment, local politics appears to be the only example where LDP and opposition MPs beginnings appear roughly compatible. LDP MPs who started in local politics have mostly graduated from Waseda (21), followed by Chuo (10), Todai (9), Keio (7) and Nihon (6). Other reputable universities attended were: Tohoku, Hosei and Hokudai (two each) and Meiji, Gakushuin and Kyodai (one each). Twenty-two MPs attended less well-known regional or private universities and colleges. Five dropped out of college. Five attended specialist colleges and seven went to specialist vocational schools. Eight made it through high school, and five only got through middle school (thus being barely able to read the *kanji* in the ministries' official communications).

Subjects studied by the LDP MPs commencing in local politics were law (30), followed by economics (14), agriculture and political economy (7 each). While not quite as elitist as the Todai Law-based central bureaucracy recruits, the LDP's 'local politicians', defying their image as country bumpkins, are fairly well educated, if somewhat closer in level to Japan's Mr Toshio Average.

It should be noted that in Japan's local politics ex-central ministry bureaucrats are prominent. Among the city mayors (*shicho*) 37 are ex-ministry officials compared with 44 from prefectural administrations and 87 from the town governments proper. Among the 47 governors a majority (25) come from the Tokyo ministries (Home Affairs figuring prominently), followed by the prefectures' own administration (12). Consequently Todai Law (22) is the governors' most frequent alma mater.

BUSINESS BACKGROUND

Most LDP MPs are busy and fully occupied with their political pursuits. Hence few remain enterpreneurs, but quite a handful are heirs to sizable business fortunes which grant an independent source of funding as well as a certain electoral base among employees and business associates.

Some 50 MPs in both Houses control or are affiliated with large business operations in family property. Most frequent are close links to *sake* brewing, construction and transportation businesses. These businesses vary in size and profitability. Faction chief Toshio Komoto in 1985 managed to create the then largest bankruptcy case in postwar Japan with his Sanko Steamship Corporation going down with 290 billion yen of bad debts. Still eight major corporations listed in the first section of the Tokyo stock exchange remain controlled by Dietmen and their families. They are:

Daishowa Paper Co. of Fuji City (Shizuoka prefecture), controlled by the Saito family – current MP: Toshitsugu Saito, son of a construction minister and mayor of Fuji City, the 'corporate castle town', and grandson of the company's founder (and a great-grandson of the founder of the Toyota Motor Co.).

Shin-Etsu Chemical, which together with other Nagano-based businesses, is controlled by the Kosaka family – current MP: Kenji Kosaka, son of former foreign minister Zentaro Kosaka and nephew of ex-transport minister Tokusaburo Kosaka.

Tonami Unyu, a Toyama-based trucking company, whose owner/president is Tamisuke Watanuki MP, ex-minister of state of the National Land Agency.

Fuji Kyuko Co., a bus, railroad and resort development company operating around Mt Fuji in Yamanashi, Shizuoka and Kanagawa prefectures. Its president, Mitsuo Horiuchi, a former minister of labour, narrowly lost his third-generation seat in Yamanashi in 1990.

Sato Construction, a Gunma-based contractor specialising in road-building and other public works. Its executive director, Genichiro Sato, represents Gunma 1 (Maebashi) in the Diet.

Kumagai Gumi, a major national construction company. Tasaburo Kumagai MP, ex-director general of the Science and Technology Agency, owns a sizable chunk in this family-controlled company and its affiliates.

Kajima Construction, one of Japan's top contractors, controlled by the Kajima family, into which Wataru Hiraizumi MP for Fukui and ex-minister of state (Science and Technology Agency) married. Hiraizumi also served as Vice President to Kajima Construction as well as Director of the Kajima Institute of Peace.

Fukuda Gumi, the largest contractor in Niigata prefecture, specialising in public and civil engineering projects. The president's two daughters are married to Noburo Takeshita's oldest son and to ex-LDP Secretary General Ichiro Ozawa respectively, the matchmaker being none other than Kakuei Tanaka.

This list of Keibatsu linking LDP MPs and their offspring to big business (*zaikai*) is by no means exhaustive.

At the other end of the scale there are rural *sake* businesses, which often only indicates an MP's social origin in the local landed gentry: an old landlord family which knew how to turn its tenants' rice rents into a good drink: Noburo Takeshita (Shimane), Sosuke Uno (Shiga), Shin Kanemaru (Yamanashi), Shin Hasegawa (Niigata), Kabun Muto (Gifu) and Kunio Tanabe (president of Tanabe Shuzo in Yamanashi) are among them. Obviously the product also makes a good gift item and serves as a visible symbol of a local quality craft with which most male voters can readily identify.

Nine more MPs control regional transportation companies, six own construction businesses, including the former construction ministers Shin Kanemaru and Ihei Ochi (Shikoku Tsushin Construction). Other family company owners are ex-MITI ministers Okonogi (Okonogi Shoten), and Nakao (Nihon Network Service), and Yoshida's grandson Taro Aso (Aso Cement).

Other business lines include mineral oil distribution, liquor wholesaling, radio stations, fishing operations, forestry, manufacturing, and golf course and *ryokan* management.

A relatively small number of LDP Lower House MPs (29 in total) display a rare phenomenon: they claim to have been straightforward 'salarymen', ordinary employees in Japan's mainstream corporations (Sumitomo Bank, Mitsui Bank, Mitsui Bussan, Kawasaki Steel, Matsushita Electric, Sony, Fuji Heavy Industries, Bridgestone, JAL, Nippon Kokan, Seiko, Dentsu, Kyushu Electrical Power, Odakyu Bus Co. and so on), in which a handful even rose to respectable managerial rank (*kacho*). Most of these seemingly ordinary white-collar workers were in fact sons of incumbent MPs and/or were later seconded by their companies to become political secretaries to senior Dietmen or ministers to learn and to prepare for the political trade – an opportunity rarely afforded (or aspired to) by Japan's average salarymen.

IDEOLOGIES AND POLITICAL PROGRAMMES

As is evident in their presentations in campaign material and in the parliamentary handbooks, there are variations in the sales pitches of conservative MPs, in which they interpret their political careers:

- the grateful son who respectfully follows the footsteps of his illustrious political ancestors and eagerly learns from the great *sensei* in Tokyo;
- the local boy who made good on the elite track in Kasumigaseki and now returns to serve humbly as a 'pipe' to central politics;
- the local politician who is proud of his manifold titles and achievements in Nagatacho and openly boasts of the numbers of dams he got out of the Ministry of Construction for his constituency;
- the hardship story (ever more rare as biographical evidence becomes less plausible with the prewar generation fading away): growing up fatherless in poverty and working his way up (in construction) the hard way;
- the ordinary story: just a straightforward local boy from Shitamachi who happened to have served as *kacho* at MOF, but who still loves *karaoke*, *sake* drinking and baseball playing.

While country MPs rather stress their distinguished ancestry, their personal elite track and pork-barrel references to an audience judged impressionable, the metropolitan Dietmen put emphasis on their 'achievement-cum-ordinariness' personality – stressing invariably that they too have shared the salaryman existence which is so common and inescapable to most of their constituents.

Cornelia Meyer, in her banking newsletter, has pointed to a related difference between city and countryside LDP MPs.[22] City MPs stress the virtues of small government, fiscal frugality and reduced taxation (as their urban salaried constituents have little to gain from public works and regional development). Rural MPs rather focus on spending projects and do not seem to mind higher taxation (which seems to have less effect on local businessmen and farmers).

As LDP MPs in their current multiple-seat constituencies must compete as personalities with fellow conservative MPs for similarly orientated mainstream votes, little attempt is made at ideological definitions, except for oblique references to peace, prosperity, international understanding, regional advancement and a stronger Japanese economy and world role in their individual slogans. They profess deeply held beliefs and motivations for political involvement. Whenever Dietmen talk publicly about their political 'philosophies', substance tends to become so philanthropist as to become implausible.

The senior representatives of the LDP after all represent a party intimately tied to the status quo and are set to benefit handsomely from the current distribution of power and wealth. There is little wrong with this if Japan's electorate is not fooled by the party's fraudulent slogans and is content with the status quo (and distrusts those who want to change it). The chances are that Japan's well-educated voters know what they are doing. Most voters will face a choice between three different LDP candidates, a Socialist, a Komeito man and a Communist.

Quite likely in his/her secret vote Mr or Mrs Average will favour a candidate who appears level-headed, friendly, approachable, presentable, successful, who has proved helpful in the past, and is likely to be even more helpful (both personally and locally) in the future. It is probable that your friendly Dietman then is from the LDP.

There are no leftwingers in the LDP. (They are by definition in the opposition camp.) While most of the LDP's parliamentary party will be safely centrist, who will not rock the boat (and lose finance and votes) by professing silly and only emotionally satisfying ideological right-wing beliefs, there is also a handful of unrepentant right-wingers in the parliamentary party. Who are these people? A 'right-winger' in Japan's political firmament believes in the divinity of the emperor; in the revision of the constitution; in worship at Yasukuni shrine; in the necessity for purified history textbooks; in the national anthem and the national flag being ceremoniously regarded at Japanese schools; in a larger military budget; and in an enhanced overseas role for Japan's military. While this current symbolic and real agenda seems to make Japanese right-wingers a pale copy of their more fearsome and belligerent right-wing brothers elsewhere, the gradualist, consensus-shifting notion typical of Japanese political decision-making makes even trivial ideas relating to the minutiae of imperial etiquette become portents of potentially frightful consequences.

Thanks to transparent symbolic issues, the LDP's right-wingers can be easily identified: they were members in the Seirankai and in Ichiro Nakagawa's short-lived faction. Although often of advanced age, many are still influential in the Fukuda/Abe/Mitsuzuka faction[23] and in the Nakasone/Watanabe faction. Prominent activists are Masayuki Fūjio (born 1917), ex-minister for construction, for labour and for education – fired by Nakasone; Takeshi Hasegawa (born 1911), ex-minister of transport, labour and justice;

Motoharu Morishita (born 1922), ex-minister for health and welfare; Eichi Nakao (born 1930), ex-minister of MITI and the EPA; Masaaki Nakayama (born 1932), ex-minister of posts and telecom; Seisuke Okuno (born 1913), ex-minister for justice, education and the National Land Agency (from which he was dismissed in 1988); Tatsuo Tanaka (born 1910), minister of education, MITI, son of prewar General Giichi Tanaka and close friend of PM Nobusuke Kishi (who was a minister of industry and of ammunitions in Tojo's war cabinet). Shintaro Ishihara MP ('The Japan that can say No'), a popular novelist and former MHW minister, whom the US media labelled as a diehard nationalist, is considered too much of an intellectual individualist to be part of the LDP's organised right. Ichiro Nakagawa's valiant and ultimately self-destructive attempt to organise the LDP's right wing in 1980 produced a faction of 25 members, which one year later had shrunk to eleven. After his suicide, most reverted to their previous factions (Abe and Nakasone). So much for the right-wingers' self-advertised endurance and perseverance in adversity. Given their generational set-up, the current bunch will be gone before long.

WAY OF LIFE

Between 8 a.m. and midnight an ambitious member of parliament will easily clock in 100 hours a week on the job. His life is essentially the life of a busy executive. There are attractive perks to the job: chauffeured cars; wining and dining on others' expense accounts; a spacious home; overseas travel; media attention and public recognition. There is also a gruelling, tedious work-week with endless Diet plenary and committee sessions; weekly factional, PRC commission and sub-committee meetings; LDP headquarters obligations; and a lengthy list of constituency, business and diplomatic visitors to be handled; lobbying matters to be pursued with central and regional administrations; and in the evenings, human relations to be furthered with peers, with the party's almighty, with old friends and with potential financiers. At the same time personal finances have to be kept in good order; a staff of some 12 assistants ('secretaries') to be managed, motivated and kept paid; while manning some four offices (two in Tokyo and two in the constituency). Also, an MP must set time aside for his own policy study and reflection, for reading and speech-writing. During week-ends, it is 'paddy weeding' time in the constituency: not only to show the flag and a caring, generously contributing face at weddings, funerals, sports events and local festivals, but also to talk and to listen to key supporters (to make sure that nobody relevant defects to rivals and possible new contenders). Normally the Dietman's wife or his son (and heir-apparent) as well as the bulk of the underpaid secretaries take care of constituency business during the week – yet weekend visits by the *sensei* himself remain indispensable.

For family affairs and private life proper this leaves little more than Saturday afternoons (which if taken regularly for family purposes merits a biographical mention). Unfortunately the favourite pastimes of the rich and powerful in Japan (golf at weekends and tea houses followed by *karaoke* bars at night) are very time-consuming, if the essential human relations are to be maintained at the appropriate intensity. During the Diet's summer break inevitably an extended period of overseas travel ensues. One of the purposes of these foreign 'study' trips is to have photographs taken with the world's mighty and famous. These are then reproduced in the Dietman's newsletters, campaign literature or in his political books, sometimes with sensational captions. Koji Kakizawa, for instance, in his *Deai Newsletter*, headlined his snapshots with presidents Mitterand and Bush as 'Koji meets François in Tokyo' and 'Koji met George last May'.[24]

Also, unsuspecting constituency folks will receive planeloads of postcards from exotic locations signed personally by their *sensei* which enhances his credentials as a leading international personality still further. (Normally these postcards are pre-printed in Japan. A hapless secretary has to carry them in suitcases to the destination, affix local stamps and post them. The suitcases then will be refilled with *omiyage* – low-priced souvenirs to be distributed to supporters back home.)

There is no decent Diet member who has not yet published his book containing his very own deep thoughts on how this world in general and Japan and his particular constituency within it should develop in peace and prosperity. All of them seem to have produced such books of which they invariably appear very proud (and think it a suitable gift item for all k*oenkai* members as well as for the business and diplomatic community). Normally these books (typically entitled '*Japan and the World in Twenty-first-Century Politics*', echoing the catch phrase of the great *sensei* in question), contain the summer vacation VIP photographs described above, documenting the author's earnest worldwide study in the quest for truth and international understanding.

Sometimes an MP produces a book which rises above the junk. Sosuke Uno, the ill-fated prime minister of July 1989, has produced remarkable books on local history. Some Dietmen, such as Shintaro Ishihara, have written decent literary works or have shown themselves good polemicists. Former senior bureaucrats are obviously good at publishing usable and accurate policy works on their particular field of (former) administrative expertise. As regards decent programmatic writings, very little appears to be published. The books of Governor Takahiro Yokomichi (a right-wing socialist) on more independent policies for Hokkaido and the decentralised evolution of Japan still seem a rare occurence.

PASTIMES

Hobbies listed by LDP MPs make fascinating reading. By far the most popular are sports (91 mentionings in the parliamentary handbook). Among sports, golf predictably ranks first (33), followed by tennis (15), baseball (12), judo (8), soccer and kendo (7 each), swimming and rugby (6 each) and skiing (5). Other types of sports mentioned are: cycling, basketball, roller-skating, weight-training, horse-riding, marathons, wrestling, boxing, jogging, Aikido, sumo, karate, motorsports, as well as spectator sports. Many MPs hold advanced degrees in the more regulated sports or are presidents/senior advisors to a prefectural sports federation. Second most popular is reading (45), with only a few specifying that they prefer either historical themes or literary works. Music (15) is another favourite pastime, with preferences being singing (4), *karaoke* (3), guitar, piano or *shakuhachi* (one each). Among games *igo* (18) ranks first, followed by *shogi* (Japanese chess) (4), mahjong (2) and bridge (1).

Cultural pursuits are more rare: painting (8), writing (5) – among which are listed *haiku*, essays and 'books' – calligraphy (3), photography (2), movies, fine arts, ceramics, sculpture, theatre-going, *kiyomoto* (ballad dramas) and *rakugo* (story-telling).

More down-to-earth is travelling (4), gardening (3), *bonsai* growing (2), rod fishing (4), walking (2), *sake* drinking (2), cooking, driving and stamp collecting (one each). It is sometimes difficult to associate this crowd of mostly elderly and very busy gentlemen with this wide range of attractive sporting and cultural pursuits. Some, such as Sosuke Uno, actively maintained quite demanding hobbies at an accomplished level (*haiku*, essay writing). For others, especially former elite bureaucrats, the public pursuit of popular pastimes appears as an important element in presenting a folksy and approachable image to their new rural constituencies.

With the resignations of PM Uno and of Chief Cabinet Secretary Tokuo Yamashita in 1989 after talkative ex-partners revealed their regular involvement in the Tokyo *geisha* scene, hints abounded that similar comforts in the enforced bachelorhood of Dietmen were more frequent than previously thought. Opportunities for heavy and regular drinking and woman-ising abound in Tokyo's nightlife, and are particularly encouraged if most of the expenditure is carried by corporate friends and sponsors. Normally a Dietman's favourite nightspot will tend to be an exclusive, discrete *ryotei* staffed by 'high-class' hostesses. Not all political contributions end nec-essarily as political expenditure. Uno was reported to have paid his *geisha* 'advance money' of 2 million yen, and a monthly stipend of 300,000 yen during their four-month affair in 1986. In return she had to be available and ready to come any time he called.[25]

FAMILY LIFE

In spite of a heavy load of on- and off-duty pursuits, a responsible LDP Dietman will think of the next century, and in view of his own regrettable mortality will pursue eternity by reproduction. Judging from the bio-data published in the monthly *Liberal Star* on LDP senior MPs in the Lower House – almost all of whom had been ministers – the 121 MPs who had listed children in their entries had 300 offspring in total (153 sons and 121 daughters, the remainder was unspecified), an average of 2.5 children per family. Dynastic survival obviously depends on a sufficient level of regen-eration. As political and/or bureaucratic talents and inclinations are not a genetic disposition, an increase in the number of children (relying either on a son willing and able to take over, or a daughter willing and able to marry an acquiescent husband to continue the family business), will reduce the risk of not having a suitable successor with the desired blood lineage. Hence LDP politicians' marital fertility appears higher than Japan's aver-age. Some, such as Masumi Esaki (5 sons, 1 daughter), Takeo Fukuda (3 sons, 2 daughters), Ryotaro Hashimoto (2 sons, 3 daughters), Kosei Amano (the same) and Hikozaburo Okonogi (4 sons, 1 daughter) have been par-ticularly blessed. Most of them, except Hashimoto, however, belong to an older generation of politicians (born between 1905 and 1928). Younger politicians' reproductive behaviour – like that of Japan's society in general – tends to be less fertile, thus inevitably reducing the talent pool of heredi-tary politics (which none the less remains in the ascendant). Relatively high numbers of children among Japanese politicians are still somewhat puz-zling, given the fact that their fathers already in their 30s will be occupied full time on a 7-work-days a week basis with their political or administra-tive careers. Also their mothers carry a considerable load of constituency work, which in many cases hardly allows them to be full substitutes for the absentee fathers.

DIETMEN PERSONALITIES

What are LDP MPs like? The answer is very much in the eye of the beholder, depending on whether he/she is foreign or Japanese, whether interactions are structurally hostile or friendly, and how political perceptions are coloured.

As a subjective view, there are many senior LDP politicians on the more sympathetic side: MPs Koji Kakizawa, Toshio Yamaguchi, Kosuke Hori, Yoshiro Hayashi, Kiichi Miyazawa, Yuji Tsushima, Yohei Kono, Koichi Kato, Tsutomu Hata, Kazuo Aichi, and others. They appear to be friendly, open-minded (not necessarily always meaning 'internationally minded') and intelligent. For each of these very pleasant personalities there are others who are either so shy and unassuming as to remain nondescript or who stay unresponsive in their utterances, or again a few others who appeared fairly arrogant and overbearing. Sometimes, however, appearances can be deceiving: Noburo Takeshita, for most of the late 1980s Japan's most powerful politician, in public consistently displays the air of a shy, retired elementary school principal from the countryside. For a foreign diplomat, however, who meets most of Japan's senior politicians in an essentially friendly and non-controversial setting, the perception is certainly different from that of a Japanese bureaucrat who is subjected to their bullying, from a corporate manager who is being solicited for contributions, and from a voter who sees his vote for a sympathetic personality alienated to a vote for a regime which at times turns out to be corrupt and is even occasionally repressive.

There is a global professional disease of politicians, which arises from their vanity and ambition (reflecting a desire to be liked and respected), and from their opinionated and lecturing approach to problem analysis. In Japan this disease appears slightly less pronounced than elsewhere – judging from experience when Japanese and foreign politicians meet and compete for speaking time. Still, the consensus of Japanese bureaucrats appears to be that politicians are fairly unintelligent. The business view is that they are greedy and inefficient, and the general public perceives them collectively to be corrupt and devious, while seeing their local MP as rather honest, hard-working, helpful – and useful.

In fact, LDP politicians' social origins, the limited recruitment channels (hereditary, political secretaries, political journalists, elite bureaucrats and regional business owners), their upper-class way of life and their particular ways as ritualist busybodies makes them a breed apart from ordinary Japanese wage-earners and businessmen. While the Dietmen know the needs and preferences of their regional and local henchmen and business clientele fairly well, there is precious little interaction with the man in the street, who will invariably treat a visiting MP with awe and overt respect, and will rarely openly speak his mind. Hence voter identification is fragile and so is the LDP's legitimacy. Serious policy misjudgements due to misreading the popular mood (the consumption tax of 1989 is only one example) are likely to be repeated, as are corruption scandals which will further erode the LDP's capacity to lead the country.

POLITICAL BIOGRAPHIES

In order to illustrate some of the points advanced above, the CVs of three distinct 'ideal types' of up-and-coming 'new' LDP leaders are reproduced:

- Kosuke Hori, ex-minister of education: a private-sector manager-turned-politician;
- Ichiro Ozawa, ex-LDP secretary general, a professional politician;
- Koichi Kato, ex-minister of state for defence, a diplomat turned politician.

The careers of an older generation – Masayoshi Ohira, the last elite bureaucrat before Miyazawa to become prime minister, and Yasuhiro Nakasone, Japan's most recent prime minister to have made significant policy impacts – will be described later. Typically, both Ohira and Nakasone are first-generation politicians, while Hori, Ozawa and Kato are sons of political fathers.

Kosuke Hori[26]

Born:	23 September 1934 in Tokyo
Education:	Graduated 1958 from Keio University (Department of Law)
Career:	
1958	Entered Nippon Seiko KK
1974	Transferred to NSk France SA and then became its President (until May 1979)
1979	Elected to the House of Representatives from Saga Pref. and since then re-elected five times; member of Takeshita faction

1980–1	Deputy Director, Labour Division of the Policy Research Council, LDP
1981–2	Deputy Director, Agriculture and Forestry Division, Policy Research Affairs Council, LDP
1982–5	Deputy Director, Science and Technology Division of the Policy Research Council, LDP
1983–5	Whip, Standing Committee on Rules and Administration
1985–6	Parliamentary Vice-Minister of Agriculture, Forestry and Fisheries
1986–7	Acting Director, Agriculture and Forestry Division of the Policy Research Council, LDP
1986–7	Deputy Director, Defence Division of the Policy Research Council, LDP; Deputy Chairman, National Organisation Committee, LDP
1987–90	Director, Agriculture and Forestry Division of the Policy Research Council, LDP; Deputy Director-General, International Bureau, LDP
Feb/Dec 1990	Minister of Education (second Kaifu cabinet)

Ichiro Ozawa[27]

Member of the House of Representatives, Takeshita faction

Born:	24 May 1942 in Mizusawa city, Iwate Prefecture
Education:	Graduated 1967 from Keio University (Department of Economics)
Career:	
1969	Elected to the House of Representatives from Iwate Prefecture and since then re-elected six times
1975–6	Parliamentary Vice-Minister, Science and Technology Agency
1976–7	Parliamentary Vice-Minister of Construction
1978	Director, Science and Technology Division of the Policy Research Council, LDP
1978–9 & 1980–1	Director, Fisheries Division of the Policy Research Council, LDP

1980–1	Deputy Chairman, National Organisation Committee, LDP
1981–2	Deputy Chairman, Policy Research Council, LDP
1982–3	Director-General, Election Bureau, LDP
1983–5	Chairman, Standing Committee on Rules and Administration (House of Representatives)
1985–6	Minister of Home Affairs
1987–9	Deputy Chief Cabinet Secretary
1989–91	Secretary-General, LDP

Wife:	Kazuko
Family:	3 sons
Interests:	Reading, *Igo*

Koichi Kato[28]

Member of the House of Representatives, Miyazawa faction

| Born: | June 1939 in Tsuruoka City, Yamagata Prefecture |

| Education: | Graduated 1964 from Law Department, Tokyo University; 1966 MA, Political Science, Harvard University |

Career:

1963	Passed the Senior Diplomatic Service Examination
1964	Served at the Japanese Embassy, Taipei
1966	Served at the Japanese Embassy, Washington, DC
1967	Vice-Consul, Japanese Consulate General, Hong Kong
1969	Deputy Director at the China Desk, Asian Affairs Bureau, Foreign Ministry
1972	Elected Member of the House of Representatives from the 2nd District, Yamagata Prefecture
1978	Deputy Chief Cabinet Secretary (the first and second Ohira cabinets)
1980	Director, Standing Committee on Rules and Administration; Deputy Chairman, Diet Affairs Committee, LDP
1981	Director, Agriculture, Forestry and Fisheries Committee; Director, Agriculture and Forestry Division, Policy Research Council, LDP
1983	Director General, Election Bureau, LDP
1984	Minister of State for Defence (second Nakasone cabinet)
1986	Acting Chairman, Policy Research Council, LDP

1987	Acting Chairman, Research Commission on Comprehensive Agriculture, LDP; Chairman, Subcommittee on Liberalisation of Agricultural Products
1989	Chairman, Research Commission on Comprehensive Agriculture, LDP
1990	Chairman of the Special Committee on United Nations Peace Co-operation
1991	Chief Cabinet Secretary, Miyazawa cabinet

Political Biography 1: Masayoshi Ohira

Masayoshi Ohira was born in 1910, the third son of a poor farmer in Wada village in Kagawa prefecture.[29] With an arable holding of 1.3ha his family was considered 'middle ranking' at the time. While not destitute, all six surviving children had to work to make ends meet. His sisters were all married off at the age of 16. With considerable hardship his family made it possible for Masayoshi, who showed academic promise, to go on to middle school. When he was 17 Ohira's father suddenly died, but the extended family still supported him so that he could attend Takamatsu Higher School of Commerce. During these years he was converted to an evangelistic branch of Christianity (Servants of Jesus) and was active in prayer meetings and street proselytising. (Ohira as a university student later joined the 'no-church movement' and has treated his religious convictions as a private matter ever since.)

After a year as a pharmaceutical salesman, at the age of 23, supported by prefectural scholarship funds and by his older brother, Ohira entered Tokyo University of Commerce (today's Hitotsubashi University), which in the Tokyo of the early 1930s provided an intellectually stimulating environment for an inquisitive student from the provinces. The serious problems and turmoil faced by Japan at the time solicited a constructive, if somewhat conformist, response in the young scholar, and after considerable preparation, Ohira passed the highly competitive Higher Civil Service Examination in 1935.

With an introduction from a member of the House of Peers from Kagawa, he called on the vice-minister of finance who also happened to hail from Kagawa prefecture, and thus became the first Hitotsubashi graduate ever to join the ministry of finance. At the time the ministry took only ten elite-track recruits per annum. His first year, according to Ohira was 'half work, half play': only the mornings were spent in the office. During his second year Ohira, at the tender age of 27, was made head of the Yokohama tax

office with 80 subordinates, his superior being Hayato Ikeda, then head of
the Tokyo Tax Supervision Bureau. At that time Ohira married Shigeko
Suzuki, daughter of the founder of a firm of stock brokers. One year later,
in 1938, he became head of the indirect taxation department in Sendai's
tax supervision bureau, his main – and unloved – task being to chase illicit
distillers. Yet, with some satisfaction Ohira, three years after joining MOF,
saw himself being treated as a social equal by local notables in Tohoku.

In 1939, however, Ohira found himself in Zhangjiakou, a muddy transportation centre north-west of Beijing, where as the finance minister of
Inner Mongolia he was put in charge of financial matters for the Japanese-
occupied Federated Autonomous Government of Mongolia, which nominally managed its own budget, taxation and currency. Japan was then most
interested in the region's iron ore and coal-mining, most of which was
exported to Japan, and in the local opium production, which was sold to
Central China.

In 1940 Ohira was relieved of this difficult post and back in Tokyo was
made to supervise Japanese 'special corporations' in occupied China which
were active in mining, railroads, harbours, transportation, electricity and
communications. 'Continental management', which was the euphemism for
the colonial development undertaken by the Asia Development Board to
which Ohira was seconded, certainly suffered from wartime constraints, yet
with the Board's officials (amongst whom were also Masayoshi Ito (later
Foreign Minister) and Yoshitake Sasaki (later MITI Minister), all friends
and later political allies of Ohira), a genuine developmental commitment
seemed to prevail over the military's more exploitative imperatives.

In 1942 Ohira returned to MOF and was appointed chief budget reviewer
for the ministry of education and the South Seas agency. During his early
years with MOF Ohira had shown himself relatively 'soft' on taxpayers,
with a great deal of respect for their resourcefulness and ingenuity in the
face of the adversity that afflicted Japan during the prewar depression. As
a budget reviewer, however, he became severe in scrutinising budget proposals for sensible cuts in government spending. This frugal fiscal attitude
remained part of Ohira's basic political philosophy throughout his public
career.

In 1943 Ohira – with Ikeda again as his superior – headed the indirect
taxation department of Tokyo's local finance bureau. In this function he
created the *Kokumin Sakaba* (people's taverns), the spartan drinking establishments that were the only exemptions to the closure of all entertainment
facilities ordered by the Tojo cabinet. In 1945 as a first encounter with high
politics, Ohira – together with Kiichi Miyazawa – briefly served as a
secretary to finance minister Tsushima.

Ohira's postwar administrative career continued without interruption and, except for losing his family home in one of the Tokyo fire-bombings, his family suffered no losses during the war. In November 1945 Ohira worked on fiscal policies in MOF's finance bureau, where he wrote a memorandum advocating deflationary politices: he recommended the sale of public enterprises; a greater reliance on indirect taxation; a balanced budget; and fiscal self-reliance in local government. At the time the good advice of the middle-ranking official went unheeded. The recommendations for increased indirect taxation were not implemented until 1989, nine years after Ohira's death.

One year later, in 1946, he served a brief stint as chief of the welfare section in MOF's compensation bureau, where his task was to adjust pay and welfare benefits for the new administrative career ranks which had replaced and narrowed the rigid and arbitrary prewar ranking system. In 1948 Ohira became chief of the public works section at the economic stabilisation board, the powerful predecessor of today's toothless EPA. In this function he oversaw all public construction projects undertaken by central and local governments. It was a job which was easily more influential than the Ministry of Construction. The main task was to repair war damage. Yet Ohira found resources to support his pet priority: afforestation, which he felt was essential for water management, disaster prevention and rural employment.

Also in 1948, together with 40 other ex-bureaucrats, Hayato Ikeda was elected to the National Diet. These bureaucrats were to form the core of the LDP's 'Yoshida school': hand-picked elite bureaucrats whom Yoshida selected as his personal powerbase to replace and to protect himself against the return of the wartime politicians, military men and aristocrats, which had been purged by SCAP. By 1949 Ikeda was made minister of finance. He picked Ohira and Miyazawa as his political secretaries. Minister Ikeda's main task was then to implement the deflationary policies commonly labelled 'Dodge line'. Ohira later openly admitted that he had taken a liking to the backstage political dealings in which he had to engage as Ikeda's secretary, and disliked the prospect of having to return to administrative routine assignments.

With the active support of Ikeda, who in 1950 began to build his own faction, Ohira at the age of 40 decided to enter politics. Starting with relatives, school and university friends, professional MOF connections (*sake* and tobacco businesses), Ohira built up his support organisation in his native Kagawa 2 district. In 1952 he ran successfully for a Diet seat for the first time.

As a trusted lieutenant of Ikeda (who had become the Liberal Party's secretary general) his first major political role was to help manage the backstage functions for final merger of the Liberal Party and the Democratic Party in 1955. In his early political years, Ohira – by his own admission a poor public speaker – made himself a name as an unpretentious fiscal expert and member of the Diet's budget committee. He also worked on tobacco and forestry issues, which were of constituency interest. By the end of the 1950s Ohira had become one of the senior members of Ikeda's faction, the *kochikai* (formed in 1954). He was chairman of the Diet's education committee, when in 1960 student-led mass demonstration brought down the Kishi cabinet. Then he diagnosed the 'spiritual emptiness' of the Japanese people as a root cause of the disturbances. The perceived lack of spiritual depth among his countrymen continued as a *leitmotiv* in Ohira's future political rhetoric.

A more immediate concern was to secure Ikeda's succession as prime minister. An alliance between the Ikeda and Sato factions – agreed between Ohira and Kakuei Tanaka, his lifelong political friend – after a bitter battle between the 'bureaucrats' and the 'politicians' factions, finally proved decisive. After Ikeda's victory, Ohira was appointed Chief Cabinet Secretary. Solving the prolonged Miike miners' strike was one of Ohira's tasks. From 1962–4 he served as foreign minister, preparing the way for Japan's membership of the OECD (which in 1964, together with the Tokyo Olympics, represented a symbol of Japan's finally catching up with the West).

The year 1964, however, with Ikeda's resignation for health reasons (he died one year later of cancer) marked an interruption in the steep upward curve of Ohira's political career, and the sudden death of his oldest son and political heir-apparent Masaki spelt personal tragedy.

Out of favour with premier Eisaku Sato and seen as a rival by his new faction boss Maeo, whom the dying Ikeda had appointed as a caretaker of the *Kochikai*, Ohira spend the next two years in the wilderness as an ordinary Diet member occupying no senior posts. His come-back as a senior party leader took off in 1967 with his appointment as chairman of the LDP's Policy Research Council. In this function he public advocated import liberalisation and an end to the public subsidisation of Japan's industry. Made MITI minister in 1969, he continued this liberal approach, which however did not endear him to his American counterparts, who in the late 1960s insisted on Japanese export restraints on textiles to protect the ailing US industry – a trade conflict which would ultimately lead to the 'Nixon shocks' of 1972.

In 1970 finally a revolt of young Turks in the *Kochikai* forced Maeo into 'voluntary' retirement, and in 1971 made Ohira *de facto* chief of the old Ikeda faction. As such he promptly ran in the contest to succeed Sato as prime minister. Ohira's main programme was his declared intent to create a 'nation of garden cities', which meant opposition to ruthless urbanisation, gardens being brought into the cities, villages being improved and, in general, localism being promoted. His other campaign slogans were: 'Heart to heart politics' and 'Politics without lies'.

After a first unsuccessful round of voting at the party convention, Ohira shifted his support to Tanaka. With Tanaka as prime minister, Ohira in 1972 became foreign minister for the second time. This time Ohira left a more forceful mark: allied with Tanaka, he pushed the LDP's then powerful Taiwan lobby aside, and achieved the normalisation of relations with the People's Republic, with which a new peace treaty was concluded. Similar talks with the Soviet Union remained unsuccessful.

In 1974, 22 years after he had previously left the ministry, Ohira became minister of finance. Shortly afterwards, a series of shady financial dealings involving prime minister Tanaka was revealed. After Miki and Fukuda had deserted Tanaka, Ohira continued his support.

After Tanaka's resignation, the LDP's mediator, Etsusaburo Shina, then chose Miki in preference to Ohira. Ohira remained as minister of finance. With the recession following the first oil crisis, Japan experienced a shortfall in tax revenue. Ohira proposed his old idea of a general consumption tax to stabilise government finances. After lengthy intra-cabinet and interfactional discussions only a draft bill providing for increased tobacco and alcohol taxation remained. This bill, due to the lack of lobbying efforts by prime minister Miki and other LDP chiefs, failed to be passed by the Diet. Ohira, a fiscal conservative, hence had to preside over a record budget shortfall of 3.5 trillion yen in 1975 – one-third of the budget had to rely on government bonds to cover the deficit.

In 1976 the Lockheed scandal peaked. The main LDP factions, including Ohira, tried to force Miki to take the blame and to resign in remorse for the collective shame that had fallen on the party. Instead, in July 1976 Miki had Tanaka arrested. In the view of the LDP's mainstream factions, this was not an act to serve justice, but rather an evil Miki plot to decimate his foremost opponent's faction.

In November 1976 Ohira and Fukuda concluded a vaguely worded half-written, half-oral alliance agreement, which provided for Fukuda to succeed Miki. In the Ohira camp's view, the agreement provided only for a two-year term for Fukuda's prime ministership who thereafter was to be succeeded by Ohira (who had the largest following among LDP Diet members at the time, commanding both his own and Tanaka's support). In accordance with the agreement, Fukuda was elected prime minister and Ohira in 1977 was made LDP secretary general, a position which put him effectively in control of the party apparatus and of the selection of Diet candidates. While the party was shaken by the turmoil of the Lockheed revelations and their public disapproval, Ohira never addressed the party's corruption as the root cause; instead he referred publicly to procedural details or delivered non-consequential, lofty moralist exhortations. At one point however, he gave a more worldly assessment of his LDP:

> [It] cannot be said to be a clean or good-looking party. . . . it is [not] a truely popular party among the people. Nevertheless, our nation's postwar management has been accomplished with this party at the helm [which] succeeded in achieving economic balance and self-reliance. . . . [The LDP] may not have the graceful carriage of a thoroughbred, but it has the performance of a study, ordinary work cow.[30]

Ohira's view was surely shared with a majority of Japan's voters, who continued to vote for the party.

In 1978 Ohira found out that Fukuda's interpretation of their 1976 agreement differed from his. In a bitterly contested membership poll both then competed for party presidency. Fukuda as incumbent felt assured of victory. Stunned by his unanticipated failure, his camp blamed Tanaka's unscrupulous resource use as decisive in the defeat.

In December 1978 Ohira was elected prime minister, eight years after he had assumed the helm of the *Kochikai*, the previous Ikeda faction. Although he tried to mend fences – including the adoption of 'Trust and consensus' as the slogan of his prime ministership – the bitterness of the Miki/Fukuda camp remained. Soon the second oil shock followed, plunging Japan anew into a fiscal crisis, which in 1979 required 40 per cent of the government's expenditure to be bond-financed. Again faced with the re-sistance of the opposition parties which held half the seats on the Diet's budget committee, Ohira failed in his proposal for a general consumption tax in order to reduce the deficit.

After the Tokyo summit of June 1979 – attended by Jimmy Carter, Helmut Schmidt, Giscard d'Estaing and a youthful Margaret Thatcher, that dealt almost exclusively with energy issues in the wake of the Iranian revolution – Ohira felt encouraged to dissolve the Diet at an early date. This move was strongly opposed by Fukuda and Miki. Inspite of Ohira's retractions, the election campaign was dominated by the public suspicion that a sales tax was in the offing, with LDP candidates being put on the defensive in their denials.

When in October 1979 the LDP lost one seat, the media instantly termed the result a 'defeat'. Faction chiefs Fukuda, Miki and Nakasone asked for

Ohira's resignation. When he refused, in November 1979 for the first time ever two LDP prime ministerial candidates were fielded in the Diet: Ohira and Fukuda. Ohira found the support of his own and of Tanaka's faction and the New Liberal Club. Fukuda was supported by the LDP sidestream factions. The other opposition parties in their usual doctrinaire fashion voted for their own party chiefs. In the final round, with these parties abstaining, Ohira won over Fukuda.

While pushing energy-saving policies at home – including the short-lived fashion of short-sleeved jackets – like any embattled prime minister, Ohira worked hard on external relations. His pet theme was improved Pacific Rim relations. He cultivated ties with the Peking leadership (Deng Xiaoping and Hua Guofeng) and in January 1980 visited Australia, New Zealand and Papua New Guinea. For the Pacific he proposed an 'open and flexible co-operation . . . in economic and cultural areas, without intruding into political or military matters.[31]

In May 1980 Ohira undertook a strenuous trip to Mexico, Canada, Yugoslavia (for Tito's funeral) and Germany. Upon return, he found bills stalled in the Diet – opposition parties and LDP sidestream factions remained unco-operative. Finally the Socialists introduced a motion of no confidence against the Ohira cabinet. The LDP's sidestream factions wished two scandals – one involving irregularities at KDD, and the other Dietman Hamada of the Tanaka faction – to be brought before the Diet, hoping that they would embarrass the Ohira camp. Dissatisfied with Ohira's usual vague assurances, the Fukuda and Miki factions decided to stay away during the no confidence vote. To the Socialists' consternation and subsequent dismay, the vote passed. The Lower House was dissolved, and elections were set for 22 June 1980, coinciding with previously scheduled elections for the Upper House. With his extensive foreign travels and domestic political problems, the strain began to show on Ohira, as the first prime minister ever to be publicly abandoned by sections of his own party. On 30 May 1980, the first day of the official election campaign, Ohira, after several campaign speeches in Shinjuku and Yokohama, collapsed with a heart attack. With intense media and party speculation about whether he would be able to attend the forthcoming Venice summit, rejoin the campaign and remain fit as a prime minister, Ohira, with his party split and crucial elections coming up, was unable to recover from the strain, and succumbed on 10 June 1980.

In the 22 June double elections the LDP increased its score by 36 seats to 284 in the Lower House, and to 70 seats among the seats up for re-election in the Upper House, thus assuring his successor – Zenko Suzuki – the stable working majority in the Diet Ohira had always wanted.

Masayoshi Ohira was Japan's prime minister for one year and seven months only. Until 1991 he was the last of the old Yoshida school of ex-elite bureaucrats to become prime minister. His five immediate successors (Suzuki, Nakasone, Takeshita, Uno and Kaifu) essentially had made their political careers through parliamentary party careers. Yet for economic policy advice, Ohira went beyond classical bureaucratic briefings. As prime minister, Ohira maintained close relations with ex-bureaucrats of economic ministries, who had gone on to a business career, such as Teiichiro Morinaga, governor of the Bank of Japan. Other members of his informal 'brains trust' of regular non-official advisors included senior supporters of Hayato Ikeda, Ohira's mentor, such as Takeshi Sakurada, chairman of Nikkeiren, Hiroki Inazato, chairman of Nippon Seiko, Osamu Shimomura, a member of BOJ's policy board, and Masaya Ito, Ikeda's former chief secretary.[32]

Ohira's distinguished administrative and political CV was a superb qualification for Japan's top slot. Yet his political achievements were overshadowed by failures – a fiscal conservative who had to preside over two record fiscal deficits, an advocate of decentralised 'garden cities' who only saw metropolitan concentration and the peripheries' depopulation increase during his tenure, and a closet intellectual and philosopher who had his career and his own life brought to a premature end by brutal factional-interest politics.

It was only through and after his death that the LDP gained a new lease of life in voter confidence, and that his successors were able to implement administrative reforms (Nakasone) and introduce a general consumption tax (Takeshita). Other political themes of Ohira – decentralisation and the revitalisation of Japan's regions, Pacific co-operation, and effective import liberalisation – still await implementation.

With an eye on posterity, conservative Japanese politicians pursue strongly dynastic ambitions. Ohira was no exception. After the death of his oldest son and political heir-apparent in 1964, his son in-law, Hajime Morita, formerly a promising MOF official, became his political secretary. Mr Morita today is a fourth-term MP from Kagawa 2 district, having inherited Ohira's local support organisation. Ohira's second son married the daughter of the president of Kanzaki Paper Co., one of Japan's largest paper-makers, the president having been one of Ohira's early supporters. Ohira's third son finally married the daughter of Upper House Dietman Uehara. Through *keibatsu* his family thus became firmly tied to the national elite.

Political Biography 2: Yasuhiro Nakasone

Yasuhiro Nakasone was born in 1918, the son of a wealthy timber merchant in Takasagi, Gumma prefecture. With a good scholastic record he entered the local grammar school, from which, after graduation, he entered the Law Faculty of Tokyo University where he studied political sciences.

Having passed the senior civil service examinations, after graduation in 1941 Nakasone joined the Interior Ministry where he was delegated to the Tokyo metropolitan administration. In April 1941 he was drafted into the Imperial Navy in which, after attending the Navy General Accounting School, he served safely as a quartermaster until he was decommissioned with the rank of lieutenant commander in August 1945. His younger brother was killed in action during the war.

After the war, Nakasone rejoined the Interior Ministry and ran the police department of Kagawa prefecture. His subsequent and final administrative posting was as an inspector in Tokyo's Metropolitan Police Headquarters. In December 1946 he left the ministry to run for election in his native Gumma 3 district.

He joined the conservative Democratic Party, which stood in opposition to Yoshida's Liberal Party. As a local support organisation in his home district, Gumma 3, Nakasone founded a then youthful *Seiun Juku* (Society for Ideals), and appealing to patriotic values, wearing his navy officer's uniform and touring his constituency on a white bicycle, he impressed his electorate sufficiently to be voted into the Diet in April 1947 at the age of 28.

His polished rhetoric and a penchant for spectacular, if somewhat showy, actions soon became Nakasone's trademark. He continued to attend Diet sessions and to vote in his Imperial Navy uniform, and wrote indignant letters to Douglas MacArthur. In 1950 Nakasone, together with a handful of Democratic party members who remained opposed to a coalition with Yoshida's Liberals, became a member of Miki's Co-operative Party, which was to be part of the conservative party merger of 1955. Originally a lone wolf, Nakasone joined the small right-wing 'politicians' faction of Kenzo Matsumura and later of Ichiro Kono, whose faction he ultimately took over after Kono's death in 1965. In 1954 Nakasone was pronouncing himself in favour of nuclear power – then anathema in nuclear-allergic Japan. He was rewarded by prime minister Kishi – who was then allied with Nakasone's mentor Kono – with his first cabinet appointment as state minister of the Science and Technology Agency in 1959, when he was only 41.

In Eisaku Sato's cabinets he served as minister of transport (1967–8) and as state minister of the Defence Agency (1970–1). Although considered hawkish on defence matters and nationalist in outlook, favouring a revision of the constitution, Nakasone was often seen to adjust his views to suit his changing tactical alliances, in which as a leader of one of the small, less well-financed and connected factions he had to stay flexible in order to survive. Although denounced by the media as an opportunistic weathercock

(*kazamidori*), Nakasone managed to enhance his influence gradually and the size of his faction by managing to come down on the winner's side at most interfactional fights. In 1971–2 he served as chairman of the LDP's Policy Research Council. In this function he initiated Japanese programmes for space research and for the exploration of Antarctica. For many years Nakasone continued to serve as the chairman of the LDP's commission for science and technology.

Having supported Tanaka in his bid for the prime ministership in 1972, Nakasone was rewarded by obtaining his first senior ministerial post as minister of international trade and industry (1972–4). Japan had been hit by the first oil crisis and he energetically pushed for active Middle Eastern resource diplomacy and for energy conservation policies at home. During his ministerial tenures he had, as *the Financial Times* observed,[33] 'the uncommon attribute of boning up on his briefs and forming his own opinions, rather than simply serving as the mouthpiece of his bureaucrats'. Although publicly suspected of having been a recipient of Lockheed money, but not indicted, Nakasone weathered this crisis, and served his old political friend, 'clean' Mr Miki, in the key function of LDP secretary general from 1974 to until his resignation in 1976. With his arch-rival Fukuda – who usually beat Nakasone comprehensively in the shared Gumma 3 constituency for the coveted top position – succeeding Miki, he would only serve in a senior party position of lesser importance: as chairman of its executive council (1977–8).

He used this time to recharge his batteries and to strengthen his factional organisation. In the 1978 LDP presidential elections, Nakasone came third, after Ohira and Fukuda. In programmatic terms, he advocated 'neoconservatism', which in his view should consist of transparent action-orientated policies responsive to popular wishes, thus echoing his earlier campaign for the election of the prime minister by direct popular vote. Having campaigned against Ohira, he obviously could not serve in a cabinet position under him. Although a strong contender to succeed Ohira in 1980, party chieftains – including Tanaka – decided in Suzuki's favour; he appeared more malleable to their requests. In Zenko Suzuki's cabinet Nakasone held consequently the relatively junior post of state minister of the Administrative Management Agency (1980–2). This position allowed him to push his ideas for administrative reform.

When in November 1982 Suzuki finally resigned from his unloved and lethargic prime ministership, it was essentially Tanaka's support which put Nakasone into the saddle by helping him to gain 58 per cent of votes in the LDP members' ballot. Within a year, however, thanks to his formidable political skills – acquired in the tough school of survival as a sidestream faction chief for more than 20 years – he was able to free himself from the 'Tanakasone' label which an initially hostile press had awarded to his first cabinet, in which Nakasone had been forced to give seven positions to Tanaka people (including Masaharu Gotoda as chief cabinet secretary) and appoint Nikaido as LDP secretary general.

Nakasone served as prime minister for almost five years until October 1987, when he was able to hand-pick his successor, Noburo Takeshita, over Kiichi Miyazawa, Shintaro Abe and Susumu Nikaido. Unlike most of his predecessors, Nakasone as prime minister succeeded in giving Japan a stronger international profile and in increasing his fellow citizens aware-ness for the need to modernise Japan's way of life and to do business commensurate with her new-found prosperity and enhanced world role.

In May 1986 Nakasone hosted the second Tokyo summit, in which Ronald Reagan, Helmut Kohl, François Mitterand, Bettino Craxi, Margaret Thatcher and Jacques Delors also took part. Discussions focused on issues such as international terrorism and on appropriate reactions to the Chernobyl disaster. While the agenda was of no particular consequence, the summit allowed Nakasone (and fellow summiteers) to bask in the international publicity which the event inevitably attracted and – unlike his predecessors – to appear at ease and as an equal of his foreign peers. This was Nakasone's fourth summit. At earlier ones (Williamsburg in 1983, London in 1984, and Bonn in 1985) he found in Ronald Reagan and Mrs Thatcher jointly held conservative beliefs and a shared distrust of the Soviet Union. The 'Ron–Yasu' relationship successfully pretended a trans-Pacific cameraderie, which was replayed in dozens of bilateral encounters. In fact, Nakasone in word and in deed attempted to alleviate a great deal of the official American preoccupations and concerns.

He called his country an 'unsinkable aircraft carrier' in the Western alliance. He raised defence spending above Japan's self-imposed 1 per cent of GNP threshold, thus removing one of the many bureaucratically defined taboo totems in Japanese politics. Nakasone also effectively promoted Japan's internationalisation as a desirable policy objective, accepting the need for effective import liberalisation, for more generous foreign aid programmes and for a cultural opening of the country. During his tenure, Nakasone visited most of the countries of the Pacific Rim, of Western Europe and of Southern Asia. On several occasions he developed a theme of an East–West cultural merger, which would develop out of the trilateral co-operation between Japan, Western Europe and the US during the twenty-first century.[34]

In commissioning a report from an advisory council chaired by Mr Maekawa, a former BOJ governor, on the necessary restructuring of Japan's so far export-led economy, Nakasone attempted to lay the necessary domestic groundwork that would prevent his 'internationalisation' slogan remaining an empty promise. He in fact committed himself to implement the Maekawa report's courageous recommendations one by one.[35]

The report asked for: increased domestic demand; reduced fiscal incentives for savings; reduction of restrictions to building permits; inducements for overseas productive investments; reduced work time; import liberalisation for foodstuffs and coal; and a permanently revalued yen.

While many recommendations still await implementation, the Nakasone administration began to tackle in earnest problems such as market access through a series of action programmes, reducing tariffs unilaterally and cutting non-tariff barriers. Nakasone privatised inefficient state enterprises such as JNR, NTT and Japan Tobacco. Runaway deficit spending was brought back under control in five consecutive tight fiscal budgets.

He finally changed the atmosphere of public debate in Japan, de-legitimising its parochial and self-serving small-country trade and security outlook on the world (which had conveniently justified free rides on both). Nakasone's landslide victory in 1986 further proved that his approach was more popular with the populace at large than with the ministerial bureaucracy or his fellow faction chiefs, who in his early prime ministerial days had usually been successful in watering down his more audacious schemes. During his early days as prime minister, Nakasone had been rather restricted to rhetoric and symbolism (like praying at Yasukuni Shrine in his official capacity). In his latter days – helped by Tanaka's incapacitation by a stroke and by his election victory – he became gradually more effective.

Nakasone appeared to mellow many of his earlier more strident views: he did not attempt to change the constitution, which he had previously criticised as foreign imposed and in need of revision; his earlier proposed national day of mourning for the war dead (15 August) was not introduced. Nakasone also curtailed his previously extensive contacts with prominent right-wingers (Yoshio Kodama and others). Rather than attempting to militarise society as his critics had feared, Nakasone worked at modernising and improving the SDF in their circumscribed constitutional role.

As a relative outsider to the bureaucracy, to the *zaikai* business circles and to his own party's establishment, Nakasone set up his own external group of non-mainstream advisors (newspaper editors, younger academics and some old conservative mentors):

Throughout his career he also maintained close ties, and listened to the advice of successful contemporaries with whom his path in life once crossed and with whom he shared common old-boy bonds. Part of this brains trust to whom he referred for policy council during his premiership were Nobuo Mochida, president of Mochida Pharmaceuticals, and Goro Koyama, executive director at Mitsui Bank, both, like Nakasone, graduates of the prewar Shizuoka High School; Shoichi Akazawa, chairman of JETRO, and Ryozo Seijima, senior advisor at C. Itoh, who served as naval officers with Nakasone; the late Noboru Goto, president of Tokyu and of the Japan Chamber of Commerce, Koichi Nakagawa, head of Nomura Research Institute, and Jiro Ushio, chairman of Ushio Electrics, who were contemporary graduates of Todai. Close Nakasone confidants also were Todai professors: Seizaburo Sato and Shinpei Kumon.[36]

Nakasone equally had to secure his own finance systems for his expanding faction: a source of various allegations of shady dealings and of close encounters with the law, such as the Shokusan Jutaku Sogo tax-evasion case, the Lockheed scandal, and later, the Recruit scandal.

With his retirement from the prime ministership in 1987, Nakasone had secured Takeshita's support for the foundation of a non-governmental strategic foreign policy thinktank, which was ultimately named the International Institute for Peace. This institute was intended to develop more brainpower in the international strategic field and to offer sound advice to the Japanese cabinet on foreign and security issues. It was presumably also intended to lend Nakasone's planned foreign ventures a suitable background and intellectual respectability. In June 1988 the Recruit scandal broke. Soon Nakasone and some of his lieutenants (Fujinami, Yamaguchi, Watanabe) were implicated as well. Nakasone as prime minister in fact had to admit that through his aides he had purchased 29,000 preflotation Recruit Cosmos shares (which later netted some 60 million yen profits after being sold on the stock exchange). Nakasone was later grilled in the Diet about his involvement in appointing Recruit chairman Ezoe to key government advisory councils, and in the bargain-priced resale of supercomputers from NTT to Recruit Co. While Nakasone denied any wrongdoings and was not indicted by the public prosecutor, he had to resign his position as 'supreme advisor' of the LDP, as well as most other public functions. He was forced to leave the party, and in the February 1990 Lower House election ran in his seventeenth re-election as an independent candidate.

Sensing that his political career was at risk, Nakasone undertook an intensive grassroots campaign in rural Gumma to ensure his political survival. Still, in spite of his re-election, Nakasone was forced to hand over *de facto* control and the formal chairmanship of his faction to his unloved successor Michio Watanabe, after having been at the helm for 25 years. Ten of his factional followers lost in the election.

While Fukuda's son Yasuo had successfully taken over his father's jiban in Gumma 3 in February 1990, Nakasone's son Hirofumi, formerly a manager with Asahi Chemical, still serves his first term in the Upper House.

Two Days in the Life of Prime Minister Nakasone
Monday, 1 June 1987[37]

10:18   Visits the Japan Art Academy in Ueno to deliver a speech at the academy's award ceremony and see works on display;

11:50   Returns to Kantei;

11:51   Meets Yoshihiko Ebihara, new deputy vice-minister of the Prime Minister's Office, and his predecessor Ryoji Fujii;

12:33   Visits Ginza to join the LDP's spring street campaign for garden and greenery;

12:58   Returns to Kantei;

13:10   Meets LDP Lower House member Taku Yamazaki;

14:43   Meets Kazuo Iwata, chief of the Japan Society for the Promotion of Machine Industry, who is heading a business mission to Yugoslavia;

15:08   Receives a United Nations Environment Commission report from Saburo Okita, one of its members, and Environment Agency Director General Inamura;

15:25   Studies in preparation for the Venice summit;

17:31   Meets Han Nianlong, a member of the Chinese Communist Party's Central Advisory Commission;

18:10   Meets LDP Upper House member Eizaburo Saito;

18:32   Arrives at Matsuya Salon in Hirakawacho to attend a meeting of alumni of the former Shizuoka High School (now Shizuoka University) supporting Nakasone;

19:40   Returns to Kantei.

Tuesday, 2 June 1987[38]

9:25   Meets a group of town and village assembly speakers from Gumma Pref. at Kantei;

10:00   Attends a regular Cabinet meeting;

10:19   Meets separately with Coordination and Management Agency chief Yamashita, Construction Minister Amano, Agriculture Minister Kato and Labour Minister Hirai;

10:34   Meets an LDP Youth Department mission to South Korea, led by his son, Upper House member Hirofumi Nakasone;

10:42   Meets Home Affairs Minister Hanashi;

10:51	Meets Jinemon Konishi, head of the Konishi International Exchange Foundation;
11:50	Meets LDP Lower House member Moriyoshi Sato;
12:00	Meets economic news editors of Tokyo-based news organisations;
2:55	Meets Deputy Chief Cabinet Secretary Fujimori;
3:04	Meets LDP Lower House member Yoshio Sakurauchi;
3:16	Meets Jiro Tsunekura and Muneyuki Matsushita, present and former political news editors of the *Asahi Shimbun*;
3:27	Meets Yoshifusa Kunigo, vice-chairman of the Central Union of Agricultural Co-operatives (Zenchu);
4:03	Meets former Prime Minister Fukuda;
4:40	Meets Toyoo Gyohten, finance vice-minister for international affairs;
5:14	Meets LDP Upper House member Bunbee Hara;
5:17	Meets Bank of Japan Gov. Satoshi Sumita in connection with the Venice summit;
5:50	Meets JAL President Susumu Yamaji;
6:38	Arrives at a Kioicho restaurant to attend a gathering of Diet members who used to be officials of the defunct Interior Ministry;
7:42	Returns to Kantei.

From these tightly set and meticulously organised schedules it is evident how little room for spontaneous decisions or improvisation there is for a Japanese prime minister (or for any other senior political figure). He will normally follow with self-discipline the strict time management arranged by his helpful staff.

4 Legitimacy Crises

With its incessant and ever-increasing financial needs, Japan's political system is structurally corrupt. The extent of personal corruption of an individual politician is then a discretionary matter in a very grey area. Yohei Kono, an intelligent and therefore cynical actor in this elite, compared the implication in the Recruit scandal to a speeding ticket: except for cyclists all are sinners, and a few unlucky ones get caught.[1] While corruption – the trade-off between corporate and private donations for special favours and services by the politician – is a daily occurrence, an affair which qualifies as a major scandal that is played up by the media and subsequently brings down a government happens on average only once a decade. While the material is plentiful, it is only a very few select stories that make it into a scandal and a national obsession.

The dynamism of this process is a worthy subject for a book of its own. Yet, in comparison with many small stories, such as irregularities and kickbacks involving beef imports through the LIPC, Taiwanese pork shipments through Nagoya, the stevedores' privileges in Japanese harbours, the award of transportation licences, public monopolies' operations (KDD, NTT, JT etc.), corporate tax frauds, stock exchange rigging, and a never-ending saga of public works cum real estate collusion with hundreds of local variations, to generate a national scandal the following criteria must be met:

- figures of national importance (an ex-prime minister preferably) must be implicated;
- overt evidence must be available, so that public prosecutors are forced to investigate officially; and
- the media must be free from any other fascinating subject (hence they will only deal with one major scandal at the time).

Almost all politicians (and some senior bureaucrats and *zaikai* business leaders) have skeletons in their closets. Most of them have learnt the proper techniques of self-protection (including designated fall-guys among their assistants), of discretion, and of suitable countermeasures to assure their career survival under most circumstances. Hence the job of an investigative journalist or public prosecutor is by no means easy. In order to pre-empt unwanted publicity or indiscretion, indirect gangland links may come in useful at times (see the third section of this chapter).

With a scandal unfolding – implicating the very top of Japan triade power elite: the LDP, central ministries and big business – public revulsion runs deep. Salaryman-san and his wife have a rare – and usually passing – realisation that they are being cheated of a good deal of their life's work through a system which favours the allocation of these societal riches to the corporate sector and some of its propertied families in a biased fashion. In other words, we witness the periodic reoccurrence of crises of legitimacy for Japan's power elite which, if the opposition camp (parties and labour unions) have been competent and prepared for a takeover, could at times have led to a change of regime in Japan.

The Lockheed scandal and the Recruit scandal are both interesting in their own way: while Lockheed revealed the corruption of a relatively small number of senior politicians, and is more interesting for the drama of the various bribery techniques employed, Recruit proved the wholesale corruptibility of almost the entire political, senior bureaucratic and business executive class, be it as agents of influence or in the form of straight favours for cash. Culprits caught by media and public prosecutors' attention in each occurrence seemed genuinely surprised and initially unaware of guilt. (This only, if hesitatingly, turned into shame during exposure and humiliating media, Diet and police investigations.) Why were these minor contributions improper, while everybody knew that much worse things were underway on a larger scale, most recipients of Lockheed's and Mr Ezoe's favours seemed to ask?

THE LOCKHEED SCANDAL

In October 1983 former prime minister Kakuei Tanaka was found guilty by the Tokyo District Court of taking a bribe from the Lockheed Corporation and was sentenced to four years of prison and fined 500 million yen – the amount he had received from Lockheed ten years earlier when, while prime minister, he had persuaded All Nippon Airways to buy 21 Lockheed jets. With Tanaka were found guilty: his secretary Toshio Enomoto (a suspended sentence of one year); the former chairman of Marubeni Corporation, Hiro Hiyama (two and a half years in prison); as well as two former managing directors of Marubeni, Lockheed's agent in Japan, who had offered the bribe to Tanaka. Ten other defendants had been convicted in earlier separate trials.

The Tokyo District Court declared itself convinced that Tanaka as a result of the bribe had given official instructions to ANA to buy Lockheed

Tristar aircraft. The amount had been given to Tanaka by Marubeni in four instalments in cash through Enomoto, Tanaka's private secretary. At the time this must have appeared to Tanaka a routine operation of a minor sort. His annual intake of contributions from Japan's big business had been a hundredfold in comparison. New was the fact that the donor was a foreign corporation that entered bribery payments in their account ledgers, and was subsequently compelled to reveal these data in February 1976 before a subcommittee of the US Senate charged to investigate the business practices of US-based multinationals.

At the time Carl Kotchian, a vice-president of Lockheed Corporation, confessed that the company had paid 2.5 billion yen to senior Japanese officials in order to promote the sales of Tristars during 1973–4. The payments went through three distinct channels:

(a) via Kenji Osano, a billionaire in the tourism sector, who owned hotel chains, travel agencies and bus lines, as well as significant minority shareholdings in several airlines (KAL, JAL, ANA), and who formed part of Tanaka's pervasive circle of friends;

(b) via Yoshio Kodama, a right-wing deal-maker and 'unseen wirepuller' (*Kuromaku*), who since 1958 had acted as a secret agent for Lockheed to promote the sales of military aircraft to the Japanese navy and air force; and

(c) via Marubeni, at the time Japan's third largest general trading company (*sogo shosha*) and Lockheed's official sales agent.

The Osano Connection

At Los Angeles airport in November 1973 Kenji Osano received in cash US$200,000 from John Clutter, the representative of Lockheed in Tokyo. In return he used his influence with ANA vice-president Naoji Watanabe and other ANA managers to obtain a purchasing decision in Lockheed's favour.

In 1981 Osano received a one-year sentence for lying under oath before a Diet investigation committee. In his trial he was convicted due to circumstantial evidence and with the help of Clutter's diary.

Osano used the Lockheed money to cover the gambling debts of Tanaka's faction member and underworld link, Koichi Hamada. MP Hamada in October 1972 had lost US$1.5 million during a wild night in Las Vegas (eight years later his gambling habit would once again make Japanese political history and contribute to the downfall and subsequent death of PM

Ohira). Unfortunately, at the time he did not possess this amount. However, Hamada as a member of the LDP's Diet Policy Committee, whose function it is to contribute discreetly to the non-communist opposition parties to secure their co-operation in ongoing diet business, could not be left alone in disgrace since he simply knew too much. At Tanaka's request, Osano, who held enough US dollar notes in cash, covered Hamada's debts. Tanaka now owed a *giri* (a moral obligation requiring a return) to Osano, who was then able to use his influence in favour of Lockheed more effectively.

The Kodama Connection

Yoshio Kodama was less honour-bound. In prewar days he experienced jail repeatedly due to his right-wing violence and murder attempts. In 1946 he was arrested for three years by the US occupation authorities as a suspected war criminal. During the war he built up his notorious Organisation Kodama in occupied China, which engaged in plunder and espionage on account of Japan's Navy Flyers Corps.

With a part of his war loot, consisting of diamonds, platinum and other precious metals which he managed to transfer to Japan before the war ended, Kodama in 1945 financed the reconstruction of Hatoyama's Liberal Party. Ever since he had maintained close and friendly relations with leading LDP politicians. Kodama also kept equally close relations with Japan's right wingers. For years he remained president of their umbrella organisation, the Greater Japan Patriotic Federation, some of whose members were closely linked with the *yakuza*, Japan's feudally organised crime syndicates. At times the *yakuza* and their battalions came in handy to crack picket lines and to intimidate dissenters. Kodama was hired in 1958 as a secret marketing consultant by Lockheed in order to promote the sales of military aircraft. For these services he received a consultancy fee of 2.4 billion yen during 1969–74. Of this, 1.9 billion yen had been paid to promote the Orion aircraft to be used for antisubmarine combat and for the sale of Tristars. With respect to the Tristars, Kodama contacted the LDP's leadership through the good offices of Yasuhiro Nakasone who, when these services were made public, had to resign from his position as LDP secretary general in September 1976.

Kodama, who was in poor health, died before his trial was conclusively terminated. Kodama himself had always denied any relationship with Lockheed and characterised all incriminating Lockheed documents as fabrications of vengeful US imperialists who were jealous of the rise of the right in Japan.

The Marubeni Connection

The third channel of bribes led with Marubeni's mediation to MOT minister Tomisaburo Hashimoto (5 million yen) and to his parliamentary vice-minister Takayuki Sato (2 million yen). In return, in 1971 on the recommendation of ANA they prohibited JAL, ANA's foremost competitor, from introducing highly profitable jumbos on domestic routes, which ANA, due to liquidity problems, could not afford at the time. ANA president Tokuji Wakasa had conducted a systematic policy of political contributions. All members of the LDP's and of the Diet's transportation committees received free annual ANA passes and generous contributions in cash and in kind. Leading MOT officials upon retirement were hired for highly paid advisory and management functions for ANA. As a result of these sustained efforts, ANA received exclusive licences to operate on the more lucrative inner Japanese destinations, with JAL and TDA (today, Japan Airsystems) being permitted to operate less lucrative routes only. Tetsuo Oba, Wakasa's predecessor with ANA, had decided in May 1970 in favour of the McDonnell Douglas DC10 as a new wide-bodied aircraft for ANA. But after the receipt of 163 million yen for five ANA top managers and himself, his successor Wakasa became more inclined to follow Tanaka's instructions and purchase Lockheed Tristars instead of DC10s. In January 1982 Wakasa was condemned to three years in prison on probation, for committing perjury before the Diet and for violating foreign exchange regulations. MOT minister Hashimoto and his parliamentary deputy Sato received suspended sentences of two and a half years and two years respectively in May 1982.

In order to play safe in their struggle against McDonnell Douglas, Lockheed vice-president Carl Kotchian and Marubeni president Hiro Hiyama agreed to offer 500 million yen (which was considered habitual on public contracts of that order) to the prime minister. As Marubeni had been a major benefactor of Tanaka's faction since 1969, the new offer came as little surprise. President Hiyama visited prime minister Tanaka in his Mejirodai residence in Tokyo's Toshima ward on 23 August 1972. A good-humoured Tanaka reportedly agreed ('*Yosh, yosh*' – *OK, Ok*) when it was proposed that he should give ANA binding 'administrative guidance' to purchase Tristars. Since Japanese airlines relied on subsidised public credits to purchase new aircraft, they depended on government approval for their purchasing decisions.

At the same time, in autumn 1972, Mitsui's vice-president Kiichi Ishiguro attempted to persuade Tanaka in a personal conversation to intervene on behalf of McDonnell Douglas, for which Mitsui conducted the sales negotiations in Japan. Tanaka appeared to be positive, but did not keep his word, as Ishiguro later bitterly remarked in the court proceedings.

Six weeks after the conversation between Tanaka and Hiyama had taken place, in September 1972 a Cabinet committee in which Tanaka and Hashimoto participated decided to recommend ANA the purchase of Tristars. Later, in October 1972, ANA announced its decision to purchase Tristars. On 12 January 1973 the contract with Lockheed was signed.

The Transmission to Tanaka

Lockheed, however, was tardy in honouring Tanaka's services. In May 1973 Tanaka, through his secretary Enomoto, told President Hiyama that if Lockheed wished ever to do business again in Japan, it should pay without further delay.

During the next nine months Lockheed inconspicuously organised the necessary cash, which was handed by John Clutter, Lockheed's representative in Tokyo, to Marubeni manager Hiroshi Itoh in four instalments against a receipt ('I received 100 peanuts' – 100 million yen). After the first hand-out on 10 August 1973, Itoh with the 100 million yen in cardboard cartons drove to the agreed meeting point behind the UK embassy in Tokyo's central Chiyoda ward, where he was met by Enomoto and Tanaka's driver, who later, after his confession, committed suicide in suspicious circumstances. While Enomoto and Itoh was chatting, the chauffeur put the cartons from Itoh's car into the trunk of Enomoto's car. Later, the cash was put into a safe in Tanaka's Tokyo residence. The next transaction of 125 million yen took place in a telephone box in Chiyoda-ku in October 1973. A further payment of the same amount in January 1974 changed hands on a parking lot at Hotel Okura, close to the US embassy. The last instalment of 150 million yen was picked up by Enomoto from Itoh's private residence in March 1974. As reported, Hiyama and Itoh both received sentences of two and a half years and two years respectively for their roles in actively soliciting bribery. Enomoto for his intermediary role received a suspended sentence of one year.

Factional Fights During the Lockheed Trial

In November 1974 Tanaka was forced to resign following the public uproar triggered by his numerous dubious real-estate deals subsequent to highly advantageous public development decisions. His resignation was unrelated and happened prior to the disclosure of the Lockheed payments. The US Senate's Lockheed hearings and their revelations in February 1976 became known to the Japanese public only through their coverage in a smallish political weekly, *Bungei Shunju*. Once the Japanese media caught on to the story, embattled prime minister Miki saw his opportunity to improve his popularity and 'Mr Clean' and to crack the power of the adversial Tanaka faction. In July 1976 he had Tanaka arrested, and in September 1976 Hashimoto and Sato were put behind bars. As public and media passions ran high during the televised Diet hearings, Miki wrote a letter to US President Ford, requesting the submission of all confidential US data on corruption cases in Japan. Miki also arranged for both countries' public prosecution authorities to conclude an information exchange agreement.

For the LDP establishment this was going too far. In May 1976 the Tanaka, Fukuda and Ohira factions had concluded a tactical alliance and had threatened Miki that he would be toppled instantly if he permitted the investigation of further suspects by the public prosecutor. Miki complied, thus saving the heads of Nakasone, Gotoda and Nikaido, who had already been strongly implicated as suspected recipients of Lockheed funds.

Late in 1976, the LDP suffered a serious setback in the Lower House elections. To the LDP's mainstream, Miki was clearly the culprit. He was overthrown by Fukuda in December 1976. Miki's hopes for a curb on Tanaka's powers did not materialise either. Having been released on bail and having relinquished nominal faction and party membership, his faction none the less increased from 80 members (1976) to 118 (1983). Tanaka remained the decisive kingmaker for the cabinets of PMs Ohira, Suzuki and Nakasone. Also in his constituency of Niigata, as a nominally independent candidate he continued to receive the largest vote of all of Japan's Lower House candidates. His last and best result he achieved in 1986 with 168,000 votes (when he was already too ill to do any campaigning, let alone to do any parliamentary work).

THE RECRUIT SCANDAL

While Lockheed appeared as a single event, in which only a handful of senior politicians, businessmen and their intermediaries were implicated, Recruit was more far-reaching. To the general public it was the final proof of what everybody had expected all along: evidence of the corruptibility of almost the entire political, administrative and managerial elite. It was particularly among its best, its brightest and its most hopeful members that Hiromasa Ezoe had spread his favours.[2] Hence the legitimacy crisis triggered by Recruit almost caused a regime change in 1989–90 – had it not been for the incompetence of the alternatives.

Recruit Co. during 1988–90 was involved in one of the biggest political scandals in Japan's postwar history. The myth that Hiromasa Ezoe, Recruit's founder, was one of the most successful businessmen of the 1980s, and the miraculous growth of his business, made the company one of the most popular private firms with new university graduates who were looking for a promising career. Recruit appeared as the symbol of the new high-tech information-orientated society.

Recruit was first set up in March 1960 as an advertising agency specialising in university newspapers. Through the 1970s and 1980s Recruit grew at a rapid pace. What began as a small firm with only three employees finally became a huge information and publishing business of 27 separate companies with 6200 employees and total sales of 184 billion yen in 1987. Total turnover of the Recruit group, including the data-communication and real-estate business, probably amounted to more than 500 billion yen.

One of Recruit's subsidiary companies, Recruit Cosmos, in 1988 had become Japan's second largest real-estate developer of apartment buildings. After the privatisation of NTT in 1985, Recruit was able to purchase two Cray Research megacomputers, which marked its start in the lease of computing time. With the help of NTT it also was able to supply on-line housing information services and circuit leasing in data communications. Recruit's rapid growth and successful business diversification coincided with and directly benefited from the real-estate boom and the selective deregulation opportunities which took place during Nakasone's rule (1982–7).

The Recruit scandal consisted of two major elements: the widespread pre-flotation share transactions involving politicians and bureaucrats, and the large numbers of politicians' fund-raising party tickets purchased by Recruit.

In December 1984 Ezoe offered 1.25 million unlisted Recruit Cosmos shares to 76 persons, including politicians, bureaucrats and business executives, for an obviously nominal price of 1200 yen per share. He also sold some 7 million shares to member companies of his Recruit group. When Ezoe realised that the distribution of further shares was necessary and helpful, he bought back 760,000 shares from his companies and offered them to another similarly select group of 83 persons for the price of 3000 yen per share in September 1986. This was just one month before their listing on the Tokyo stock exchange, where their officially traded price jumped to 5270 yen per share on 30 October 1986, their first trading day. Most beneficiaries are known to have sold immediately, thus realising profits of between 2300 and 4000 yen per share. Privileged share offers varied between 5000 and 30,000 shares per person. Profits were hence between 10.6 million and 120 million yen per beneficiary.

Chronological Development of the Scandal

1988

18 June	The *Asahi Journal* discloses that Hidenori Komatsu, deputy mayor of Kawasaki City, purchased pre-flotation shares of Recruit Cosmos, a subsidiary of Recruit Co., and thus effortlessly realised high profits. In return he had offered Recruit 'special conditions' for the construction of an office building.
6 July	Newspapers report that Recruit Cosmos's pre-flotation shares were also purchased by aides of former prime minister Nakasone, LDP secretary general Abe and by finance minister Miyazawa. Ezoe retreats into a hospital and remains unavailable for comment.
5 September	United Social Democrat (*Shaminren*) Diet member Narazaki reveals that he was approached by Recruit Cosmos with the obvious intention of bribery.
October–November	Newspapers report that former administrative vice-ministers Takashi Kato (MOL) and Kunio Takaishi (MOE), and Hisashi Shinto, chairman of NTT (Nippon Telegraph and Telephone) also benefited massively from preferential Recruit share offers. These reports follow the public prosecution's confiscation of some 1700 boxes of Recruit files, the questioning of Ezoe, and the arrest of his chief secretary, Hiroshi Matsubara. Other stories cover the involvement of major Diet members, including leading LDP and opposition party figures. Socialist Diet member, Takuni Ueda, resigns from the House of Representatives because of his secretary's purchase of Recruit Cosmos unlisted shares.
9 December	Finance minister Kiichi Miyazawa resigns (after his earlier story about an anonymous friend of his secretary abusing his personal seal for purchases was found to be fictitious).
14 December	NTT chairman Shinto resigns.
27 December	PM Takeshita reshuffles his cabinet. The common factor among new appointees is that they do not appear to have been tainted by the scandal.
30 December	The new justice minister, Hasegawa, resigns after it is discovered that he too benefited from Recruit.

1989

24 January	EPA minister Ken Harada resigns when it is revealed that his fund-raising organisation continued to receive Recruit funds until well after the scandal broke.
7 February	Implicated DSP (Democratic Socialist Party) chairman Tsukamoto announces that he will not run for the next term of chairmanship. This amounts to a *de facto* resignation.
12 February	LDP loses the by-election for a vacant Upper House seat in Fukuoka Prefecture, a traditional LDP stronghold.
13 February	Arrests of Hiromasa Ezoe, former chairman of Recruit Co. and of Hiroshi Kobayashi, vice-president of First Finance (a subsidiary of Recruit) on suspicion of offering bribes to Hisahiko Hasegawa and Ei Shikiba, former executives of NTT who are arrested at the same time for taking bribes.
15 February	Shunjiro Mamiya and Seiichi Tateoka, executives of Recruit Co. and of Recruit Cosmos respectively, are arrested on charges of violating the Securities and Foreign Exchange Law.
17–18 February	Arrests of Shigeru Kato (MOL officer) on suspicion of taking bribes, and of Toshihiro Ono (private secretary of Ezoe) for violating the Securities Law.
6 March	Arrests of Hisashi Shinto (ex-NTT president) and of Kozo Murata (Shinto's secretary) on suspicion of having taken bribes.
8 March	Arrest of Takashi Kato (ex-administrative vice-minister, MOL) on suspicion of having accepted bribes.
19 March	Gubernatorial elections in Chiba and Miyagi prefectures: in Chiba the LDP-backed candidate wins only 200,000 votes ahead of the only competitor, a communist, who was able to triple his party's score. In Miyagi the Recruit-implicated LDP candidate, Kazuo Aichi, withdrew at the last minute, thus allowing his socialist competitor to win by a wide margin in this conservative heartland.
28 March	Arrest of Takashi Kato (ex-administrative vice-minister, MOE) on suspicion of having taken bribes.
10 April	PM Takeshita admits that his support organisation has received 150 million yen in cash from Recruit Co.

14 April   Secretary General Abe concedes that his wife during
              1982–8 received a total of 23.7 million yen as con-
              sultancy fees from Recruit.

22 April   Takeshita has to admit further that he received 50
              million yen as a loan from Recruit in 1987.

25 April   Takeshita announces his intention to resign after the
              passage of the budget for FY1989 (likely to be late
              in May 1989).

26 April   Takeshita's finance secretary Ikei Aoki commits
              suicide.

25 May   After months of refusal, Nakasone finally testifies
              before the Diet under oath. Opposition questioning
              turns out to be unexpectedly harmless. Nakasone
              gets away with his claims of not having been in-
              formed about his secretaries' purchasing decisions,
              of not having been involved in NTT/Recruit trans-
              actions nor of having had a role in Ezoe's appoint-
              ments to government councils. The Minister of Justice
              announces the forthcoming conclusion of the Recruit
              investigation: the only politicians charged will be
              Nakasone's crown prince, Takao Fujinami, and
              Katsuya Ikeda of the Komeito.

30 May   The LDP decides that Recruit-implicated party mem-
              bers will not be allowed to hold party or government
              posts for one year.

31 May   After the resignation of Takeshita, foreign minister
              Sosuke Uno is nominated LDP prime ministerial
              candidate.

8 June   The public prosecutor announces the end of inves-
              tigations with only two politicians, Fujinami (LDP)
              and Ikeda (Komeito), having been indicted for sus-
              picion of bribery.

23 July   Upper House elections; LDP loses Upper House
              majority. PM Uno announces his resignation.

8 August   Toshiki Kaifu is elected prime minister.

1990

18 February   Lower House elections. LDP wins comfortable ma-
              jority. Most Recruit-implicated MPs are safely re-
              elected (sole losers: Keishu Tanaka of the DSP and

Kunio Takaishi, former administrative vice minister at MOE).

9 October Hisashi Shinto, ex-NTT chairman, is given a two-year suspended prison sentence by the Tokyo District Court and fined 22.7 million yen for having taken bribes.

1991

25 April Ei Shikiba, ex-director of NTT is sentenced to an 18-month suspended prison term, and fined 11.4 million yen for bribery by Recruit.

Beneficiaries

The Diet members who have been reported in connection with the Recruit scandal are shown in Table 4.1.[3]

Outline of the Scandal

As mentioned, Recruit took two difference avenues to buy the favours of a large number of politicians, bureaucrats and executives. The first was the sale of unlisted shares of Recruit Cosmos, a real-estate subsidiary of Recruit Co., with a full financing service provided by First Finance, a finance subsidiary of Recruit Co. This type of transaction was provided for politicians such as Nakasone, Takeshita and Miyazawa and for bureaucrats such as Takaishi, then administrative vice-minister of MOE. The politicians and bureaucrats who purchased Recruit Cosmos's pre-flotation shares did not have to pay any cash for the transactions because First Finance provided interest-free loans. They subsequently earned large capital gains after the company was listed. The second type of contributions were political donations in various forms, including the purchase of politicians' fund-raising party tickets.

For the direct business interests of Recruit Co. two groups of bureaucrats and politicians were bribed. The first group consisted of NTT executives: chairman Shinto and executive directors Hasegawa and Shikiba in connection with Recruit's new venture of data communication services by leasing NTT facilities. The second were Labour Ministry and Education Ministry officials in relation to Recruit's job information services to university and high school students.

Compared with other political scandals such as Lockheed, the Recruit scandal has three outstanding features: the wide-ranging distribution of the

Table 4.1 Beneficiaries and benefits provided by Recruit Co.

Name	Faction	Pre-flotation shares (no.)	Party tickets (million yen)	Donations (million yen)
Yasuhiro Nakasone (ex-prime minster)	Nakasone	29,000 (through his aides)		110
Michio Watanabe (ex-chairman of Policy Research Council)	Nakasone	5,000 (through his son)		
Takao Fujinami (ex-chief cabinet secretary)	Nakasone	12,000 (through his aide)		
Toshio Yamaguchi (ex-labour minister)	Nakasone			1
Kiichi Miyazawa (ex-finance minister)	Miyazawa	10,000 (in his own name)		
Koichi Kato (ex-defence minister)	Miyazawa	5,000 (in his own name)		
Yuko Kurihara (ex-labour minister)	Miyazawa		1.2	1.5
Shintaro Abe (ex-secretary general of LDP)	Abe	17,000		100 plus 23.7 (consultancy fees to his wife)
Mutsuki Kato (ex-agriculture minister)	Abe	12,000 (through his aides and family)		
Yoshiro Mori (ex-education minister)	Abe	30,000 (in his own name)		
Takashi Hasegawa (ex-justice minister)	Abe			6.24
Noboru Takeshita (ex-prime minister)	Takeshita	12,000 (through his aide and family)		151 + 50
Ken Harada (ex-minister for EPA)	Takeshita		1	1

Table 4.1 (cont'd) Beneficiaries and benefits provided by Recruit Co.

Name	Faction	Pre-flotation shares (no.)	Party tickets (million yen)	Donations (million yen)
Keizo Obuchi (ex-chief cabinet secretary)	Takeshita			2
Ichiro Ozawa (deputy chief cabinet secretary)	Takeshita			2
Saburo Tsukamoto (ex-chairman of Democratic Socialist Party)	DSP	5,000 (through aide)		
Kazuo Aichi (LDP Dietman)	Takeshita			7.6
Fumiaki Ibuki (LDP Dietman)	——	30,000 (in his own name)		
Tokujiro Hamada (LDP Dietman)	Miyazawa	30,000 (in his own name)		
Hideo Watanabe (ex-deputy chief cabinet secretary)	Nakasone	10,000 (in his own name)		
Takumi Ueda (ex-Dietman)	JSP	5,000 (through aide)		
Kenshu Tanaka (ex-Dietman)	DSP	5,000 (in his own name)		
Katsuya Ikeda (ex-Dietman)	Komeito	5,000 (through brother)		
Kakuei Tanaka (ex-prime minister)	Tanaka/ Nikaido	20,000 (through aide)		
Kunio Takaishi (ex-admin. vice-minister, MOE)		10,000		
Takashi Kato (ex-admin. vice-minister, MOL)		3,000		
Hidenori Komatsu (ex-deputy mayor of Kawasaki City)		30,000		

unlisted shares and cash; the 'outsider' standing of the principal culprits (Nakasone was a sidestream leader of the LDP and Ezoe was clearly not in the mainstream of *Zaikai*, the big-business elite; and the closeness of relations between Nakasone's reformist political projects and Ezoe's innovative business activities.

The political donations of the Recruit group focused on the labour experts (*rodo zoku*) and education experts (*bunkyo zoku*) among LDP Diet members. Since Recruit had become a comprehensive employment information giant and had been rapidly diversifying business operations to include data communications and real estate, the number of related bureaucrats and politicians turned out to be large.

Kunio Takaishi, as an administrative vice-minister at MOE, systematically prepared his post-retirement career. He befriended Nakasone and energetically pushed for the latter's 'educational reforms', including 'moral education' and the reintroduction of nationalist symbols into Japanese schools. For his (ultimately unsuccessful) campaign to gain a Lower House seat in Fukuoka as a prospective member of the Nakasone faction, his financial needs had been high. Not only did he request his MOE underlings to buy his fund-raising party tickets, he also asked construction companies and private universities for generous contributions. Among them, the Teikyo University figured prominently. Its rapid expansion in the late 1980s had benefited from 2.4 billion yen of public subsidies and unusually quick licensing decisions by MOE. Recruit's relatively minor contribution of 10,000 shares finally ended Takaishi's political career with his arrest for taking bribes. It was he who had appointed Ezoe to various MOE advisory councils in return.

Together with Takaishi, his former opposite number at MOL, Takashi Kato, was arrested. For an even smaller amount of bargain-priced shares (3000), Kato had used his power to water down draft regulations for job-matching in magazines, which had threatened to restrict Recruit's primary business activities.

Hisashi Shinto, previously president of the Ishikawajima Harima Heavy Industries shipbuilding company, was charged with the privatisation of NTT. In introducing more competitive sourcing policies at NTT, he broke the 'Denden family' cartel of telegraph and telephone-orientated companies (NEC, Fujitsu, Oki and Hitachi), which had supplied political funds to the LDP's Tanaka (later Takeshita) faction. In return for being able to introduce competitive bidding, Shinto established a 'voluntary' NTT fund for political donations to which NTT managers as well as new clients were asked to contribute. Mr Ezoe's Recruit Co. was prominent among the new business friends and contributors to the fund which operated at President Shinto's discretion for mutual benefit. Shinto probably perceived that acceptance of the Recruit contribution was for the good of NTT and not for his personal gain.

Beyond his immediate business concerns, Ezoe seemed have been preparing for the post-Nakasone political scene. The relatively larger contributions indicated the direction of his unrealised future political ambitions. With most of his largesse going for the benefit of the Nakasone and Abe factions, the unlisted share transactions that were set up for other leading LDP figures such as Miyazawa and Takeshita can be seen as an attempted investment to secure his political future, as he set out to prepare an Upper House career in the Iwate constituency, in which Recruit Co. began systemically to develop business projects (golf courses, ski resorts, and so on.)

For his eventual admission to the faction he made considerable cash contributions to faction chiefs Nakasone (for entry into the faction) and to Takeshita and Abe (for not raising objections). The size of these contributions were only known in the latter stage of the scandal's public unfolding. Their individual amounts certainly dwarfed the share scheme's more widely spread and smaller benefits. While these 'straight' political donations were probably business as usual in influence-peddling Japanese politics, PM Nakasone in addition was suspected (but as usual was never indicted nor sentenced) to have pressured NTT into buying two Cray Research supercomputers from the US and reselling them cheaply to Recruit. As a previous 'non-mainstreamer' Nakasone was frequently rumoured to be involved in dubious transactions. This was indicative of the fact that the financial resources of Nakasone and his faction were not stable, compared to, for instance, the mainstream Miyazawa faction. It was believed that Nakasone had long planned to set up his own economic power base by privatising NTT and Japan National Railways and by reforming the politico-economical framework, which had been established by the mainstreamers.

At the same time, the leaders of the new service industries, such as Ezoe's Recruit, similarly suffered from a much lower status in *zaikai* than the leaders of the traditional industrial sectors. Their political influence had been limited to reflect their financial contributions to the LDP. Hence it is not surprising that Nakasone and Ezoe found common interests. Ezoe's financial contributions to politicians did not follow the conventional routes of the mainstreamers of *zaikai*. He bypassed the control of *Keidanren* to ensure his direct access to leading politicians. As essentially a self-made man, the multibillionaire Hiromasa Ezoe, who in 1987 was estimated to be Japan's twenty-ninth biggest taxpayer with a taxable income of 1.3 billion yen, felt personally humiliated by the lack of establishment contacts and recognition. He went out to buy himself the social status he yearned for by paying for nominations to government committees and to prepare a career in national politics.

Ezoe was appointed a member of four important government advisory committees related to Nakasone's NTT privatisation and education reform policies. By playing a key role in these committees, Ezoe strengthened his access especially to Nakasone and his followers, such as Fujinami, the chief cabinet secretary in the Nakasone cabinet. Ezoe had become a member in the key *zaikai* organisations, *Keidanren*, *Nikkeiren* and *Keizai Doyukai*, in 1984. Yet he remained far from positions of influence and prestige. In setting up a club of entrepreneurial 50-year-olds, among whom figured prominently his friends and beneficiaries Jiro Ushio (chairman of Ushio Electric Machines) and Ken Moroi (chairman of Chichibu Cement), who were set to replace the septuagenerians at the head of *Keizai Doyukai* and *Nikkeiren* respectively, Ezoe attempted a generational and business change in these venerable *zaikai* institutions. He and his friends were considered the parvenues of an easy money/rapid growth real-estate/*zaitech* boom which, however, proved to be no match for Japan's gilded *keiretsu* (steel cum banking/general trading) elite.

Consequences

One year after the Recruit disclosures, PM Takeshita had resigned, his predecessor Nakasone had been forced to leave the party and his own faction (the leadership of which was assumed by Michio Watanabe in a less than friendly takeover), the prime ministerial ambitions of Shintaro Abe and Kiichi Miyazawa appeared to have been truncated, the careers of half a dozen 'neo-new' leaders of middle-aged LDP hopefuls were temporarily placed on hold, chairman Sabura Tsukamoto of the DSP had resigned, two administrative vice-ministers were criminally charged and a dozen prominent business and media chiefs disgraced (and partly unemployed). The LDP finally lost the July 1989 Upper House elections. Yet six months later, with all affected LDP MPs considering themselves sufficiently purified by their re-elections during the Lower House campaign of February 1990, their rehabilitation began in earnest, and was completed with the inauguration of the Miyazawa cabinet in November 1991.

UNDERWORLD LINKS

Japan's organised crime syndicates constitute tightly organised armies with a total of some 100,000 men under arms, which – for a price – are also available for (usually) right-wing-orientated political actions. In postwar Japan their political links were fairly ominous (although politics – then and now – never was the *yakuza's* primary motive or *raison d'être*).

The gangs started with black-marketeering, in ethnic or subcultural gangs, and later linked up with right-wing extremists and dubious *kuromaku* (unseen wirepullers such as Yoshio Kodama, Kenji Osano and Ryoichi Sasagawa), as well as with LDP power-brokers (most notably the former sidestream faction chiefs Ichiro Kono, Bamboku Ono and PM Nobusuke Kishi), most of whom are dead now.

David E. Kaplan and Alec Dubro have written a book[4] which describes the LDP/mob connections unearthed by the Lockheed scandal investigations. It also provides fairly impressive descriptions of the internal structure of the *yakuza* organisations, with their feudalist *oyabun–kobun*(boss–follower) ties. The authors describe the current transition of this venerable Japanese social institution (where uniform black-stripped dress codes, tattoos and cut little fingers still abound) from its traditional activities of extortion, prostitution, blackmail, strike-breaking and casual-labour exploitation (at docks and construction sites) to encompass more modern service-orientated lines of racketeering: loan-sharking, the control of entertainment facilities (from snack bars to coffee shops), real-estate operations, the control of trucking companies, drug smuggling and political activities – usually fund-raising, campaigning and occasional dirty business on behalf of selected LDP luminairies. One recent example is the case of a secretary of Hiroshi Mitsuzuka using *yakuza* to intimidate a publisher not to publish material embarrassing to certain constituency interests.[5]

Kaplan and Dubro convincingly demonstrate that the links between gangsters and right-wing politicians are based on preferences for rigid social structures (appealing to both), a shared mystical world view that worships power, and a joint resentment of foreigners and foreign ideas (socialism or liberalism in particular).

The gangs primary motivation, however, is clearly based on straight profit: the defence of their rackets and the opening of new business ventures, facilitated by political protection. While the *kuromaku* of old may be a dying breed, the prominence of LDP Dietman Koichi Hamada (Takeshita faction, also of Inagawa-kai) and others, as well as the omnipresence of black loud-speaker trucks manned by right-wing thugs in all major Japanese cities, suggest continued links between gangland and politics.

Koichi Hamada in the 1950s served one year in prison on charges of embezzlement, infliction of bodily injury, assault and battery. Promoted by Kanewaru to become chairman of the Diet's budget committee, he had to resign in 1988 after insulting opposition Members of Parliament. Still Hamada continues to operate as an intermediary between the LDP's leadership and major gangs and rightist groups. Knowing too much about other parties' skeletons in the closet, the Socialists also appear careful not to rub Hamada the wrong way.[6] Yet it is probably fair to say, as Professor Yukio Hori has done, that with the decline of the militantly fought public controversies since the 1960s, the LDP's need for right-wing thuggery has declined, as has their past reliance on money raised by the *kuromaku*,[7] with more or less clean *zaikai* cash being readily available.

Reflecting this changed outlook, the LDP in 1988 actually managed to introduce legal measures against the use of loud-speaker trucks (a favourite instrument of right-wing extortionists); in 1991 it introduced measures against money laundering and produced fairly toothless regulations against professional crime syndicates.

POLITICAL REFORM

In the aftermath of the Recruit scandal, which dented some of their careers (most prominently Mr Abe's, who died in May 1991 before he could realise his prime ministerial ambitions) and led to the loss of their Upper House majority in 1989, it dawned on the LDP's higher echelons that a less costly, and less scandal-prone electoral system would be of benefit. Such a political reform would also attain other objectives:

- assure the likeliness of continued LDP victories;
- guarantee the re-election of most incumbent LDP MPs;
- reduce intra-LDP frictions (that is, the power of the factions) so as to facilitate more determined political decision-making;
- rebalance the urban and rural votes;
- eliminate the communists, the socialists' left wing and the mini-parties from Japan's political scene;
- exercise a moderating influence on Japan's remaining opposition party (ideally through a merger of the centrist parties with the JSP's right wing); and
- assure the opposition's collaboration in the passage of the reform.

Obviously, these objectives were difficult to square. The impossible mission was assigned to the LDP's most prominent 'idealists', Masayoshi Ito and Tsutomu Hata, as well as to Masahara Gotoda, who subsequently headed policy reform committees in the LDP's Policy Research Council (PRC). PM Kaifu, secure in the knowledge that these deliberations and their acceptance would take time, in the spring of 1990 defined 'political reform' as the new priority objective which he wanted to see through during his prime ministership.

After a year of intensive deliberations, Hata came up with an ingenious compromise. Each voter would have two votes: a vote for his constituency MP and a vote for a party list (either nationwide, regional or based on old constituencies – the options were left open). Three hundred MPs would be elected in single-seat constituencies, and 171 MPs on the lists based on proportional representation.

Againsts all the odds and against considerable intra-party resistance – particularly by those MPs fearing to lose their seats (typically being less-prominent, junior-ranking MPs with no clearly localised electoral base) – this proposal was steamrollered through the LDP's executive council and was thus formally endorsed by the LDP in June 1991, until it was disawoved by the party's leadership two months later in what appeared to be a plot to get rid of PM Kaifu.

Also, acceptance by the opposition was – and remains – less than assured. It appears that the socialists and the centrist opposition parties – understandably – prefer the German system of combining proportional representation with single constituencies (which, if it were in force, would have forced the LDP to run coalition governments decades ago).

Mr Kunio Hatoyama,[8] grandson of a prime minister, son of a foreign minister (and current Upper House MP), himself a fifth-term MP and currently the minister of education (Takeshita faction), volunteered the following views about political reform in 1991: a two-party system of alternating centrist parties along US lines should develop in Japan. It was unfortunate for Japan that the LDP had been in power without interruption for more than four decades. Political reform was a major historical chal-lenge, equivalent to the reforms of the Meiji period. Successful political reform would allow improved foreign policy decisions, which would permit Japan's foreign policy role to become commensurate with its economic strength. At the moment, Japan's foreign policy instruments were essen-tially limited to ODA allocations complementary to one-sided US policies.

As the government's failures during the Gulf crisis proved, it was es-sential that political decision-making in Japan be streamlined in order to allow a more active and constructive international role. Hatoyama said that if everything went well, in ten years' time the right wing of the JSP would have merged, with the small centrist opposition parties, such as the DSP, Komeito, Shaminren and the Rengo MPs forming a constructive alternative to the government. Within the LDP even his faction (led by Mr Takeshita) could leave the party, thus reconstituting the pattern of two opposing conservative parties (which prevailed in Japan until the merger of the

Liberal and of the Democratic Party in 1955). This corresponds to an idea already put forward by LDP strongmen Ozawa and Kanemaru at regular intervals since 1989.

Part II
The Bureaucratic Elite

5 The Civil Service System

Japan's civil service combines in a unique yet pragmatic fashion the inherited traditions of a formerly Confucian mandarinate, which stressed the virtues of paternalism, hierarchy, seniority, consensus, personal loyalty, dedication to detail and precedents and enjoyed the high social prestige accorded to public officialdom by society at large. This tradition was blended with Franco-Prussian elements of centralism, legalism, professional training, public interventionism and administrative sophistication which were introduced in the late nineteenth century. This fairly authoritarian amalgam was supplanted after 1945 by elements of American inspired participatory democracy and civil rights, and laws providing checks and balances. The system now operates in contemporary Japan's workaholic and hedonist metropolitan way of life.

Although the liberalisation of Japan's economy since the 1960s and the enhanced political strength and management skills of senior LDP politicians – in power for more than 40 years – have eroded the ministries' past regulatory and budgetary power, still their elite track ('class I officials') career bracket continues to attract many of the best and brightest of Japan's university graduates. As officials they appear as impressive as those of the French and British 'fast-track' administrative grades, the only two other truly professional civil services remaining in major industrialised countries.

Recruitment and promotion of class I officials in the central ministries, which follow a largely identical pattern, are the source for the infusion of 'fresh talent' into the power elite. At any given time, some 500 men and a handful of women occupy the position of *kacho* (division chief) and above in the central ministries. They can claim with justification to be part of the top 2000 of Japan's power elite.

STRUCTURE

Japan employs a total of 4.5 million civil servants. 1.2 million work for the central government (360,000 for the 12 ministries and the eight major agencies; the rest are employed by the national schools, universities and hospitals (180,000), the postal service (310,000), the national forest, government printing and minting offices (40,000), the military (270,000), the Diet, Courts, Audit (30,000) and the hundred-odd public corporations

(190,000). Local governments are managed by 1.5 million officials, and prefectural governments have hired 1.7 million. In total 3.7 per cent of Japan's population has civil servant status, which is a fairly low rate among comparable developed countries (the privatisation of JR and NTT in the 1980s has helped to take 780,000 people off the public payroll).

In 1969 the Diet passed a 'Total Staff Number Law', fixing the maximal limit of non-industrial government personnel (that is, ministry, agency, education and hospital staff) at 506,000. In response, the National Personnel Authority continuously screens ministries and agencies for redundant positions to be scrapped and pooled and later reallocated to areas of increased administrative demand (for example, diplomatic staff, hospital and airport personnel, and so on). As a result of the law, the total figures for government employees declined somewhat (−1 per cent by 1987), while the GNP since the enactment of the law almost doubled in real terms.

There are, however, ways to beat the law: a lot of manual maintenance work has been subcontracted. Local/regional civil servants (to whom the law does not apply) increased by 36 per cent (or 840,000) during 1968–83.

HIERARCHIES

Japan's public administration (like any other social organisation in Japan) is thoroughly hierarchised (see Table 5.1). Rank depends on current grade, seniority in this grade, strategic importance or size of the administrative unit in charge, the type of entrance examination passed, seniority in the institution, academic background, special skills, gender and age.

The basic administrative unit is the division (*ka*), of around ten to twenty officials (including one or two part-time female clerks) sharing one office with their division chief (*kacho*).

There is also a range of counsellor positions (at *kacho* level) and of 'senior counsellor' positions available with often no particular job description or corresponding support staff. They appear to be tranquil, high-level positions while waiting for other assignments to come along.

Next to the *kacho*, his two or more deputies (*kachohosa*) are seated, overlooking the sections (*kakari*) consisting of four to six desk officers (one of them acting as a section chief (*kakaricho*), which they are supervising. In some ministries the section chiefs (called *hancho* instead of *kakaricho*) serve concurrently as junior deputy division chiefs.

Three to eight divisions – in the case of ministries – form one directorate general (*kyoku*) headed by a director general (*kyokucho*), and his deputy

Table 5.1   Ministerial hierarchy

(a)   Political appointees

    (1)   Minister

    (2)   Parliamentary vice-ministers

(b)   Administrative career officers

    (1)   Administrative vice-minister (*jimujikan*)

    (2)   vice-minister for International Affairs

    (3)   Deputy vice-minister

    (4)   Director general (*kyokucho*)

    (5)   Deputy director general

    (6)   Director general (head of department) (*bucho*)

    (7)   Director (head of division) (*kacho*)

    (8)   Deputy division chief (*somu kachohosa*)

    (9)   Section chief (*hancho/kakaricho*)

    (10)   Senior desk officer (*han in*)

(*jicho*), or – in case of prefectural administrations – a department (*bu*) with a department director (*bucho*) as chief. *Kyokucho*, *bucho* and their deputies have separate offices and, with the exception of an assistant ('secretary'), no staff of their own. The same applies to the administrative top layer: the administrative vice-ministers (*jikan*), deputy vice-ministers, and the prefectural vice-governors (*fukuchiji*). Whenever they request information or wish to give instructions, these will be directed to the director (*kacho*) in charge, who will delegate this task without fail to the competent section chief of his division, while passing on the senior hierarchy's views on how the issue should be dealt with (to the extent that this is known).

All officials have a very strong sense of hierarchy and of their own position within it. Even staff members of the same formal rank will be acutely aware of who is the more senior (in terms of seniority in the ministry's service) among them. Yet up to the *kakaricho* and the more junior *kachohosa* inclusive, the status differences (in terms of work content, salaries, ways of life) are not very pronounced. The *kacho* and possibly his most senior deputy (*somu kachohosa*) are more aloof and, although sharing the same office, have a distinct professional role and are no longer directly but rather in a supervisory function involved in the team work of the division and its sections. The subordinates' feelings towards their *kacho* may vary from sympathy and admiration to antipathy and fear. *Bucho*, *kyokucho* and higher-ups with separate offices are out of sight of the ordinary desk officers and middle management. These senior grades are often feared and treated with great deference and respect.

RECRUITMENT

Recruitment to a civil service career is, almost without exception, through competitive examination at entry level. The examinations are essentially held for three professional career brackets: class I for future middle and top management functions (university graduates or graduate school); class II to fill clerical and administrative positions, essentially for university and a few college graduates; and class III for manual and maintenance tasks (high school graduates mostly). These exams are held annually, containing written, oral, aptitude and physical tests, and – particularly for class I – are extremely competitive: only one in 19 applicants will succeed (see Table 5.2).

The written exams for class I candidates consist of a gruelling mixture of multiple-choice questions on a broad range of factual questions requiring an almost encyclopaedic knowledge and a series of essays to be written on more general topics and to be completed within tight time limits. While participation in the exams is in principle open to any Japanese citizen aged between 21 and 33, *de facto*, however, the (unspecified) educational requirements are very exacting – and limiting – for those who wish to pass and to be actually hired as well.

Among class I applicants, 3400 were women (a new record in 1987) of whom 116 (3.4 per cent) were successful. In 1988 the number of successful women increased to 150. Apart from gender, the class I exams have a clear bias favouring national university and science/engineering graduates.

While 60 per cent of applicants are from national universities (10 per cent from other public universities, and 30 per cent from private universities), 85 per cent of the successful candidates hail from these traditional suppliers of elite bureaucrats (2 per cent from other public and 13 per cent from private universities). Todai, in fact, was established in 1886 with the explicit purpose of training government personnel in order gradually to replace the Choshu and Satsuma clansmen in senior administrative posi-

Table 5.2   Central government recruitment, 1987

Category	No. of applicants	Successful in examinations	Received and accepted employment offer
Class I	32,000	1,700 (1:19)	840
Class II	46,000	5,000 (1:9)	2,000
Class III	130,000	18,000 (1:7)	13,000

tions in Tokyo. Other imperial universities were founded in the regions to provide qualified officers to man the prefectures. Until this day, for instance, Hokudai graduates will dominate the administration of Hokkaido prefecture, and Tohokudai graduates the prefectural administrations in Tohoku, in much the same way as Todai Law dominates the core ministries in Tokyo.

In 1988 among the 1814 successful class I applicants 32 pre cent were form Todai, 11 per cent from Kyodai, 5 per cent from Tohoku University, 5 per cent from Waseda, and 4 per cent from the Tokyo Institute of Technology. After interviews with the ministries and agencies, eventually some 1030 of the total were expected to be hired.

Depending also on the subjects studied, the odds on succeeding vary considerably. Among 3900 students of public administration only 50 (1.3 per cent) were successful, but among 500 information engineering graduates, 95 (19 per cent) succeeded. Other physical science and engineering majors were similarly privileged. Most of them had graduate school experience (59 per cent), while the law, economics and liberal arts candidates usually apply in their fourth year of undergraduate studies.

The stricter selection of law/economics/administration candidates is compensated for by their preferred recruitment to the more prestigious classical ministries: MOF, MITI, MHA, MOE, EPA, the Cabinet Office, and so on, which prefer generalists in their elite grades. MAFF's class I officials are essentially (78 per cent) agricultural science graduates. The Science & Technology Agency, the Agency for Industrial Technology and the Patent Office predictably recruit mostly science specialists, while public works, engineering and architecture graduates are the majority among MOT and MOC freshmen. Sociology, education and psychology majors are hired almost exclusively by the Ministry of Justice.[1]

Special exams are held for specialist positions in the customs service, for airport management and air traffic controllers, immigration officers and prison guards. There are also special exams for class I officials in the Imperial Household Agency and in the Foreign Ministry (where among some 1000 class I applicants only 40 or less – again mostly Todai Law graduates – survive each year).

Since their introduction in 1948, 9.5 million Japanese have experienced the pleasure of undergoing civil service examinations. Yet since their peak in 1978 (388,000) the number of applicants for all examinations is in continuous decline (down to 243,000 in 1987), reflecting improved salary and working conditions in the private sector. Not surprisingly, the reduction is particularly pronounced among class I applicants (–57 per cent over the last decade) from science and engineering graduates.

Successful candidates are entered on eligibility lists and appear before selection boards of ministries of their liking. An attractive ministry, such as MITI, renowned for its relatively open atmosphere and wide field of competence, will attract around 500 candidates for the 45-odd elite-track openings (25 of them for law/economics generalists, and 20 for scientists and engineers for the technology-related agencies. MOF will attract fewer candidates: it is known to consider only the 50 best placed exam candidates for the recruitment of its annual intake of 25 class I officials. Among them Todai graduates (85 per cent in 1985) predominate.[2] The rest are largely from Kyodai and Hitotsubashi. Less-attractive ministries and agencies take the rejects from these ministries.

Quite a number of those who passed the exams, however, will fail to receive any governmental employment offers at all, while an even larger number – particularly scientists and engineers – will opt for more lucrative and more promising private-sector career offers.

In selecting the members of their annual class I entry group, ministries will go to great lengths to recruit and to chose bright, able candidates with the 'right' character profile desired by the institution. Employment is for professional life; members of the entry class in question will contribute to the atmosphere and working style of the ministry over the next 25 years. Ultimately the class will produce a crop of bureau chiefs and most likely an administrative vice-minister as well. Mistakes and misjudgements could be very costly and unforgivable in the light of the ministry's standing among its peers and in view of the general public's respect, as there will be no lateral entrants nor political appointees of any sort to correct possible shortfalls in leadership talent.

CAREER PATTERNS

After graduation, preferably from Todai's Faculty of Law (which is not a law school, but after a two-year generalist course a thorough compulsory training in public law is given, as well as options offered on a broad range of law/economics/social science subjects) class I officials enter their ministry at the age of 23. They start low down the pecking order, and spend their freshman year using word processors, copying machines and carrying their bosses' briefcases. After their first assignment of two or three years as a junior desk officer, they are often rewarded with a one-year stint at a research or graduate institution in Japan or at an overseas university, preferably in the US (Ivy League names figure prominently), or in the UK (Oxbridge) and a few other continental European, Australian and Canadian institutions. There, few duties are expected of them, except for learning the language and culture of the host country. Upon return in their late twenties, promotion to a (junior) *kachohosa* rank awaits them.

They usually get married now. Options range from courting the office lady (part-time, tea-serving, two-year college graduate, usually attractive), to *omiai* matches arranged by a paternalist *kacho* or by other well-placed family friends, at times even the eligible daughters of leading businessmen or politicians, or – as a last resort – to consulting the *omiai* list of available potential brides in the personnel department. In any case, the prospective bride is fully aware of the fact that her future husband will hardly see her (and the subsequent one or two children) except very late at night or very early in the morning on weekdays during the next 20 years. The *kachohosa* are in fact the workhorses of the ministries: they do the essential research, direct the operational work details, do most of the footwork for negotiations, do legislative and other drafting, and deal with the personnel management of the divisions.

Every one to two years, the class I *kachohosa* rotate (*sotomawari*) their jobs (class II or prefectural officials stay in their posts much longer). This happens four to six times (the last assignments will be more of a genuine deputy division chief), usually to completely unrelated fields within the ministry: operational divisions, research divisions, administrative divisions, budgeting, PR; also possibly stints with prefectural governments, exchange with other ministries, or a three year term at a Japanese embassy abroad as a first secretary. Decisions for promotions and assignments are taken by each ministry's personnel department – according to criteria which sometimes mystify even those concerned. While individual preferences on locality and content for future assignments are told to the personnel department through annual questionnaires, these wishes are not always taken into consideration. The system also implies that a *kacho* has no influence whatsoever on who will become his deputies or on other assignments to his division. His entire staff – including himself – may be confirmed or reassigned at the whim of the personnel department. On average, each year one-third of staff change assignments (normally in July), so his team is in constant transition. Individual class I job assignments may last between nine months and three years. While complaints about the murkiness of personnel management are frequent among ministry staff (a phenomenon not exclusive to Japanese administration), criteria for promotion, however, still appear sufficiently motivating to encourage extremely dedicated work in the central ministries, perhaps with the possible exception auxiliary staff, class II officials and sidelined *kacho* in their late forties who realise that a further promotion is not be in store for them.

Depending on performance (and other criteria for promotion), the class
I official will be promoted *kacho* between the ages of 37 to 46 (14 to 20
years after joining the ministry). Those who are promoted earlier may again
serve as *kacho* in up to eight different divisions (changing every one to two
years), or as a counsellor at a Japanese mission abroad.

Reflecting the ministries' preference for generalists with broad experience in several divisions, assignments to head general affairs/co-ordination/
personnel affairs divisions in the Minister's secretariat are indicative of
higher laurels to come. At the age of 48 (or 25 years after joining the
ministry) promotion to *bucho* (director general) or *jicho* (deputy director
general) are made. Less-fortunate class-mates (who joined the ministry in
the same year) either get their tap on the shoulder to retire voluntarily at
around the age of 50, or are shifted to head some regional office or management position in an agency or public corporation related to the ministry.
There are five to ten bureaux per ministry (except for the MHA which has
only four departments). The top level officials remaining in the ministry
after their promotions to executive ranks are shifted on an annual basis.
They may serve twice as deputy director general, possibly twice as director
general and then either be retired or promoted deputy vice-minister, and
subsequently administrative vice-minister, a function in which they serve
for one year (in rare cases, two years) only, to be retired – the last survivors
of their 'class' – inevitably at the ripe old age of 55–6.

After 20 years of long hours spent working reliably and hard in what
is not the world's most pleasant office environment, but remaining co-
operative, communicative and resourceful, mastering the details of ever-
new assignments, identifying with the ministry, but also learning the cynical
political ropes of the job, elite bureaucrats emerge in the ministry's top
assignments, demonstrating the survival of the fittest. The techniques of
deferred gratification which they have practised during their high school
and university days will finally be brought to fruition in the final months
of their ministry careers.

There are, of course, class I officials who take things easy, who are jolly
good fellows, ready to wine and dine. They leave the office on any justifiable occasion, and are happy to be assigned to senior positions in quiet
provincial capitals. While their quality of life may be higher, they usually
never make it beyond *kacho* or into the national power elite.

Class II officials normally continue to work until 60, the mandatory
retirement age (introduced by law only in 1981, when it was realised that
the informal 'shoulder tapping' needed some legal back-up). Class II officials serve much longer in their divisions (their last rank is usually in the
ka*chohosa* category) – ten years is not exceptional – and are essential to

maintaining the continuity of administrative operations amidst the hectic pace of change affecting their superiors. A class II official only in rare cases and with an exceptional performance record may be promoted to *kacho* (director) level at the end of his career. The division which he heads is likely to be of lesser importance in his ministry's priorities.

Job performance of officials is regularly reviewed (in a division, usually the task of the most senior *kachohosa*). It covers not only actual professional performance, but also the evaluations of character, ability and aptitude. Next to objective criteria covering the quality and efficiency of work performed, and cognitive factors, such as general intelligence and levels of knowledge (including foreign languages), personality variables such as co-operative behaviour, willingness to do hard and dedicated work (as evident in long hours overtime), physical and mental health and a stable family life play an important role. The very fact that co-operative behaviour and teamwork are valued highly in staff evaluations and that the overt display of ambition is frowned upon and actively discouraged (with less than desirable new assignments, for instance), puts an effective lid on aggressively competitive behaviour. In fact, only among the peer group of each entry class is non-hierarchial camaraderie practised (since everybody else in the ministry is either senior or junior in seniority and rank). The seniority rule also ensures that no class I official ever needs to fear being overtaken by his junior staff. Hence he can always remain supportive and share information.

Promotions are formally decided by the administrative vice-minister and the director-general of the minister's secretariat (or the director of the general affairs department, in the case of prefectures) at the recommendation of the personnel department, which is the recipient of the regular staff reports. For junior- and middle-management promotions the most important decisions are made conjointly by the *kacho* of the personnel division and the senior directors of the other horizontal divisions.

The system ensures that staff are under continuous scrutiny. With various assignments and frequent changes, the possibilities for individual superiors' patronage and favouritism are minimised. Those officials who eventually reach senior ranks have been carefully selected and screened – after all, they spend the better part of some 25 professional years at junior and middle levels in large office environments with their colleagues (and sometimes also spend a good deal of off-duty time in their company) – and are carefully groomed through selected appointments as generalists for leadership positions. Anybody lazy, incompetent or unbalanced will surely be spotted in time, remain assigned to 'safe' positions and be 'out-placed' at the earliest possible opportunity.

Leadership ability will be tried and tested: through learning on the job by observation and imitation, with gradually enlarged responsibilities during early low-risk assignments in running branch offices or heading units in attached organisations, young fast-track officials experience gradually increasing responsibilities. They are carefully monitored with respect to their skills and attitudes in handling sensitive files and delicate or challenging situations and in motivating and caring for their subordinates. At any given time, for instance, MITI has some 25 officials on temporary management assignments in prefectural administrations; 170 MITI officials serve in senior positions in Japanese embassies abroad, in JETRO offices, with international organisations, in EPA, in MOF, in the cabinet secretariat, the Environment Agency, JICA, MITI-related agencies (SME Agency, Energy Agency, the Patent Office) and with national oil companies.

It is surprising, when observing the sometimes idiosyncratic or semi-despotic leadership behaviour of Japanese government organisations, that this should be possible after such careful long-term scrutiny of the person in question. Presumably such attitudes have been acquired after promotion and becoming used to the long-term exercise of power.

A few ministries prefer specialist careers. To some extent MOF is an example: class I officials after reaching *kachohosa* level stay in one bureau only, where they become specialists in taxation, budgeting, tariffs, banking, securities or international finance. Only in a few ministries do genuine specialists by university training have a fair chance to move above *Kacho* level. While the majority of class I officials in all ministries are such 'specialists' (*gikan*), 'generalists' (*jimukan* – that is, law/economics graduates) fill 75 per cent of all senior positions, including virtually all vice-ministerships. Only MOT and MOC as technical ministries will allocate evenly and alternately specialists and generalists to the most senior administrative levels, including the vice-ministership.

In the national government, class I officials for the first three years work as straight desk officers. In prefectural administrations their role is less privileged. Promotion to section chief (*kakaricho*) will only be in their early thirties. Work content is essentially identical with class II officials, who may also reach *kakaricho* rank in their late thirties, and possibly *kacho* positions in their late forties. In local administrations *kacho* and *bucho* ranks mean much less: in small towns a *bucho* may have only ten subordinates or fewer. Also educational requirements are less stringent. In a centralist country like Japan, the further down one moves on the central–local scale, the lesser are the powers of discretionary decision-making, as well as the qualifications and the motivation of officialdom.

REMUNERATION

Public sector unions do not have the right of collective bargaining and strikes. Instead wage levels are decided annually by the cabinet and the National Diet on the recommendation of the National Personnel Authority (NPA). The NPA's recommendations (in 1990, for instance, a pay increase of 3.7 per cent[3]) are based on equivalence with comparable private sector pay and (except for some years in the early 1980s) are usually approved unchanged.

Net of allowances and bonuses, the basic monthly salary for a university graduate is a meagre 130,000 yen in his first year of public service (at the age of 23). At 35 the official will make 250,000 yen; at 45 he earns 360,000 yen and ten years later, close to retirement, his basic pay is 460,000 yen on average.

In terms of hierarchy, a desk officer's basic pay moves in the 200,000 yen bracket. A *kakaricho/kachohosa* (section chief) earns around 300,000 yen; a *kacho* (division chief) makes 400,000 yen; a *bucho* (department director) gets 500,000 yen; and the top – *kyokucho* (director generals) or *jikan* (vice-ministers) – receive 800,000 yen as their basic monthly salaries.

In addition, there are allowances, depending on family situation (20,000 yen as the household allowance) and regional adjustments (+10 per cent in Tokyo). More importantly, summer and winter bonuses increase the annual pay by 41 per cent (or to 16.9 times the monthly salary per annum).

Including basic allowances, the average official (40 years of age, with 19 years of service and a high school or college education) will earn 277,000 yen per month (some US$2000).

There are altogether 17 different pay scales for central government employees; the lowest are for nurses, the highest for vice-ministers. On average, government researchers, university professors and medical doctors are on better scales than the administrative ministry personnel. According to Koh's own and other investigations quoted by him, 'financial reward does not appear to figure prominently in [the higher civil servants] incentive structure'.[4] Officials were aware that their salaries were 30 per cent to 50 per cent below that of their peers in the private sector; however, most were not able to quote their income figures properly. They are also many possibilities for legitimate side-incomes and quasi-monetary renumeration offered by clients (royalties for publications, honoraria for speeches, extensive gifts, all-expenses-paid travel, invitations to entertainment, and so on).

By and large, however, class I officials – who, when at work in Tokyo, have little opportunity to spend money in large amounts (even for nightlife, time is scarce) – appear more strongly motivated by non-material considerations when opting for the lower-paying civil service career (which offers compensatory higher pay prospects only in the uncertain event of a successful secondary, post-retirement business or political career). More powerful motivators are probably higher social prestige, wider-ranging job content and the great societal role and impact which Japanese ministry officials exercise compared to their private sector peers.

WORKING HOURS

Officially, the hours of work are 42 hours of regular office work per week. But except for part-time ladies in clerical work (who work 30 minutes less per day than the full-timers), almost all officials work overtime for one or two hours each day. In the ministries they sometimes work until 2.00 a.m. (after which they sleep on sofas in the office).

The introduction of a five-day working week began in 1975 in earnest and is progressing with the usual speed. Bulky official studies have been produced forecasting a societal revolution emanating from this new system.

Currently 34 per cent of officials work a system of taking alternate Saturdays off (in four weeks six days are free); 18 per cent enjoy a real five-day week already. But others have three (7 per cent) or only one (13 per cent) Saturday off in four, and 23 per cent still work all Saturdays (and many continue to go to their offices on Sundays as well).

Recently, given the increasing incidence of nervous disorders among officials and of adjustment problems among their fatherless offspring, the excessive use of overtime has been criticised by the unions and has also been officially frowned upon: in MITI, the ministry most notorious for overtime, for instance, *kachos* are reprimanded if four or more of their staff are discovered working after 10 p.m.

Officials are also encouraged to take off their eight or so days of holiday. Yet high costs of domestic and overseas travel and housing conditions (appropriate where there is an absentee husband) discourage most from taking more than the usual three days off. This is usually done in combination with national holidays, around New Year, during Golden Week (early May), or in mid-August (*Oshogatsu*).

A major stumbling block for extending the five-day week was the legal requirement to keep all public offices open on Saturdays (which has been amended in FY1989 to alternating Saturdays). In addition to their time in the office proper, in metropolitan areas another three or four hours are spent commuting every work day. In the provinces, both commuting and overtime needs are much reduced.

WORKING STYLE

Japan's office culture resembles a total institution: some 40 to 50 people share a densely packed office for most of a long ten-hour working day. Desk officers' small metal desks are grouped together with their section chief's (*kakaricho*). Supervisors' (*kacho/kachohosa*) desks are set apart. The officials sit with their backs to the windows, so that they can observe their staff at any moment. Space is so scarce that there is no privacy for staff members (except for the toilet and a small personal locker). Everything he or she does is seen or heard. After long shared office hours – interrupted only by a brief lunch-break in the canteen (jointly taken) – and often followed by communal evening drinking sessions, few secrets remain. Almost all personal details become public knowledge: personal histories, family life, educational background, housing situation, habits with regard to drinking, womanising, sports, vacations, the state of health, moods, interests, approach and attitude to work, past achievements and possible misdeeds.

Total supervision, the lack of privacy and the need to be considerate to one's desk neighbours create strong pressures for conformism. The office norms are both public and private: there are dress codes, norms about appropriate political views, drinks, cigarettes, sports to be practised, the right approach to work and, most importantly, the right way to deal with colleagues and with superiors. In spite of an education system which encourages conformity, the pressures to conform are felt to be burdensome by many officials: there is an almost boyish hilarity when a feared *kacho* leaves the office or – even better – is away on a business trip. To junior officials it is a constant worry what their hierarchy – and their *kacho* in particular – thinks about them.

On the face of it, a Japanese government office appears fairly chaotic. It is not only the paper mountains which pile up in the superiors' in-trays, the rows of files which cover the officials' desks – leaving an effective clear writing space of some 200 cm² – and the cardboard boxes into which newspapers, files, magazines, cigarette packs, empty lunch boxes and *ringi* drafts are thrown for temporary storage in corners, on shelves, and in the office's meeting room. More importantly, there is no clear and strict delineation of competences. Each division has horizontal and vertical sections. Each bureau similarly is divided into horizontal and vertical divisions. Officials in charge of planning, co-ordination, research and general affairs – who make up one-third of each division – always seem to be in charge of everything and of nothing in particular. Tasks are allocated *ad hoc*, and may be reallocated or shared out. Officials' duties are never limited explicitly to their (usually vague) job descriptions. Other duties can be added temporarily, and the working orders of superiors cannot be refused, even if they constitute a *de facto* down-grading. The advantage of the system of diffused responsibilities is that someone in the division always appears to be involved and is informed about the issue in question (which also reflects the advantage of overhearing most telephone calls and conversations with visitors).

There is a constant noise of office chatter, telephones ringing, street noise, computer printers rattling, as a continuous stream of visitors (local government officials, parliamentarians, lobbyists, retirees, life insurance sales girls, delivery boys for name cards, lunch boxes, cleaned suits and so on) floats through the office. Concentrated work or the study of files is hence only possible after official office hours – once the noise and distraction provided by visitors, colleagues and telephone calls have subsided.

Japan's administration produces few formal reports, there are no written position papers, few inter-office memos. Most letters received will never receive a reply in writing. In fact, the Japanese bureaucracy does very little note-writing. If a written record is needed, the minutes spontaneously taken at a meeting will be added to the file. Most internal communication is oral, not written. Leadership information and briefings are also done orally. For inter-ministry co-ordination, therefore numerous meetings and mutual visits/telephone calls are essential. This also applies to the ministries' client groups and industries (they all have to visit Tokyo) and to the general public at large. Anything put formally in writing is habitually submitted to the *ringisho* procedure, which is cumbersome and slow. *Ringisho* supplies daily stacks of information or approval circulars to all concerned, and is normally limited to formal and inevitable routine communications. Officials stamp their 'seen and approved' sign usually only after reading these documents cursorily and at great speed (assuming that the documents in question have already been seen as drafts and are *de facto* approved by the senior hierarchy).

Japanese office staff do not have the time and concentration to prepare well-reasoned, written reports (there are also no professional secretaries to type anything anyway) as their Western counterparts would do – where leadership information is normally given in writing and management responses are returned orally or as scribbles in the margins.

Reliance on oral communication may be time-consuming; however, in the Japanese context it does not create a shortfall in information. Rather the opposite: in large offices most conversations are overheard. Regular meetings at all levels make sure that information on relevant issues and projects is freely circulated within a bureau, and that potential intra-ministry objections will be raised, heard and accommodated. Joint lunch outings and after-office drinking assures that gossip – containing important informal information – is freely aired throughout the ministry via the numerous old and young-boys networks.

A division has only one filing system, the folders of which are placed in metal cupboards and are accessible to all members of the department. (The notion that desk officers maintain semi-personal files is unheard-of in Japan). Such files are always kept accessible in the office and are never taken home (commuting conditions in crowded public transport and the absence of time and of proper work space at home prevent much office work being done at home anyway.) Due to high staff turnover, files are usually kept very carefully. Care is also taken to procure as much outside information as possible on any subject under consideration.

Hence smooth working relationships are maintained with all organised interests and clientele industries/groups concerned by the administrative unit in question. Industry or other interest groups, in turn, will make sure that there is a continuous flow to the ministry in charge of information on the situation of the sector and its needs and that the administration has update documentation on any given subject of industry interest. Standard briefing documents sent to ministries are often attractively laid out and written in a prose suitable for intelligent laymen: just the type of information a newly appointed *kacho* would need in order to familiarise himself with a sector's basic issues, its jargon and its problems in a few hours of concentrated reading. High information input is required by the Japanese ministries' tendency towards the meticulous preparation of drafts, publications, meetings, visits and so on. Nothing is left to chance or to gifted improvisation. On any visitor a director general or minister will receive a briefing containing the visitor's CV, background information on the country or the organisation he represents, a presentation of the issues the visitor is likely to raise, and a draft statement and draft replies, which he is likely to follow to the letter. If questions are asked outside the prearranged scope, the responses are likely to become empty standard phrasing ('Difficult problem. Will study/consider the matter . . . ') or the junior officials present at the meeting will be asked openly for an appropriate reaction. Official visits are organised meticulously to the last minute, as are the daily agendas of all senior officials and ministers. Strict punctuality forms a core element of bureaucratic norms, to which even prime ministers are expected to adhere. (One way to demonstrate intentional rudeness in Japan is to be late for appointments, if one can afford this.) Also draft regulations, legislation and budget proposals are expected to demonstrate the thoroughness of their preparation by voluminous accompanying documentation. Often the purpose of such documentation, including the research data, is merely to *look* impressive, as it is safely assumed that nobody outside the originating division will have the time to study the data in sufficient detail.

On budgetary proposals form then often overtakes reality. Bureaux tend to defend their established programmes vigorously and resourcefully to ensure their continuation (which includes absurdities typical of centralist administrations, such as building roads from nowhere to nowhere, and fishing ports where there are neither fishermen nor fish, constructing new paddy fields while others are ordered fallow, modernising coal mines which are being closed, and so on). MOF's budget bureau's personnel resources, for all their renowned brilliance and power, are too stretched and the auditing mechanisms too weak to detect and prevent the continuation of most public spending follies. In-house criticism of a ministry's own programmes is almost unheard of. Memos will almost invariably support the official party line – which has already received the blessing of the hierarchy. Questioning it would possibly lead the author and his unit into conflict with very senior ministry colleagues.

The annual budget cycle and the need for political acceptance-seeking (*nemawashi*) require that all spending projects be prepared well in advance. There is no room for sudden adjustments or modifications in response to late information. As bureaucracies are usually at their best in dealing with routine situations, they are at their worst when sudden crises require fast responses, quick fixes or deals on the spot. In international multilateral conferences (such as G7), therefore, when the outcome is least foreseeable by the Japanese side, the cumbersome nature of the system renders it most inefficient and dysfunctional. The same certainly applies to genuine international crises or to domestic catastrophies (of which fortunately there have been only a few in Japan in the postwar years).

Japanese ministries have at their disposal the same means of sanctions and incentives as fellow ministries in other democracies: applying laws and regulations, issuing directives, lending budgetary and other project support. Although Japan's public sector and its spending powers are relatively smaller than in most other OECD countries, its powers for discretionary decisions are larger: laws are drafted in a deliberately vague fashion by the ministries themselves, so as to allow their implementation by ministerial regulations and ordinances which, due to their technical nature, will be largely outside political attention and control. These regulations will be discussed with advisory bodies (*shingikai*) on which independent experts and interested parties are represented. It is, however, the ministries themselves that will nominate the members of their advisory committees. Finally, administrative guidance (*gyoseishido*) is the most famed among Japan's extra-legal instruments for bureaucratic intervention. Such guidance may, for instance, take the form of a MITI director calling in representatives of the Japanese steel industry to inform them formally (after informal consultations have taken place) that voluntary steel export restraints have been entered *vis à vis* a third country. He supplies them with a list of monthly corporate shipment quotas and requests compliance. Non-compliance by any participant implies that either a more rigid legal control instrument would be applied or that an individual company refusing to co-operate would risk being put on an informal governmental blacklist, and would face potential disadvantages when asking for public subsidies, requesting licences, or applying for loans from semi-public banks, getting unwelcome tax audits, and so on in the future. Since there is no legal status for 'administrative guidance', compliance in formal terms is voluntary and no legal recourse is possible.

As in other administrations, decisions are made at the levels judged appropriate by the institution. There are political decisions on issues such as rice prices, public sector spending, beef liberalisation, the consumption tax, the opening of diplomatic relations, and so on which are taken at a political level; decisions such as the amount of ODA for the Philippines, the tariff levels for imported cheese, whether to open a consulate general in Leipzig, and to allocate landing slots at Narita, which are taken at senior official or administrative vice-minister level; there are the middle-management decisions on more technical issues – subject to subsequent confirmation at the senior level – such as whether to build new quarantine facilities, streamline labelling regulations, ban certain food additives, or introduce new safety standards for car brakes; and finally these are routine decisions that are left to junior officials, such as nominating the participants of a study mission to Japan, redesigning official forms or repainting MOF's interior walls. On important issues senior officials will often tell their subordinates how the problem should be resolved on general lines, and leave to their discretion the details of implementation with room for negotiation with the parties and other ministries/bureaux (often at *kachohosa* level). Once they come up with a reasonable and mutually acceptable solution, it will usually be agreed and supported by the senior hierarchy without much further ado. A few issues judged politically sensitive will, however, often be personally dealt with by senior officials (*kacho*, *bucho*, *kyokucho* level) working for a positive resolution.

On any given subject a *ringi sei* procedure will only be initiated once the section in charge is reasonably confident of its acceptance by the hierarchy throughout the institution. Only then is a folder prepared, containing the decision and its documented reasoning, with space on the cover for the personal seals (*hanko*) to be stamped indicating 'read and approved' by all the officials concerned, starting with the drafting desk officer and up to the minister. The *ringi sei* form is also used for administrative trifles, official letters, technical notifications, and so on. It is part of the function of a secretary to a director general or minister to sort out the routine and trivial *ringi sho* and to stamp the boss's seal without bothering him. He also has to sort out and mark the politically sensitive or potentially controversial files which will require his chief's personal attention. Approval in such cases is by no means assured. This author once witnessed a *bucho* tearing off a *ringi sho* cover (with almost all seals stamped), throwing it into the waste-basket and returning what was left, crossed through with red ink, to the hapless expeditor. Only a very timid newcomer to a senior post will be so impressed by the number of *hanko* attached (which is mostly done routinely and with little reading) as not to dare to refuse a draft with he considers faulty. In any case, the frequently heard belief that *ringi sei* represents a bottom-up decision-making procedure appears to be thoroughly mistaken.

WORKING CONDITIONS

Almost inevitably, ministerial and prefectural offices in Japan are unappealing, ferroconcrete, high-rise buildings consisting mostly of large offices into which 40 or more officials are squeezed. Metal desks are grouped together, half submerged in disorderly piles of paper. Metal filing cabinets and lockers line the walls of separate off a battery of word-processors, photocopiers and on-line computers. As mentioned previously, phones are constantly ringing, and an unending stream of visitors and *ad hoc* meetings continue to absorb the attention of *kacho* and his deputies. There is constant private and work-related chatter across the desks, loud-speaker announcements (including five minutes of daily gymnastics which no one observes), regular visits from women selling life insurances, investment advice (during bonus time), fermented milk drinks, as well as the regular trolley lady. Other daily services include the delivery of lunch boxes, laundered shirts and dry-cleaned suits or freshly printed name cards.

In spite of all the noise, distraction and cigarette smoke, miraculously some officials manage to do concentrated and meticulously detailed work (some of the attractions of overtime are that offices become quieter and visitors and phone calls are rarer); others – even more of a miracle – succeed in falling into a deep sleep, until their phone or a visitor wakes them up.

Most ministry and other large public office complexes contain their own cafeterias, supermarkets (for all the necessities of life), book and stationery shops, banks, travel agencies, post offices and barber shops in the basements, as well as sports facilities (often on the roof). This attempt at self-sufficiency is understandable, given the fact that most of the officials' day is spent within these buildings. This also contributes to a generally blurred distinction between private and public matters handled on and off duty.

All ministries and key agencies are located in Tokyo's Kasumigaseki area within walking distance of each other and Nagatacho, the centre of political Japan. Kasumigaseki is easily accessible by major subway lines. Some newly built ministry buildings (such as MITI and MHW/MOL) have their own direct subway entrances. The area's wide avenues can accommodate hordes of pedestrians and a heavy load of daily traffic at the same time. Nearby Hibiya Park offers little-used opportunities for quiet walks. Towards Yurakucho station, the major JR station in the vicinity, there is a wide range of cheaper drinking establishments for refreshment in the early evening. For larger budgets and the cultivation of political contacts, the entertainment areas of Akasaka are equally within easy reach. For contacts with the business world and their mega-expense accounts, the Ginza establishments are likewise conveniently located.

OPENNESS AND ACCESSIBILITY

Contrary what is said by its detractors, the Japanese administration in many respects is one of the most open and accessible in the world. Except for *Gaimusho* and the prime minister's office, government buildings and ministers' offices are loosely guarded by unarmed watchmen, who do not even check visitors' bags or ID cards. As long as one wears a tie and a suit, one can easily proceed to the necessary office. Location guides for all the bureaux and the divisions are posted on all of the ministries' floors. At each office's entrance a map will indicate the names and seats of its officers. The seating arrangement reveals their ranks. An office girl or junior clerk will receive the visitor's name card and, if deemed important enough, even if the visit is unannounced will usually arrange for the visitor to see the *kacho*, his deputy or at least the section chief in charge. It is, of course, always advisable to have arranged an appointment, to bring some documentation, a personal letter and a gift, in order to gain the *kocho*'s and his staff's attention. Department chiefs and higher-ups have secretaries in their antechambers so that they are shielded from unwanted visitors.

During budget time, ministries are flocked by lobbyist groups – and MAFF flooded by farmers – who march from division to division, deliver petitions and hand over name cards and small token gifts to all concerned in the decision procedure. Most ministries also have their international department, which acts as a window (*madoguchi*) for their international contacts. Their officials are most accessible to foreign diplomats and to visiting senior foreign officials. It is through this avenue that foreign business interests are most efficiently represented with GOJ.

Each ministry has its journalist (*kisha*) club, which is made up of re-porters from the general and the specialist press accredited to the ministry. They have their own working room on the premises, and are allowed to roam the building, searching for leaks, gossip and other revelations. While the journalists in question know most of the ministry's secrets, there is a code in force not to reveal them in the papers, for risk of being expelled from the *kisha* club and from the ministry. Only once a scandal has been made public by some other medium, will the *kisha* club-affiliated journalists begin to feel bold enough to write about what they knew all along. Japanese newspapers always manage to publish the ministries' annual promotion lists to senior positions as tolerated leaks, before they are notified to the individuals concerned.

Compared to other countries, ministries and their internal working are covered to a larger extent in the general press than elsewhere. Senior bureau chiefs and administrative vice-ministers, although career officials, rise to public prominence in Japan. Outspoken former administrative vice-minis-ters such as Toyoo Gyoten (MOF) or Makoto Kuroda (MITI) are household names, and were more prominent than some of their ministers.

The ministries also accept a good number of young employees from related banks and industries on secondment for a limited period to work in the less-sensitive departments. Some ministries have recently granted internships even to a handful of foreign researchers and resident diplomats.

The ministries publish handbooks which survey comprehensively the competences of all bureaux and their divisions. They also contain photo-graphs, professional CVs, including place and date of birth, schools and universities attended, home addresses and home telephone numbers of all senior ministry officials. This degree of transparency is unheard of even in the most liberal and open-minded of European administrations.

In a country of civility and domestic peace like Japan, this openness does not offer an open invitation to terrorists or pranksters. Instead, it gives useful pointers to the donors of gifts, which keep the officials' bars at home well-stocked throughout the year.

All bureaux and divisions have update briefing material ready, including basic statistics and descriptions of the policies they pursue, and formal descriptions of the problems they face and current and planned projects. These official sanitised (*tatemae*) versions of policies constitute the demarcation line where transparency ends and where the investigative story for the true (*honne*) version begins, which may involve politics and at times corruption and incompetence. Yet if one knows the sector, has learned the official versions and does some parallel investigations, it is not so difficult to gain the respect and the liking of the junior and middle-level officials involved and then learn, preferably at social occasions, step-by-step and through cross-checking, an approximation of the true background and the real version of events.

RETIREMENT

Upon voluntary or compulsory retirement officials receive a lump sum of – depending on their length of service – 34 times (in the case of 24 years) to 41 times (30 years) of their final monthly salary. For a *kacho* retiring at the age of 53 this may be a sum of 16 million yen (US$100,000), enough to pay off his last mortgage and his children's university tuition. Yet he will not receive a pension until reaching 65 when, as a typical example, he will begin to receive 174,000 yen (US$1000) per month,[5] after a reform in 1986 cut such pensions by 10 per cent and postponed their payment from age 60 to 65 years.

The retired officials' habitual response is to seek secondary careers as *amakudari* (descendants from heaven), most of which are based on past experience, expertise and connections. (Yet there is a mandatory two-year period after retiring from office when an official cannot work in a profit-making enterprise which relates to the previous posts. This is a rule from which, however, dispensation is given frequently).

Elite-track class I ministry officials usually have little difficulty – given their qualifications and experience – in embarking on a lucrative career in private industry (particularly in the growth industries seeking outside management talent or in those sectors in need of maintaining extensive ministerial contacts), as well as in related business associations, research institutes, semi-public organisations, or in professional activities (for example, as consultants, lawyers, professors or writers) or finally, in increasingly rare instances, in national politics (one-third of LDP Dietmen are former bureaucrats with at least 25 years of ministerial service).

At the other end of the scale, however, lower-grade officials in the provinces may have to open coffee shops, return to farming or become night-watchmen. For the welfare of their officials, ministries and other public institutions will therefore exercise considerable pressure on related private and semi-public enterprises to offer adequate employment to their deserving retirees. Such attempts are increasingly being resisted.

In 1988, 233 government officials at division chief level or above switched to the private sector upon retirement. Forty-four of them changed to companies which were close to their previous official roles, thus requiring an NPA-authorised exemption from the mandatory grace period. Table 5.3 shows (top 4 positions) the *amakudari* placements of former bureau chiefs and vice ministers.[6]

Table 5.3   *Examples of administrative elites' retirement positions*

Ministry	Name	Last post before retirement	New position
MITI	Makoto Kuroda	Vice-minister for international affairs	Adviser to Long-Term Credit Bank of Japan
MITI	Ryuji Anraku	Director-general of industrial location and environmental protection bureau	Adviser to Sumitomo Bank
MOT	Teiichi Kuribayashi	Director-general of the Maritime safety agency	Vice-president of Airport Facilities Co. President of Narita Airport Facilities Co.
MPT	Tetsuro Tomita	Director-general of the postal bureau	Executive director of Fuji Television Network Inc
MOF	Satoshi Sumita	Administrative vice-minister	President Ex-Im Bank (1972–9); Deputy governor BOJ (1979–84); Governor BOJ (1984–9)
MITI	Shohei Kurihara	Vice-minister for international affairs	Vice-president, Toyota Motors
MITI	Shoichi Akazawa	Director general	Executive director/ vice-president/ vice-chairman, Fujitsu (1973–83), JETRO chairman

Table 5.3 (cont'd) Examples of administrative elites' retirement positions

Ministry	Name	Last post before retirement	New position
EPA	Isamu Miyazaki	Vice-minister	Chairman, Daiwa Securities Research Institute
MOF	Takashi Hosomi	Vice-minister for international affairs	Advisor, IBJ (1974–81); chairman, Overseas Economic Co-operation Fund (1981–7); chairman, Nippon Life Insurance Research Institute
MFA	Bunroku Yoshino	Vice-minister, (ambassador to Germany)	Chairman, Institute for International Economic Studies
MFA	Yoshio Okawara	Deputy vice-minister and (ambassador to the US)	Advisor to Keidanren and Kobe Steel
MITI	Naohiro Amaya	Vice-minister for international affairs	Executive director, Dentsu Institute for Human Studies

MOF customarily occupies the largest number of total *amakudari* positions in the private sector each year that require a derogation by the NPA, followed by MITI, MOL, MAFF, MOT and MPT. Yet, with respect to the banking sector which forms a key part in the pool of companies accepting former MOF officials, there is keen competition between the ministry and the Bank of Japan that also seeks to place its retirees in key positions. In fact, BOJ provides more bank presidents than does MOF. In MOF's camp are the Bank of Yokohama, 116th Bank, 18th Bank, Hiroshima Bank and Hokkaido Bank with ex-MOF officials as either chairman or president (or both). BOJ banks are: Chiba Bank, Kanto Bank, Shiga Bank, Fukuoka Bank, Awa Bank and Sanin Godo Bank. While these regional banks are firmly in their respective *amakudari* camps, cultivating special relationships with the supervisory institutions in question, some national banks have begun to shake off these ties: the Bank of Tokyo and Kobe Bank (following the latter's merger with Mitsui Bank) are deserting MOF, while Kyowa Bank has begun to shed its BOJ *amakudari* ties.[7]

A less-arduous, if temporary, way of seeking post-retirement employment is to be hired by a ministry-affiliated public organisation whose senior posts are customarily occupied by the ministry in question. Koh quotes a study according to which 379 out of 489 executives in 83 selected public organisations in 1986 were retired higher officials. Most of them were from MITI, followed by MAFF, MOF and MOL.[8]

An individual ex-bureaucrat can repeat such employments, collecting attractive separation allowances upon resignation in the process. This system severely limits promotion prospects for the regular personnel in these organisations. In certainly impedes their recruitment and hampers staff motivation.

A more attractive, though more demanding, post-retirement career is in local and national politics. While some 80 LDP MPs in the Lower House are former ministry career officials (mostly from MOF, followed by MITI and MAFF), a much larger group will eventually be elected governors or city mayors, typically as LDP-backed 'independents'. Local politics appears to be particularly attractive to former MHA officials.

6 Government Operations

Japan in theory and in form adheres to the principle of unitary government. Cabinet meetings are held every Tuesday and Friday, and the conference of administrative vice-ministers, which prepares the cabinet meetings, takes place on Mondays and Thursdays. In reality, however, Japan's central administration has pushed departmentalisation to the extreme. Each ministry does its own planning, budgeting, policy execution and has its own personnel policy. Stories about interministerial disputes over policies and competences abound. There are very few among the core ministries that do not harbour bones of contention *vis à vis* other ministries.

The more formalistic and less-substantial cabinet and vice-ministers' meetings apart, there are only four institutions to create a semblance of unity on policy matters in Japan's government:

(1) the prime minister's secretariat in the PMO;
(2) the cabinet secretariat;
(3) the budget bureau of MOF;
(4) the PRC of the LDP (as well as ultimately the decisions of the LDP faction leaders).

THE PRIME MINISTER'S OFFICE (PMO)

The prime minister's office consists of a small secretariat, which serves to brief the prime minister on political issues and exercises some interministerial policy co-ordination. It handles the prime minister's PR, reviews draft bills and legislation and does a bit of policy-related research of its own. Staff and budgetary resources are so limited, however, that the prime minister's secretariat, true to its name, fulfils this secretarial function only. For the rest, the PMO is an umbrella for an odd collection of agencies and institutions for which by chance no other ministry is in charge: the Decoration Bureau, the National Archives, the Science Council of Japan, the Fair Trade Commission, the Imperial Household Agency. Nominally it also supervises those agencies headed by a Minister of State: the Defence Agency, the Economic Planning Agency (EPA), the Science and Technology Agency (STA), the National Land Agency, the Environment Agency, the Management and Co-ordination Agency, and so on. At the administrative level the prime minister's secretarial was headed in 1991 by a previous director general of the PMO's Decoration Bureau, who had begun his career at the Statistical Office.

The prime minister has three private secretaries, two of whom are politically appointed assistants, and one who hails from Gaimusho with *kacho* rank. He also has two administrative 'secretaries' (that is, assistants), one each from MOF and from MITI. These three ministry officials all have assured career prospects. The senior staff of the prime minister's secretariat is again composed of *kacho*-class officials mostly on secondment from central ministries and agencies (Personnel Authority, MHW, MOT, MOC, MOF, MHA, Police Agency, MFA, and so on, thus assuring close ministerial links and *ipso facto* preventing an independent role for the prime minister's secretariat.

THE CABINET SECRETARIAT

The cabinet secretariat has a total staff of 170. While it is nominally headed and directed by the prime minister himself, this task is taken care of by the chief cabinet secretary. He is usually a trusted senior political ally of the PM and a Member of Parliament of cabinet rank who acts as the government's spokesman.

The secretariat is divided into six units (offices on cabinet matters, on internal affairs, on external affairs, on security affairs, on public relations and on information research).

In the cabinet secretariat almost all senior officials are seconded from central ministries and agencies for a limited period of service. In 1991 the principal councillor of the Cabinet Affairs Office was a bucho-level officer from MHW. The three other councillors were from MOT, MOC and MHW respectively, all at *kacho* level. The internal affairs office was led by a *kyokucho*-class MOF official. He was assisted by one councillor from each of the relevant domestic ministries: MOF, MOE, MHW, MAFF, MITI, MOT, MPT, MOC, MOL and the Police Agency – all of *kacho* rank – and 12 councillors, who share this assignment only on a part-time basis, remaining principally occupied in their ministries of origin. The Office on External Affairs was managed by a director general of MFA. The other councillors hailed from MAFF, MITI, EPA, PMO, MOF and MFA. There were six part-time councillors.

The security affairs office was run by a Ministry of Home Affairs official, who had previously served as a director general at the Defence Agency. His four *kacho*-level colleagues were from the Defence Agency, MFA, MOF and the Police Agency.

The Cabinet's PR office was managed by a deputy inspector general of the Police Agency. There were no other full-time councillors in this unit. The information research office is subdivided into sections for general affairs, internal matters, external matters, economics and science. In the first three sections security-linked officials dominated. The office itself was managed by a *kyokucho*-class police officer as well. He was assisted by two councillors from the Police Agency, four from the Defence Agency, and one each from MFA, MOF, MAFF, MITI and the PMO.

The secondment system obviously prevents the development of the Cabinet Secretariat's 'own' administrative enclave. It facilitates co-operation and the flow of information with the ministries represented. Yet this system and the very limited staff numbers ensure that secretariat functions are also limited: policy initiatives are very unlikely to emanate from the cabinet secretariat.

On draft decisions of political significance, ministries will always consult with the cabinet secretariat office (in which there is usually a senior official from their own ministry on secondment), prior to their formal adoption by the ministry. Through this avenue the chief cabinet secretary and the prime minister remain formally informed about major ministerial initiatives, which the PM can veto at this stage should he wish to exercise the powers entrusted to him by the Cabinet Act. (In fact, however, he is unlikely to do so at this stage, since on any subject of political significance the party's hierarchy will already have given its blessing at a conceptual stage; see chapter 2).

The Cabinet Secretariat is also theoretically empowered to act as a final arbiter if ministries persistently disagree over policy decisions that need to be taken urgently. It also maintains a legislation bureau which examines all draft bills and cabinet orders, in order to ascertain legal continuity and constitutionality.

THE CABINET

The cabinet proper is subdivided in various *ad hoc* groups – such as external economic affairs – to which the cabinet secretariat offers administrative co-ordination and assistance. At these meetings, however, ministers will usually only read out the statements prepared by their respective administrations, and will normally leave the differences to be sorted out by their officials.

The policy disinterest and/or incompetence of many prime ministerial incumbents also contributes to making the cabinet secretariat a fairly ineffective and formal institution. It was only under a forceful prime ministers with genuine policy interests, such as Yasuhiro Nakasone who attempted 'top-down' operations, that the cabinet and the ministries followed an agenda set by the cabinet secretariat at Nakasone's instructions.

Attempts under Nakasone to institutionalise a strengthened policy-making role of the cabinet by creating a special external affairs office and by integrating the moribund National Defence Council into a Security Council along US lines, which would have allowed an increase in Japan's responsiveness to international crises[1] largely failed. Due to the ministries' opposition, these proposals which emanated from the Administrative Reform Council, were implemented only in a watered-down version in July 1986 as a decision-making body in case of national emergencies.

THE MINISTRY OF FINANCE (MOF)

With its class I officials representing the 'elite of the elite', MOF stands at the apex of Japan's bureaucratic power structure. Its principal source of influence is its role in budget formulation: any policy proposal with a spending component will need to find MOF approval.

Of MOF's seven bureaux, the budget bureau (whose director general normally succeeds to the administrative vice-ministership) is therefore most important: it receives demands for funds from all ministries and agencies, and decides according to its own priorities and criteria which requests will be satisfied in the light of limited budgetary resources. Two further bureaux are involved in public finance: the tax bureau which has to supply annual revenue programmes and work on the tax structure and its rates (with actual tax collection being done by the National Tax Administration Agency, a MOF subsidiary); and the finance bureau which is in charge of non-fiscal revenues: it issues bonds to cover the annual deficit and supervises Japan Tobacco Inc., a major fiscal cash-cow. It also administers the government's loans and investment programme which channels post office savings funds into semi-public institutions and public banks.

Japan's public calendar is determined to a large extent – more so than in any other country – by the annual procedures and rituals of the budget process. The EPA each April publishes its growth forecast for the coming fiscal year (which runs from 1 April to 31 March). Based on these figures, MOF's budget bureau estimates the likely fiscal revenues, and the ministries and agencies compile first-guesses on the following year's expenditures and possible incomes.

In the summer MOF hands a total figure for next year's budget to the cabinet. This will usually be approved subsequently. Within this overall ceiling, by the end of August ministries have to submit their detailed budget requests, which the budget bureau will examine throughout September and

October. During this period lobbying activities with the bureau will be intense, first by desk officers and middle-management people of the ministries and interest groups; later – if issues remain unresolved – at a more senior administrative and political level. By November agreement will have been reached on most items. The few points of disagreement will be cleared up at the most senior administrative and political level during that month. By December a draft budget will be submitted to the cabinet for approval. In direct negotiations with the finance minister, the ministers will squeeze out some more money for a few pet projects (a regular occurrence for which MOF will already have made allowances).

In January, the cabinet-approved budget will be discussed by the budget committee of the Lower House, in the televised deliberations of which the opposition parties will raise almost any subject under the sun (except a serious budgetary discussion). The budget will then be submitted to the plenary session of the Lower House which will do likewise. Depending on the LDP's majority, its passage will either be smooth and unchanged, or the opposition parties may be able to threaten it with delays and to force some – usually populist and window-dressing – adjustments at the last minute for example, tax rebates of 3000 yen for each citizen (in 1978) or additional welfare spending).

Discussions in the budget committee and in the plenary of the Upper House – where the LDP's majority is usually (except since 1989) more substantial – are a more perfunctory affair.

The budget is normally approved in late March. If it is not (as during the heat of the Recruit scandal in 1989), then for a while the government may continue on monthly instalments (based on one-twelfth of the previous year's budget), until the prime minister and his cabinet are forced to resign.

MOF is also in charge of banking and monetary policies (the latter conjointly with the Bank of Japan). The banking bureau supervises Japan's insurance businesses and banks, including the Bank of Japan and other governmental financial institutions (Ex-Im Bank, Japan Development Bank, and so on), while the securities bureau (more in theory than in practice) watches over Japan's securities houses and their markets.

The international finance bureau deals with questions relating to Japan's balance of payments and exchange rates, and with international monetary policies in general. It co-ordinates Japan's position with fellow G7 countries. It also deals with the indebtedness problems of third world countries and represents Japan at monetary conferences and institutions, such as the IMF, the World Bank and the Asian Development Bank.

Finally, the customs and tariffs bureau deals with the implementation of Japan's trade policies. It manages Japan's tariff code and supervises the customs houses.

MOF's influence still works wonders when administrative guidance is issued to Japan's city banks or securities houses. Its budget bureau still carries clout with budget-hungry ministries. Japan's taxpayers, live in fear of the NTAA's ingenious tax inspectors. Senior MOF officials still secure the most lucrative *amakudari* post-retirement careers.

Among the ex-bureaucrats of the LDP's parliamentary party, one-third are former MOF class I officials (30 in total). Former premiers Ikeda, Fukuda and Ohira began their professional careers at MOF, and so did Kiichi Miyazawa, the current prime minister. For all these credentials of power and influence and the undisputed top-class professionalism of most of its elite track staff, MOF, with the deregulation of Japan's financial markets and the earlier abolition of exchange rate controls, has lost some of its regulatory instruments which it freely used prior to the 1980s (credit allocation, interest rate regulation, and so on), Also on exchange rate and monetary policies BOJ has repeatedly and successfully defend its anti-inflationary course against what it probably perceived as unduly politically influenced MOF positions.

Further, the once-almighty budget bureau appears to have succumbed to the unrelenting onslaught of top-level pork-barrelling: while officials can prove their tough professionalism on the more technical spending items, the strategic definition of priorities and the larger spending programmes are clearly decided at a senior political level by the LDP, to which the bureau and its director general can only acquiesce. Seizaburo Sato, for instance, argued that, due to the LDP's increased government experience, by the late 1950s the centre of the budget-making process shifted from MOF's budget bureau to the LDP.[2]

THE MINISTRY OF INTERNATIONAL TRADE AND INDUSTRY (MITI)

The ministry proper consists of the minister's secretariat and seven bureaux. There are also four affiliated agencies: the Agency of Natural Resources and Energy, the Patent Office, the Small and Medium Enterprise Agency and the Agency of Industrial Science and Technology. The minister's secretariat contains all horizontal functions and assures effective policy co-ordination within the ministry. It is in charge of personnel, general co-ordination, budgets and accounts, data processing, statistics and public relations.

MITI's international work is handled by the international trade policy bureau and by the international trade administration bureau. While the first is in charge of trade policy formulation, conducts trade negotiations and contains all regional divisions, the latter manages trade policy instruments: it deals with trade promotion, export control, trade finance and export insurance.

The other five bureaux deal with domestic industry: the industrial policy bureau (in charge of basic industrial policies, restructuring, consumer policies, chambers of commerce); the industrial location and environmental protection bureau (competent for industrial land and water development, industrial pollution and waste, public safety, safety in mines; the basic industries bureau (dealing with iron and steel, light metals, chemicals and industrial alcohol); the machinery and information industries bureau (handling precision equipment, industrial machinery, electronics, cars, aircraft, and cast and wrought products); and finally the consumer goods industries bureau (which deals with textiles, paper, pulp and printing, household and recreational goods, ceramics and construction materials, as well as the housing industry).

Of all ministries, MITI has the largest number (18) of affiliated public corporations. These non-profit-making enterprises also serve as training grounds for aspiring MITI careerists and offer coveted – lucrative and stress-reduced – if only temporary *amakudari* executive resting-grounds for newly retired senior MITI officers. MITI also maintains the second largest number (20) – MHW ranks first – of advisory councils, ranging from the industrial structure council to the high pressure gas and explosives safety council.

Ministry-appointed industry and consumer representatives, as well as academics and knowledgeable journalists sit in these councils, and advise the ministry on any newly drafted bill or planned regulation which falls within the council's competence. These advisory councils are an important vehicle for direct formalised industry–government links. Bureaucracy benefits from the assembled know-how and expert input, while industry gets advance information on government plans and a genuine chance to present amendments and modifications.

Like most other ministries, MITI also maintains regional bureaux, which are located in Sapporo, Sendai, Tokyo, Nagoya, Osaka, Hiroshima, Takamatsu and Fukuoka. These bureaux deal with regional economic development and supervise the local implementation of MITI policy. The administrative division of Japan into 47 mostly small prefectures gives these regional MITI offices a unique regional co-ordinating role – particularly in areas such Kyushu with strong interprefectural rivalries, thus effectively enhancing Japan's centralist power structure. (A more sensible regionalised and decentralised approach to Japan's regional development exercised in full by autonomous regional authorities would, in Sato's view entail the need to dissolve the regional ministry offices.[3]

Through JETRO's 97 overseas offices MITI also maintains an international information and communication network of its own, independent of MFA control.

MITI, during its 'golden era' in 1935–55,[4] followed a consciously foresighted industrial policy furthering the heavy industrialisation of Japan. Initially, the policy instruments were provided by the wartime organisation of the economy. After the war the preferential allocation of foreign exchange, cheap credits, public infrastructural investments and low-priced industrial land were suitable means to implement such industrial policies. MITI's subsequent and current role in guiding the continuous restructuring of the Japanese economy has been made possible by its earlier spectacular success and the creation of business confidence in MITI's strategic advice. MITI throughout the period from the 1950s till the 1970s, orchestrated a skilful if somewhat single-minded economic diplomacy which succeeded in opening Japan's export markets while delaying reciprocity until the moment when the Japanese industry in question was confident of withstanding any import competition. The re-establishment of the *keiretsu* and setting up sectoral cartels whenever it was felt necessary for adjustment reasons were part of the concomitant domestic structural policies.

Partly a victim of its own success, with Japan's top-ranking companies flush with cash, freed from formal bureaucratic shackles, sophisticated in their own strategic production and marketing decisions and turning rapidly into global operators, the good advice of bright MITI boys in their mid-30s will continue to be listened to politely by the captains of Japanese industry. MITI's formal policy instruments, however, have lost most of their clout. Current MITI visions and industrial policy designs ('technopolis', retirement colonies abroad, the promotion of advanced technologies and internationalisation) are part of corporate Japan's enlightened mainstream orientation, and big business's actual adherence and involvement is purely voluntary.

Although MITI's mission appears to have been fulfilled – with its officials experiencing increasing difficulty in securing adequate *amakudari* positions in industry – most of Japan's MITI- related businesses will still be careful not to antagonise the ministry for fear of its residual regulatory powers and because of its potential for punitive arbitrary decisions: a delinquent company could soon find itself at the receiving end of some *ad hoc* administered export cartel with its shares being squeezed by a disadvantageous formula. It could also find a few protective industry standards being removed overnight. Attractive sites in MITI sponsored industrial parks might no longer be available.

THE MINISTRY OF FOREIGN AFFAIRS
(MFA – *GAIMUSHO*)

The Ministry of Foreign Affairs is an awkward player in Japan's administrative power structure, remaining almost completely bereft of any domestic constituency. Except for the Japan Foundation and the JICA there are no affiliated public corporations.

MFA's strength lies in its high public exposure and the prestige which its international role entails. Travelling abroad, Dietman and other politicians need to rely on the Japanese embassies' logistical support and briefings. All official communications between the Japanese government and the rest of the world in principle need to be channelled through the (slow-moving) diplomatic channels of *Gaimusho* (and are therefore often cut short in practice). Like all foreign ministries in the world, MFA takes its formal rights very seriously, more seriously usually than the substance of many of the economic and technical issues which form an increasing part of Japan's international intergovernmental communication. MFA's only significant budget item constitutes the bulk of Japan's development aid, which the ministry is joyfully mismanaging while jealously guarding its administrative incompetence.[5]

A *Gaimusho* official is different from (and in his own eyes superior to) his colleagues in other ministries, usually being able to speak better English and to comprehend the menu and wine cards in Tokyo's French restaurants. As diplomats stationed abroad they have had time to read novels and to play tennis, and the money and space to collect antiques which their contemporaries at home obviously do not have. Being staffed by gentlemen (and gentlewomen) of great cultural standing, *Gaimusho* has for a long time decided that its internal factions should not be based on the banal ties of *kyodobatsu* (shared local origin), *gakubatsu* (shared schools/universities), or *keibatsu* (family/marriage links), as in other ministries and institutions, but on 'schools' based on one's favourite linguistic leanings and overseas postings. Consquently there are mutually hostile French, American, British, German schools in existence. Looking at officials' CV's, it is usually not difficult to spot the school they adhere to. As befits the alliance ties to the US, the American school is naturally the most powerful postwar school in *Gaimusho* (having inherited this role from the previously dominant 'German school'). However, these cliques are of little consequence to the substance of Japan's sophisticated foreign policy, which is to make no enemies and to remain friends with everyone, in particular with the United States (which is why MFA is deeply aggrieved once the US has chosen a confrontational stance to a third country in their international dealings).

With slightly less than 4000 officials, MFA is reassuringly small for the foreign ministry of a nation of 120 million people. Japan maintains 163 embassies and 65 consulates general abroad. The ministry proper is organised into a powerful minister's secretariat and ten bureaux.

The Ministry is run by the administrative vice-minister of foreign affairs, who is in turn assisted by two deputy ministers (one dealing with political issues, the other devoting himself to economics). The minister's secretariat is headed by a deputy vice-minister. The title of this *kyokucho*-class official indicates the primacy of this horizontal institution over the bureaux. The secretariat is in charge of policy co-ordination, personnel, finances, public relations, cultural affairs, protocol and archives.

Five regional bureaux cover Asia, North America, Latin America and the Caribbean, Europe and Oceania, and the Middle East and Africa respectively. The five sectoral bureaux deal with: economic affairs (foreign trade, international transportation, energy, fisheries, matters related to GATT, OECD and the European Community); economic co-operation (development aid and overseas investments); treaties (legal affairs), the united nations (subjects related to the UN family); and finally with information, analysis, research and planning (conceptual and analytical tasks for foreign policy formulation).

Some of the attractions of an elite-track *Gaimusho* career is that every year, in addition to normal HQ executive posts, some 50-odd ambassadorships or consul general positions are redistributed. In consequence, the infamous 'tap on the shoulder' for voluntary retirement is slightly later in *Gaimusho* than elsewhere. On the other hand, a definite shortage of domestic branch offices, dependent public organisations and political pork-barrel budgets limits *amakudari* options and secondary career prospects for Japan's ex-ambassadors and ex-consuls general.

OTHER MINISTRIES

There is a general consensus that MOF, MITI and MFA constitute Japan's most prestigious ministries. This is also reflected in the numbers of applicants and in the general quality of manpower. Ministership in at least one of these ministries is considered a precondition for assuming the position of prime minister, who thus is viewed as having proven his credentials on difficult dossiers before the eyes of the world.

The purely domestic ministries suffer from a US occupation-inflicted legacy. The powerful wartime and prewar interior ministry (*Naimusho*) had, not without reason, been considered by MacArthur and his lieutenants as the stronghold of an authoritarian, centralised police state. In order to democratise and decentralise Japan, the hapless *Naimusho* was duly dismantled and its composite bureaux hived off as independent ministries (health and welfare, labour, transport, construction, home affairs) and agencies (national land, national police, and so on). As inheritors of *Naimusho*'s great regulatory traditions, the new ministries remained equally disinclined to liberalise, to democratise or to decentralise. However, with five well-budgeted new ministerships up for annual redistribution, LDP politicians remained very content with the new arrangements, as were the sectoral business communities concerned. Now closer and cosier relations were possible with 'their' ministry with fewer checks and balances provided by other bureaux, and without the administrative discipline forced by the earlier in-house police presence. LDP politicians at times even managed to colonise the weakened left-over ministries as *factional* fiefdoms, making sure that factional sympathisers were promoted in personnel decisions, that public projects and budgets were allocated to benefit foremost factional MPs and benefactors.[6] The ministry of construction, for instance, was long considered to be firmly in the pocket of the Tanaka faction.

Little wonder that such ministries rank pretty much at the bottom of public esteem and have difficulty attracting suitable staff. The difference in dealing with, say MITI/MOF officials on the one hand and MOT officials on the other is striking. With the first there is quick problem identification, fast, intelligent responsivess (if not always of the desired sort) and a thorough investigation of the issues concerned; with the second, policy responses are slower, resort to *tatemae*-type explanations (face-saving untruths, unbelievable by all parties concerned) is more frequent, as are open admissions that the ministry is unable to resist vested interests (even be they semi-criminal in nature – as in the case of Japan's stevedores association). Some MOT bureaux are not even ashamed to front for Mr Ryochi Sasagawa's benevolent operations. Foreign officials are invited to MOT junkets, and only learn later that their pleasures have been paid for by one of this former war criminal's numerous foundations and that they ought to be grateful to this great philanthropist.

Other ministries (justice, agriculture, education, post and telecommunication) are of distinguished prewar lineage, but have since had to pander to parochial LDP interests as well. MOE is a playground for right-wing

LDP ideologists, whose principal passions lie in doctoring Japanese history textbooks, in reintroducing as much nationalist symbolism as possible into Japan's public schools and in annoying *Nikkyoso*, the leftist and equally doctrinaire teacher's union as much as possible.

MAFF, whose policies I have analysed elsewhere,[7] through its LDP masters is obliged to design its policies mainly to benefit the all-powerful *nokyo* (agricultural co-operatives) bureaucracy and the part-time (rice) farmers whose interests are represented by this lobby. Against the officials' own better judgment, the interests of the full-time professional farmers, who form the backbone of Japan's agricultural structure proper, remain neglected.

Individual variations notwithstanding, all ministries are organised along similar structures with a minister's secretariat performing horizontal tasks, and a number of semi-autonomous bureaux dealing with their respective vertical sectors and clienteles.[8] This structure has been fixed by law and – in contrast to Western administrations – is unlikely to be altered quickly or frequently.

AGENCIES AND PUBLIC CORPORATIONS

All ministries have their share of dependent or semi-dependent public institutions (sometimes shared between different ministries), which are used as depositories of redundant senior staff or as training grounds for young hopefuls. The regular staff in these institutions are correspondingly demotivated.

Let us take a sample of five out of the 87 public corporations in existence in 1988.[9] Their executives had the following career background:

The Forest Development Corporation

The president hails from MAFF; among the four vice-presidents three are from MAFF, one from MOF. There are three directors (*bucho*): one from MAFF, one from Wakayama prefectural government, and one in-house. This position appears to be the corporation staff's most senior career possibility.

The Water Resources Development Corporation

President: MOL
Vice President: MAFF;

Executive directors: MAFF (3), MOL (3), MOF (1), MITI (1), management
agency (1), MHW (1), Shimane Pref.-Govt. (1)
Directors (*bucho*): MOL (9), MAFF (3), supply agency (1), other public
corporations (2), in-house: none.

The Shipping Consolidation Corporation

President: MOT
Executive directors: MOT (4), MOF (1)
Directors (*bucho*): MOT (4), MOF (1), in-house, none.

The Japan Foundation

President: MFA
Executive directors: MFA (1), MOF (1), MOE (1)
Directors (*bucho*): MFA (2), MOE (2), NTAA (1).

Ex-Im Bank

President: MOF
Vice-President: BOJ
Executive directors: MOF (1), MITI (1), MFA (1), in-house (3).

For most public corporations it appears that presidents and vice presidents
invariably hail from the supervisory ministry. Among executive directors,
usually one top achiever is promoted from within the public corporation's
own staff. At *bucho* level, the generalist departments are frequently headed
by ministerial implants, while the technical departments are usually run by
in-house staff.

The same pattern – though to a lesser extent – applies to the national
agencies, which are often headed by a minister of state, but whose senior
positions are occupied to a significant extent by mainstay ministry men.

Let us look at six major agencies, four of which (defence, science and
technology, economic planning, and environment) are headed by a minister
of state with cabinet rank

The Fair Trade Commission (FTC)

Chairman: MOF
Members of the Commission: legal studies expert (1), MOF (1), MITI (1),
FTC (1).

Kacho/counsellor-class officials: FTC (31), PMO (4), MOF (2, of which
  one is the *bucho* of the economics department), MITI (2), other ministries: MFA, MOT, MOE, EPA, MOL, MAFF, MHA, MOJ, DA,
  MHW and the (former) Supply Agency (1 each).

Eighty per cent of the FTC's executives and 38 per cent of the *kacho/bucho*-
class officials are transplanted. Their placement assures that an early alarm
is sounded when one their ministry's client industries is targeted by an FTC
investigation. They can then have a mitigating influence on the course and
outcome of this investigation, if it is to be permitted to proceed at all.

The Police Agency

All management, including the director general (*kancho*) are in-house elite-
track professionals. The agency has successfully stayed clear of both politicians and management transplants from other ministries.

The Defence Agency (DA)

Headed by a minister of state who, as a member of the cabinet, is aided
  by a parliamentary vice minister.
Administrative director general: DA
Executive counsellors: DA (2), MFA (1), MOE (1)
Head of director general's secretariat (*kanbocho*): Police Agency
Defence policy bureau (*kyoku*): MOF
Education/training bureau: DA
Personnel bureau: DA
Finance bureau: DA
Equipment bureau: MITI

Among *kacho* officials in the Defence Agency's Akasaka headquarters, 20
are from the Agency proper, two are from MOF, and one each from the
Police Agency, MHW, MITI and the (former) Supply Agency. Hence 40
per cent of the administrative executives are transplanted, as are 23 per cent
of the *kacho*-class. It should be noted, however, that in spite of their
numerical inferiority, the most strategic administrative positions covering
defence policies, procurement and overall intra-agency co-ordination are
occupied by civilians, who in a draft-free Japan don't even know how to
load a pistol, let alone fire one. MITI's positioning in running the equipment bureau gives it a Pentagon-type hold on military procurement deci-

sions and suits its pet projects to develop a Japanese aviation and high-tech armament industry. This standard MITI posting confirms the notion that a lot of the defence budget can safely be assumed to operate as effective subsidies for industrial R&D. Historical experience, however, still speaks for strong civilian control of the Japanese – or any other – military administration.

The Economic Planning Agency (EPA)

Headed by a minister of state of cabinet rank, who is assisted by a parliamentary vice-minister. (Administrative) director general (*jimujikan*): MOL Head of director general's secretariat (*kanbocho*): MOF. Other directors general (*kyokucho*): MITI (2), the former Supply Agency (1), promoted from EPA's ranks (2).

Among *kacho*-class officials, 40 are from EPA proper, 8 from MITI, 6 from MAFF, 3 from MOF, two from MOL and MOT, and one each from MPT, MOL, MHW and the (former) Supply Agency. The transplants account for 78 per cent of senior EPA executives and 38 per cent of *kacho*-class officials.

The Science and Technology Agency (STA)

Again this is an agency worthy of a minister of state and of a parliamentary vice minister.
Director general (*jimujikan*): MOF
Deputy director general: MITI (science and technology in Japan is, after all, a matter of public finance and industrial policy)
Head of the director general's secretariat: MITI
The other directors general:
    Science/technology policy bureau: STA
    Science/technology promotion bureau: MITI
    Research and development bureau: STA
    Atomic energy bureau: MOF
    Nuclear safety bureau: STA.

Non-scientific transplants comprise 63 per cent of STA's executives. Among *kacho*-class officials in the agency proper (not counting research institutes) their share stands at 42 per cent (most of whom are from MITI).

The Environment Agency (EA)

Created in 1971, it is headed by a minister of state, assisted by a parliamentary vice-minister.

Director general (*jimujikan*): MHW

Senior advisors: MPT, MOE and MOF (one each).

Kyokucho-class officers come from MHW (3), MOF (1) and MAFF (1). One *kyokucho* is from Niigata Prefectural Administration. Among the 49 *kacho*-class officials, five are from the Agency proper (10 per cent); the remaining 90 per cent are mostly from MHW and from other assorted ministries and some prefectural administrations.

Agencies vary in their ability to ward off 'colonial' management invasions by related (and unrelated) ministries. The Police Agency, which 'knows too much', is obviously the most successful. The Environment Agency, due to the relative short period of her existence and the youth of her own class I staff, has so far been the least successful. Still, the agencies do better than the public corporations.

   Political expediency explains the lower status of some agencies. The Hokkaido Development Agency was created precisely when a socialist governor came to power for the first time in Hokkaido. Decision-making and administration of all public projects financed by Tokyo was shifted away from the prefecture and centralised in Tokyo in the Agency in order to benefit the LDP friends of the new state minister. The same applied *mutatis mutandis* to left-leaning Okinawa once it rejoined the motherland in 1973. It saw the creation of the Okinawa Development Agency in Tokyo. Both are usually headed by the same state minister – an LDP backbencher who has served his time – who, almost as a rule, has ties to neither prefecture. The agencies' (except for the Police Agency) and the public corporations' lack of autonomy and their essential dependence on one or more 'parent ministries' largely excludes them from decision-making on issues of importance. Their senior staff (political and administrative heads apart) should not normally be considered part of Japan's power elite.

HORIZONTAL CO-ORDINATION

There are two agencies dealing with horizontal *administrative* management among Japanese ministries (in addition to the *policy*-co-ordinating institutions, the Management and Co-ordination Agency (MCA) and the National Personnel Authority (NPA).

The National Personnel Authority (NPA)

The NPA acts as the principal personnel agency of the government: it organises the entrance examinations, produces annual pay recommendations, organises training courses and welfare programmes, and supervises disciplinary and complaints procedures for all government officials. The authority is led by three commissioners who are appointed by the cabinet and approved by the Diet for terms of four years. The presiding commissioner hails from the former Home Ministry. His fellow commissioners are an ex-journalist and a former MITI official. These arrangements have been made and fixed by law to assure the authority's independence and the integrity of Japan's civil service. Indeed, the NPA was highly successful in defending the meritocratic tradition of Japan's central administration. Yet within the rules of seniority-based promotions and recruitment through examinations only, ministries are autonomous in their concrete personnel decisions. The NPA was thus unable to prevent the emergence of a particular inequality among Japanese civil servants, namely inequality by institution: central ministries outrank agencies, which in turn take precedence over public corporations. Central government has supremacy over prefectural governments, which in turn lord it over local administrations. Here, city (*shi*) governments are more important than town (*machi*) administrations, which in turn look down on village (*mura*) management. Central offices of any sort always take precedence over branch offices. The meritocratic mandarinate has ultimately produced a comprehensive administrative caste system.

The Management and Co-ordination Agency (MCA)

Complementing the NPA's more formal tasks, the MCA is charged with improving the efficiency of Japan's civil service system. It reviews staffing levels, organograms and administrative institutions, and recommends changes where appropriate. The agency also handles pensions for retired officials and a number of odd jobs such as the population census and co-ordinating the government's policies on traffic safety, the aged, and the discriminated-against '*dowa*' stratum in Japan's society. Most important for our concerns is the agency's *administrative inspection bureau*, which carries out inspections of government institutions, public corporations and their direct or indirect (subsidised) programmes and projects. The bureau also has to respond to citizens' complaints about governmental or governmentally sponsored activities.

The agency carries out inspections and, transcending traditional audit operations, reviews the subject matter of current public projects: examining the 'appropriateness of policies', the goal attainment of stated policies, and the fairness and efficiency of operations.[10]

Malfunctions and inefficient practices are supposed to be pointed out. The bureau is able to investigate about 20 projects per annum. This review is innovative, as MOF's budget bureau only scrutinises *new* programmes, while ongoing programmes receive adequate funding without much further questioning.

The board of audit finally provides classical independent auditing, which was established in Japan in 1889 following the Prussian pattern. Its dependence was further strengthened in 1947, this time following American models.[11]

MINISTRIES: ORGANISATIONAL AUTONOMY AND POWER POSITION

Although most members of the national bureaucratic elite originate from the same alma mater (Todai Law), are of the same generation (in their early to mid-fifties), follow similar work patterns, and have similar career cycles and professional experience, this homogeneity does not create a closeness of minds. Interbureaucratic conflicts between ministries and between bureaux are frequent and are often taken personally. In fact there is a rich folklore of interministry wars, with winners and losers in terms of budgets, competences and administrative fiefdoms. Such wars trigger strong public interest and are covered extensively in the newspapers. The vice-minister or bureau chief of a ministry or bureau that has just lost a battle appears as about as disgraceful as a general returned from a bungled military campaign. In the heat of such battles allies are sought wherever possible – from politics, business, the media or even by soliciting foreign governments' support.[12]

Within the loose constraints of cabinet and sub-cabinet co-operation, and respecting the basic rules of personnel and budgetary management prescribed by law and the constitution, Japan's central ministries are fairly autonomous on administrative matters. As regards policies, considerable discretionary administrative power and exclusive policy expertise are still left with the three elite ministries: MOF, MITI, and MFA. As concerns the rest of the crowd – particularly the dismantled former *Naimusho* bureaux (MHW, MOT, MOC, MOL and MHA) – as well as the ministries of justice, agriculture, education, and posts and telecom, political intervention is higher and the incidence of administrative influence is correspondingly reduced.

While Japan's handful of key power brokers are members of the LDP's upper crust, the top members of the administrative elite constitute some 20 per cent of the core elite of Japan's top 400 power holders. This band of elite bureaucrats is currently headed by the deputy chief cabinet secretary, Mr Nobuo Ishihara (a former vice-minister of MHA), who is sometimes called the 'unofficial prime minister' of Japan for his essential institutional backstage role[13] in inter-ministry co-ordination.

Other members are the administrative vice-ministers of MOF, MITI and MFA, as well as the directors general of the BOJ and the Police Agency and the director general of MOF's budget bureau. The administrative vice-ministers of the other ministries as well as the directors general of the PMO's agencies belong more to the second tier of Japan's administrative power elite. In this group are included the deputy vice-ministers, the heads of the minister's secretariats and the directors general of the three core ministries. As part of Japan's power elite at large, we find other ministries' directors general, key *kacho* of the three core ministries, the PMO and the cabinet secretariat, the heads and deputies of the other agencies and the major public corporations, the ambassadors to Japan's most important allies, the vice-governors of the prefectures and the supreme court judges, making a total of about 400 individuals.

The *temporary* nature of the administrative elite has to be understood: incumbency in top administrative positions is transitory, and shorter than for the political or business elite. There is a long period of aspiration, and a relatively short time of one, or at the most, three years of actual exercise of power. In fact, only a few incumbents manage to maintain their elevated status in secondary (mostly political) careers. Yet the administrative elite (unlike the political elite) enjoys high meritocratic legitimacy and public status. Their power is little personalised but role-bound. The – temporary – incumbents have the full institutional support of their ministries and of the affiliated institutions. As such, they have considerably more resources at hand than the self-financing LDP politicians. On policy issues the business elite is usually more disinterested and starved of intellectual resources due to other, profitable, priority concerns. In short, the administrative elite is very powerful in its proper – central administrative – domain. In a developmental capitalist state this makes their senior members full and legitimate participants of the national power elite.

7 Elite Civil Servants

THE SENIOR MANDARINATE

Promotions in their mid-forties to senior *kacho* positions constitute forebodings about class I officials' future career path. Some 23 years after joining a ministry, appointments to the most senior *kacho* level are due. Only those who are appointed *somukacho* (director of a bureau's general affairs division) will be considered for promotion to head the minister's secretariat's personnel division or general affairs division one year later. In MITI's case the first selection to *somukacho* eliminates 17 out of 24, the second selection picks from the remaining seven the two survivors who will remain in the restricted race to the vice-ministership and to the (junior) position of vice-minister for international affairs respectively, some eight years later. Four years after being promoted to *bucho* rank (department chief), directors general (in MITI's case – see table 7.1) are *almost* assured of whichever of the two coveted positions they will ultimately reach.

Having an established structured and preprogrammed clockwork type of succession has two major benefits. It limits the pool of people available for the top slots and therefore restricts the competition and likely antagonisms between the members of the ministry's top echelon: any director general who has not headed either the minister's secretariat's personnel or general co-ordination divisions, *knows* that he will not become vice-minister and he will not even try. It also limits the scope for political intervention in senior personnel appointments, which are resisted by the self-respecting core ministries (MOF, MITI, MFA).

In principle, the incumbent minister is responsible for all personnel decisions within his ministry. Prior to submitting his proposals, for example, for promotion to *somukacho* to the minister, the head of the personnel division will have consulted and have sought the agreement of all *kyokucho* and the vice-minister. When picking his successor and filling key bureau chief posts, the outgoing administrative vice-minister will not only consult with his predecessors but also with his minister. Ministers may be activist and interventionist (like Michio Watanabe during his tenure at MAFF) or inclined merely to rubber-stamp the administrative consensus. In any case, even if he is only a recently appointed know-nothing backbencher, prudence dictates that he consult on all important personnel changes with his *zoku*, the leading experts and power-brokers of the ministry in question in

Table 7.1 The way to the top at MITI

Age	Seniority in ministry (years of service)	Position
22–24		Todai Law graduation/enter ministry
37–42	14–18	First kacho assignment
46–47	23	Kacho, General Affairs Division (*somukacho*)
47–48	24	Kacho, Personnel Division/General Co-ordination Division, minister's secretariat
48–49	25	Bucho
49–50	26	Deputy director general (*shingikan*)
Vice-minister track		
51	28	Director general, minister secretariat (*kanbocho*)
52	29	Director general, machinery and information industries bureau
54	31	Director general, industry policy bureau
55	32	Vice-minister
International vice-minister track		
52	30	Director general, basic industries bureau
54	32	Director general, international trade policy bureau
55	33	Vice-minister, international affairs

the LDP's parliamentary party (that is, a large part of his predecessors and successors).

These LDP MPs know all senior ministry staff through year-long contacts. They regularly receive briefings by ministry officials at PRC committee meetings and at Diet committee meetings. They have met all *kacho*, *bucho* and *kyokucho* when they were parliamentary vice-ministers or ministers themselves, or when lobbying for specific constituency projects or national causes. Being politicians, they will not fail to make their personnel preferences known and, if they want to remain effective, will support their choices actively. Knowing the system, they know that political intervention has already taken place for appointments at senior *kacho* level. This tendency has not remained unnoticed among junior *kacho* who, when entertaining career ambitions, actively seek and cultivate political contacts with LDP *zoku* members.

While some ministries, such as MOC or MOT with large pork-barrel budgets, have been virtually 'colonised' by the LDP and sometimes even by its factions (such as MOC by the Tanaka faction in the 1970s), the more professional-minded ministries face a tactical dilemma between either soliciting LDP support in their perennial battles with fellow ministries or staying aloof and rejecting LDP intervention (and potential support). Since the ministry and its LDP *zoku* usually go along quite well in practice, the ministry's senior officials in their personnel decisions will anticipate their political partners' preferences and reward those officials who have earned the *zoku*'s respect by displaying both professional competence and unbureaucratic responsiveness to essential pork-barrel requests.

Given the 'Todai-sation' of all senior positions (the higher the ranks, the larger the percentage of Todai Law graduates), sometimes the career strategy of the non-Todai cohort may be to rely on political patronage as the only effective resort for career enhancement. This also applies to the specialists (*gikan*), who in most ministries and agencies have almost no prospects of ever reaching vice-ministership (at best, they may aspire to manage 'their' specialist bureau).

However, the rule of generalists of the Todai Law persuasion continues to hold sway over all key ministries (thus demonstrating certain limits to political intervention). (Note that in any given cabinet one-third to one-quarter of ministers are ex-ministry officials themselves, who are often exacting on bureaucrats' performance, but are unlikely to rock the system.)

Senior ministry officials will delegate all the routine decisions to the divisions in their charge. A *bucho*, *kanbocho*, *jicho* or *kyokucho* will see it as their main professional duty to represent and defend their units at the interministerial, private sector and political interfaces. They will study in depth and intervene only on a handful of politically sensitive dosiers – or on those which hold special personal appeal. While delegating the technical details to subordinates, their power for promoting budgets and projects are considerable: such decisions can be initiated, vetoed or altered selectively.

In a centralist system like Japan, a powerful position in the national administration exercises even more leverage at the regional level, where the projects of financially dependent local administrations can either be promoted, expanded, or nipped in the bud.

Nationwide representative tasks, such as making speeches and attending formal functions at inaugurations and anniversary celebrations – but also at weddings and funerals of staff – and receiving cohorts of visitors both domestic and from abroad are important components of senior administrative activity. The job is to win acceptance for the ministry's budgetary and legislative projects both from the power elite and from the public at large.

Thanks to an antechamber staffed by an assistant and a secretary, they enjoy a quiet office, filled with status symbols, with fewer pressures to conform. The office will be conservatively furnished with a dominant (and often untidy) desk and by seating for visitors and chairs for his own staff. Executive offices regularly feature a TV set (often turned on, especially during Diet deliberations) and stacks of newspapers and journals, indicative of having more reading time available.

Life at *kyokucho* level appears to be less stressful than as a *kacho* or *kachohosa*. Work can easily be delegated ('do something') and briefings requested at little notice. Official residences are available in downtown Tokyo, and commuting and official travel is possible in chauffeured cars. They are no longer commuting for up to four hours each day, nor is there any need to hail and squeeze into taxis for out-of-office appointments. The director general will receive VIP treatment in the prefectures (eager for subsidies) and in his home town: the local boy who made good. He will be treated with great deference by his subordinates and by the ministry's associated institutions. There will be plenty of opportunities for international travel and regular invitations for golf. In the late afternoons there are regularly receptions (up to three consecutively) to be attended at the major Tokyo hotels, as well as potentially more influential but restricted meetings at the Akasaka or Ginza teahouses. These occasions are no longer the welcome moments for free drinks and opulent food that the young *kachohosa* may have cherished; they have become part of a senior-level networking chore for the *kyokucho*. Drinks and food are treated with strict discipline. Most receptions will be left after a short symbolic attendance.

It is the *kyokucho* who maintains the political contacts – invisible to the eyes of his divisional staff in their collective offices. To them he will eventually pass on the instructions received. (Still, it must be remembered that 95 per cent of all decisions are considered administrative and remain delegated to the desk officers and their team leaders. The remaining 5 per cent of political decisions are taken at the top – as they probably should be.)

The actual leadership behaviour of the senior grades is often fairly enigmatic to the desk officers concerned. It is frequently seen as aloof, distant and often intimidating. While the jovial paternalistic type may be the ministry's role model, actual behaviour is often authoritarian, sometimes bordering on the despotic. Yet, to the relief of their subordinates, their rule is only for a limited time of one to two years until the next job rotation or until the eventual retirement of the executive office holder. It appears difficult for many in executive ranks not to succumb to the temptation of vanity due to the loss of social constraints after having become more successful than their peers. They preside over ministries in which only 'juniors' are left in seniority and rank, and this affects actual leadership behaviour. There are also role expectations which junior officials and society at large have of their senior ministry officials: they are to behave with benevolent authority and rectitude. In fact, the directors' lifestyle during their later *kacho* period in their mid-forties makes a drastic change from the hustle and bustle and the social and financial constraints of their earlier salaryman life to one befitting the upper classes of Japan. The professional environment, the salary, the fringe benefits and the social company are all transformed during the official's last decade in ministerial life.

Now he is immaculately dressed and coiffured. He will make beautiful speeches and toasts. He has more time for leisure and cultural pursuits as befits a senior representative of his powerful ministry. The 16 most senior MITI officials in 1988 listed golf (10 times), music (7), reading (6), spectator sports (4), go (3), painting (2) and travel (2) as their favourite pastime.[1] Their list of interesting recent books is a selection of well-written popular history, science and contemporary Japanese novels.

To the hard-driven *kachohosa*, his *kyokucho*'s professional and private life must appear sufficiently attractive and motivating to spark continued deferred gratification as the engine for often only mildly interesting, relentless work. Their outstanding position, knowledge, connections and command over public budgets and authorisations allow some senior officials also to prepare for a political career – be it at national level (Upper or Lower House) or a senior local position (governor, mayor), normally in his district of origin. As a director general or administrative vice-minister, he is in a position to visit frequently a prospective constituency and to allocate public projects and other well-targeted ministerial favours. His position also permits the right political contacts to be made which ultimately might permit factional (and party) endorsement of an official candidacy. Conservative beliefs and an affinity to the LDP come naturally at this career stage.

For some 30 years the official has worked successfully with the one party in power, the LDP. During these years he had learned to despise and to manipulate the often ignorant and populist opposition parties. Also his general outlook on life and life experience – having witnessed his career prospering alongside a Japan which has risen from the ashes and from the miseries of the postwar period of his youth – will support a conservative and pro-business view of life and politics in general. As a senior ministry official there are few attractions in social equality. Having worked a long, hard and successful professional life for the societal status quo and its only incremental improvement through the established power, there is little cognitive dissonance in beginning to work overtly and publicly for the LDP.

ADMINISTRATIVE ELITE CAREERS

Table 7.1 shows the regular top career pattern at MITI. MITI is more predictable than other ministries for promotions to its two top slots: promotions to senior key *kacho* positions (heading the ministry's personnel and general co-ordination divisions) are indicative of higher laurels to come. All other 'class' members by then get the message that their careers will fall short of the highest positions available. In other ministries the situation is less clear, with competition remaining intense between senior directors general about who will ultimately be designated by the outgoing vice-minister (in agreement with the incumbent minister and the LDP *zoku*) as his successor. MITI's earlier pre-selection system appears to attempt to reduce this last-minute political influence by creating a certain 'traditional' vice-ministerial career track, thus obliging the incumbent vice-minister and minister to honour the pre-established line-up (which, however, is sometimes still being altered, either by surprise appointments or by extending the term of incumbents).

Our focus on the top slots crowing class I careers should not make us lose sight of the fact that the majority of class I officials are retired at *kacho/bucho* rank at around 50. Table 7.2 contrasts the ideal types of such 'truncated' careers with those of high-flyers. The fast-tracks' promotions to middle and then to senior management functions happen earlier in professional life. As a result, their experience in senior management will be more extensive before they reach the executive level (*kyokucho* and above). Also their post-retirement (*amakudari*) careers are usually (but not always) more attractive and successful than those retiring without reaching executive ranks.

BIOGRAPHICAL SKETCHES

Six short biographical sketches follow, two each from senior MOF and MFA men, and one each from MOL and MITI. While some careers have led to vice-ministerships and to distinguished careers beyond, others have fallen short, while most of the careers sampled here are still unfolding. While top career tracks may vary between ministries, there is a clear indication in these CVs that consecutive important generalist assignments in mid-career correlate with overall career success. The MOF careers clearly differentiate between tax/budget and international finance specialisations. In the case of *Gaimusho*, special qualifications are also visible (international law; Asian/North American area specialists; economic affairs/inter-

Table 7.2   Variation in career patterns, class I officials

Graduation, senior high school, age 19
Graduation, national university, age 23
Entry ministry, age 23
Promotion Section Chief (*hancho*), age 28

top 5 per cent		**lower 60 per cent**	
Post	*Age*	*Post*	*Age*
Promotion dep. div. chief,	33	Promotion dep. div. chief (*kachohosa*)	37
Senior management			
Promotion div. chief (*kacho*)	37	Promotion div. chief (*kacho*)	45
Promotion dep. chief (*bucho*)	48	Promotion director general, regional ministry office	48
Executive level		Retirement from ministry	50
Promotion director general (*kyokucho*)	51	Director, public corporation	51
Promotion vice-minister	53	2nd retirement	54
Retirement from ministry	55	Director, SME business association	55
President, public corporation	55	3rd retirement	56
Senior advisor, 'Big name' private firm	57	Managing director, public foundation/minor research association	57
Vice-president, 'Big name' private firm	59	Final retirement	65
Retirement from private sector	66		
Honorary senior advisor (*komon*) to previous employer, other advisory public functions	66		

	Years		Years
Time spent in middle management	9		17
Time spent in senior management	14		11
Executive functions	15		0

national organisations), yet they are less obvious in terms of career advancement. MITI careers in their early to middle stages appear fairly generalist, with a great variety in consecutive assignments. The example of MOL (women and labour standards) in turn stands as an example of more 'specialist' careers, reflecting this ministry's narrower competences. This observation also applies to the other sectoral (non-core) ministries.

Hisashi Owada, deputy minister for foreign affairs[2]

Born:	18 September 1932
Education:	Graduated from Tokyo University, Faculty of Education, March 1955

Career:

1955	Entered foreign service (the ministry of foreign affairs)
1971	Executive assistant (private secretary) to the minister for foreign affairs, Takeo Fukuda
1972	Director of political affairs division, United Nations Bureau
1974	Director of treaties division, treaties bureau
1976	Executive assistant to the prime minister, Takeo Fukuda
1979	Minister, Japanese embassy in US
1981	Envoy-extraordinary and minister-plenipotentiary to USSR
1984	Director-general of treaties bureau, and director-general for law of the sea
1987	Deputy vice-minister
1988	Ambassador of Japan to the OECD
1989	Deputy minister for foreign affairs

Academic activities:

1962–5, 1973–7, 1984–8.	Lecturer in international law and International organisation, University of Tokyo
1979–81, 1987–8, 1989–	Visiting professor at Harvard Law School (international law), and at Harvard University Center for International Affairs

International law specialist

Koji Watanabe, deputy minister for foreign affairs[3]

Born: 1934 in Shizuoka Prefecture

Education: Graduated from Tokyo University, Faculty of Liberal Arts, 1956

Career:
1956   Entered ministry of foreign affairs
1971   Director, second international organisations division, economic affairs bureau
1973   First secretary, embassy in the United States of America; Fellow Center for International Affairs, Harvard University
1974   Counsellor, embassy in the Republic of Vietnam
1976   Director, first North America division, North American affairs bureau, ministry of foreign affairs
1978   Deputy director-general, Asian affairs, bureau, MFA
1981   Minister, embassy in China
1984   Director-general, information analysis, research and planning bureau, ministry of foreign affairs
1986   Director-general, economic affairs bureau, MFA
1988   Ambassador-extraordinary and plenipotentiary, embassy in Saudi Arabia
1989   Deputy-minister for foreign affairs, ministry of foreign affairs

Marital Status: Married with two sons

Asia/North America specialist

Shigeo Muraoka, vice-minister of international affairs, ministry of international trade and industry[4]

Born: 7 July 1933, Akita Prefecture

Education: Graduated from Tokyo University, Faculty of Law, March 1957

Career:
1957   Entered MITI
1971   Director, consumer economy division, enterprises bureau
1973   Director, paper and pulp and printing industry division, consumer goods industries bureau

1974	Member of the minister's secretariat
1975	Consul, consulate-general in New York
1978	Director, international economic affairs division, international trade policy bureau
1981	Jan: Director, general affairs division, international trade administration bureau
1981	June: Director, general co-ordination division, minister's secretariat
1982	Director general, international economic affairs department, international trade policy bureau
1983	Deputy director general, international trade policy bureau
1984	Director general, international trade administration bureau
1986	Director general, international trade policy bureau
1988	Vice-minister of international affairs

Toyoo Gyoten, former vice-minister of finance for international affairs, ministry of finance[5]

Born: 2 January 1931

Education: Graduated from Tokyo University, Faculty of Economics, March 1955

Career:

1955	Entered the ministry of finance
1964	Seconded to IMF Washington office
1967	Assistant to president of Asian Development Bank (ADB) in Manila
1972	Head, Haneda branch, Tokyo Customs House
1973	Director, international organisations division, international finance bureau
1975	Director, second fund planning and operation division, financial bureau
1977	Director, research division, international finance bureau
1978	Counsellor, minister's secretariat
1980	Deputy director general, international finance bureau
1983	Deputy director general, banking bureau
1984	Director general, international finance bureau
1986	Vice-minister of finance for international affairs (until July 1989)

Ginko Sato, assistant vice-minister of labour[6]

Born:

Education:　　　University of Tokyo (majored in international relations)
　　　　　　　　New York State School of Industrial and Labour Relations,
　　　　　　　　Cornell University (Fulbright scholarship)
　　　　　　　　London School of Economics, London University

Career:
　1958　　　　　Entered the ministry of Labour
　1958–77　　　(1) Labour relation bureau
　　　　　　　　(2) Labour standards bureau
　　　　　　　　(3) Statistics and information department
　　　　　　　　(4) Women's and young worker's bureau
　1977　　　　　Director, industrial homework division
　1978　　　　　Director, women's division
　1979　　　　　Director, women workers' division
　1984　　　　　Director, international labour affairs division
　1985　　　　　Ministerial councillor
　1986　　　　　Director-general, women's bureau
　1990　　　　　Assistant minister, MOL
　1991　　　　　Japan's Ambassador to Kenya

**Fujio Yoshida, executive vice-president Suntory Limited, Osaka;
advisor, Fukoku Mutual Life Insurance Company, Tokyo[7]**

Born:　　　　　　5 July 1924, Tokyo

Education:　　　Graduated in March 1947 from Tokyo University,
　　　　　　　　Law Faculty in political science

Public Career:
　1947　　　　　Joined ministry of finance
　1950　　　　　Director, Onomichi district tax office
　1960　　　　　Director-general (*bucho*), department of administra-
　　　　　　　　tion, Yokohama Customs House
　1961　　　　　Director-general (*bucho*), department of investiga-
　　　　　　　　tions and audit, Osaka regional tax administration
　　　　　　　　bureau
　1962　　　　　Director of property tax division, national tax ad-
　　　　　　　　ministration agency

1964	Director of indirect taxation division, taxation bureau, ministry of finance
1966	Director of inward investment division, international finance bureau, ministry of finance
1967	Councillor, permanent delegation of Japan to the OECD, Paris
1971	Councillor for international finance minister's secretariat, ministry of finance
1972	Director-general (*bucho*), department of direct taxation, national tax administration agency
1973	Deputy director general (*jicho*), national tax administration agency
1974	Director-general (*kyokucho*), custom and tariff bureau, ministry of finance
1975	Retirement from MOF

Business career:

1978	Senior managing director, Suntory Ltd.
1979–	Executive vice-president, Suntory Ltd, and advisor to Fukoku Mutual Life Insurance

Functions at business associations:

Since Sept. 1979	Chief director, Japan Spirit and Liquor Makers association
Since May 1986	Managing director, Brewing Society of Japan

Public service:

Since Oct. 1984	Member of Japan Environment Corporation, Environment Agency
Since Nov. 1986	Member of Central Council on Alcoholic Beverages, National Tax Administration Agency

Part III
The Business Elite

8 The *Keiretsu* Business Conglomerates

THE ORGANISATION OF BIG BUSINESS

Japan's economy is characterised by a dual structure: a top tier of large-scale, heavily capitalised and usually very profitable big corporations (providing one-third of private sector employment) coexisting with a majority of small and medium-sized enterprises which often operate as subcontractors and frequently enjoy less profitability and offer comparatively worse working conditions and wages.

Most of the top-tier industries are organised in tightly knit *keiretsu* enterprise groups, centring either horizontally around a city bank and a general trading company (*sogo shosha*) – largely reconstituting the *zaibatsu* pattern of old – or comprising vertically upstream and downstream companies, controlled closely by a major manufacturing enterprise.

It is the core companies of the *keiretsu* which form the centre of corporate Japan and which dominate *zaikai*, the four major organisations of big business, thus being able to act as acknowledged spokesmen for Japan's aggregate economic interests, be it *vis à vis* the political establishment, the central bureaucracy or Japan's international partners.

Today some 1.8 million companies exist in Japan. Of these some 20,000 companies are directly affiliated with the 16 major *keiretsu* groups. In terms of *employment* the core companies of the six horizontal *keiretsu* account for 1.6 million jobs (5.9 per cent of Japan's total) and the ten industrial (vertical) groups for 1.1 million jobs (3.6 per cent).

As regards *paid-up capital*, the six major *keiretsu* made up 18.5 per cent of Japan's total. The ten other vertical industrial groups add another 7.5 per cent (banks and insurance companies not included) to a total *keiretsu* share of 26 per cent.

In *annual sales*, these 16 *keiretsu* account for 24 per cent of Japan's total (slightly less than their total of 26 per cent in capitalisation, but far in excess of their 9.5 per cent share in total employment). The six major *keiretsu* alone account for some 18 per cent of Japan's total annual sales.

Net profits for the big six reached 1.1 trillion yen (or 16.4 per cent of Japan's corporate total) and 950 billion yen (13.6 per cent of Japan's total) for the ten other groups, corresponding to 30 per cent of corporate Japan's

Table 8.1   The six horizontal keiretsu (FY1986)

Group	No. of member companies in presidents' club[a]		No. of employees (in 1000)		Sales (trillion yen)		Current profit (billion yen)	
Mitsubishi	29	(25)	244.0	(204.5)	–	(22.9)	867	(435)
Mitsui	24	(20)	242.0	(212.9)	–	(25.9)	988	(702)
Sumitomo	20	(16)	155.9	(116.7)	–	(18.8)	516	(161)
Fuyo	29	(25)	332.3	(295.7)	–	(26.5)	841	(492)
Sanwa	44	(41)	391.4	(358.0)	–	(27.1)	688	(429)
Daiichi-Kangyo (DKB)	47	(42)	495.1	(449.5)	–	(44.2)	615	(396)
Total[b]	188	(164)	1617.2	(1403.7)	–	(150.5)	4300	(2041)
Japan Total			–	(31,804.3)	–	(1057.3)	–	(21,045)

Notes

[a]   Figures in parentheses exclude banks and insurance companies.

[b]   The sum of the groups does not correspond to totals because some companies (Hitachi, Kobe Steel, Nissho Iwai, etc.) participate in more than one group.

total net profits (FY1982). Expressed as a share of annual sales and as net profits per employee, the *keiretsu* then by far exceed Japan's corporate average. Increased productivity and profitability (particularly pronounced in the Matsushita and Toyota industrial groups) in turn enhance the groups' corporate growth and societal standing.

The figure in Table 8.1 only refer to the 188 core companies as represented in the six presidents' club. If one adds the 12,000 direct subsidiaries and affiliates of these companies, their shares in the Japanese economy, according to FTC data, is increased considerably: they account for 32 per cent of all paid-up capital, 27 per cent of total assets and 25.2 per cent of total sales in FY1987.

HISTORICAL ORIGINS

It is instructive to follow the historical emergence of Mitsui and Mitsubishi, Japan's two leading prewar *zaibatsu*, whose postwar successor conglomerates (*keiretsu*) today directly account for 7 per cent of the turnover and paid-up capital of the Japanese economy.

Mitsubishi is the younger of the two and the more successful competitor. Its current *keiretsu* appears to be more coherent and to have a stronger manufacturing and finance base than its bitter – and originally superior – competitor for all of its corporate existence, the Mitsui Group.

Mitsui was founded in the early seventeenth century by a *samurai* who renounced his nobility to become a merchant and later went into textile trading and money exchange. By the end of the seventeenth century it had become a fiscal agent for the Tokugawa government, a function which Mitsui expanded by becoming the *de facto* monetary authority of Meiji-Japan until the Bank of Japan was set up in 1882. Roberts consequently claims that 'Mitsui is the world's oldest large-scale business enterprise'.[2] This claim could obviously be contested by Sumitomo, which began as a copper refiner in Kyoto in 1590. All other Japanese *zaibatsu* or later *keiretsu* are, however, of more recent origin. Mitsubishi was founded only in 1882.

Yataro Iwasaki, the founder of Mitsubishi, started out as a commercial officer of the Tosa Han (today's Kochi prefecture on Shikoku island). Following the Meiji Restoration he was able to benefit from the privatisation of foreign-induced shipping, shipbuilding and mining interests, which previously had been the public property of this feudal domain.[3]

Mitsui, in turn, was able to purchase cheaply the Miike coal mines in Kyushu, and later became the exclusive government agent for the importation of strategic imports (railway and military equipment, engines, medicines, ships, patents and so on). For this privilege, both Mitsui and Mitsubishi proved their worth to the new Meiji government by supplying essential financial and logistical help to suppress various regional uprisings. Later each went their separate ways to cultivate their political ties.

Mitsubishi maintained close links with the Satsuma clan (originating from what is today Kagoshima prefecture) and with the Democratic Party (*Minseito*). Mitsui in turn cultivated the Choshu clan (of the contemporary Yamaguchi prefecture) and the Liberal Party (*Seiyukai*). Depending on the clan and party in power, their economic fortunes benefited correspondingly. In the mid-1870s, for instance, Mitsubishi's domestic maritime transportation monopoly was approved by the government, and foreign competitors were actively discouraged. Following the privatisation of the coal mines at nominal prices, the government's investments and lands in recently developed Hokkaido were sold off cheaply in the 1880s to the emerging *zaibatsu*. Mitsubishi began its diversification 'from sea to land' by expanding its ship-repair facilities in Nagasaki to become fully fledged shipyards and engine works. Helped by beneficial public orders and profits from mining and shipping, it organised warehousing, banking, marine insurance, trading and railway operations.

Mitsui, which from an early stage capitalised on its support for Japan in the wars with China and Russia, was able to secure an interest in the South Manchurian Railroad and to procure low-priced coal and iron ore from Manchuria and China for its nascent Yahata Steel Works. By 1909 Mitsui had set up a holding company which directly controlled their banking, mining and trading companies. They in turn controlled the manufacturing subsidiaries. Later, separate subsidiaries for shipbuilding, marine insurance (Taisho Marine) and cotton trade (Tomen) were set up, and financial help was extended to a struggling automatic loom-maker – today's Toyota Motors.

Mitsubishi had in 1907 set up a family-controlled holding company, having gradually set up its specialised departments as subsidiaries: a railroad company, a stock-farm   (Koiwai), Mitsubishi Paper, Asahi Glas, Mitsubishi Zosen (shipbuilding), Kirin Beer, Nagasaki Steel Works and so on. By the time Japan's First World War boom ended, Mitsui, Mitsubishi, Sumitomo, Yasuda, Kawasaki and the rest were fully fledged diversified business conglomerates, all tightly controlled by family-owned holdings but effectively managed by a class of professional managers. They were at the same time challenged by the emergence of *nouveau rich* risk-taking entrepreneurs setting up 'new *zaibatsu*', such as Nomura, Hitachi, Nissan and Suzuki Shoten.

Japan's interwar economic depressions brought with them labour unrest and right-wing terrorists who objected to the *zaibatsu* families' feudalist opulence and cosmopolitan lifestyles. Some *zaibatsu* heads, including Takuma Dan of Mitsui, and their political allies were assassinated. The military also disliked the *zaibatsu*'s unpatriotic profiteering and, after the conquest of Manchuria, initially permitted only the aggressive new Nissan *zaibatsu* to invest and to exploit the new protectorate.

Yet as war preparations progressed, even the army realised that it had to rely on Mitsui's trading expertise to exploit China's riches and to manage its requisitioned factories profitably, and that it needed Mitsubishi's heavy and aircraft industry for the production of warships and military aircraft (which finally produced some 17,000 Zero-fighters).

Benefiting from handsome profits from military procurement, colonial exploitation, remunerative crises and wartime cartels, by the late 1930s Japan's eight *zaibatsu* families controlled 50 per cent of the country's financial capital. Yet the capital needed to advance heavy industrialisation forced in particular the Iwasaki of Mitsubishi to issue substantial public stock offers. By 1937 the board of (employed and Iwasaki-appointed) directors of the affiliated companies became Mitsubishi's supreme deci-sion-making body, thus securing postwar cohesion. In contrast, in Mitsui's case, the clan and the family head, Baron Hachiroemon Mitsui, continued their often incompetent personal rule over the conglomerate. By the end of the war, the Iwasaki families held only 48 per cent of their holding company's stock, while the Mitsuis still owned 64 per cent of their (larger) holding.

Holding the *zaibatsu* responsible for Japan's wartime imperialism, in November 1945 the US occupation authorities ordered the 'voluntary' dissolution of the holding companies of the four biggest *zaibatsu*; broke up production monopolies; and with particular thoroughness engaged in the destruction of the *zaibatsu's* general trading companies: Mitsui Bussan and Mitsubishi Shoji were cut up respectively into 140 and 170 new small trading houses.

The *zaibatsu* families and their senior managers also fell under the occupation's general purge that prohibited them from holding any public or managerial office until the conclusion of the San Francisco Peace Treaty of 1951. While the *zaibatsu* families lost most of their assets and manage-ment roles permanently (the less-competent Mitsui more completely than the more resilient Iwasaki, Sumitomo and Yasuda), most of the former *zaibatsu*-affiliated companies quickly regrouped with the revision of the Anti-monopoly Law once Japanese sovereignty was re-established. Mitsubishi Shoji quickly re-emerged, and jointly with Mitsubishi Bank and Mitsubishi Heavy Industries in 1954 established a presidents' council (*kinyo-kai*) of core affiliated companies to co-ordinate policies and to encourage mutual share acquisition, interlocking directorates and joint projects. As a result of their dynamism and cohesion, today the Mitsubishi *keiretsu* is Japan's – and the world's – largest and most successful business conglo-merate.

It took Mitsui Bussan, in contrast, until the late 1950s to reunify. When subsequently reorganising the Mitsui group, together with Mitsui Bank, some of the former affiliate corporations – Toyota, Toshiba, General Sekiyu (oil) and Toshoku (food) – chose to remain separate, aided by the relative weakness of Mitsui Bank which forced them to shop for finance elsewhere.

The Mitsui clan's mismanagement can probably be blamed for allowing Mitsubishi to gain the undisputed top slot in Japan's postwar *keiretsu* system. However, this system, whether horizontally organised around the old *zaibatsu* (Mitsubishi, Mitsui and Sumitomo) or, more loosely, around the new city banks, Fuji Bank (formerly Yasuda), DKB (comprising the former Furukawa, Kawasaki *zaibatsu* and so on) and Sanwa Bank, or vertically around big independent industrial groups (Nippon Steel, Hitachi,

Nissan, Toyota, Matsushita, Toshiba-IHI and so on), has allowed Japan to operate the world's most formidable system of industrial organisation. This system eliminates the need for sizable dividend payments, quarterly return figures, or fears of hostile takeovers. It allows significant captive markets, cheap intragroup finance, labour flexibility and joint strategic long-term planning and the systematic conquest of overseas markets and competitors. Having put this superlative economic machinery into motion is by no means a small achievement for the handful of swordsmen who founded or preserved these empires some 120 years ago, or who, when briefly in positions of government authority, had the foresight to help these nascent businesses to prosper.

With their shareholdings and most other assets expropriated, the *zaibatsu* families were banned by SCAP from holding any managerial function in any of their former (or any other) enterprises. Behind the scenes frantic efforts were undertaken by the *zaibatsu*'s former clans to rescue as much wealth and retain as much influence and group coherence as possible in the adverse circumstances. Such efforts by their loyal retainers were, however, never encouraged by the Mitsui clan head, Baron Hachiroemon.[4] Even before the Pacific War, the Mitsuis active in business were considered an 'average lot'. The infrequent gatherings of Mitsui family heads consisted of 'polite, but none the less spiteful wranglings' about questions of status and power, but rarely about business strategy.[5]

While some of the assets in the postwar era still managed to survive hyperinflation and the clan remained linked by blood and marriage to Japan's social elite, the Mitsui did not succeed in assuming any prominent business positions after the purge (apart from some initial honorary posts for elderly ex-company heads and some residual influence on Mitsui Real Estate). Most family members pursued white-collar or professional careers in the arts or in academia, typical of many upper-middle-class families in Japan.

Other *zaibatsu* families fared better: Iwasaki members held high positions in Mitsubishi Real Estate, Mitsubishi Paper, Asahi Glass and Tokyo Marine and Fire Insurance. Currently, Ikino Iwasaki is chairman of Mitsubishi Plastics, and Tadao Iwasaki is senior advisor to Mitsubishi Monsanto Kasei KK.

The head of the Sumitomo family, Kichizaemon Sumitomo, due to his clan's personal large forestry ownership (strangely, forest property remained unaffected by the land reform) remained one of the richest men in Japan, and headed Sumitomo Real Estate as chairman, a company in which he as the largest shareholder in late 1981 still held 9.7 million shares (or

12 per cent of the total). Hisayoshi Sumitomo currently works as president of Sumitomo Chemical. Motoo Sumitomo is chairman of Sumitomo Precision Products, and Yoshio Sumitomo is auditor to Sumitomo Electric Industries. Hajime Yasuda became chairman of Yasuda Mutual Life Insurance. Members of the Asano, Shibusawa and Okura families also made a comeback to some extent.

The *zaibatsu* dissolution created the illusion of a renaissance of nineteenth-century-style free competition in postwar Japan – the most unlikely object for such an ideological concept (which had proved unattainable even in New Deal America at the height of its trust-busting). More importantly – and lastingly freeing Japan's industry from clan domination – the advent of full managerial control represented a necessary step towards modernisation. As independent enterprises, companies were free to raise the enormous amounts of external capital needed for the heavy and chemical industrialisation of Japan's light industry structure that was predominant in the 1950s. Their greater autonomy subsequently also allowed corporate management more entrepreneurial initiative and faster reactions to events and business opportunities.[6]

With Japan's sovereignty re-established in 1951, rehabilitated former *zaibatsu* managers returned to their previously held management positions. The first revision of the Anti-Monopoly Law also permitted the revival of intercorporate stockholding, the formation of presidents' clubs, the rebuilding of the trading companies, and the promotion of intragroup loans by banks and other financial institutions. The scarcity and heavy regulation of capital enhanced the strength of financial institutions and the importance of ties to *zaibatsu* banks (which had not been subjected to the break-up orders by SCAP). Consequently, the placement of *zaibatsu* bank managers on fellow group members' corporate boards began a postwar tradition of interlocking directorates.

In 1953 the share of intragroup loans for the Mitsui group stood at 36 per cent, for Mitsubishi at 23 per cent and for Sumitomo at 24 per cent.[7] By 1955 ten Mitsubishi bankers were appointed directors to 11 Mitsubishi companies, as were the same number of Mitsui Bank managers to 14 Mitsui group members. In 1957 member financial institutions held the following shares of group member companies: Mitsubishi: 8.5 per cent; Mitsui: 16.7 per cent; Sumitomo: 14.8 per cent. At the same time non-financial group companies owned the following shares in the financial institutions of their member *keiretsu*: Mitsubishi: 10.2 per cent, Mitsui: 5.2 per cent; Sumitomo: 10.5 per cent. During this period, Shibagaki sees the presidents' clubs as exercising 'a sort of collective leadership [which] was formed around the groupings' core bank'.[8] Since 1953 'new' banking *keiretsu* were brought into existence by systematic intragroup loans made available by city banks, which supplemented this strategy by corporate stock holdings and interlocking directorates:

Fuji Bank: (formerly Yasuda Bank), merged the remnants of the Yasuda and Asano zaibatsu (the latter consisting of Nippon Steel Tube and Oki Electric), as well as of Nissan and Hitachi.

Dai-Ichi Kangyo Bank (DKB): gathered the companies belonging to the Furukawa, Kawasaki, Suzuki Shoten (Kobe Steel, Amagasaki Steel, Nissho Trading), Fujiyama (Nitto Chemical, Dai Nippon Sugar), and of the Meiji zaibatsu (Meiji Sugar).

Sanwa Bank: assembled previously independent companies (Nisshin Steel, Sekisui, Teijin, and so on).

KEIRETSU STRUCTURES

Japan's contemporary *keiretsu* structure has evolved into three types: (a) the classical *keiretsu*, cutting horizontally across industries and sectors, which are of direct *zaibatsu* origin: Mitsubishi, Mitsui and Sumitomo; (b) the 'new' city bank orientated horizontal groups: Fuyo (Fuji), DKB and Sanwa, which are of mixed origins; and (c) single-industry vertically organised groups dominated by large independent industrial concerns, which have outgrown the needs of near-exclusive affiliations with city banks or general trading houses: Nippon Steel, Hitachi, Nissan, Toyota, Matsushita, Toshiba-IHI and so on. They are typical of the capital-intensive car, steel and electronic industries, which rely to a great extent on exclusive subcontracting operations in Japan. Sometimes these industrial *keiretsu* remain loosely affiliated with one (or, as in Hitachi's case, with three) horizontal *keiretsu*. There is also a lengthy list of smaller bank- or industry-centred groups and groupings, which have *keiretsu* ambitions but, either through lack of scope or coherence, still have not yet quite made it.

The six major horizontal *keiretsu* engage in an entire spectrum of business activities ranging from manufacturing, finance, insurance, trading, to transport, real estate and services,[9] with the core companies liaising closely with each other. Banks and general trading companies are usually central to this organising function. While traditionally *keiretsu* presence was (and remains) dominant in the heavy and chemical industries, today most groups prominently feature joint investments and R&D activities in the new future-orientated industries.

Table 8.2   Cross shareholdings among Mitsubishi core companies

Shareholders:	M. Bank	Tokyo Marine & Fire Insurance (%)	M. Shoji	M. H. Industries	M. Trust
M. Bank		4.8	4.9	3.6	3.1
Tokyo Marine & Fire	4.3		6.0	2.0	1.9
M. Shoji	1.7	2.3		1.5	3.1
M. H. Indus	3.0	1.8	3.1		2.7
M. Trust	1.7	3.3	5.4	6.7	
Meiji Life Ins.	5.6	4.5	5.7	3.0	4.8

M. = Mitsubishi

Among the six major *keiretsu* the ratio of crossholdings of shares by fellow group companies was stronger among the ex-*zaibatsu* groups than among the city bank groups: Sumitomo 21.4 per cent; Mitsubishi 20.0 per cent; Mitsui 17.4 per cent; Fuyo 16.2 per cent; DKB 14.6 per cent; and Sanwa 13.5 per cent (FY1982). Table 8.2 gives breakdown of crossholdings among major Mitsubishi firms (as of September 1990).[10]

PRESIDENTIAL COUNCILS

During 1951–78 the presidential councils (*shacho kai*) were set up for each *keiretsu* (see Table 8.3). The presidents of core-group companies can take part in discussions and vote (if ever) as equal partners. They usually meet once each month to discuss the macroeconomic situation, the groups' financial outlook, progress in R&D, the maintenance of group trade marks and company names, labour problems, joint investments in new industries, political donations, PR activities, top personnel appointments and rehabilitation programmes for troubled member companies.

Minutes of these meetings have never been disclosed. Officially the councils are being downplayed as if they were mere social events to foster friendship between the presidents. Takeshi Nagano, president of the newly merged Mitsubishi Metal and Mitsubishi Mining & Cement, in 1990 told the *Financial Times*, when asked about his views on the US request to make public the minutes of the *shacho-kai*, that these minutes would make uninteresting reading: 'The fact is that we hold a very small amount of stock in each other. We don't have any obligations to each other. There is no

Table 8.3   Keiretsu presidential councils

Group	Name	Number of members
Mitsubishi	*Kinyo-kai* (Friday Society)	29
Mitsui	*Nimoku-kai* (Second-Thursday Society)	24
Sumitomo	*Hakusui-kai* (Whitewater Society)	21
DKB	*Sankin-kai*	45
subgroups	Furukawa *Sansuikai*	41
	Kawasaki *Mutsumikai*	4
	Jugosha Shachokai	15
Sanwa	*Sansui Kai*	42
Fuyo	*Fuyokai*	29

contract. If someone wanted to take over a Mitsubishi company, then we would help. A *keirestsu* is a good thing.'[11] Yet it is difficult to imagine that some 30 highly paid executives would waste half a working day each month to discuss trivia.

PERSONNEL POLICY

At senior management level, personnel exchange exists as a means of strengthening group cohesion. Sending senior personnel to supervise affiliated subsidiaries serves to exercise effective control. In some groups the *shacho-kai* is influential in appointing personnel to top ranking positions.[12] Among the 4726 representative directors of all listed companies 245 were sent from city banks and 84 from general trading companies. This compares with 155 *amakudari* executives from the central ministries and the BOJ and 54 from Japan's public corporations (including JR and NTT, since privatised), who have successfully reached these executive levels during their secondary careers. At director level, out of a total of 30,192 directors in all listed companies, 1066 were of city bank origin and 427 hailed from *sogo shosha*. In comparison, the number of *amakudari* directors from the central ministries and the BOJ (535) and from the public corporations (421) was again smaller.

JOINT INVESTMENTS

Initially most of the six major *keiretsu* undertook group ventures into nuclear energy development. In the 1970s and 1980s this was followed by group projects in information processing, real-estate development, ocean prospecting and oil exploration. Typically the *sogo shosha* played a driving force in these ventures, in which also large semi-dependent vertical industrial groups took part within their respective *keiretsu* affiliation (Toshiba with Mitsui, Hitachi with Fuyo, and so on).

THE INDIVIDUAL *KEIRETSU*

The Mitsubishi *Keiretsu*

The group is organised around three core companies: Mitsubishi Bank, Mitsubishi Shoji and Mitsubishi Heavy Industries (MHI). The *shacho-kai* (*Kinyo kai*) meeting on the second Friday each month is attended by the presidents of an inner group of 29 Mitsubishi companies (Table 8.4) with 244,000 employees. The group in total comprises some 150 major companies (excluding affiliates and subsidiaries). Excluding financial institutions, the 25 core Mitsubishi industrial and service enterprises accounted for 7.9 per cent of Japanese industries' total listed assets. The full group of 150 Mitsubishi affiliated companies account for 12.7 per cent. In terms of sales, their respective shares stood at 9.2 per cent and 14.2 per cent[13] among Japanese industrial companies listed on the stock exchange, thus making Mitsubishi the foremost industrial organisation in Japan (and in the world).

The group's main focus is on heavy and chemical industries, yet the comprehensiveness of sectoral coverage of member companies indicates a great potential for vertically integrated group operations: From cotton spinning and synthetic fibre production to finished fabrics and clothing to textile wholesalers and department stores. Equally impressive also is the comprehensive array of in-group business services available: banking, insurance, leasing, marketing, construction, real-estate development, transportation, warehousing, data processing and so on. Still, some Mitsubishi companies, including Mitsubishi Shoji and MHI through subsidiaries maintain subgroups under their own control within the entire group. For instance, MHI subsidiaries are M. Steel Mfg, Mitsubishi Motors and Toyo Engineering. Two semi-independent subgroups are also linked with the Mitsubishi *keiretsu*: the Morimura group, focusing on ceramic products (including Noritake, Toko, NGK Insulators, Inax, and so on) and Shimadzu (leading makers of precision and scientific equipment).

Due to their continued reliance on heavy and chemical industries, and as mature industries have low growth and profit prospects, the Mitsubishi companies face an image and profitability problem. Employees' salaries are

Table 8.4   Mitsubishi Group companies

Banking	Mitsubishi Bank
	Mitsubishi Trust and Banking
Insurance	Tokyo Marine and Fire Insurance
Trading & commerce	Mitsubishi Corp.
Food	Kirin Brewery
Fibres & textiles	Mitsubishi Rayon
Pulp & paper	Mitsubishi Paper Mills
Chemicals	Mitsubishi Chemical Industries
	Mitsubishi Petrochemical
	Mitsubishi Gas Chemical
	Mitsubishi Plastics Industries
	Dai Nippon Toryo
Petroleum products	Mitsubishi Oil
Glass/cement	Asahi Glass
	Mitsubishi Mining & Cement
Iron & steel	Mitsubishi Steel Mfg.
Non-ferrous metals	Mitsubishi Metal
	Dainichi-Nippon Cables
Machinery – general	Mitsubishi Kakoki
	Toyo Engineering Works
Electrical & electronics	Mitsubishi Electric
Transportation machinery	Mitsubishi Heavy Industries
	Mitsubishi Motors
Optical instruments	Nippon Kogaku
Marine transportation	Nippon Yusen
Real estate	Mitsubishi Estate
Warehousing	Mitsubishi Warehouse & Transportation
Construction	Mitsubishi Construction
Service	Mitsubishi Research Institute

lower than for financial institutions. In addition, a conservative management style and a staid image (including the practice of sending young MHI recruits to SDF bootcamps for weeks), hence serve to deter able university graduates from joining the Mitsubishi *keiretsu*.[14]

Efforts at modernisation and internationalisation are, however, feared to weaken Mitsubishi's legendary cohesion. The gradual retirement of company presidents who began their careers in the *zaibatsu* structure and their replacement by the postwar genration who joined independent companies may possibly have a more centripetal effect. Still, their *keiretsu* organisation has brought the Mitsubishi companies advantages more tangible than a sentimental get-together for their superannuated chiefs. In the immediate postwar period it brought protection for the undercapitalised, dismantled enterprises against hostile takeovers. Japan's high growth period after 1955 saw a wide range of public support (import protection, cheap credits, low-cost industrial site developments, preferential taxation, and so on) for those companies which, like Mitsubishi, were geared towards heavy and chemical industries. In fact, Mitsubishi has always identified with the national interest, as is evident in Koyata Iwasaki's impassioned defence of Mitsubishi in 1945. In 1934 he established three main guidelines as the corporate motto, the first of which was '*shoki hoko*' (promote the national interest). Iwasaki's motto remains valid today, and is framed in most Mitsubishi offices, but its English translation has been rendered more acceptable to a foreign audience as 'corporate responsibility to society'.

The Mitsubishi group at an early stage felt confident enough to enter into joint ventures with overseas partners. Its first ventures were into oil trading (with Tidewater/Getty Oil), petrochemicals (Shell), power generation machinery (Westinghouse), cars (Chrysler). More recently a cooperation agreement with Daimler of Germany, was concluded. Mitsubishi, as Japan's strongest *keiretsu*, can rightly feel confident in its organisation and in the quality of the staff which (until very recently at least) it has been able to attract. If Mitsui is considered to be strong in able individuals, Mitsubishi's forte is perceived to lie in teamwork and in harmonious group decisions. This also applies to the *Kinyokai*, whose function it is to ensure continued cohesion through mediation and final decision-making.[15]

For operational reasons the *Kinyokai* has appointed ten advisors from its number. Two of them serve as representative manager and as co-manager respectively. They operate as the effective spokesmen of the *Kinyokai*, and hence of the Mitsubishi *keiretsu*.

Member companies of the *Kinyokai* on average hold 24 per cent of each others' shares (compared to 15 per cent of mutually held shares at Mitsui). The sense of group solidarity and of shared business objectives permeates the employees' ranks. At the symbolic level, Mitsubishi men will own Mitsubishi Motors' cars and drink Kirin beer only. Intragroup preferences enable tax advantages and strategic pricing options through suitable in-house transfer pricing. For Mitsubishi Shoji, importing raw materials and Mitsubishi producers of base and semi-finished materials for industrial use, in-house downstream companies offer a stable and foreseeable outlet. Member companies with excess labour in mining, shipbuilding and so on can offer alternative employment opportunities to their redundant work force within the group. Also if there are potential financial corporate problems, fulltime mainstream employees can rest assured that the group will eventually bail out the troubled company, and this contributes to an overall sense of job security and group identification. The latter is facilitated by the fact that the Mitsubishi *keiretsu* ranks indisputably first in Japan's corporate group hierarchy. Corporate unions seem to share this presumably pervasive employee identification: at Mitsubishi there have been hardly any major labour problems in the postwar years.

Mitsui

The Mitsui *keiretsu* is headed by three companies: Mitsui Bussan, Mitsui Bank (today's Mitsui Taiyo Kobe Bank – the future Sakura Bank) and Mitsui Real Estate Development. Its presidential council (Nimoku-kai – Second-Thursday Society) is composed of 29 group companies (see Table 8.5). The total number of official Mitsui *keiretsu* enterprises comprises 110 companies. Executive directors of 66 of these companies form a *getsuyo-kai* (Monday Society). Similar to Mitsubishi and Sumitomo, the Mitsui *keiretsu* covers a wide range of economic sectors, but it remains relatively weak in heavy industries and in banking.

After the postwar dissolution of the Mitsui *zaibatsu*, only very gradually did formerly Mitsui-affiliated companies return to the fold, sometimes only tentatively (Oji Paper, Toshiba, and Mitsukoshi in 1973; Toyota in 1974; Onoda Cement in 1980; and General Sekiyu (oil) and Toshoku (foodstuffs) in the early 1980s) with Tomen at the same time becoming a leading member of the merging Tokai Group (and Toshiba and Toyota running their own semi-autonomous groups). Also Mitsui OSK Lines, created in 1964 as a government-sponsored merger of the previous Mitsui Steamship and Osaka Shosen Kaisha (a Sumitomo group company), has shared loyalties to both groups. The lack of cohesion of the postwar Mitsui group was caused by Mitsui Bussan's delayed merger (in 1959) and its subsequent internal management problems, and by the Mitsui Bank's small capital base, which forced ex-Mitsui *zaibatsu* companies to shop for credit elsewhere and to develop new loyalties. In particular, this applied to Asahi Breweries and Sapporo Breweries, which were successor companies to the prewar Dai Nippon Breweries of the Mitsui *zaibatsu*. After their credit request had been turned down by the Mitsui Bank, they turned to the Sumitomo and to the Fuyo *keiretsu* instead.

Table 8.5   *Mitsui Group companies*

Banking	Mitsui Bank Mitsui Trust & Banking
Insurance	Taisho Marine & Fire Insurance
Trading & commerce	Mitsui & Co. Toyo Menka (also in Tokai Group) Toshoku Ltd Mitsukoshi Ltd
Mining	Mitsui Mining
Construction	Mitsui Construction Toyo Engineering
Food	Nippon Flour Mills Mitsui Sugar
Fibres & textiles	Toray Industries
Pulp & paper	Oji Paper
Chemicals	Mitsui Toatsu Chemicals Mitsui Petrochemical Industries Daicel Chemical Industries
Petroleum and coal products	General Sekiyu
Glass/cement/ceramics	Onoda Cement
Iron & steel	Japan Steel Works
Non-ferrous metals	Mitsui Mining & Smelting
Electrical & electronics	Toshiba Corp. (also in Toshiba-IHI Group)
Transportation machinery	Mitsui Engineering & Shipbuilding Toyota Motor (also in Toyota Group) Ishikawajima Harima Heavy Industries (also in Toshiba-IHI Group)
Real estate	Mitsui Real Estate Development
Marine transportation	Mitsui OSK Lines (also in Sumitomo Group)
Warehousing & transportation- related business	Mitsui Warehouse Mitsui Wharf

Figures for interlocking stockholding among Mitsui companies are relatively low at 15 per cent, as is the ratio for internal financing from affiliated financial institutions (18 per cent). Sometimes management links between *keiretsu* companies are personal: the president of Nippon Flour Mills, Toshiyuki Yahiro, is the younger brother of Tohikuni Yahiro, ex-president (and current senior advisor to the board) of Mitsui Bussan.

None the less Mitsui Bussan and Mitsui Bank have found it rewarding to sacrifice management time, capital and efforts generously to the rebuilding of the *keiretsu*, although one of the group's most prominent joint foreign investment projects, the Bander Khomeini petrochemical complex, turned out to be a disastrous flop.

Mitsui Bank as fund raiser and Mitsui Bussan as distributor are exercising crucial roles for the group, which in turn determines their own growth and corporate standing in the Japanese economy. Mr Goro Koyama, then Chairman of the Mitsui Bank, explained the group's rationale:

In order to rebuild the Japanese economy from the ashes of World War II, it was necessary to somehow put together considerable amounts of capital. As capital is a very timid creature, however, it gravitates only to the safest places. We, therefore, had to deal primarily with those whom we knew very well and whom we could whole-heartedly trust. The *Nimokukai*, therefore, is a group of close friends. The *Nimokukai* is the place where Mitsui group companies can take up a variety of common problems and try to jointly solve system to their mutual satisfaction as well as to cooperate with one another in a wide range of fields. If the *Nimokukai* were a mere salon, no Mitsui executive would spare his precious time and attend it regularly.[16]

Former Mitsui Real Estate chairman, Hideo Edo, seconded this view with an added motive for the Mitsui group's re-emergence: 'As long as Mitsubishi and Sumitomo steadily consolidated themselves as groups, someone in the Mitsui group would sooner or later have been forced to take similar steps to those we took.'[17] In the absence of a *keiretsu* organisation, obviously Mitsui's financial institutions, the trading company and the other service companies (such as real estate, warehousing, marine transportation, industrial insurances, would lose their 'natural' corporate clientele.

With the merger of Mitsui Bank and Taiyo Kobe Bank in April 1990, aiming at the 'survival of the fattest',[18] 50 per cent of all senior management positions were occupied by former Taiyo Kobe managers, who have no affinity or previous affiliation with the Mitsui group. Although the Bank's organigram shows a network planning division in its planning headquarters, which presumably deals with *keiretsu* matters, only 14 of the 22 members of the Bank's senior advisory council are from Mitsui companies. Among the ten largest shareholders five Mitsui *keiretsu* companies are left, accounting for a mere 9.1 per cent of total stockholding. Mitsui traditionalists appear worried about the Bank's forthcoming renaming as the stylish and ahistorical Sakura Bank.

Some industrial manufacturers such as Toyota or Toshiba, have gown into (Japanese-style) multinationals, which allows them to organise their own exports, overseas investments, and the direct sourcing of parts through their affiliated subsidiaries. They are so profitable that they are able to finance their investments from their own cash flow, so the old-style horizontal *keiretsu* have outgrown most of their economic usefulness. Their size and profitability has permitted them to set up their own vertical *keiretsu*, so that membership in the larger horizontal *keiretsu*, such as Mitsui's, becomes more or less nominal.

Sumitomo

The core of the Sumitomo *keiretsu* consists of 21 companies (Table 8.6) whose executives at three levels meet regularly: presidents (*hakusui-kai*), chairmen and advisors (*hakusen-kai*) and executive directors (*itsuka-kai*)/

While this traditionally Osaka/Kansai-based and heavy industry-orientated group boasts a financial and organisational cohesion similar to Mitsubishi, it was handicapped originally by the weakness of its *sogo shosha*, the Sumitomo Corporation, which was set up only in the postwar era. For most of the 1950s and 1960s, the *keiretsu* hence had to rely on C. Itoh as a general trader, until Sumitomo Corp. was able to generate sufficient strength to take over. In response, C. Itoh shifted gradually a *keiretsu* core function with the Dai-ichi Kangyo Bank group. However, among the three leading companies of the Sumitomo *keiretsu*, the Sumitomo *sogo shosha* remains conspicuously absent. It is the Sumitomo Bank, Sumitomo Chemical and Sumitomo Metal which play this organisational key role.

With its traditional focus on heavy and chemical manufacturing, the group's four financial corporations – Sumitomo Bank, Sumitomo Trust & Banking, Sumitomo Mutual Life Insurance, and Sumitomo Marine & Fire Insurance – had ample opportunity to bail out and restructure ailing member-industries (aluminium smelting, copper operations, coal mining, shipbuilding, and so on). More recently Itoman, a textile and meat trader, with

Table 8.6 Sumitomo Group companies

Banking	Sumitomo Bank Sumitomo Trust & Banking
Insurance	Sumitomo Mutual Life Insurance Sumitomo Marine and Fire Insurance
Trading & commerce	Sumitomo Corp.
Forestry	Sumitomo Forestry
Mining	Sumitomo Coal Mining
Construction	Sumitomo Construction
Chemicals	Sumitomo Chemical Sumitomo Bakelite
Glass/cement	Nippon Sheet Glass Sumitomo Cement
Iron & steel	Sumitomo Metal Industries
Non-ferrous metals	Sumitomo Metal Mining Sumitomo Electric Industries Sumitomo Light Metal Industries Sumitomo Aluminium Smelting
Machinery	Sumitomo Heavy Industries
Electrical & electronics	NEC Corp.
Real estate	Sumitomo Realty & Development
Warehousing	Sumitomo Warehouse

the generous support of Sumitomo Bank, ventured massively into real estate speculation and golf course development. In 1990 the bubble burst, leaving 700 billion yen of bad debts and forcing Sumitomo Bank president Ichiro Isoda to resign in disgrace in October 1990. However, in 1981 Mr Isoda asserted of his bank: 'We are always prepared to help out whenever group companies are in trouble. We won't allow any group member companies to fail.'[19]

While finance proved to have a cohesive effect, joint large-scale development projects undertaken at home and abroad (especially in South-east Asia), often with a steering role supplied by Sumitomo Corporation, further increased intragroup collaboration. As a result, mutual stockholdings, intramural financing and interlocking directorships actually intensified over time.

Mr Isoda, when still in office with Sumitomo Bank, reinforced the hierarchically supreme function of the *Hakusuikai*, the presidents club, over the more formal and august chairmen's club:

> At the time of the *Hakusuikai*'s start in the immediate postwar years, presidents were at the very top of the corporate hierarchy. They did not have to worry about others' reactions to their decisions. When such powerful presidents became chairmen in their turn, the succeeding presidents apparently had to put in extra effort to keep the *Hakusuikai* functioning as the group's supreme decision-making organ.
>
> When I myself joined the intragroup association, I remember often going out of my way to remind other members that they were making the group's final decisions and that they could not take back their words even if they faced opposition in their own companies.[20]

Fuyo

The Fuyo group is managed conjointly by Fuji Bank (the prewar Yasuda Bank) and Marubeni Corporation as the general trading company. The Fuyo *keiretsu* has 29 core members (Table 8.7) constituting the presidents' council, the *Fuyo-kai*, and encompasses some 130 companies in total. Some days before the *Fuyo-kai* meetings, the vice-presidents (*Fuji kai*) and directors of the planning departments (*Fusui kai*) of the 29 meet in order to prepare the agenda for decision-making. Also the heads of the general affairs departments of the same core companies meet once a month. Being a relatively loosely structured 'banking *keiretsu*', the group, unlike other *keiretsu*, has no presiding executive and no formally designated secretariat (these functions *de facto* are exercised by the Fuji Bank). Originally a conglomerate of members of the prewar Yasuda, Asano and Okura *zaibatsu*, the Fuyo group in the early 1960s was enlarged by a series of independent businesses (such as Nissan and Hitachi, who form vertical *keiretsu* of their own), with the core group being restricted to one company for each business category (a restriction which was intended to enhance group cohesion). For the second-tier members no such restriction applies.

While Fuji Bank served as a main banker to the group, Marubeni until 1982 claimed that its business with group members amounted to only 9 per cent of its total sales and saw scope for growth, particularly in supplies of raw materials to the *keiretsu*.[21]

Table 8.7 Fuyo Group companies

Banking	Fuji Bank
	Yasuda Trust & Banking
Insurance	Yasuda Mutual Life Insurance
	Yasuda Fire & Marine Insurance
Trading & commerce	Marubeni Corp.
Construction	Taisei Corp.
Food	Nisshin Flour Milling
	Sapporo Breweries
	Nippon Reizo
Fibres & textiles	Nisshin Spinning
	Toho Rayon
Pulp & paper	Sanyo-Kokusaku Pulp
Chemicals	Showa Denko
	Nippon Oil & Fats
	Kureha Chemical Industry
Petroleum & coal products	Toa Nenryo Kogyo
Cement	Nihon Cement
Iron & steel	Nippon Kokan
General machinery	Kubota Ltd
	Nippon Seiko
Electrical & electronics	Hitachi, Ltd (also in Hitachi Group)
	Oki Electric Industry
	Yokogawa Hokushin Electric Corp.
Automobiles	Nissan Motor (also in Nissan Group)
Optical instruments	Canon Inc.
Real estate	Tokyo Tatemono
Land transportation	Keihin Electric Express Railway
	Tobu Railway
Marine transportation	Showa Line

DKB

In 1971 the Dai-Ichi Bank and the Nippon Kangyo Bank merged to form
Japan's largest bank, the Dai-Ichi Kangyo Bank (DKB). It took DKB years

to digest this merger, and its *keiretsu* remained a collection of sub-*keiretsu* which were cohesive in themselves but together remained a grouping of the 'loosely attached and free', brought together only by their individual financial ties to DKB and by the usual PR group gimmicks (logos, group journals, joint exhibits and so on) rather than by shared and synergic business interests and traditions.

The major subgroups – similar to the Fuyo group – derived from separate smaller prewar *zaibatsu*: Furukawa (consisting of Furukawa Co., a non ferrous metals maker, Furukawa Electric, Fuji Electric, Fujitsu, Nippon Light Metal, Yokohama Rubber and Nippon Zeon, a synthetic rubber maker) and Kawasaki (Kawasaki Steel, Kawasaki Heavy Industries and Kawasho Corporation, their trading company). As mentioned earlier, C. Itoh (formerly of the Sumitomo *keiretsu*) has increasingly become the DKB's major general trading company (thereby displacing Nissho Iwai). However, Kanematsu Gosho, which specialise in textiles, metals and machinery trading, services as a complementary *sogo shosha*. Yet another subgroup of the DKB *keiretsu* consists of 14 companies which maintained close credit relations to the previous Nippon Kangyo Bank, forming the *Jugosha Shachokai* (the 15 Company Presidents' Club). The Furukawa and Kawasaki subgroup equally kept their separate presidential councils.

The DKB group as a whole also contains a number of major independent companies, such as Hitachi, IHI, Nissho Iwai, Kobe Steel, and the smallish Meiji group (Meiji Seika and Meiji Milk Products). In total, 41 companies form the core *Sankin-kai* of the DKB *keiretsu* (Table 8.8). The *Sankin-kai* (Third-Friday Conference) of company presidents meets four times a year on the third Friday of January, April, July and October. Its main characteristic ten years after its set-up seemed to be little more than the conviviality of the meetings.[22]

The DKB *keiretsu* has among its members competitors in such important areas as trading, steel and insurance. This is also evident from the list of core members in Table 8.8. The *Sankin-kai*'s secretariat is situated in the DKB, with other group companies, including C. Itoh, seconding staff members for the tasks of formal co-ordination and joint action. Mr Shuzo Muramoto, ex-president of DKB, described his *keiretsu*'s *raison d'être* as follows:

As you know, we have in Japan two distinct kinds of business groups. There are on the one hand what might be called the *zaibatsu*-related groups that are solidly united in pursuit of a definite purpose, with no duplication in business category, and functioning much in the manner imagined to be that of 'Japan Inc.' The other type is like ours, an assemblage resulting not from any desire to form a group of similarly

Table 8.8 DKB Group companies

Banking & insurance	Dai-Ichi Kangyo Bank
	Nissan Fire & Marine Insurance
Security brokerage	Nippon Kangyo Kakumaru Securities
Trading & commerce	C. Itoh & Co.
	Nissho Iwai Corp. (also in Sanwa Group)
	Kanematsu-Gosho
	Kawasho Corp.
Construction	Shimizu Construction
Fibres & textiles	Asahi Chemical Industry
Pulp & paper	Honshu Paper (also in Mitsui Group)
Chemicals	Denki Kagaku Kogyo (also in Mitsui Group)
	Nippon Zeon
	Asahi Denka Kogyo
	Sankyo Co.
	Shiseido Co.
	Lion Corp.
Petroleum products	Showa Oil
Rubber products	Yokohama Rubber
Cement	Chichibu Cement
Iron & steel	Kawasaki Steel
	Kobe Steel (also in Sanwa Group)
	Japan Metals & Chemicals (also in Nippon Steel Group)
Non-ferrous metals	Nippon Light Metal
	Furukawa Co.
	Furukawa Electric
General machinery	Niigata Engineering
	Iseki & Co.
	Ebara Corp.
Electrical & electronics	Hitachi, Ltd (also in Hitachi Group)
	Fuji Electric
	Yaskawa Electric Mfg
	Fujitsu Limited
	Nippon Columbia (also in Hitachi Group)

Table 8.8 (cont'd)   DKB Group companies

Transportation machinery	Kawasaki Heavy Industries
	Ishikawajima-Harima Heavy Industries (also in Toshiba-IHI Group)
	Isuzu Motors
Optical instruments	Asahi Optical
Land transportation	Nippon Express
Marine transportation	Kawasaki Kisen
Warehousing	Shibusawa Warehouse
Service industry	Korakuen Co.

motivated businesses but engendered by the shared experience of being served by the same bank, the aim being to promote mutually cordial relations and access to profitable opportunities, to encourage exchange of information, and to facilitate the undertaking of projects beyond the capability of any single business, all on an equal footing with the older tightly united groups. Our approach is rather that of a federation.[23]

Seiki Tozaki, then president of C. Itoh, backed this up: 'It is our belief that close internal unity and the exclusion of outsiders do not make the right pattern for a viable and effective group of businesses.' We can deduce how the operations of the former *zaibatsu keiretsu* and of the cohesive Fuyo group appear to fellow executives.

Sanwa

It was only in 1967 that the Sanwa *keiretsu* was organised, when the *Kansai*-based Sanwa Bank set up the *Sansui kai* (Third-Wednesday Society), composed of the presidents of the 42 group companies (Table 8.9). For the discussion of more concrete joint projects, the executive directors of the 42 met as *Clover kai* to prepare decisions for the *Sansui kai*. For PR and welfare purposes a third institution, the *Midori kai*, has been set up. Similar to the DKB *keiretsu*, the Sanwa Group is a fairly loose grouping, without even the advantages of close subgroup cohesion, as is evident in the DKB's Kawasaki *Mutsumi-kai* and Furukawa *Sansui kai*. Again we find ample competitors within the group as in life insurance, general trading, construction, pharmaceuticals, textiles, steel, electrical appliances, which is indicative of weak *keiretsu* cohesion. Hitachi, for instance, finds it worth-

Table 8.9   Sanwa Group companies

Banking	Sanwa Bank
	Toyo Trust and Banking
Finance	Orient Leasing
Trading & commerce	Nissho Iwai Corp.
	Nichimen Corp.
	Iwatani & Co.
	Takashimaya Co.
Construction	Toyo Construction
	Ohbayashi-Gumi
	Sekisui House
Food	Ito Ham Foods
	Suntory Ltd
Fibres & textiles	Teijin Ltd
	Unitika Ltd
Chemicals	Ube Industries
	Tokuyama Soda
	Sekisui Chemical
	Kansai Paint
	Tanabe Seiyaku
	Fujisawa Pharmaceutical
Petroleum products	Maruzen Oil
Rubber products	Toyo Tyre & Rubber
Cement	Osaka Cement
Iron & steel	Kobe Steel
	Nakayama Steel Work
	Nisshin Steel (also in Nippon Steel Group)
General machinery	Toyo Umpanki
	Tsukishima Kikai
	NTN Toyo Bearing
Electrical & electronics	Hitachi (also in Hitachi Group)
	Iwatsu Electric
	Sharp Corp.
	Nitto Electric Industrial
	Kyocera Corp.

Table 8.9 (cont'd)   Sanwa Group companies

Transportation machinery	Hitachi Zosen Corp.
	Daihatsu Motor (also in Toyota Group)
	Nippon Express (also in DKB Group)
	Hankyu Corp. (also in Hankyu-Toho Group)
	Nankai Electric Railway
Marine transportation	Yamashita-Shinnihon Steamship
Warehousing & transportation	Nissin Transportation & Warehousing
Service industry	Midori-Kai

while not only to form its own vertical *keiretsu* but also to be part of the *Fuyo kai*, of DKB's *Sankin kai* and of Sanwa's *Sansui kai* as well. Apparently Hitachi presidents have plenty of time to spare for convivial get-togethers.

The Sanwa Bank itself is the result of a 1933 merger of three Osaka retail banks (the 34th Bank, the Yamaguchi Bank and the Konoike Bank) which in the 1960s, in order to address its shortcomings in corporate finance, began to assemble and purchase equity of other independent Kansai companies (to the extent that they were not already in the Sumitomo camp). Still, with a share of only some 14 per cent mutual stockholding, mutual financial links remain relatively weak. Apparently there are also no interlocking directorships in the Sanwa Group. The Sanwa Bank's annual report for 1990 mentions only good corporate citizenship (public tree-planting, international scholarships and cultural exhibitions) as worthwhile activities of its *Midori kai* – which, by coincidence, is very much in line with the *keiretsu*'s law-profile policy subsequent to the US's SII attack of 1989–91.

Previously, Sanwa Bank chairman Kenji Kawakatsu had pushed his group to imitate the Mitsubishi *keiretsu*'s 'Buy Mitsubishi' policy:

As part of our good partnership policy, our bank has initiated a highly successful campaign to promote sales of Suntory beer and whiskies among Sanwa group member companies. Suntory's shares of the market have increased significantly in the areas where our bank's offices are located. My favourite restaurants also have come to always stock Suntory beer and whiskies. Many of Sanwa group companies, moreover, have switched to Suntory beer and whiskies as a result of our 'Drink Suntory' campaigns ... Suntory, for its part, urged its employees to deposit their summer allowances with Sanwa Bank and the campaign also proved to be a big success. This type of mutually beneficial accommodation and exchange of territories, managerial knowhow and clients is what we call good partnership, a true way of attaining maximum co-prosperity.[24]

Also 'Our bank, moreover, uses only Hitachi-built computers and our on-line system is operating in close co-operation with Hitachi Ltd. Mutual confidence in each other over this closely knit relationship ought to be exceptionally high.' Former chairman Takao Nagato of Hitachi Zosen explained some further relevant functions of this loose *keiretsu*, as seen from his corporate vantage point:

> Shipbuilders are naturally required to have close relationships with shipping companies. By joining the Sanwa group, we have been enabled to get ship orders from such traditional Sanwa affiliates as Yamashita-Shinnihon Steamship and Taiyo Kaiun Kaisha. Conversely, our company pulled Yamashita Steamship away from the group headed by Dai-Ichi Kangyo Bank and made it join the Sanwa group instead. Maruzen Oil, on the other hand, started placing tanker orders with our company, instead of Mitsubishi, when we joined the Sanwa group. Even in the field of land machinery, we, through our joining the Sanwa group, have come to have close relations with Ube Industries and other leading Sanwa group companies. In the time of the shipbuilding industry slump, from which our company suffered seriously, we were able to temporarily relocate our surplus personnel in such Sanwa group companies as Hitachi, Daihatsu Motor and Shin Meiwa Industry.[25]

Also, '[Sanwa] Bank, for example, is making loans to Ube Industry so that the latter can place orders with our company.' Mr Nagato further observed: 'It is a well known fact that presidents' meetings of an industrial group rarely lead to actual intragroup transactions, although they are certain to foster friendship among the participating presidents. Meetings of managing directors etc. in charge of sales and supplies, on the other hand, are highly likely to result in intragroup transactions. Regular meetings of managing-director-class people are highly recommended for bolstering intragroup solidarity.'

In addition to the six major *keiretsu*, regularly surveyed by the Fair Trade Commission with a series of unchanged and increasingly meaningless indicators, there are two more intersectoral corporate groupings (Tokai and IBJ) and eight vertical industry groups (Nippon Steel, Hitachi, Nissan, Toyota, Matsushita, Toshiba-IHI, Tokyu and Seibu, as well as a series of smaller bank- or industry-centred groups (Hankyo/Toho, Kintetsu, Daiwa/ Nomura, Kyowa-Saitama Bank, Tobu, and so on).

Tokai Bank, together with Toyo Menka as a general trading company, attempts to assemble Nagoya-area-based businesses for its five company-strong *Satsuki-kai*, the presidents' club, and for its 23-member *Wakaba kai*, the executive directors' club.

The *Industrial Bank of Japan* (IBJ), while not maintaining a formal presidents' club, has in fact organised close long-term financial links with key businesses in Japan's heavy and chemical industry. In these industries IBJ has strong managerial influence through personal appointments, loan policies, financial rehabilitation, as well as through organising joint communication, research and overseas investment projects.

Nippon Steel, Japan's largest steel maker, which was created in 1973 through the merger of Yahata and Fuji Iron & Steel, controls some 180 companies which deal with steel processing and related activities (downstream processing or services). Control is exercised through shareholding and key personnel appointments.

Hitachi, a prewar Nissan *zaibatsu* company, in its postwar strategy followed an active policy of creating its own corporate empire by spinning off subsidiaries, which are mostly subcontractors, diversified end-users or lending services, to this largest manufacturer of electronics and electrical equipment in Japan. Hitachi through shareholdings and senior management appointments maintain a controlling interest in its *keiretsu*.

Nissan's group member companies are closely linked to the core company's automotive interests: producing cars, car parts or organising their marketing. Fuji Heavy Industries, with its manufacture of Subaru cars and Nissan Diesel as a truck-maker, forms part of the Nissan *keiretsu*. Nissan successively increased its financial control over these companies and placed senior management into leading positions in affiliated companies. When it encounters resistance (as in the case of Ichikoh, a rear-mirror maker in 1991) it showed little hesitation in throwing out the old family management and replacing it with its own men.

Toyota remains a conglomerate controlled by the Toyoda family. Most of the subsidiaries were in fact spinn-offs of Toyota Motors or of the older Toyoda Automatic Loom Works, covering, besides automotive parts, steel, precision machinery, textiles, household products, housing units and so on. Since the mid 1960s, however, Toyota has also acquired controlling interests in Daihatsu Motor and in Hino Motors, a leading truck-maker.

Matsushita Electric has a controlling interest in about 25 major companies, mainly specialised electronics and electrical appliance makers, spin-offs from the core company, which is still controlled by the family of the founder, the late Konosuke Matsushita.

Toshiba-IHI (Toshiba and Ishikawajima-Harima Heavy Industries) are members of two different *keiretsu* (Mitsui and DKB respectively). Both maintain diversified groups of affiliated subsidiary companies of their own which focus on the groups' respective core businesses (electronics and electrical machinery, and shipbuilding and heavy industrial machinery). Yet both groups have decided to team up through crossholding shares, interlocking directorships and joint ventures, such as nuclear energy development.

Tokyu started out as a family-owned suburban railway company, linking Tokyo with Yokohama and with its southwestern suburbs. The Tokyu group, in which the Goto family still has a strong influence, today consists of transportation (including Japan Air Systems), department stores, housing and tourism development interests. Although one of the smaller *keiretsu*, the Tokyu companies in 1990 employed 96,000 people, which achieved a revenue of US$21 billion.[26]

The *Seibu Group* was in many ways similar to Tokyu, until the group's founder, the late Yasujiro Tsutsumi, in his last will separated the Seibu railway and the real-estate group from the Seibu department store/retail group by awarding the dividing the management between his two hostile sons, Yoshiaki and Seiji. Any appearance of group unity was lost in 1988 when Seiji's Saison group bought the Intercontinental Hotel chain and with other leisure and real estate schemes entered the area of Yoshiaki's corporate interests.

Other smaller corporate empires are: the *Hankyu-Toho group* focusing on Kansai-based railways, department stores, real estate and entertainment centres and movie productions); the *Kintetsu group* (with railways, tourism facilities and department stores in the Kinki area); the *Daiwa-Nomura group* (operating in banking, securities, insurance, construction and real estate); the *Kyowa-Saitama group* (with a Saitama-based diversified industrial grouping, the *Gyokusen-kai*); and the *Tobu group* (yet another suburban railway cum department store/real estate group in Kanto).

THE IMPORTANCE OF *KEIRETSU*

Core *keiretsu* in 1983 controlled 53.4 per cent of Japan's banking loans, 67.3 per cent of all life insurance income and 82.5 per cent of non-life insurance income. Sectorally the role of *keiretsu* is very differentiated. If we look simply at the presence of *keiretsu*-affiliated companies among the top ten in annual sales in each sector an interesting picture emerges. *Keiretsu*-dominated sectors (with six or more *keiretsu* companies among the top ten) are: trust and banking, leasing, securities, non-life insurance, life assurance, general trading (*sogo shosha*), machinery wholesaling, steel trading, electrical appliances/electronics trading, automobile wholesaling, department stores, mining, general construction, dredging and reclamation, housing construction, plant engineering, flour and feed milling, sugar refining, beer brewing, edible oils, synthetic fibres, pulp and paper, inorganic chemicals, petrochemicals, plastic products, fats and detergents, paints, coal products, tyres, rubber products, glass, cement, carbon, ceramics, iron and steel, non-ferrous metals, engines, metalworking machinery, construction machinery, bearings, electrical home appliances, measuring equipment, batteries, electrical components, shipbuilding, rolling stock, cars, auto parts, records, videos, cassettes, real-estate development, private railways, marine transport, warehousing, and data processing.

Sectors in which *keiretsu* companies are less prominent (four or less among the top ten) are: regional banks, textile trading, food wholesaling, pharmaceutical/chemical wholesaling, energy trading, trading in sports goods, supermarkets, book stores, oil industry, electrical construction, confectionery, fisheries, other processed foods, cotton textiles, packaging materials, inks, cosmetics, footwear, steel structures, building materials, nuts and bolts, tools, springs, other metal products, valves, computers, office automation equipment, bicycles, scientific and optical instruments, printing, shoes and leather goods, musical instruments, furniture, stationery, other sundry goods, bus/taxi transport, other road transport, broadcasting, electrical power, city gas, theatres, cinemas, travel agencies, restaurants, advertising, and publishing.

These lists indicate the very strong influence of *keiretsu* ties in key service industries (finance, insurance, general trading, maritime transportation, warehousing, construction), as well as in capital-intensive primary processing of imported raw materials (iron and steel, non-ferrous metals, basic chemicals, pulp and paper, cement, glass and so on) and in capital- and R&D-intensive large-scale final production (cars, ships, electrical appliances, communications equipment, industrial machinery, and their key components). In many ways these sectors are closely linked to the functioning of the basic equation of Japan's industrial economy: the importation of raw materials, the domestic processing thereof, and their export as high value added mass-produced consumer or industrial products. In this function, the *keiretsu* are often able to operate in a fully integrated fashion furnishing and executing all necessary processing and related services 'in-group', ranging from up-stream raw-material sourcing to downstream domestic and overseas marketing of the end products.

In contrast, non-*keiretsu*-dominated sectors appear to be doing traditional and/or light industrial manufacturing (textiles, furniture, bicycles, leather goods, other sundry products) or to be representative of sectors typical of SME activity (industrial standard components, transport services, other consumer services) or of knowledge-intensity and creativity (broadcasting, theatres, advertising, publishing, scientific instruments and so on), for which organisation as industrial conglomerates is of marginal – if any – benefit.

The picture emerging from this analysis points to an almost complete coverage of the key value added sectors of the top layer of the Japanese economy by *keiretsu* organisation. While individual *keiretsu* may vary a lot in terms of internal cohesion, ranging from tight organisations, like Mitsubishi and Sumitomo, to the loose house-bank clubs of the DKB, Sanwa and Tokai sort, their implications for competition, foreign trade and political power in Japan are considerable.

The first two issues were raised by the US during their Strategic Impediments Initiative of 1990–91. As horizontal *keiretsu*, if effective, include only one company per sector (vertical *keiretsu* being one-company-centred anyway), it is difficult to deduce if *keiretsu*-type organisations form horizontal cartels. In fact, one could more plausibly argue the opposite: the very fact that there is a set of six or seven horizontal, mostly-exclusive, one-company/one-sector *keiretsu* allows them to fight each other murderously in certain key competitive sectors (such as cars and electronics) in allocating strategically the groups' financial, R&D and marketing power. In terms of product innovation and marketing, inter-*keiretsu* competition is surely keen (as all overseas competitors in these sectors had to learn to their disadvantage both within Japan and abroad). Horizontal cartels (on public works construction, cement, domestic aviation, beer pricing, and so on) whether legal or not, do exist aplenty in Japan, but it is not certain whether *keiretsu* structures *per se* have any significant effect on these distortions. It is more certain that *keiretsu* as such have a restrictive effect on merchandise imports and on the (non-)use of foreign supplied services in Japan.

Vertically organised industrial *keiretsu* (in cars, electronics, steel and so on) do not place orders with foreign parts suppliers (except for a few symbolic items or in case of domestic shortfalls), but rather stick to their dependent and partly owned/managed domestic subcontractors and suppliers. (They may, however, use the existence of foreign offers to squeeze prices even further or to tighten specifications.)

For the horizontal *keiretsu*, in most cases the 'in-group' facilities/offers will be preferred, *ceteris paribus*, over external offers. This safely prevents any significant foreign penetration of the Japanese industrial and service sectors in which the presence of *keiretsu*-affiliated companies as industrial suppliers has been dominant. These effective restrictions apply to corporate finance, non-life insurance, marine transport, warehousing, raw material import handling, export marketing, leasing, construction and real estate development, as well as to the supply of semi-processed materials (textile fibres, pulp/paper, basic chemicals, paints, cement, iron/steel, non-ferrous metals). After year-long bilateral talks on the *keiretsu*, US negotiators concluded in a report, made public in June 1991: 'The *keiretsu* system remains a formidable barrier to entry into the Japanese market.'[27]

Keidanren, a keiretsu dominated institution as we shall see, in a position paper on the SII talks went so far as to admit:

> Exclusive business practices: Keidanren has maintained that Japanese business practices, which emphasize stable, long-term relationships based on trust, constitute a rational economic response by individual companies in the marketplace and that such practices do not contravene the Antimonopoly law. However, we also need to address the criticism from the United States that the importance placed on long-term trading relationships poses some disadvantages for newcomers, in particular foreign companies to get in.[28]

A paper by Robert Lawrence of the Brookings Institution[29] estimated that, in the absence of *keiretsu*, Japanese imports in 1985 would have amounted to some US$61 billion instead of the actual value of $27 billion. Lawrence's assumptions appear to be slightly heroic. His quantified conclusions on trade, in any case, are more plausibly argued than the Japanese public attempts to downplay the *keiretsu*'s role (regularly using FTC surveys which only cover the core president club companies, and neither their host of subsidiaries nor further affiliated companies). There is little doubt that the *keiretsu* in total put a brake on manufactured imports and on foreign services: the *vertical keiretsu* (cars, electronics) restrict access for foreign part suppliers. Their control over domestic distribution limits foreign penetration effectively to niche products. The *horizontal keiretsu* limit the access of semi-manufacturers (and hence reduce the foreign value added for imported raw materials) and the scope for a whole range of foreign supplied services. The actual quantification of net import reductions, however, only very detailed sectoral analyses could show. The *keiretsu* effect certainly is not the only barrier to import penetration. Government behaviour in public procurement, administrative guidance and setting up visible barriers (quotas/tariffs) and a wide array of less-visible (non-tariff) barriers (which testify to the existence of a considerable amount of creativity and ingenuity of Japan's civil service), and the organisation of Japan's distribution system in aggregate may be similarly effective.

Mr T. Boone Pickens' ill-fated attempt to take over Koito, a Toyota *keiretsu*-affiliated supplier of car lighting systems during 1979–91, proved the *keiretsu* to be an effective defence against 'greenmail' and hostile takeovers (which may be necessary, given the Japanese securities houses' (such as Nomura's) now well-known sponsorship of major gangster syndicates).

For two years Pickens was Koito's largest shareholder, owning 26 per cent of its shares (compared to Toyota's 20 per cent). Yet, the solidarity of other major Japanese shareholders (Matsushita, Nissan, insurance companies) prevented Pickens taking seats on the board of Koito or purchasing additional shares. The rationale of Pickens's bid was not altogether plausible: as a famed corporate raider he claimed to be able to make Koito more profitable. Yet he knew that Koito was an almost exclusive supplier to Toyota, which enjoyed preferential pricing. Implausibly, he claimed to be able to end this dependence. Pickens's bid none the less served to shed light on the vertical *keiretsu*'s in-house business practices, which seem to follow the motto: 'Harmony through ruthless domination'. The owner of a car-parts maker testified before the US House Judiciary Committee that his auto parts business started by making parts for a number of companies. Once one car-maker became his largest customer, it offered to 'improve' his supply process and began to send in quality control officers, then auditors, then board directors. Eventually his company was held captive, its profit margins set by the *keiretsu* along with every other facet of his business. Asked why he didn't break away, he explained: 'No one else would buy from me. All my family wealth is in my company. It would be economic suicide.'

Too-close *keiretsu* affiliation also boded no good for the previous family owners of Ichikoh Industries, a maker of car rear-mirrors. The equity share of Mr Tetsuya Tsukatani, the previous owner and president, had been whittled down during successive enlargements and a merger, with Nissan owning some 20 per cent of the stock in February 1991, when Nissan felt it appropriate to retire the 71-year-old Mr Tsukatani forcibly in order to avoid his son Takuro, who was previously involved in a Nissan labour dispute, taking over at the company's helm.

These incidents, though singular, are indicative of certain structures in the normally taciturn and discrete world of *tatemae* harmony in internal *keiretsu* relations, and reveal a clear power hierarchy in vertical *keiretsu*. Among horizontal *keiretsu*, the same hierarchy applies to relations between parent companies (*honsha*) and their subsidiaries (*kogaisha*).

What then is the situation in the formally egalitarian society of *keiretsu* core company presidents? The downfall in 1982 of Shigeru Okada, president of Mitsukoshi, Japan's most prestigous department store, was triggered by the discovery that some exhibits in its celebrated exhibition of ancient Persian artefacts were fakes. The press also suddenly found out that Mitsukoshi suffered from unsellable inventories acquired expensively from companies linked with Okada's girlfriend. In a palace coup, orchestrated by a Mitsui Bank adviser, Okada was fired by his own board of directors,[30] in order to defend the good name of the Mitsui group and the financial interests of Mitsui Bank. In the case of financially troubled *keiretsu* companies, the rescuing bank's or general trading company's reaction is similarly swift and unscrupulous. When Ikeda Bussan, a car-seat maker got into trouble in 1990, Kyowa Saitama Bank, its *keiretsu* cheerleader, came to the rescue and replaced one of its senior executives by a banker. A rougher fate in 1991 awaited Itoman, a textile and meat trader turned real estate speculator, whose many shady deals (including tax evasion) ultimately brought down also the chairman of Sumitomo Bank who had lent his support to these and similar bubble economic ventures. In order to rescue Itoman from receivership almost all its senior executives were replaced by Sumitomo bankers.

Ultimately, the power structure and the supreme decision-making within a *keiretsu* group is a curious mixture of corporate standing and of the personality traits of the core companies' leading executives. Ten years before his downfall, Mr Isoda, chairman of Sumitomo Bank, explained leadership in Sumitomo's *Hakusui-kai*:

> I try not to be too obtrusive. As Mr Yoshifumi Kumagai and Mr Takeshi Hijikata, present heads of the two remaining pillars [Sumitomo Metal Industries and Sumitomo Chemical, respectively] of the Sumitomo triumvirate, are modest men, the *Hakusuikai* is operating smoothly without serious troubles. In times of real crisis, leadership will naturally emerge on its own on the basis of the ages of the presidents represented and the history, real prowess and social position etc. of the corporations involved. The group's 'triumvirate', moreover, is undergoing subtle changes with such lively personalities as Sumitomo Corporation's Mr Mitsuo

Uemura, Sumitomo Electric Industries' Mr Masao Kamei and Nippon Electric's Tadahiro Sekimoto gradually coming to the fore.[31]

The *keiretsu* attempt to translate their considerable economic leverage into political power. At the domestic Japanese level this is done in the most transparent way through their domination of the four *zaikai* organisations, *Keidanren*, *Nikkeiren*, *Keizai Doyukai* and *Nissho*. Most senior positions in these four key organisations are filled by top *keiretsu* executives. The same applies to sectoral business associations (banking, automobiles, electronics, steel, chemicals, shipping).

Individual *keiretsu* companies offer well-paid and prestigious second careers to 'retired' elite bureaucrats, but it is *Keidanren* and the sectoral industry federations which supply key finance to the LDP and to its political allies.

THE *SOGO SHOSHA*

Japan's general trading companies originally reflected the nationalist import substitution objectives of Japan's Meiji modernisers, who wanted to break foreign companies' domination of Japan's external trade. The *sogo shosha* were made privileged commission merchants to market the output of Japan's internationally unsophisticated manufacturing sector, and to supply the resource-poor country with the raw materials and the industrial technologies it needed.

By the early 1970s the ten largest *sogo shosha* had been so successful in this role that they accounted for 50 per cent of Japan's exports and for two-thirds of its imports. Typically they dominated the importation of the energy and bulk raw-material requirements for affiliated *keiretsu* enterprises, amongst which the capital-intensive heavy and chemical industries figured prominently. For exports they supplied a whole range of transport, finance and marketing services abroad, which Japan's internationally inexperienced industry at the time did not possess itself.

It was clear by the mid-1970s, however, that the *sogo shosha*'s so far indispensable role was being made increasingly redundant by Japan's economic success which they had helped to engineer so effectively. The challenge came in three forms:

- Japan's export-orientated industries were awash with cash and no longer required the *sogo shosha*'s trade finance;
- the manufacturers – particularly in the booming consumer products sector – had also acquired sufficient overseas marketing know-how, that

they (the Hondas, Sonys and Toyotas) increasingly preferred to manage their international sales themselves;

- at the same time, Japan's economy was restructuring away from the bulk processing of heavy and chemical industries towards a more diversified technology-intensive industrial and service structure, a structure which obviously depended less on imported bulk raw materials.

With the writing clearly on the wall, almost all of Japan's *sogo shosha*, however, refused to go the way of the dinosaur, and, after a few lean years of trial and error and reduced returns, managed to stay afloat and continued to grow in a suitably adjusted role. Their own readjustment was again aided by the pivotal roles they acquired in the *keiretsu* realignments of the 1950s and 1960s.

The top nine *sogo shosha* play a leading organisational role in the following *keiretsu*: Mitsubishi Shoji (Mitsubishi), Mitsui Bussan (Mitsui), Sumitomo Corporation (Sumitomo), Marubeni (Fuyo), C. Itoh (DKB), Kanematsu Gosho (DKB), Nissho Iwai (DKB and Sanwa), Nichimen (Sanwa) and Tomen (Tokai and Mitsui).

Their *keiretsu* core service role has allowed the *sogo shosha* to go both upstream (into contract manufacturing to produce certain products satisfying foreign or domestic market niches) and downstream (into retailing joint ventures). Notable examples of these latter operations is Mitsubishi joining in the successful establishment of Kentucky Fried Chicken and of Sutor Coffee Shop chains across Japan. The main motive is less corporate growth than returns on investment. Instead of focusing on low-risk/low-yield trading credits, some *sogo shosha* (in particular the ill-fated, junior-ranking Itoman Corporation) turned to *zaitech* financial speculation, which sometimes provided valuable lessons on the virtues of risk reduction. For upstream sourcing and natural resource development investments, the *sogo shosha* usually made good use of Japan's rapidly expanding ODA budget[32] which they used to procure low-interest loans or grants to organise the construction of related public infrastructure or of turnkey plants in Asian and other LDCs. They also ventured increasingly into intra-third-country off-shore transactions, which often included complex barter deals. The *sogo shosha* offered their information know-how on foreign markets for overseas services (banking, finance, insurance, transport, warehousing, and so on) and for various sorts of real-estate development, ranging from commercial building to golf courses and tourist resorts, both at home and abroad.

Mr Kazuo Haruna, president of Marubeni Corporation, declared in 1986:

We have diversified rapidly into these areas [leisure and entertainment] in the past few years. A Corporate Development Department established in 1983 plays a main role in such areas as hi-tech, biotech, new services and information industries. For example, we have finished laying cable TV lines in Tokyo and Nagoya and we established an auto leasing company and a joint venture with Vittel for mineral water and health care systems. Providing management and maintenance services to hospitals may create new demand in Japan. And even producing movies is also included in such new fields. In the bio-tech area, it is just the right time to import and sell automatic diagnosis systems.[33]

Mr Isao Yonekura, president of C. Itoh, explained his company's new high-tech role:

At C. Itoh, we created a task force within the trading group to co-ordinate and follow advanced technology. We have added a New Technology Department to handle new developments in other areas such as new materials, biotechnology, alternative energy and space. Some examples are seeds, foodstuffs, medicines, agricultural chemicals and amorphous alloys. We have close relations with a number of manufacturers to exchange information and analysis on technology. We also invest in high-tech venture businesses in Japan and abroad. It takes time and money to develop high-technology business, but we want a bigger share of the high-tech market. Our biggest strengths are again information and the money needed to underwrite risks.[34]

It is fairly obvious that it was their extensive *keiretsu* ties which facilitated the *sogo shosha*'s new roles in these high-growth sectors. Their respective *keiretsu* made possible the complex operations necessary for turnkey plant exports, collected the capital for overseas resource and real-estate developments, and provided the technical know-how and specialist manpower for various high-tech joint ventures. Without the *keiretsu*, Japan's *sogo shosha* would have gone the way of obsolete general trading companies in the rest of the world: into oblivion and economic history monographs.

9 *Zaikai* – the Organisation of Big Business Interests

Zaikai, Japan's business world, consists of four major organisations: *Keidanren*, the Federation of Economic Organisations; *Nikkeiren*, the Federation of Employers' Associations; *Nissho*, the Japan Chamber of Industry and Commerce; and *Keizai Doyukai*, the Association of Corporate Executives. There is also a large number of regional and sectoral associations within each of these national umbrella organisations.

As voluntary organisations, in personnel policy and policy stance they have to reflect the consensus of key corporate members. Decision-making is hence often cumbersome and tends to reflect the lowest common denominator. Yet *zaikai*'s financial power (demonstrated to the political establishment) and its ability to offer secondary *amakudari* careers to elite-track bureaucrats, assure its continued core role in the political economy of modern Japan.

KEIDANREN

Set up in 1946, with its 120 associations and 940 corporate members, *Keidanren* stands at the apex of Japan's organised business interests. Its chairman is often referred to as the 'prime minister of business' – a description which, in a Japanese context, appropriately reflects not only the public role but equally the effective constraints of such a consensual position. *Keidanren*'s effective top-level decision-making body is its executive council, consisting of the chairman and his 12 vice-chairmen. Formally, all decisions have to be blessed by monthly board of directors meetings which, with 461 'directors' is clearly too unwieldy to have any effective deliberations or decision-making role. Roughly, one in two 'directors' (or 206 in total) also serve on the board of executive directors which meets monthly in parallel; 486 *Keidanren* members also serve as 'councillors', whose main function appears to be to attend an annual plenary meeting each December and to listen to the addresses of Japan's political leaders. More effective work seems to be done in *Keidanren*'s committees, which report to the board of directors. Currently there are 44 such committees, covering almost all general corporate concerns: corporate ethics, political reform, economic policy, public affairs, administrative reform, economic research, industrial affairs, environment, information and telecommunication policy, energy, natural resources, distribution, transportation, housing and land development, agricultural policy, taxation, international finance, foreign relations, corporate philanthropy, defence production and so on. With the help of *Keidanren*'s small secretariat, the committees produce position papers reflecting Japan's business circles' consensus. These are subsequently submitted to the government and published. *Keidanren* also maintains 17 bilateral committees and participates in 26 other bilateral committees jointly with other economic organisations and groups. Their function is to undertake 'private economic diplomacy', to monitor events in a particular country, to cultivate ties with its political and economic leadership, and to encourage bilateral trade and investment (and to receive foreign honours and medals in return).

The composition of *Keidanren*'s two leading councils – the executive council, composed of the chairman and his 12 vice-chairmen, and the board of councillors – is clearly dominated by *Keiretsu*-affiliated executives. While chairman Gaishi Hiraiwa is from a (neutral) utility company (Tokyo Electric Power), five of his deputies are with horizontal *keiretsu* (Mitsubishi, Mitsui, Sumitomo, Sanwa and Tokai), four with vertical *keiretsu* (Nippon Steel, Toshiba IHI, Toyota and Nomura), with only the remaining three unaffiliated (the chairmen of Sony, Komatsu and Ajinomoto). It is a similar story with the ten member board of councillors: seven are with horizontal *keiretsu* (Fuyo, Sumitomo, Sanwa, Mitsubishi and DKB (3), including senior executives from the DKB Kawasaki and Furukawa subgroups), one is president of a vertical *keiretsu* (Yutaka Kume of Nissan), and only two are unaffiliated: a senior councillor from the Long Term Credit Bank of Japan and the Japanese president of IBM Japan. The composition of both these boards obviously reflects a careful balance among various *keiretsu* groups. Most committee chairmanships are also firmly in *keiretsu* hands.

During *Keidanren*'s golden days it was claimed by serious scholars that *zaikai* was more or less able to decide on who would become prime minister of Japan.[1] This was in Japan's high-growth period, during which Taizo Ishizaka was *Keidanren*'s chairman (1956–68). Originally an official with the prewar Ministry of Communications, Ishizaka first became president of Dai-Ichi Life Insurance and later of Toshiba, where he led the management victory in a major battle with militant unions. He was known for his strong dislike of government interventionism, and advocated capital liberalisation and opposed MITI controls in industrial restructuring.[2]

Since then, Keidanren's influence has suffered from an increasing diversity of business interests (created by a more differentiated economic structure), from the strengthened government role of the LDP, and from a series of chairmen who preferred to sit out problems and wait for a business consensus to emerge, instead of leading and forcing decisions. *Keidanren* chairmen do not come from the major horizontal *keiretsu*, but for the sake of balance are usually from smaller *sangyo keiretsu*, such as Toshiba (Toshiro Doko) and Nippon Steel (Yoshihiro Inayama, 1980–6), and Eishiro Saito, 1986–90). Mr Hiraiwa, chairman since December 1990, hails from Tokyo Electric Power Co., a utility which is dependent on MITI for rate approvals and other key decisions. Inayama and Saito as steel men were used to cartel arrangements in production and exports, which also depended on MITI approval and goodwill. Saito in particular during his chairmanship was attacked publicly for his lack of leadership and his inability or unwillingness to stand up to politicians.[3]

Keidanren chairmen are not elected. They are selected by their predecessors, who are free in principle to decide whether to continue for yet another term or to retire gracefully and appoint a successor. A lot of intensive backstage negotiations, covering the selection of vice-chairmen as well are necessary for the appearance of consensus. As part of a complex deal with Tokyo Electric Power, which was pushing for Hiraiwa to take over, Saito agreed to resign in December 1990,[4] after he had enjoyed the full honours as chairman of the Osaka Expo '90 during April–September 1990 and having been gratified by an honourable place alongside foreign dignitaries during Emperor Akihito's enthronement ceremonies in November 1990. Implausibly, *Keidanren* tried to sell the transition from Saito (79) to Hiraiwa (76) as 'rejuvenation'. Also the average age of the 12 vice-chairmen remained stubbornly at 75.

At least in terms of sectors represented, *Keidanren*'s old heavy industry bias had been discarded. The vice-chairmen since May 1990 represent general trading, retail distribution, banking, securities, and the manufacturing of food, chemicals, cars, electrical appliances, heavy machinery and steel. Hiraiwa also announced that 'the entire *Keidanren* organisation must be revitalised'.[5] In July 1991 he had one of his deputies, Nomura chairman Tabuchi, expelled, after the latter had to admit publicly to large-scale preferential Nomura loans and stock price manipulations for the benefit of the *Inagawa-kai* crime syndicate.

However, it seems unclear whether *Keidanren* can reassert itself as Japan's business opinion leader, given the diversity of conflicting interests on crucial issues such as land prices, distribution reform, public works, regionalisation and effective environmental protection.

Although clearly the most affluent and status-orientated among Japan's power elite, *zaikai* appears politically weak on issues beyond sectoral parochial interests (which can be facilitated by straight contributions in money or in kind): Japan's big business remains awestruck *vis à vis* the central administration, fearful of having licences revoked and its tax accounts audited, so it dutifully continues to follow the whims of administrative guidance. Towards the LDP, *Keidanren* – the party's principal paymaster – periodically issues stern admonitions to stop political in-fighting and lead Japan more earnestly (also by reducing its demands for political donations). Yet LDP chieftains, by threatening increased corporate taxation, were able to laugh off such well-meaning exhortations, and succeeded in extracting increased new levies from the *Keidanren's* fundraising arm, the *Kokumin Seiji Kyokai*, which allocates shares to its member associations and industries for political contributions. Allowing LDP MPs to consider *Keidanren's* cash as 'basic salary' and outside contributions as additional 'allowances' requiring special efforts, *Keidanren* continues to waste most of its potential for direct influence.

While some of *Keidanren's* positions have resembled gratuitous and implausible sloganeering, such as Saito's pledge in 1990 to work for 'democracy in the business world'. others appear to be more sensible and honest if taken seriously. Mr Hiraiwa said in July 1990 at a reflective summer seminar, at the foot of Mount Fuji, where annually the *Keidanren* top brass meets for a weekend:

> The reforms that have taken place in the Soviet Union and Eastern Europe since last year have proved the superiority of the free-enterprise economy over the socialist economy. This does not mean, however, that there is nothing wrong with the present free economic system. In Japan, for example, we have many problems such as the land problem. In order to make the needed reforms it is essential that each business tries its best to improve itself in the realisation that it is a social presence and to help change society for the better. Therefore it is important to live up to the principle of self-accountability and establish business ethics.[6]

One of his predecessors, Yoshihiro Inayama, hit the nail on the head: 'An economy jacked up with pork-barrel civil engineering and housing projects is not going to stay healthy for long.' And on Japanese politicians: 'The obsessive fear of not getting elected makes them tend to put their constituents' narrow interests first. We need more broad-minded and well-informed politicians to debate the crucial issue of how to manage the economy.'[7]

Yet for all its common sense in public consensus papers and executive interviews, *Keidanren* has frequently been criticised for coming out with too little too late. *Keidanren's* land tax proposals of May 1990, for instance, proposed higher taxes on unused corporate land and reduced taxation for land for residential purposes. This fuelled speculation that *Keidanren* was seeking yet another tax break for corporations selling their land while prices were still high.[8] Both on the consumption tax and on a reform of Japan's cumbersome distribution system, *Keidanren* remained positive. Yet it failed to persuade *Nissho*, Japan's Chamber of Commerce and Industry, to change its adamant opposition. With a great fanfare in April 1991, *Keidanren* adopted a 'global environment charter',[9] full of high-minded principles aimed at making environmentalism an integral part of business philosophy. Yet the charter failed to provide a clear idea of how businesses would actually work to protect the environment, or how they would act to dispel effectively their past (and current) reputation for using any available means to emasculate effective environmental legislation. On trade issues *Keidanren* had been consistently supportive of the trade liberalisation objectives of the GATT Uruguay Round,[10] whose failure it feared, as it would encourage North American and European regionalism in trade and unilateral trade sanctions. *Keidanren* also asked for Japanese contributions to facilitate the Round's conclusion, including a partial opening of the rice market. A *Keidanren* delegation, led by Jiro Kawake (Oji Paper) and Akio Morita (Sony) made this request officially to MAFF minister Kondo in April 1991. The minister listened politely, but replied predictably that Japan's policies on banning rice imports would not change.[11] This type of reaction to *Keidanren's* political requests now appears to be the rule. Even on technical issues, junior ministry officials easily dismiss *Keidanren*-backed trade petitions (which after all will only be submitted once they have been carefully vetted by *Keidanren's* secretariat, making sure that no domestic industries and member companies are negatively affected).

Foreign dignitaries making their compulsory stop at *Keidanren's* Otemachi HQ when on a visit to Japan, hence ask less often for *Keidanren's* policy intervention on their behalf, but rather advertise their investment and ODA opportunities to Japan's monied elite.

On the requests emanating from the US under their Structural Impediments Initiative of 1989–91, *Keidanren* (rightly) was quick to admit the shortfalls in Japan's social capital formation, the government's inadequate deregulation efforts and its wasteful rigidities in public works decisions. Yet on the US criticism of Japan's toothless competition policy and its exclusive *keiretsu* system, *Keidanren* confronted with its own vested interests, turned defensive: it judged the current version of the Anti-monopoly Law to be 'adequate', and called the 'so-called' *keiretsu* nothing but shifting arrangements in the interests of 'long-term ties and vertical co-operation',[12] which were a reflection of a laudable Japanese preference for 'quality, competitive pricing, reliability of supply and delivery, and trust-worthiness'. For the rest, the US should shape up, and solve its budget deficit and declining labour quality, as Akio Morita, head of *Keidanren's* SII committee, helpfully pointed out.[13]

Keidanren has its counterparts in all major regions of Japan, such as in Kansai (*Kankeiren*), Kyushu/Yamaguchi (*Kyukeiren*), Hokkaido (*Hokukeiren*) and so on. These regional associations are structured very much like *Keidanren's* model, yet they insist on their independent status. *Kankeiren* with 540 corporate members, sees itself as the representative of the Kansai business community, with the mandate to made its consensus opinions known on any national or international socioeconomic subject of mutual interest. Hence it also maintains a structure of committees covering subjects such as administrative reform, industrial policy, taxation, land use, national security, education, culture and international trade. While proud of its input on national affairs, *Kankeiren's* most intensively felt concerns lie in the regional development of the Kansai economy and generating public support for large public infrastructural investments (Kansai International Airport, the construction of a Kansai Academic City, urban restructuring in Osaka) and for the public works contracts associated with it. This function is even more pronounced among the other regional business federations. With *Kankeiren* chairman Hosai Hyuga being chairman of Sumitomo Metal, four of his six vice-chairmen represent major Kansai-orientated *keiretsu* firms (Sanwa Bank, Matsushita Electric, Mitsui Taiyo Kobe Bank and Nippon Shinyaku – Mitsubishi *keiretsu*).

Most of the other regional federations, in the absence of any *keiretsu* headquarters outside the Japanese metropolises of Tokyo, Osaka and Nagoya, are usually headed by the chairman of the regional electricity company, with the heads of regional banks acting as vice-chairmen. In *Kyukeiren*, for instance, the chairman is from Kyushu Electric Power Co. Eight of his nine vice-chairmen head their respective prefectural banks. The lone industrialist on the board is the president of Japan Steel's Kokura plant. *Kyukeiren* also maintains dozens of counsellors and senior advisors, a system whose main function appears to be to supply member-company presidents with a good-sounding new title.

Kyushu is administratively divided into seven small prefectures. *Kyukeiren*, together with Kyushu Power Co., thus acts as one of the few institutions which is in a position to lobby effectively for the integrated regional development of the island. As such, it focuses on the construction of a Shinkansen extension from Fukuoka to run along Kyushu's west coast to Kagoshima, and to build a highway from Kokura to Miyazaki along the east coast.

While the development plans pursued in Japan's regions all seem to share identical futurist slogans ('technopolis', 'biopolis', 'sunresort', 'new mediapolis', 'greentopia' and so on), most of the corporate executives involved in these regional promotions appear to be gerontocrats, anchored firmly into traditional concepts of economic development and management styles.

NIKKEIREN

Nikkeiren, Japan's Federation of Employers' Associations, is composed of 47 prefectural associations and 53 sectoral associations, representing virtually all employers in industry and services. *Nikkeiren* deals essentially with wages, labour relations and working conditions as the counterpart of *Rengo*, Japan's trade union confederation. *Nikkeiren*, however, does not directly negotiate with *Rengo* or with any other national union. The annual *Shunto* ('spring offensive') talks are effectively held between sectoral unions and their corresponding employers' organisations and between individual enterprise unions and their corporate management. *Nikkeiren* and *Rengo* aim to co-ordinate their respective sides' requests and offers, and to supply their causes with intellectual studies and PR support. *Nikkeiren* regularly cautions that 'wages that are set higher than economic and business performance warrant could result in inflation, tighter money, and a downturn in the economy'.[14]

Nikkeiren was set up in 1948 at the height of Japan's labour struggles. (It still has its headquarters in a stately old building reminiscent of prewar *zaibatsu* splendour near Tokyo Station.) In the 1950s it was successful in co-ordinating the effective destruction of Japan's militant postwar unionism in the private sector. The strategy pursued at the time simply meant engaging a prominent left-wing union in a prolonged labour dispute, locking out the striking employees, and re-hiring only those who were willing to become members of a new tame enterprise union. Eventually the militants were left out in the wilderness. Today *Nikkeiren* prides itself in the establishment of 'orderly and harmonious labour–management relations'.[15] It focuses on 'better management and training', in order to instil and propagate 'scientific personnel management practices'.[16] *Nikkeiren* strives to achieve co-operative relations with *Rengo* through joint studies on prices, welfare, taxation, real-estate costs and so on. For its member companies it urges a 'people-orientated style of labour relations',[17] which in the top-tier companies is based on lifetime employment, seniority-based management and enterprise unions. Company-wide joint consultation procedures, workplace meetings (including quality circles), grievance procedures and suggestion systems are supposed to enhance management–labour communication and to instil in workers a sense of responsibility and corporate identification. It is no accident that Japan has not seen any major labour struggles since 1977 (the breakup of the tough JNR unions in the context of Nakasone's privatisations of 1985–6 hardly caused a ripple), and that its unionisation rate has fallen below 25 per cent, as all-too-co-operative unions fail to instil any meaningful purpose of union membership into post-industrial employees.

Nikkeiren takes a wide view of its labour-orientated mandate, and with confidence publicly comments and advises the government on labour-related issues, ranging from land prices to rice import liberalisation. *Nikkeiren* was sensible enough to recognise publicly that the soaring land and stock prices of Japan's too liquid 'bubble economy' created classes of haves and have-nots, with 'workers starting to lose interest in working, because they know that the asset gap will never be filled, even with a lifetime of work'.[18] Understandably, *Nikkeiren* also recognised: 'While nominal wages in Japan are among the highest in the world, high prices and other factors prevent workers from feeling that their standard of living is truly affluent'.[19]

The yen's weakness in terms of purchasing power parities obviously constitutes a threat to *Nikkeiren's* (usually attained) objective of keeping aggregate real wage increases in line with productivity gains. In fact, *Nikkeiren's* retail price statistics when compared with other OECD countries makes interesting reading, as the retail prices possible in Tokyo compared to Hamburg and New York reveal considerable overcharging to Japanese consumers, the indicative of widespread dual pricing systems practised by Japanese manufacturers between captive domestic markets and overseas markets they wish to conquer, not only in foodstuffs and utility charges but also for recreation, household and 'other' equipment, clothing, footwear, transportation, rents, recreational facilities, and 'other services'.[20] In order to deflate the unions' wage claims, *Nikkeiren* has repeatedly asked the government to deregulate the transport, telecommunications and utilities sectors (which would lead to reduced private users' costs), to liberalise imports (including rice), and to enact a more rational land-use system (in order to decrease workers' costs for housing, commuting and recreation). Eiji Suzuki, *Nikkeiren's* previous chairman, frequently criticised *Keidanren* under Saito's chairmanship for failing to speak out and lobby forcefully on these issues.

More strongly even than *Keidanren*, *Nikkeiren* has been under *keiretsu* management. The current chairman, Takeshi Nagano (chairman of Mitsubishi

Materials), in office since May 1991, as well as his two immediate predecessors, Eiji Suzuki (Mitsubishi Chemicals) and Bunpei Otsuki (Mitsubishi
Mining), are Mitsubishi men. Takeshi Nagano himself hails from one of
Japan's gilded clans, which includes his late father, the former transportation minister Mamoru Nagano, his late eldest son Iwao, who was an
Upper House member, and his late uncle, Shigeo Nagano, a former president of Japan's Chamber of Commerce and Industry who played an active
role as one of the Big Four in *zaikai* business circles in the 1970s.[21]

Among Nagano's seven vice-chairmen there is one SME representative
and one from a (privatised) JR regional company (Kinki JR), but three
senior executives of vertical *sangyo keiretsu* (Nissan, Toshiba and Japan
Steel) and two from horizontal *keiretsu* (Fuji Bank (Fuyo) and Oji Paper
(Mitsui). The average age of new board members of *Nikkeiren* was 68.8
years on average when appointed in May 1991 (replacing the previous
Suzuki board who averaged 72.5 years). Seven of its eight members are
Todai graduates – three from the economics faculty and two each from
engineering and law – together with one lone Keio Law graduate.

NISSHO

Japan's Chamber of Industry and Commerce (*Nissho*) is the federation of
488 local chambers, one of which exists in each Japanese town. They
comprise a total of 1.3 million member companies, most of which naturally,
are, small and medium-sized. This structure makes *Nissho* the spokesman
of Japan's SMEs and of its often-neglected regional economies. As Rokuro
Ishikawa, *Nissho's* president, puts it: 'The size of our member companies
varies greatly, as do their opinions.'[22]

However, *Nissho* attempts to provide unified views on economic policy,
taxation, regional development, external trade and so on, to the government.
Reflecting the interest of Japan's SMEs in tax evasion, *Nissho* remained
adamantly opposed to the introduction of a sales tax in 1989, thus breaking
zaikai's ranks which in a low-key fashion had generally been supportive
of the tax in its crucial stages (while the introduction of a value added tax
had been loudly demanded earlier by prominent business leaders for more
than a decade), thus triggering the fury of senior LDP leaders, who felt
abandoned in their highly unpopular efforts to introduce the tax.

For the main part, however, Japan's Chambers of Commerce at the
central and local levels operate their various services for SMEs, providing
consultancy, arbitration, vocational examinations, technical training, access
to government-supplied SME-specific preferential loans, and general and

business information, including on foreign markets, and (through *Nissho's* Japan Economic Co-operation Centre) on access to ODA funds.

Yet, in spite of its regional and SME focus, *Nissho* is also clearly in *keiretsu* hands. The current chairman, Rokuro Ishikawa, is a member of the Kajima clan, which controls Kajima Corporation (Sumitomo *keiretsu*). His predecessor was Noboru Goto, president of Tokyu Corporation, who controlled the Tokyu *keiretsu*. The *Nissho* chairmanship, in fact, is not considered suitable for a salaried executive from the mainstream horizontal *keiretsu*. The job requires plenty of discretionary funds, which only family-controlled enterprises (but not their hired managers) can supply to their owner-executives.[23] This requirement does not seem to apply to *Nissho's* vice-presidents who all during Goto's reign in 1985 (except Mr Soichiro Honda), were *keiretsu*-affiliated executives (one from Toshiba and two from Mitsui).

KEIZAI DOYUKAI

Keizai Doyukai, the committee for Economic Development, was set up in 1946 to provide a forum where individual corporate chieftains could meet and discuss economic and social issues. In February 1991 Takeshi Ishihara (Nissan) chose Masaru Hayami (Nissho Iwai – Sanwa *keiretsu*) as successor to head *Keizai Doyukai*. Mr Hayami, a Hitotsubashi graduate, after 34 years with the Bank of Japan, entered Nissho Iwai, the company which his father-in-law Kotaru Nagai had established, as president in 1981.[24] Some vice-chairmen were equally exchanged, so as to 'rejuvenate' the Committee's executives from an average age of 66.3 years to 61.1 years. Five vice—chairmen are from the following *keiretsu*: Toshiba, Sanwa, IBJ and Fuyo (2). Only three other vice-chairmen are unaffiliated with the *keiretsu*.

The *Keizai Doyukai* saw its golden age of influence and prestige during 1963–75 under the chairmanship of the late Kazutaka Kikawada (Tokyo Electric Power), when its study group on industrial problems outlined corporate adjustment strategies to deal with Japan's changing industrial structure.[25] Indicative of the organisation's decline in standing and power was an 'incident' in 1991 when Hayami, *Keizai Doyukai's* new chairman, was forced by LDP chieftain Takeo Nishioka to retract publicly and apologise for his earlier mild criticism of the LDP's obvious inability to tackle political reform in earnest.

However, *Kaizai Doyukai* carries sufficient prestige in the eyes of Japan's corporate elite and provides enough coveted top-level interaction to warrant valuable executive time and efforts to occupy its senior positions and to attend its various study meetings and social functions.[26]

OTHER BUSINESS ORGANISATIONS

Apart from the four top-level *zaikai* organisations, there is a wide range of horizontal and sectoral business associations in which the Japanese business elite satisfies the networking and socialising needs which are so essential for doing business (or anything else) successfully in Japan. In fact, all major companies have external relations sections headed by sociable senior managers, whose main functions are to cultivate such ties, to stay in active contact with the major associations, to gather and evaluate the information received, and to prepare their chairmen's briefings, speeches and *zaikai* schedules.

Some younger executives find the classical *zaikai* organisations too ossified, gerontocratic and too wedded to the interests of manufacturing industries in general (and of heavy industry in particular). The newly set-up alternative organisations include groups such as the *Nijuiseki Keizai Kiban Kaihatsu Kokumin Kaigi* (Association for the Development of Economic Foundations for the 21st Century), in which academics and executives aged below 55 (such as the chairmen of Fuji Xerox and Chichibu Cement) are socialising,[27] or the New Business Conference (NBC) which Tadahiro Sekimoto, president of NEC, set up in 1985 to assemble young executives from new high-tech venture firms. The NBC hence organises a wide range of committees, seminars, symposia, overseas missions and publications that allow its members to study earnestly industrial innovation and to propagate the public policies and deregulation measures needed to foster new industries.

Sectoral business associations cover virtually all economic activities. Among the most influential ones, let us look at the *Nihon Boeki Kai*, the Japan Foreign Trade Council (JFTC), and at the Kozai Club, the Iron and Steel Mill Products Association, as examples.

The JFTC has 56 formal corporate members, which include the general trading companies and major specialised trading houses, accounting for more than 60 per cent of Japan's total external trade. With president Yohei Mimura (chairman of Mitsubishi Shoji) and his deputies Toshikuni Yahiro (Mitsui Bussan), Kazuo Haruna (Marubeni), Tadashi Itoh (Sumitomo Corp.), Isao Yonekura (C. Itoh) and Masaru Hayami (Nissho Iwai), the JFTC is clearly managed by the major *sogo shosha* (which in turn are key *keiretsu* organisers). The president and the vice-presidents form an 'executive board of directors' together with some senior staff, and meet every month to discuss urgent issues to be presented to Japan's business leaders and to the government. There is also a structure of specialised and regional committees supplying reasoned opinons to the JFTC president. In addition, the JFTC carries out its share of private economic diplomacy (a past focus having been China), as well as general PR and trade-orientated information-gathering and research work done through its affiliated institutes, the International Trade Institute and the Fair Trade Centre, both of which are located in Tokyo.

The Kozai Club is Japan's major iron and steel trade association, including 30 manufacturers and 90 trading companies which handle 80 per cent of the steel produced in Japan. With a small headquarter in the *Tekko kaikan* in Nihonbashi, the Kozai Club's staff regularly surveys steel market developments and promotes new applications for steel, ranging from artificial reefs for fish farming to new energy technology applications (geothermal, wave, tidal, solar) using steel. The Kozai Club also lobbies the government for large-scale infrastructural projects, for example, linking the Japanese main islands with bridges and tunnels, and promoting high-rise urban redevelopment, including the utilisation of space above public railway tracks.

Chairman of the Kozai Club is Hiroshi Saito (president of Nippon Steel). His vice chairmen are from Nippon Steel, Kawasaki Steel, Sumitomo Metal, Mitsubishi Shoji and C. Itoh. At the same address as the Kozai Club are other steel associations, such as the Japan Iron and Steel Exporters Association, which also shares the same chairman. Yet it focuses rather on more specific export-orientated questions, such as foreign market analysis, maritime transport and export insurance. Hence its membership is slightly more restricted. Here, Mr Saito's deputies also vary slightly, hailing from Nippon Kokan, Kobe Steel, Mitsui Bussan and C. Itoh. The composition of the executives of the two fraternal associations makes sure that all major steel-makers and the principal *sogo shosha* are in constant contact on key sectoral questions and can react instantly where common interests are concerned.

The multitude of this and other sectoral organisations serves as a sort of training ground for those executives of the top-notch *keiretsu* companies who will ultimately make their way through horizontal associations (like *Keizai Doyukai*) to the very top of *zaikai* at *Nikkeiren* and finally *Keidanren*.

10 Executive Careers

Unlike the central bureaucracy or national politics, the elite track for corporate Japan appears to be relatively more accessible: each year tens of thousands of university graduates enter the white-collar ranks of the major top-tier corporations, to be told at each corporate entrance ceremony that one of the crop of freshmen could end up as company president some 40 years later. For those who do not wish to wait four decades, there are plenty of rags-to-riches stories of legendary postwar enterpreneurs such as Konosuke Matsushita, Akio Morita (Sony), Soichiro Honda, Kanichiro Ishibashi (Bridgestone), Tadao Yoshida (YKK), Kazuo Tajima (Minolta), Kazuo Inamori (Kyocera) and the rest, whose successful blend of engineering ingenuity, commercial talent and paternalist management ethic have become common objects of veneration in Japan.

With entrepreneurs becoming a rare breed in a mature business culture like Japan (which in spite of the adulation offered to founder-members perceives successful newcomers currently prominent in real estate, golf course and resort development, *zaitech* and software engineering still as parvenus), the aspiring management candidate's typical career debut will be as a corporate soldier, with the rank of private, in the mainstream of corporate Japan. A 'good' university, membership of suitable sports clubs, a decent family and social background (that is, conventional and conformist middle- to upper-class) and an agreeable, if potentially dynamic, personality will have helped to secure job offers from large, prosperous, expanding (and therefore prestigious) top-tier companies.

Each self-respecting company has an extensive programme of initiation for its male white-collar employees. These may involve stays at military boot camps, at zen monasteries, or in other exotic and rigid disciplines that are calculated to cure an individual's bad student habits and transform him into a loyal and unquestioningly comformist employee for the rest of his working life.

PERSONNEL MANAGEMENT

With the lifetime employment system in the top-tier companies of corporate Japan – evident in its features of seniority-based remuneration and career prospects and its unwillingness to hire outsiders to its elite track – each college graduate knows that the choice of his prospective employer is likely to be the most important decision of his life. Chances are that his decision will be a carefully considered, hard-nosed one, in which his peers, professors and the senior members of his family will also be consulted and, in case of need, asked for help to secure proper placement offers.

The 23-year-old graduate will make an almost total career commitment for the next 35 to 40 years. Hence among the job offers received he will select a company with strong prospects of growth and survival in an expanding and promising economic sector. The leading companies of the sector in question in return obtain the best and the brightest of an annual crop of graduates, thus making popular perceptions about their management qualities and growth prospects almost a self-fulfilling prophecy. Companies go to enormous lengths to ensure a good intake of new recruits. In order to attract students of the leading national and private universities, some companies even offer job contracts to third-year students (knowing that graduation is more of a formality). The regular job/head-hunting season is officially on for fourth-year students only at the end of their autumn term. Jeans-clad, long-haired, relaxed students then mothball their surfboards, tennis rackets and comic collections, and line up as blue-suited, neatly shaven, timid salarymen-candidates for interview before the selection boards of Japan's major and not-so-major companies.

Corporate information replaces student club gossip as their principle topic of conversation. Japanese companies offer uniformaly low entry salaries, and equally lousy leisure time to their new entrants. Hence graduates are free to contemplate the forcible trade-off offered by corporate Japan: low wages and lengthy working time in return for economic security, carefully cultivated social relations at the workplace and – fairly remote – senior career prospects. With the evident lack of attractiveness of foreign companies' job offers for male salarymen, which offer the inverse trade-off of high initial wages with less job security, whatever the media hype about supposedly changed values of the younger generation, the graduates' preference for financial security, corporate prestige and a Japanese-style working environment remains overwhelming.

Graduates from lower-ranking regional or private universities have to compete for corporate employment with SMEs or with large companies scoring low in the popularity ratings – those operating in sectors of structural decline: notably mining, shipbuilding, textiles and steel. It is the foreign-owned companies which – sometimes for better but usually for worse – finally receive the *male* rejects of Japan's often needlessly rigid and conformity-enforcing corporate employment system.

In contrast to Western companies, Japanese corporations do not normally look for specialists during recruitment, but rather for talented and flexible human resources, who will acquire all the necessary skills in-house during extensive corporate lecturing and on-the-job training programmes.

Japan's top-league corporate system has its share of drop-outs, often highly publicised with commentators ready to diagnose a new trend. These then join smaller manufacturing or service firms. There are also middle managers who leave declining industries (often at their companies behest in restructuring programmes), to join growth industries which are short of managerial expertise. There are also, as mentioned above, bankers and other *keiretsu* managers transferred to executive positions in related or subsidiary enterprises, similar to the *amakudari* practice for the small band of elite bureaucrats retiring each year from their ministries. As a rule, however, employment in the top-tier companies of Japan's business (covering roughly 30 per cent of all male employment) is still perceived by both sides to be a lifelong affair with most senior management preferably promoted in-house. Companies go to great lengths to invest in their human capital and to train their staff through elaborate schedules of formal instructions and job rotation programmes. The training schedules are most intensive for newcomers and middle management candidates, who will have to do most of their study assignments (ranging from accounting, to business English) outside their regular office hours (at night, on Sundays or during commuting time).

Having survived his initiation boot-camp, somewhat bewildered but otherwise in good health, the new corporate recruit begins way down the pecking order: In a department store, he will start by selling socks; in a bank by bowing to customers in branch offices and helping old ladies to fill in their withdrawal forms; in an electric power company by reading the meters; in insurance by selling policies door to door; in car manufacturing by joining the shop floor, and so on. This period of endurance may last between four months and two years, depending on individual performance (the less visibly enthusiastically these chores are performed, the longer the assignment will last) and on company policy. Companies see such underqualified assignments for their new staff members as essential for their later corporate identification, their future management orientation and the companies' labour relations. It also allows the company insights into their men's reactions to hardship and frustration.

With their low starting salaries of between 170,000 to 200,000 yen per month, the new salarymen cannot afford to rent their own housing. They either have to continue to live with their parents or are offered (sometimes compulsory) accommodation in corporate dormitories, thus making their first years on the job (until marriage) a truely totalitarian experience with round-the-clock company supervision, regimentation and evaluation. Corporate discipline is strict: punctuality, obedience, quality of work, attitudes to work assignments, proper deference to the hierarchy and to customers are continuously supervised and publicly evaluated (for blue-collar workers there are often public scoreboards showing work quality). It is only the socialising experience of having successfully survived Japan's education system for two decades that teaches most recruits the self-discipline and endurance necessary to survive the first gruelling and decisive years as lowly corporate footsoldiers. There is still no absenteeism and only few examples of unsubordination or organised labour troubles. Also drop-out rates are very low: each university-trained recruit knows that his first employment is his one and only career chance in the top tier of corporate Japan. No other self-respecting big league company would take him: employment and work conditions would not be much different, and our man would only have proven his immaturity by wasting his painfully acquired seniority of a few years of work experience. Only lower-paying second or third-tier businesses and similar institutions would be available, and these would offer less prestige and job security. He would also have to compete with the graduates of the second- or third-rated universities, colleges, professional schools and high schools.

It is therefore lack of viable alternatives and the self-discipline instilled by Japan's education system that internalises the value of deferred gratification which persuades our man to soldier on. It is certainly not (or hardly ever) some mythological identification with the fairly alien corporate conglomerate which, moreover, is felt to be rather oppressive, exploitative and uncaring by most in their first years, which makes these mostly intelligent young men endure. Still, in many cases a lot of psychological counselling and family cajoling is needed to keep them on track. Corporate middle management – and in theory the *kacho* rank in particular – has the function of looking after their subordinates in a paternalist manner, and sorting out the professional and private troubles of their underlings (including also occasional *omiai* matchmaking, which can become urgent due to forthcoming overseas assignments).

After about five years of 'premanagement' toil and education, most companies begin to allow their successfully conforming manager candidates to rise to the lowest levels of junior management (assistant section chief), whereupon starts a programme of rotating job assignments, which will test their abilities, including leadership potential. Sometimes this may lead to a period of service (*shukko*) with a related company, with a government institute, or research facilities at home or abroad. Job rotation ideally should be maintained throughout an employee's working life. Such job assignments may vary greatly: alternating years in production management with years in sales, in accounting, to running affiliate companies or overseas subsidiaries, each requiring thorough new learning experiences. The company hopes that its managers will thereby acquire a broad range of experiences, personal contacts throughout the company, and an ability to communicate across departmental lines and share common corporate goals and objectives. After the initial 'premanagement' stage many personnel departments will have discreetly picked 'elite-track' candidates, whose future assignments will be particularly varied and challenging. Upon their successful completion, in their rise through the ranks many will still formally follow the seniority track, but in terms of job content and discretionary remuneration (bonuses) there will already be indications of quicker promotions. The sizable bonus payments (due in July and December) allow individual merits and achievements to be rewarded discreetly (as regards colleagues) but perceptively (as regards the beneficiary).

The virtues required from employees during their biannual evaluations also undergo a subtle shift: as a junior salaryman the only leadership quality required is obedience. At a more middle level the attainment of quantitative goals, negotiating and analytical skills and personnel management abilities are desired.

After 10–15 years on the corporate payroll and after a decade in positions of gradually increasing responsibility, including training/supervising subordinates, corporate identification will surely set in, as the company has indeed become by far the major centre of a manager's life and absorbs most of his interests. Corporate values and norms are internalised. From being discreet dissidents in their freshmen days, these middle managers have gradually transformed themselves into conformist corporate role-models. No more dreams of dropping out or of long vacations. Most would hardly know what to do with themselves during extended periods if left to their own devices.

Given their major obligation to their family (which is to deliver the pay cheques regularly to their wives), Japanese managers usually cite financial objectives as their main motivation to work in opinion surveys. As they, however, receive hardly more than pocket money in return from their wives (and plenty of frills in kind from their company and their clients), the genuineness of this convenient assertion for Japanese managers is rather doubtful. Still, as they climb the seniority escalator and the related career ladder, monthly remuneration will normally have quadrupled by the age of 40 compared with their starting salary, reaching some 10 million yen p.a.

for most managers in top-tier companies at that age.¹ With seniority-based increments, their basic salary plus allowances will peak at the standard retirement age of 55. With luck, by then the last housing mortgages will be paid and their standard two children will be out of college/university.

Finally, allowances are also paid for executive rank. They vary a lot between companies, but never reach the extreme variations experienced in the US and even in Europe between chief executive officers and the lowest blue/white-collar worker. This differential in Japan appears at most as 11:1. Still, benefits in kind (share entitlements, corporate mansions, chauffeured cars, complementary travel, golf club membership, entertainment allowances and so on) may be considerable, and increase dramatically on the top rungs of the corporate ladder.

Obviously, the age structure of a company affects its wage cost ratio strongly: the younger (and faster-growing) the company, the lower the labour costs; the older (and more stagnant or declining) the company, the higher they become. Both virtuous and evil spirals are at work.

Individual career prospects also vary widely with the employees' demographic profile and the corporate growth prospects in a largely seniority-based system. Slow-growth companies will have a bulge of unpromotable, frustrated ex-hopefuls in their mid-forties, for whom simply there will be insufficient executive posts available. Declining companies shedding labour will provide even more demotivating career prospects. The alternatives are often management titles without content or additional costly layers of management. Efforts are currently being made to shift the seniority system to a more selective meritocratic basis. But resistance among those likely to lose out is predictably strong.² There are, however, still sufficient high-growth companies, with ever-expanding staff intakes and a proliferation of subsidiaries, to make the Japanese promotion escalator system go on.

CORPORATE DECISION-MAKING

'Decision-making in large companies is in general from the bottom up, consensual and participative.'³ Statements of this level of generality, which still abound in the standard literature on Japanese management, are meaningless as they fail to qualify the type of decisions being made. If they concern technical suggestions for improving shop-floor operations made by quality circles or routine commercial decisions, the bottom-up *ringi-sho* procedure, similarly to that in public administration, surely applies.

On issues of strategic importance (that is, on new product developments, diversification projects, overseas investments, marketing strategies, corporate acquisitions, key personnel decisions and so on) it is nonsensical to assume that such decisions are not taken by the company's chairman and his board of directors. These are decisions for which only they are qualified, for which they will be held responsible and will take the credit (and rarely the blame).

As in Western companies, Japanese corporations are headed by a president (*shacho*), who acts effectively as chief executive officer, to whom the various vice-presidents (*fuku shacho*) in charge of major corporate units report. Next in the organisational hierarchy follow managing directors (*senmu*), executive directors (*jomu*), and directors (*torishimari yaku*). At the middle level are heads of departments (*bucho*), of divisions (*kacho*) and finally of sections (*kakaricho*).

The chairman (*kaicho*) of the board is usually the previous president who, after handpicking and grooming his successor, sees this new position as an honorific – and often very influential – pre-retirement stage during which he leaves the hands-on management to the president, who remains the ultimate power figure in each company. The board of directors is largely composed of the senior directors (*juyaku*), who are essentially in-house career managers, handpicked by the president and his predecessor, plus one or other fellow *keiretsu* executives and a friendly banker. If the membership of the board of directors is too large for effective decision-making, a smaller group consisting of the president, the vice-presidents and the managing directors will make the substantial deliberations and decisions.

The dominance of the president is evident in each corporate annual report photograph: he is usually seated in the centre (sometimes with the chairman), with his vice-presidents standing obediently, in hierarchical order, at his side. Even his facial expression seems to be shared by his senior underlings. If he looks sour and unamused at the camera, his deputies equally seem to suffer from ulcers or chew on lemons. If he smiles broadly, his vice-presidents also appear visibly more relaxed and cheerful.

It is only the founder-president or a wilful heir to a family-owned enterprise who will make decisions in an autocratic one-man fashion. This creates problem cases where the succession consists of groomed successors or vice-presidents who are all untried yes-men. In general, however, corporate Japan prefers commonsense-orientated consensus board decisions over the genius or folly of a company president. Major decisions will usually only be taken after all the senior managers concerned have been able to supply their relevant input (produced by their respective departments), and after extensive deliberations of the board of directors, where all members are probably aware of their president's preference. Yet in most cases he will probably be hesitant to overrule his board's majority view or consensus on a major issue. This will make any – even a very senior and powerful – president very hesitant to engage in the on-the-spot decisions which are sometimes so popular among Western CEOs who are eager to demonstrate their leadership and decision-making powers as symbols of their executive virility. As a result, Japanese corporate decisions usually take more time, particularly in the case of middle-management decisions (which require more in-house consultation and senior-level *nemawashi* acceptance-seeking), but are often better researched and evaluated. In consequence they are implemented more quickly and smoothly.

Japanese corporate promotions reflect and reward not only quantitative goal achievement, analytical abilities and demonstrated leadership qualities, but also co-operative behaviour and paternalistic care for subordinates among their middle management. Most senior executives are hence, ideally, steeped in the tradition of consultation and delegation to junior levels which they are expected to continue upon promotion to senior functions. While Japanese corporations have their share of factional schisms and intersectional conflicts of interest, the management policies of job rotation, systematic consultation and consensus-seeking tends to reduce what is a perennial problem of most corporate organisations.

On issues of corporate importance, top-down modes of decision-making and channels of communication are clearly dominant in Japanese companies. There are, however, also channels of bottom-up communication which are encouraged and, in case of the quality circles, actually run parallel to the formal organisational structure with the circle leader reporting directly via the company's quality control committee to the directors' level, thus making sure that the principal shop-floor concerns and suggestions get a fair senior hearing and are not, as in conventional suggestion systems, shot down and frustrated by middle management.

Particular emphasis is also placed on regular middle-management meetings with the sales staff, which provide valuable instant feedback on the company's situation in the market-place and on competitors' activities, the conclusions of which are transmitted to executive level.

In international comparison, Japanese companies, their employees and executives appear to be a fairly homogeneous lot. In fact, there are no known foreign board members in even the most internationalised top-league corporations. Also, recruitment policies, intensive corporate socialisation, job rotation practices and seniority-orientated promotion tend to produce (to corporate outsiders, at least) fairly uniform and conformist corporate soldiers ('Mitsubishi men' are supposedly more disciplined; 'Mitsui men' reportedly act in a more independently minded way; 'Toyota men' are Nagoya-centred, conservative nationalists; 'Nissan men' appear to be internationalist visionaries). This homogeneity facilities communication, as corporate goals are shared and perceived in predictable ways. Promotion in the private sector, similar to public administration, follows roughly the order of seniority (which is why no manager ever needs to be afraid or jealous of his subordinates' achievements), following the 'class' (year) of entry into the company. This happens usually at the age of 23 for university graduates. According to a JETRO study, promotion to *kacho* is at between 32 and 42, to *bucho* between 39 and 48, while senior directors are appointed from the age of 45.[4]

Those employees not promoted to *bucho* rank are usually retired at 55 (and often rehired as part-timers by subsidiaries with a significant pay cut). There are no uniform retirement policies for director-level people, which formally may not be until 70. In most cases, however, executives will receive a 'friendly' but determined 'tap on the shoulder' and get the message by offering their 'voluntary' retirement, which in turn will be accepted with regrets, and rewarded by a subsequent temporary executive position at one of the company's subsidiaries. It is only the president who has the privilege of determining his own retirement and appointing his successor, unless, of course, an impeding business failure or major public scandal involving the company makes his resignation mandatory. These imponderables and the vagaries of his health notwithstanding, a company president in many cases can expect to reign until the advent of senility. This makes the members of the business elite Japan's longest-serving office-holders and, by comparison, almost absolute rulers of their respective kingdoms.

Corporate succession news is subject to intense business and public speculation. Newspapers, and the *Nikkei* in particular, early in the year forewarn their readers of which presidents are likely to retire and which ones will try to stay on. Many companies have renewable tenure of office of two to five years for their presidents. This increases pressure on presidents not to seek the renewal of yet another term once they are close, or beyond, the age of 70. Once a president has decided upon retirement and has designated his successor (recently some companies like C. Itoh, Nissho Iwai, Taisho Fire & Marine, Fujitsu and Honda have picked executives in their late fifties as new presidents), all the by-passed vice-presidents and executives who are older than the new president offer their resignation, thus permitting a rejuvenated new corporate era to unfold.

As most Japanese top-tier and *keiretsu* companies own each other through crossholdings, the major shareholders (the city banks and insurance companies) are not interested in dividend payments, but in long-term asset growth. Hence companies are free to define their ultimate objectives as corporate growth and survival. For the company this translates into max-imised sales (and the achievement of market shares that permit them to dominate markets), expanded production capacities to minimise unit costs, and enhanced control of subcontractors' affiliates and sales outlets in order to assure complete upstream and downstream control – cutting input costs, and increasing the quality of components and of associated services. High-growth companies also begin to spin off a range of expanding specialist corporate divisions (property administration, PR, market research, publications, research, special productions, etc.) as nominally self-contained subsidiaries, allowing them to operate as semi-independent profit centres, to diversify and to generate new business opportunities.

For employees, corporate growth and profitability implies, in the short term, increased bonuses and, in the long term, above-average basic salary increases. It also means enhanced career prospects for its premanagement and middle management personnel, as new units are created and new subsidiaries are set up.

For a company's senior management, corporate growth means not only personal riches (through the increased value of executive entitlement shares), but more importantly enhanced personal prestige among peers and the public at large, which in Japan – almost more so than in the US – makes successful (that is, those presiding over 'number one' – ranking companies) business leaders objects of public worship and adulation.

Japan's corporate obsession with never-ending growth and its strive for ever-more-comprehensive upstream and downstream control in an open world economy obviously has international implications. Japanese compa-nies simply project their ingrained domestic habits of market domination onto world markets, and, wherever possible, through a mixture of predatory pricing, better quality and quicker service, attempt to cut down and sub-jugate their overseas competitors, eventually reducing them to the role of dependent marketing agents and subcontractors for local assembly or com-ponent production. Japan's export economy is beyond the stage of creating havoc on foreign markets with a torrent of exports, as was aptly described by a leaked Commission paper in 1979.[5] Today its major car and electronics companies are engaged in a systematic, carefully planned and orderly executed colonising conquest of the world markets in question, thus leading their corporate objectives to their ultimate conclusion. 'Japanese manage-ment style' (whatever this means to different authors) is currently being lauded as containing valuable wisdom to enable ailing US and European industries to get back on their feet (but often ignoring its basic premiss:

the regime of iron discipline for company employees – and earlier for high school students – emanating from a rigidly segregated labour market: top-tier employees constantly face the choice between 'up and doing' or 'down and out'; the latter entails being sent to a regional branch office on pro-bation, or being assigned permanently to a subsidiary, with drastic cuts in salary and fringe benefits).

Yet while foreign critics, who in the past have derided Japan's feudalist features, have become rare, today they continue to stress more the func-tional defects of the Japanese system of management. A frequent critique addresses the fact that multiple layers of management (a result of posts created for personnel due for promotion since the advent of low-growth periods in the mid-1970s) have caused considerable delays for commercial routine decisions, with *ringi-sho* procedures (already described as a routine operation in public administration) causing considerable delays in approval and enactment. This bureaucratisation served to stifle junior-level initiative and creativity. In fact, job satisfaction of white-collar employees, up to middle-management level, appears to be surprisingly low.

Reorganisation attempts to cut out needless intermediate layers of management, however, face determined opposition from the vested inter-ests of the position-holders concerned, and thus cannot be conceived of as a simple rationalisation, as in Western private organisations. For instance, as a *conditio sine qua non* in Japan, titles must be maintained: indeed, any *meishi* collection will reveal that middle-ranking managers now display a wide array of impressive sounding titles. Ken Moroi, chairman of Chichibu Cement and a former vice-chairman of *Keizai Doyukai*, has argued for a more radical solution:[6] To abolish the rigid hierarchies of rotated generalists by the horizontal assembly of project teams consisting of specialists who would find professional fulfilment in their respective fields of expertise. Promotions would be based on merit, and the companies' executives se-lected from among management specialists. Moroi sees these fundamental organisational changes embedded in a post-material societal fulfilment and in the quality of life and of the environment for the next century.

CORPORATE ELITE CAREERS

Two representative biographical sketches follow. They are for the two big-business leaders, Koichiro Ejiri, chairman of Mitsui Bussan, and Yutaka Kume, president of Nissan. These are followed by three prominent *zaikai* leaders: Gaishi Hiraiwa, Eshiro Saito and Eiji Suzuki.

Four phenomena are striking in analysing the biographies:

(1) the predominance of graduates of Todai Law in business careers;
(2) the strongly rotated, if still strictly in-house, character of these careers;
(3) the frequency of *zaikai* and government advisory activities once the vice-presidency level has been reached; and finally
(4) the importance attached to domestic and foreign honours received.

Biographical Sketches

Koichiro Ejiri[7]

Chairman, Mitsui Bussan
Chairman of *Keidanren* committee on EC–Japan relations

Born: 1 September 1920

Education and career profile:

Sept. 1943	Graduated from Law Department of Tokyo Imperial University
Oct. 1943	Entered Mitsui & Co. Ltd
April 1968	General Manager, Melbourne Office of Mitsui & Co. (Australia) Ltd
June 1971	President, Mitsui & Co. (Australia) Ltd
June 1974	General Manager, Iron Ore Department, Mitsui & Co. Ltd
May 1975	Director and concurrently General Manager, Iron Ore Department
June 1977	Executive Managing Director and concurrently General Manager, Iron & Steel Administrative Division
June 1980	Executive Managing Director, General Manager for the Americas, and concurrently president, Mitsui & Co. (USA) Inc.
June 1982	Senior Executive Managing Director, General Manager, Corporate Planning Group
June 1983	Executive Vice-president, General Manager, Corporate Planning Group
June 1984	Executive Vice-president
June 1985	President
June 1990	Chairman
Honours:	Governor's Award of the State of New York (USA) Blue Ribbon Medal of the Japanese Government

Yutaka Kume[8]

President of Nissan Motor Co. Ltd

Born: 20 May 1921 in Tokyo

Education and career profile:

Sept. 1944	Graduated from the University of Tokyo with a BE degree in aircraft engineering
April 1946	Joined Nissan Motor Co. Ltd
Nov. 1964	General Manager, Production Control & Engineering Department, Department, Zama Plant
Nov 1971	General Manager, Yoshiwara Plant (transmission and steering components)
Nov. 1973	Director and member of the board, concurrently serving as General Manager of Tochigi Plant
June 1977	Managing Director in charge of the Office of Product & Engineering Strategy; General Manager of Tochigi Plant until the end of 1978
June 1982	Executive Managing Director in charge of the Office of Product & Engineering Strategy and Quality Administration Division
June 1983	Executive Vice-president in charge of Research & Development, Diversified Operations and Corporate Planning Office and concurrently served as General Manager of Quality Administration Division
June 1985	President

Positions held outside the company:

Executive Director, Japan Federation of Employers' Associations (*Nikkeiren*)

Chairman, Japan Automobile Manufacturers' Association, Inc. (*JAMA*)

Member of the Board of Directors, Chairman, Japan–Greece Economic Committee

Chairman, Committee on Environment and Safety, *Keidanren* (Federation of Economic Organisations)

Chairman, Japan Motor Industrial Federation, Inc.

Chairman, Japan Institute of Industrial Engineering

President, Japan–Netherlands Society

President, Japan Amateur Rowing Association

Honours:

April 1986	Blue Ribbon Medal from the Emperor
June 1986	Commander of the Order of Orange-Nassau

Gaishi Hiraiwa[9]

Chairman of the Board of Directors of the Tokyo Electric Power Co. Inc.

Born: 31 August 1914

Education and career profile:

March 1939	Graduated from Tokyo University, Law Department
April 1939	Entered Tokyo Electric Lighting Co. (in 1942 renamed Kanto Electric Power Distribution Co. and since 1951 renamed the Tokyo Electric Power Co.)
May 1964	Manager, General Affairs Department
May 1968	Director
May 1971	Managing Director
Nov. 1974	Vice-president
Oct. 1976	President
June 1984	Chairman of the Board of Directors

Positions held outside the company:

April 1973	Trustee of the Japan Committee for Economic Development (*Keizai Doyukia*)
May 1973	Director of Japan Electric Association
Nov. 1976	Executive Director of the Federation of Economic Organisations (*Keidanren*)
March 1977	Member of the Economic Council, Economic Planning Agency
May 1977	Executive Director of the Japan Federation of Employers' Association (*Nikkeiren*)
June 1977	Member of the Industrial Structure Council, Ministry of International Trade & Industry (MITI)
July 1977	Chairman of the Federation of Electric Power Companies (retired in June 1984)
July 1977	Member of the Electricity Utility Industry Council, MITI.
Feb. 1978	Executive Director of the Japan–China Long-term Trade Committee
May 1978	Vice-chairman of the Federation of Economic Organisations (*Keidanren*)
June 1980	Counsellor of the Atomic Energy Commission, Science & Technology Agency
Nov. 1980	Special Member of the Industrial Structure Council, MITI.

Feb. 1981	Member of National Public Safety Commission
March 1981	Vice-chairman of Japan–China Society
Oct. 1981	Special Member of Council for Transport Policy, Ministry of Transportation
Jan. 1982	Member of Policy Board, Japan Federation of Employers' Associations (*Nikkeiren*)
Nov. 1982	Executive Councillor and no. 3 Councillor of the Tokyo Chamber of Commerce and Industry
April 1984	Member of the Customer Representative Panel, Nippon Telegraph and Telephone Public Corporation (NTT)
June 1984	Vice-chairman of Japan–China Association on Economy and Trade
July 1984	Counsellor of the Japan Development Bank
July 1984	Chairman of the Business Policy Forum
Sept. 1984	Special Adviser to Minister, Economic Planning Agency
Oct. 1984	Counsellor of Power Reactor and Nuclear Fuel Development Corporation
May 1985	Chairman, Committee for Energy Policy Promotion
Dec. 1990	President, *Keidanren*

Honours:

Oct. 1976	Medal of Honour with Blue Ribbon
March 1980	Honorary Commander of the Order of the British Empire
March 1983	Légion d'Honneur Officier
Nov. 1984	First Class Order of the Sacred Treasure
April 1985	Das Große Verdienstkreuz des Verdienstorden der Bundesrepublik Deutschland

Eshiro Saito[10]

Chairman, *Keidanren*

Born: 22 November 1911

Education and career profile:

1935	Tokyo University (Faculty of Economics)
1941	Joined Japan Iron and Steel Co. Ltd
1962	Managing Director, Yawata Iron and Steel Corporation
1970	Senior Managing Director, Nippon Steel Corporation

1973	Executive Vice-president, Nippon Steel Corporation
1975	Vice-chairman, *Keizai Doyu Kai*
1977	President, Nippon Steel Corporation
1977	Executive Director, *Keidanren*
1977–9	Chairman, International Iron and Steel Institute
1979–84	Chairman, Japan Iron and Steel Federation
1979–87	Chairman, The Kozai Club (Steel Materials Club)
1979	Chairman, Japan Iron and Steel Exporters' Association
1979	Chairman, Japan Project Industry Council
1979	Member, Trade Conference, Prime Minister's Office
1980	Vice-chairman, *Keidanren*
1980	Chairman, Japan–DDR Economic Committee
1981	Chairman, Nippon Steel Corporation
1981	Member, Council for Transport, Ministry of Transport
1982	Member, Fiscal System Council, Ministry of Finance
1984–6	Vice-president, Japan Federation of Employers' Associations (*Nikkeiren*)
1984	Honorary Chairman, Japan Iron and Steel Federation
1984	Chairman, Japan–Australia Business Co-operation Committee
1984	President, Japan–Argentina Association
1984	Member, Co-ordination Committee, Industrial Structure Council, Ministry of International Trade and Industry
1985	President, Japanisch–Osterreichische Kulturvereinigung
1986	Chairman, *Keidanren*
1986	Chairman, *Keizai Koho* Centre (Japan Institute for Social and Economic Affairs)
1987	Honorary Chairman, Nippon Steel Corporation

Honours:

1967	Medal of Honour with Blue Ribbon
1978	Ordem de Rio Branco, Brazil
1982	First Class Order of the Sacred Treasure
1983	Order of Bernard O'Higgins, Chile
1986	Grosser Stern der Völkerfreundschaft, DDR
1986	Order de Mayo al Merito en el Grado de Gran Cruz, Argentina
1988	Honorary Companion in the General Division of the Order of Australia
1988	Ordem Nacional do Cruzeiro do Sul Grand Oficial, Brazil
1988	Knight Commander's Cross First Class, Austria

| 1990 | Das Große Verdienstkreuz mit Stern des Verdienstordens der Bundesrepublik Deutschland |
| 1990 | Grand Cordon of the Order of the Rising Sun |

Personal History of Mr Eiji Suzuki

Eiji Suzuki[11]

President, Japan Federation of Employers' Associations (*Nikkeiren*) and Chairman, Mitsubishi Kasei Corporation

Born: 29 May 1913

Education and career profile:

March 1937	Graduated from Tokyo University of Commerce
April 1937	Joined Nippon Chemical Industries Ltd (subsequently renamed Mitsubishi Kasei Corporation)
Sept. 1962	Member of the Board of Directors and concurrently General Manager of the Accounting Department
Sept. 1964	Managing Director
March 1970	Senior Managing Director
Nov. 1973	Executive Vice-president
July 1974	President of the Mitsubishi Kasei Corporation
April 1982	Chairman of the Board of Directors, Mitsubishi Kasei Corporation

Positions held outside the company:

1975– present	Executive Director of *Keidanren* (Federation of Economic Organisations)
1976–7	President of Japan Urea & Ammonium Sulphate Industry Association
1976–84	Director in *Keizai Doyukai* (Japan Association of Corporate Executives)
1978–80	President of Japan Chemical Industry Association
1981– present	Member of Policy Board of *Nikkeiren* (Japan Federation of Employers' Associations)
1981–7	Chairman of the Kanto Regional Employers' Association
1984–7	Vice-president of *Nikkeiren*
1987–91	President of *Nikkeiren*

Appointments to public committees:
  more than 50 important public appointments, including:

1981–present	Member of the Electricity Utility Industry Council, Ministry of International Trade & Industry (MITI)
1984–present	Member of the Council on Population Programme, Ministry of Health and Welfare (MHW)
1986–present	Member of the Health Science Council, Ministry of Health and Welfare (MHW)
1986–present	Member of the *Ad-hoc* Committee on Life Sciences and Mankind, Science and Technology Agency
1987–present	Chairman of the Fiscal System Council, Ministry of Finance; President of the Japan Hockey Association

Honours:

1977	Blue Ribbon Medal
1986	Grand Cordon of the Order of the Sacred Treasure

A limited number of fellow *keiretsu* managers and more or less friendly bankers and an even smaller number of *amakudari* (bureaucrats-turned-executives) appear as the only sizable group of senior-level side-entrants into the closed world of Japanese in-house management. However, when not dealing with or managing straight ministry clientele industries (like public banks for MOF, oil companies for MITI, air transport for MOT), only a few of these highly qualified elite bureaucrats can be found in straight senior line-management positions. If they have not opted for the soft senior advisor (*komon*) positions straightaway, or gone to head some industry-financed research institute, then even with an executive title (senior managing director for a former deputy director general, or vice-president for a former vice-minister) they appear to be in charge of fairly advisory/representative (international relations) or governmental relations (external relations) aspects of the corporations they joined. In only very rare cases do they seem to become responsible and successful in managing straightforward core business operations. In case of *keiretsu* despatched/exchanged managers, however, these restrictions appear to apply much less – and certainly *not* in case of a subsidiary company or a firm in need of a rescue operation.

As the biographies above indicate, Todai clearly dominates among top corporate presidents as alma mater. This is confirmed by the statistics (Table 10.1).

The story is clearly different for Japanese corporate presidents in general, the largest number of whom head SMEs. Here Tokyo's private uni-

Table 10.1 *Alma maters of the presidents of top corporations (1987)[12]*

1	Tokyo University (Todai)	417
2	Keio University	172
3	Kyoto University	134
4	Waseda University	131
5	Hitotsubashi University	64
6	Tohoku University	46
7	Kobe University	43
8	Nihon University	37
9	Osaka University	33
10	Kyushu University	32

Table 10.2 *Company presidents of companies capitalised at more than 1 million yen (1987), by university of graduation[13]*

1	Nihon University	15,517
2	Waseda University	13,920
3	Keio University	10,562
4	Meiji University	10,541
5	Chuo University	8,687
6	Hosei University	6,475
7	Tokyo University	5,421
8	Doshisha University	4,741
9	Kansai University	4,092
10	Ritsumeikan University	3,379

versities with the largest enrolment also supply the largest numbers (Table 10.2).

As Ken Moroi puts it: 'Members of the business elite are now being asked to make so many personal sacrifices for their companies that they cannot lead a human life. The result is a growing number of broken families.'[14]

Compensation for the sacrifice is shown in Table 10.3.[15]

These presidential and other executive salaries are only a fraction of what US and European top managers in comparable positions would command. Fringe benefits are obviously more difficult to compare. Yet one interesting hypothesis emerges in the context of an international comparison: could it be that executive remuneration is inversely related to the long-term health of the companies concerned?

Table 10.3 Annual remuneration and bonuses for company presidents
and directors

Company capitalisation (billion yen)	President (million yen)		Vice-president/ managing director (million yen)	Executive director (million yen)	Director (million yen)
> 10	Salary	33.6	33.0	16.6	13.3
	Bonus	13.8	7.5	4.3	5.9
3–10	Salary	27.6	18.0	13.7	12.6
	Bonus	10.7	6.5	3.8	4.7
1–3	Salary	21.8	14.8	12.5	9.4
	Bonus	7.3	4.5	3.2	3.0

THE SUPER-RICH

According to Forbes,[16] Japan had 41 US$ billionaires in 1990, including the world's two richest men, Taikichiro Mori, aged 87, whose Tokyo real-estate holdings were worth US$15 billion, and Yoshiaki Tsutsumi, aged 57, owner of the railroad/real estate-based parts of the Seibu *keiretsu*, worth at least US$35 billion. Other mega-rich men from Japan include Kitaro Watanabe, president of Azabu Motor Co. (net worth US$7 billion), Kenkichi Nakajima, owner of Heiwa Corporation, a *pachinko* machine-maker (net worth US$6.1 billion), the Takenaka family, controlling Takenaka Construction (net worth US$5.4 billion), the family of Yoneichi Otani (net worth US$5 billion), and Hirotomo Takei, the chairman of Chisan Co., a speculative real-estate developer, currently indicted on tax fraud, but none the less still with a net worth of US$4.5 billion.

A Nikkei survey of 1988, which only considered the market value of stocks, land and other assets held in the names of individuals (and hence did not list Yoshiaki Tsutsumi, most of whose property is in the name of companies he controls, including his Kokudo Keikaku Holding), came up with a list of some 180 Japanese owning fortunes of 10 billion yen or more (see Table 10.4).[17]

The late Konosuke Matsushita, who at the age of 23 founded the Matsushita group in 1917, with a starting capital of 100 yen by manufacturing light bulbs and battery lamps, headed the list with his shareholdings estimated worth 370 billion yen (however, the estate he left to his family one year later, according to the Osaka Tax Bureau, was worth 'only' 245 billion yen – still constituting a national inheritance record and triggering a record inheritance tax of 85 billion yen.)[18]

Table 10.4   The richest people in Japan in terms of personal assets
(in billion yen, June 1988)

Ranking	Name	Title	Assets
1	Konosuke Matsushita	Executive Advisor/Matsushita Electric Industrial	370
2	Rinji Shino	President/Kishu Museum	300
3	Tamesaburo Furukawa	Chairman/Nippon Herald Films	200
4	Kichinosuke Sasaki	President/Togensha	150
5	Shoji Uehara	Chairman/Taisho Pharmaceutical	120
6	Kitaro Watanabe	President/Azabu Motors	100
6	Genshiro Kawamoto	President/Marugen	100
6	Isao Nakauchi	Chairman & President/Daiei	100
9	Taro Iketani	Advisor/Tokyo Steel Mfg.	97
10	Kanichiro Ishibashi	Honorary Chairman/Bridgestone	95
11	Masatoshi Ito	President/Ito-Yokado	88
12	Kenichi Mabuchi	Chairman/Mabuchi Motor	83
13	Yasuo Takei	Chairman/Takefuji	72
14	Hiroshi Yamauchi	President/Nintendo	72
15	Goro Tatsumi	President/Kosei Securities	68
16	Yoshiro Ohbayashi	Chairman & CEO/Ohbayashi	68
17	Kazuo Inamori	Chairman/Kyocera	63
18	Sae Uehara	Honorary Chairperson/Taisho Phamaceutical	62
19	Namiko Iijima	Owner & Manager/Ginza Nohgakudo	55
20	Makoto Iida	Chairman/Secom	53
21	Yohachiro Iwasaki	Chairman/Iwasaki Sangyo	50
21	Kiyobumi Moroto	President/Moroto Forest	50
23	Shoichiro Toyoda	President/Toyota Motor	46
24	Shoichi Kajima	President/Kajima	45
25	Yoshitomo Takagi	President/Chujitsuya	44
26	Saburosuke Suzuki	Chairman/Ajinomoto	44
26	Tasaburo Kumagai	Senior Adviser/Kumagai Gumi	44
28	Hideto Furuoka	Chairman/Gakken	40
29	Hiroshi Okura	President/Noevir	38
30	Ryoichi Jinnai	Chairman/Promise	37

Second on the list was Rinji Shino, the thirty-sixth head of the Shino family, which was already rich through landholdings in the twelfth century and managed to survive the US occupation's postwar land reform. Shino also controls the Meiko tourism group, operating in central Japan.

Japan's third and fourth richest men are Tamesaburo Furukawa and Kichinosuke Sasaki, two self-made real-estate and stock speculators.

In Japan the leading taxpayers are also published each year, their top scores making front page news.[19] Among the top 100, 60 made their money by selling real estate and 35 by gains on the stock exchange. The 1990 list was headed by Ryoei Saito, aged 74, chairman of family-controlled Daishowa Paper, Japan's second largest paper-maker and owner of large traces of woodland in Japan. Saito (his brother is governor of Shizuoka prefecture, and his son an LDP Dietmember) had to pay 3.1 billion yen (US$23 million) in tax after selling some of his land and Daishowa stocks to generate the funds for his 24.4 billion yen purchases of Van Gogh's *Portrait of Doctor Gachet* (US$82.5 million) and Renoir's *Le Moulin de la Galette* (US$78.1 million) in New York in May 1990. Saito subsequently created an international uproar by declaring that he wanted the paintings cremated with him upon his death (which he later declared was meant as a joke). On his top listing amongst Japan's taxpayers, Saito was quoted as worrying about next year's positioning: 'I don't want to become number 30 or lower on the list. I want to be at least number 10 or number 15. So I have already started thinking about how to generate enough money to stay at that level.'[20] While Saito's attitude may bode ill for the world's cultural heritage or for Daishowa's financial health, his vanity surely is recommendable from the National Tax Administration Agency's point of view.

As elsewhere, money in Japan gains lustre with age. Fortunes made by quick ruthless deals in land or stock speculation in Japan's bubble economy of the 1980s still have the stigma of tax evasion, political favouritism, insider trading or underworld connections attached to this new money. Although this applies much less to the entrepreneur founders who set up conglomerates in the sectors expanding most rapidly since the postwar era (cars, electronics, construction, pharmaceuticals, supermarket retailing), still the image of parvenu sticks when compared to second- and third-generation or even older money, whose often rough origins have conveniently been lost to oblivion, as these fortunes managed to survive the vagaries of the times. As Mr Shino proved, some very old money actually managed to survive in Japan, escaping the prewar banking crashs, the devastations of the war, the postwar hyperinflation, SCAP's farmland reform and *zaibatsu* expropriation, and finally Japan's inheritance taxes (which amount to a stiff 70 per cent for transfers between blood relations of one generation).

Some of the greatest riches of contemporary Japan include second-generation owners of the smaller *zaibatsu* (Tokyu, Seibu and so on) which escaped the US dissolution order. They are an integral part of the *zaikai* elite. For the first generation of super-rich, however, genuine *zaikai* membership is usually still out of question.

In 1979 Professor Hamabata undertook anthropogical fieldwork with the Japanese upper classes.[21] His study was into the mindset, the social norms and family life of the established Japanese business elite. After apparently considerable difficulties in passing through cultural, class and gender barriers, he was finally able to obtain the confidence of some – mostly female – members of one of Japan's gilded business families and came to learn the intricacies of interhousehold (*ie*) relations, the complexities of the battles to succeed as head of the household and of the family enterprise, of strategic marriage arrangements (*omiai*), and of the importance of upper-class status symbols and adherence to the appropriate way of life. The feudal rigidities of the norms and behaviour which Hamabata observed among his upper-crust associates may come as a surprise. One might have thought that Japan's cosmopolitan monied elite would have been the most emancipated from feudal *ie* concepts. Yet they appear more *ie* obsessed than even the most conservative (ex-)landowners in the Tohoku countryside.

Upon reflection, however, this apparently out-dated behaviour becomes plausible: these people owe their social status and wealth essentially to their birth and family. It is hence a feudal, not a bourgeois individual-performance-orientated, elite (the latter applies to Japan's salarymen – managers or elite bureaucrats). It is their foremost duty to preserve and enhance their family's wealth and status, to continue the family line and to appoint an able successor. Succession is not automatic: in case of unavailable or incompetent sons, the successor may be an adopted son-in-law or a more distant relative. In order to preserve the family's status, the rules are strict: premiums are placed on good education, appropriate behaviour, business acumen, the right social contacts and way of life, including the choice of the right marriage partner (which is essential for breeding a proper prospective successor one generation later). There is no place for dissidents, bohemians, other-worldly scholars or spoilt brats.

All clan members implicitly acknowledge that for *ie* survival at a socially elevated status discipline must remain iron. Hamabata reports a few incidents of rigid collective *ie* discipline enforcement *vis à vis* dissenters and individualists within the family: they quickly learn either to adjust (including in their choice of marriage partners) or to be cast aside permanently (which means running a small subsidiary company with no prospects of taking over the family and its main business).

For a smooth succession in any good feudal system legitimacy is needed, apart from abilities and proper conformity. Hamabata described the intricate struggles for symbols of legitimacy in the case of the crisis situation of an open succession struggle (which was left undecided by the deceased family head) in the family he encountered. Once decided, the new head of the family enforced his new authority ruthlessly over the reticent side-households and the businesses of his brothers, sisters and other relatives.

It is interesting to note that while men in the family deal mostly with business, it is the women who have to maintain social status, take care of family symbols, maintain a lavish and cultured life-style, are responsible for the groomed successor's education, proper marriage-making (*keibatsu*) and close social links to other peer elite families. To be accepted within this upper-crust money is essential but clearly not sufficient: the spouses of upstart land- or stock-speculating *nouveaux riches* were not welcome in *Keidanren*'s Women's National Auxiliary, to which the female members of Hamabata's family, together with the wives of other leading company presidents, LDP Members of Parliament and members of the Imperial Household belonged. Apparently, it took three generations of business success, of adherence to the right norms and of marrying upwardly to achieve this status. The women were acutely aware that this achievement could not be taken for granted, but had to be actively maintained.

Indeed, the biographies of successful members of the second generation demonstrate a self-discipline and stringency which the founder generation themselves applied. Below is the 'official' résumé of Shoichiro Toyoda, president of Toyota Motor. While family control of the company assured rapid promotion, Mr Toyoda (as is the rule in most larger family-controlled joint-stock companies) had to go through the motions of a regular corporate career.

Shoichiro Toyoda[22]
President, Toyota Motor Corporation

Shoichiro Toyoda, who was born in 1925, graduated from Nagoya University in 1947 with a degree in engineering. Three years after joining Toyota in 1952, he interrupted his business career to earn a doctorate in engineering from Tohoku University, where he wrote his doctoral thesis on fuel injection.

Dr Toyoda became managing director of the company in 1961. After promotion to senior managing director in 1967 and to executive vice-president in 1972, he became president of the company's marketing organisation in 1981. Dr Toyoda assumed the presidency of the newly integrated Toyota Motor Corporation upon the merger of the sales and production organisations in 1982.

Automotive technology, quality control and factory management have been primary emphases for Dr Toyoda throughout his career, and he received the Deming Prize in 1980 for his contributions to quality control. Dr Toyoda, who is a prominent spokesman for the automotive industry, recently served four years as chairman of the Japan Automobile Manufacturers Association, and became vice-chairman of the influential Federation of Industrial Organisations (*Keidanren*) this year. In 1984 he received Japan's prestigious Medal with Blue Ribbon for outstanding public service through business. Dr Toyoda's hobbies include *go*, gardening, and golf.

The entrepreneurial companies taking off during the postwar period (when the stranglehold which the established *zaibatsu* companies held over the market was weakened) still had to fight for finance, public subsidies and finally access to *zaikai* organisations, which the business establishment was unwilling to grant. As Woronoff rightly pointed out,[23] often with government agreement, newcomers were prevented from entering the steel and heavy industry, the chemical industry, and textiles and fibre-making.

Some founder-generation magnates (such as Akio Morita, the cofounder of Sony, Isao Nakauchi (Daiei) or Keizo Saji, who expanded and diversified Suntory) are known to speak their minds – more forthrightly than most of the salaried *zaikai* executives, who would never dare to venture off the well-trodden paths of conformist commonsense. Yet their proud management 'philosophies' offer little more than the usual homilies about the need for thorough training, good labour relations and the importance of trust rather than contracts, and of quality rather than price.[24]

While founder-presidents of the great manufacturing companies are publicly revered, public revulsion about the profiteers of Japan's real-estate bubble, which increasingly deprived middle-class salarymen and their families of the chance to own private housing in the metropolitan areas, is equally strong (as is public glee once the corporate titans have fallen from grace and landed in jail for tax evasion, fraud and the other minor infractions necessary to shortcut the long road to riches and fame). According to a 1986 poll, 70 per cent of the Japanese thought the rich were wastrels.[25] As the entrepreneurial postwar generation fades away, with speculators and conspicuous spenders coming to the fore, Japan's former 'middle middle classes', with their lack of purchasing power and stagnant living standards, begin instead to believe that they are actually 'lower middle class'. With this fundamental change, the legitimacy of the business elites' sway over the Japanese economy and over much of its public life may begin to erode before long.

Such feelings may also apply to Yoshiaki Tsutsumi, the world's and Japan's richest man, who does not fritter his wealth away on overpriced

Impressionists and tax bills, but who frugally purchased the 1998 Winter Olympics for Nagano, where he owns nine hotels, six golf courses, eight ski grounds, the Karuizawa Skating Centre, and extensive real estate, which will benefit from the anticipated tripling of land prices in the prefecture[26] as the result of public infrastructural investments. The opposition of local residents to Tsutsumi's aggressive development style, and the inevitable environmental degradation which the Winter Olympics would bring about, was subsequently swept aside by Tsutsumi's well-organised local support machine.

CORPORATE SOCIETY AND BUSINESS ETHICS

Since the early 1950s Japan has single-mindedly and most successfully concentrated on the optimisation of one single goal: economic growth through corporate prosperity. This strategic decision clearly reflected a profound consensus of its power elite, and was approved by a majority of the Japanese population (as evidenced in election results) and by its industrial unions (as visible in their industrial relations policy), which appreciated the resulting dramatic improvements in material living standards.

Often, however, Japan's pursuit of its single economic objective was at the expense of other equally worthy societal objectives (one could argue that the priority accorded to welfare policies in Western Europe and to the immediate gratification attitudes prevalent in the US are conversely to the detriment of these countries' long-term economic health). In Japan urbanism, regional development, the social infrastructure, housing standards, its education and legal systems and the quality of life for people in general still are strikingly inferior to, say, Western Europe, including countries such as the UK or Italy, which are at only 70 per cent of Japan's nominal GNP per capita.

Once most of the sensible material needs were satisfied for the great majority of the population, the continuation of almost exclusive economic growth objectives turned into a pretty mindless and wasteful exercise. There are, however, signs (as there have always been) that Japan's economic consensus might be unravelling. The (slightly left-wing) *Asahi* in its 1991 New Year editorial published the following thoughtful comments:

> There is probably no other country where companies exercise influence as they do in Japan. Corporate behavioural principles such as efficiency and profits have come to be widely accepted. Other values have been pushed aside as meaningless. Companies have tried to suppress not only

the dividends paid to shareholders but also the wages of workers. They have sought to ensure their own growth by spending most of their profits on capital investment. When domestic markets matured, they advanced to overseas markets and overwhelmed European and American companies. For many Japanese, corporations are indeed a group to belong to in place of their local community. As workers receive careful protection from companies, a thick wall forms between them and society at large, and they come to show less and less interest in problems such as social welfare and the environment.

Companies should make it daily practice to behave in a way that would be accepted by the world and to contribute positively to society. There are many characters to a person – that of a worker, member of the local community, consumer and family member. What seems to be called for is that an employee of a company should spend more time with his family and people of the local community. For this, it is necessary for corporations to allow workers to have varied facets and to shorten working hours to the level of those of Western companies at an early opportunity. Only by having workers regain their sense of daily life can initiatives emerge for reforming the taxation system and other policies which support currently the corporate-orientated society.[27]

It is a good editorial tradition in Japan to conclude with pious exhortations, but to avoid outlining strategies and conditions for political change.

Ethical standards in Japanese business are very much *sui generis*. Everything is good and proper for most Japanese salarymen which is good and proper for their company and which has been (implicitly or explicitly) approved by management. Japanese companies think little of purchasing industrial secrets stolen from a competitor (as is done by the heavy machinery makers which bought Komatsu's commercial secrets in 1991). Cement and beer companies operate open-price cartels. The construction industry is addicted to *dango* bid-rigging on public works contracts. Underworld groups control the gambling industry, stevedoring and large chunks of entertainment and road transport. The security houses run the Tokyo Stock Exchange like a rigged casino, pushing share prices up for specific clients (like the shares of the Tokyu railways by Nomura Securities for the benefit of the *Inagawa-kai* crime syndicate) or compensate political and business friends at the expense of other clients, if such plots did not work out as foreseen. All industries which depend on public licences to pursue their operations (air/sea/road transport, banking, securities, oil trading, liquor production, and so on) or which are in need of public protection (like the food and leather processing industries) or want access to public subsidies (ranging from R&D costs in heavy industries covered by the defence budget to the export of obsolete equipment by the *sogo shosha* by means of ODA funds) entertain strongly collusive ties to the government departments in charge. For most companies, including SMEs (the smaller, the worse), cheating on taxation is a common pastime, for which the only rule is not to get caught.

In general, however, Japan's way of doing business often implies an open-ended practice of gift-giving and -taking, which operates as a significant in-kind, tax-free salary enhancement for the upper ranks, and represents a major grey zone bordering on – and often amounting to – endemic corruption. For many managers, the borderline between private and corporate gifts is blurred: since they live for their companies anyway, 'private' and 'official' functions are mingled. Thus many executives would, like Hisashi Shinto, ex-chairman of NTT and previously of IHI, who was implicated in the Recruit scandal, have taken Mr Ezoe's offers of shares as normal gifts (as the average Japanese would accept complimentary towels or telephone cards), and insisted that such standard business practices could not constitute bribery.

Politicians must also be paid, and often actively offer favours and their good offices in return for a hefty fee. These payments are most sizeable in sectors in which good government relations are essential: public works, real-estate development, transport, telecommunications, finance, liquor, power generation and so on. These individually solicited contributions come on top of the funds collected by the business associations and the *Keidanren* as general goodwill money for the LDP.

As regards the underpaid bureaucracy, smaller joys and favours will be appropriate: free drinks, golf, travel and regular gift packs, as well as immaculate briefings and documentation on issues of corporate (and bureaucratic) interest to facilitate the officials' work, will do the job, as will the promise of *amakudari* postings at all levels of officialdom.

Business links to organised crime are usually very discreet, avoiding direct contacts and involving a series of shady intermediaries who are used to pay off *sokaiya* corporate extortionists or potentially troublesome 'right-wingers'. During the labour fights of the 1950s and 1960s gangsters and right-wing gangs were employed systematically and openly to beat up picket lines and to intimate trade union leaders. Today – again mostly through intermediaries – the gangs are used to 'motivate' hesitant landowners to sell their land quickly to real-estate developers, to collect unpaid debts, to recruit and control day-labourers for construction, stevedoring and other dirty or dangerous work, or to do some other unforeseen type of work requiring unorthodox methods. It was still unusual (and hence 'scandalous') that Nomura and Nikko Securities were found in the summer 1991 to have aided senior gangland figures *directly* through stock-rigging and preferential loans.

However, corruption is by no means an exclusive preserve of the Japanese elites. When Mr Yoshiaki Tsutsumi secured the 1998 Winter Olympics for Nagano, he knew that the members of the International Olympic Committee would respond favourably to the receptions, wining and dining and other favours bestowed on them by the 1.6 billion yen promotional fund he had collected from Nagano businesses, plus some unspecified amounts of his own.

A billionaire of a different standing, Mr Ryoichi Sasakawa, formerly imprisoned as a suspected war criminal and currently in control of all motor-boat racing betting in Japan, has set himself the objective of generating as much philanthropic publicity and public honours (both foreign and domestic) for himself as possible. As the largest individual donor to the UN and other charitable developmental and academic causes, his collection of honours and favourable VIP quotes (ranging from Jimmy Carter to Mother Theresa) is now quite impressive. (To Mr Sasakawa's regret, the award of the Nobel Peace Prize, in spite of unrelenting efforts, still remains elusive.) His son, whose career highlight was to head the Gumma Motor-boat Racing Association, is now an LDP Upper House member. Sasakawa is also the provider of a significant slush fund to MOT, which the Ministry can spend at its discretion without the control of MOF.

The middle classes' relative deprivation experienced as a result of the asset inflation of Japan's bubble economy of the 1980s as well as the series of business scandals revealed during 1991, have not led to any perceptible public rejection or legitimacy crisis for Japan's business elites (except for a couple of culpable executives, such as Setsuya Tabuchi, ex-chairman of Nomura, who were caught and publicly humiliated). The Japanese public was probably aware of how business was conducted anyway, and the series of relevations only served to confirm these cynical views, without affecting perceptibly the loyalty of clients or employees.

If there is to be an end to the corporate state in general and to business corruption in particular in Japan, structural change could only occur once there was political change. This change would require a wholesale exchange of Japan's political elite for a new set of individuals and policies genuinely committed to a broader diversity of societal objectives, who could design and enforce alternative norms and behaviour from Japan's public and corporate sectors. Although desirable, for lack of a viable alternative a change of political regime appears to be unlikely in the foreseeable future.

Hence 'scandals', editorial exhortations and the middle classes' eternal discreet discontent will continue, with gradual adjustments (mostly of the cosmetic sort) being undertaken as a response by corporate Japan during the coming decades.

Part IV
Conclusion

11 Elite Mobility and Elite Rule

According to Putnam,[1] the analytical model of classical elite theorists, such as Mosca, Pareto and Robert Michels, consists of five elements:

(1) Political power – like other social goods – is distributed unequally.
(2) People fall into only two groups: those who have 'significant' political power and those who have none.
(3) The elite is internally homogeneous, unified and self-conscious (shared group consciousness, coherence and common intentions).
(4) The elite is self-perpetuating and is drawn from a very exclusive segment of society (self-recruitment).
(5) The elite is essentially autonomous (answerable only to itself).

These criteria appear to apply in large measure to Japan's contemporary power elite, Japan's top 2000 decision-makers who comprise some 0.0001 per cent of the country's population. With Michels' 'Iron Law of Oligarchy' applying universally, in Japan from students' clubs and *ikebana* associations to punk rock bands and gangster syndicates (all strictly hierarchical with well-circumscribed and well-known roles for chiefs, Indians and slaves, ranked according to criteria of seniority and of merit) it is almost a platitude to observe the same phenomenon at the macro-societal level.

Living in a parliamentary democracy, Mr Shin Kanemaru, chieftain of the Takeshita faction and of the construction *zoku*, and Mr Taro Tanaka, forestry worker and part-time fisherman in Western Hokkaido, have the same vote in elections, yet when it was up to appointing the prime minister in 1991, Mr Kanemaru had his choice between candidates Kaifu, Miyazawa, Mitsuzuka, Watanabe and his estranged *keibatsu* relative Takeshita, with his decision carrying the day. Mr Tanaka, however, and with him in different circumstances some 123 million Japanese, will at most be able to write an apprehensive letter to the local edition of his *Hokkaido Shimbun* and raise funds from fellow wood-choppers and part-time fishermen for a trip to attend a demo in Tokyo. This unusual and almost un-Japanese activism would place the fictitious Mr Tanaka almost into the pre-elitist category of regional activist. Fortunately for Mr Kanemaru, there are preciously few such Tanakas left in Japan these days. This proves points 1 and 2 of the classical elite theorists' model.

ELITE HOMOGENEITY

For the administrative and business elite, graduation from Todai Law remains an essential entry condition. To go instead through other Todai faculties, other top-ranking national or private universities invites considerably more competition and significantly less effective peer support. To get into Todai Law means either discipline and the mind of a genius or iron discipline, intelligence and the sacrifice of one's youth in *juku* crammers. These are the only two first-generation ways to draw entry tickets for candidature of the national elite.

Far more elegant and mentally less strenuous is to be born into the second, third or more generations of a senior political business or administrative family, and with the necessary minimum of intelligence and ability to make maximum use of family connections, money and know-how to get into the right university (such as Waseda with its debating club) and to opt amicably for the right career track (either *keiretsu* mainstream, the three leading ministries or the right political assistantship).

After the age of 50, the duality of origins (upward achievers and second-generation beneficiaries) may unify in terms of lifestyle: inner-Tokyo apartment housing, a country retreat, provincial hometown residence, golf as a hobby, Akasaka tea houses and Ginza bars for evening entertainment, first-class foreign travel as a regular experience, and material status-symbol-orientated affluence as a regular way of life. Still, the second and more successor-generation members have enjoyed privileged political career access since the 1960s and in the current political set-up are strategically well-placed to take over wholesale from the largely postwar generation of achievers in politics, which is Japan's ultimate power centre.

Quite clearly the peak and most of the core of the power elite's pyramid is about to become limited in access to a near-exclusive preserve for a new aristocracy of second- and third-generation politicians (and to a lesser extent; to owner-presidents of major businesses), who have risen through the ranks of the LDP's parliamentary party during the last 25 years.

In many ways, Japan's power elite after the big democratising push initiated by the purges and expropriations of the US occupation allowed access to a great number of new social recruits: be it to elite bureaucrats of the Yoshida school at large, or to populist, self-financing politicians (such as Kakuei Tanaka and Yasuhiro Nakasone). In the meantime, in its continued exercise of power the political elite ossified and turned to convenient auto-recruitment, with intake of meritocratic achievers in the central bureaucracy reduced to a trickle (often in the form of a humiliating adopted son-in-law status). The senior business elites, although largely freed from the old *zaibatsu* family ties have developed certain family-orientated patterns of succession among senior *zaikai executives*. Leadership of certain vertical *keiretsu* (Matsushita, Toyota, Seibu, Tokyu and the rest) remains in owner-family hands and so are their executive functions in the *zaikai* positions in the national elite.

Japan's political culture at the constituency level, as well as in other public manifestations, requires a great deal of (fairly unreal) populist humility by politicians and ideally also of business leaders. The latter are supposed to stroll about in egalitarian blue overalls through the corporate canteen slurping the collective *miso* soup. The first are advised to meet their electorate humbly begging for guidance and inspiration and pretending deep gratitude for the good advice received from the worldly wise country folks back home. Any overt display of arrogance – be it intellectual or in status and power symbols – goes down badly. Still, as senior office-holders rise in the ranks, the increasing absence of social checks and critical voices often induces some elite members – of all three branches – into fairly idiosyncratic and, by Japanese and universal standards, overbearing behaviour.

Elite accountability appears to be limited in the last analysis to the unwritten premises of 'don't get caught', referring to the only effective control mechanism: a media campaign focusing on irregularities (corruption foremost) which could trigger the public prosecutor into action with usually terminal consequences for the bureaucratic and business elite members concerned but with only passing inconvenience to the political power-brokers. Mutual corporate ownership of the *keiretsu*, the absence of an effective parliamentary control, of a plausible political alternative to the LDP's rule as well as the lack of administrative courts and the unwillingness of the legal system to challenge bureaucratic decisions, allows for an enviably large measure of autonomy for the Japanese power elite. This proves the continued applicability of classical elite theory to Japan.

ELITE RECRUITMENT

Critics have argued that after the SCAP reforms of 1945–8 (expropriating rural landowners, *zaibatsu* families, abolishing the nobility, curbing the military's future role, and purging wartime officials, politicians, senior managers and officers), its concomitant massive intake of middle-class achievers based on meritocracy was only short-lived, and that Japan's society today has ossified to the extent that a 'new aristocratic class' is seen to be emerging. According to Fred Hiatt, it is 'an ancestral elite that is replacing the titled gentry of prewar days and challenging the meritocracy that has underpinned the nation's postwar success. The rising establishment, like the old, is based on wealth, inherited power and strategic marriages linking the two.'[2] Hiatt goes on to quote sociologist Ikko Jin: 'Japanese democracy after the war had guaranteed the opportunity for anyone to rise from farmer to prime minister'; and 'What worries me most is that meritocracy, the goal of democracy after the war, is quietly giving way to a kind of feudal, hereditary system.' Covering the extent to which sons and daughters inherit parental occupations in the Japanese traditional arts, in television and in medical practice, Hiatt claims: 'More and more bureaucrats in the foreign or finance ministries are sons or sons-in-law of former bureaucrats.' It is difficult to find more than anecdotal evidence for this assertion which, however, is plausible on three counts:

- the resources needed to afford the necessary private tuition (*juku*) throughout junior and senior high school in order to pass Todai entrance exams surpasses the means of families who are not upper and upper middle class.
- to apply for civil service examinations, due to an affinity to carry out public duties and to opt for a public service career and its way of life is instilled during early family socialisation.
- after passing senior civil service exams, employment offers from ministries are more likely to reach the sons of senior officials than those of families unrelated to the ministry in question.

As we noted before there are two principal modes for elite recruitment. The first is to be born into (a) the super-rich owner-president families; (b) senior politicians' families; or (c) old, well-connected managerial or ministry officials' families. Families may be old and of noble descent or 'just' second-generation power-holders: there are big differences in style and way of life, as there is in any country between old and new money. Yet the privileged access to socioeconomic power is identical. If aspirants accept the rules of appropriate upper-class role behaviour, they have a fair chance of reaching a position within the national power elite.

The second avenue is the hard road of the achievement-based upward climb. Here the narrow entry passes largely through Todai Law, for both the ministerial and the corporate managerial (*zaikai*) elite track. For other avenues, chances of success have become minute. Individual one-generation climbs through politics or an entrepreneurial career to the societal top have become as good as extinct after the social consolidation following the first postwar decade (when embarking on such a career was still possible). Graduating from Todai Law alone is obviously not sufficient for self-propelled upward mobility. For ministry careers it is essential to pass the senior civil service exams with high marks and to be accepted into top-ranked ministries. Similarly, hard choices have to be made by those ambitious Todai graduates embarking on a business career: to select a company which favours generalists of the Todai breed and which is likely to be a leading and respected member of the *zaikai* inner corporate circle in 30 to 40 years' time. When making this assessment, 'small' is clearly not beautiful, but foolhardy. Also, joining declining industries, companies with regional headquarters, with uncertain growth prospects or those outside the *keiretsu* core groups is definitely 'out' for the socially ambitious.

Strategic marriages may be very helpful. Often they serve to build alliances between established families or to co-opt achievers into the old elite, refreshing its blood-line (as so-called 'breeding horses') and propelling the bridegroom's career.

For both administrative and managerial careers there are periodical selective checks which effectively decide 'up', 'out' or 'sideways'. For each administrative vice-minister there are 20 to 30 of his peer entry class which did not make it (although some may still overtake him during their secondary *amakudari* careers).

The transition from the public sector to pursue either semi-public, private or political careers in their mid-fifties is yet another crucial selective stage, for the success of which political help is often sought.[3] This is aided by the fact that ministerial bureaucrats had to cultivate and to get along well with their *zoku* politicians in order to reach their ministry's executive ranks beforehand.

Obviously, for each recruit to the national power elite there must be a corresponding exit. In a limited, individual sense, this is done through resignations, retirement, death, incapacitation, incarceration, lost elections or corporate bankruptcies. Social decline to middle-class status and relative anonymity has befallen many formerly leading families. Witness, for instance, the fate of the Mitsui clan after their expropriation of 1945, and of the successors of Masayoshi Matsukata, a prominent prime minister of the Meiji period, after the banking crisis of 1927 and the devastations brought about by the war.[4] If members of these families subsequently rose to prominence it was largely on account of their personal abilities and achievement.

The war indeed constituted a major break for the power of Japan's old families, comparable perhaps only to Germany and the countries of Eastern Europe that were subjected to subsequent communist dictatorships. Of 400 prewar members of the House of Peers, only four descendants serve today in any of the two national chambers of parliament, and in the 1980s, only one of Japan's 47 governors, Morihiro Hirokawa of Kumamoto prefecture, was a direct descendant of the *daimyo* who ruled this region (formerly called Higo) before the Meiji restoration. By any Western (and particularly British) standard, this indicates a relatively high degree of pre/postwar elite discontinuity, which implies that Japan's 'new aristocracy' is essentially of postwar origin.

A major reason for this elite change is presumably that Japan's contemporary way of doing politics by trading public works and favours for cash probably holds little appeal for the grand old self-respecting families. There were also secular changes in the overall balance of power within the Japanese power elite. After 1945, as mentioned earlier, the officer corps of the military, the *zaibatsu* families, the court nobility, the landed gentry and a great many of the war politicians lost their elevated social status, which after the formal rehabilitation of 1951 only relatively few, based on individual power positions, were able to regain. The administrative elite, which as the 'Yoshida school' was able to play a decisive role in politics until 1980, was able to fill the vacuum through high achievers recruited into senior positions of both the political and corporate elite.

With the bureaucratisation of the LDP's rule and of its hereditary political careers, as well as with the affluence of Japan's increasingly deregulated corporate sector, the achievement-orientated administrative elites are in gradual decline since the 1960s, a fact which became glaringly obvious during Kakuei Tanaka's decisive if somewhat self-serving rule of 1972/4.

Shared life experiences evidently vary between generations. Almost all members of today's core business and political elite were born between 1915 and 1925. They attended the prewar school system, were often on active military duty, and experienced war, defeat and postwar deprivations as young men. The year 1964, the year of the Tokyo Olympics and of Japan's admission to the OECD, is usually cited as that in which Japan achieved affluence for its citizens and entered an lasting period of 'stable economic growth'. This affluence was surely particularly pronounced among the middle-aged parliamentarians, corporate middle managers and designated-successor owner-residents, who were then aspirants to the national power elite. A certain measure of affluence may already have been familiar to many LDP first-generation politicians, who hailed from well-established local families, owning regional enterprises (such as *sake*-brewing, commodity trading, transportation or local newspapers).

Zahl stated in 1973 that the then-active elite, which had been born between 1890 and 1910, had finished their education between 1915 and 1935 in what was still an agricultural society, with its frugal, traditional value system.[5] He found a high percentage of entrepreneurial or managerial fathers, and noted a strong *samurai* tradition in their family backgrounds as well as experience in military service during their formative years. With law graduates from Todai dominating, Zahl observed the coexistence of an authoritarian upbringing, high educational qualifications and (some) continued social exclusivity of elite positions with access to the 'inner circle' of power for descendants of the old nobility.

Currently, we witness a gradual but perceptible generational change in core elite positions towards those born between 1925 and 1935. The present members of Japan's administrative elite (vice-ministers and directors general) were born exclusively between 1935 and 1938. For this new generation the war is more of a distant memory of childhood and teenage years. The frugality, the social turmoil, the sacrifices and the hard work of the 1950s, which secured Japan's current status in the world, were more a formative experience. Most of their adult lives, however, have been lived in material ease and without existential worries for their social stratum. With most second- and third-generation politicians and, especially, with inheritors of great fortunes, the experience of continued affluence and elevated social status has occasionally led to a 'spoilt brat' syndrome, which surely is indicative of the long-term decline of the dynasty in question.

Peter Cheng compared the backgrounds of Japanese cabinet ministers of three periods: (a) Meiji (1885–1912); (b) the rise of the military (1913–45); and (c) postwar (1945–73).[6] He found Meiji cabinet members to be well-educated, frequently with university degrees from abroad (28 per cent) and with substantial exposure to and life experience in the West (61 per cent). In contrast, the postwar cabinet members had fairly limited foreign exposure, with a large majority (78 per cent) having had no meaningful foreign contacts.

The generation of interwar ministers took a somewhat intermediate position. Cheng, however, rightly forecasted that the post-1973 cabinet generations were likely to have even less foreign exposure than their postwar colleagues. Looking at regional origins, Cheng concluded that between Meiji and the postwar period a shift had taken place from Kagoshima/Yamaguchi origins (the homebases of the victorious Choshu/Satsuma clans) to Central Japanese places of birth. Contemporary methods of elite recruitment prefer a metropolitan upbringing. While the offspring of the political elite is dutifully born in provincial hometowns, the sons of the administrative and business elite are mostly born and brought up in or near the metropolitan centres of ministerial or corporate headquarters (for which, in more than 90 per cent cases, read Tokyo).

As regards gender, 99 per cent of the Japanese power elite are male (aged between 52 and 85). Women make it to a handful of senior administrative positions (such as to an assistant vice-minister in MOL or an ambassadorship to Denmark) and to a few LDP Upper House seats (which have resulted in some token ministerships). There are currently no female Lower House LDP MPs (and hence there will be no influential women ministers in the next 20 years), no female governors or city mayors, and no women as *zaikai* leaders. In major family-owned businesses, the female executive role is limited to the caretaker function until a suitable male heir assumes his role.

In the national elite, the role of women is probably stronger as an influence behind the scenes. It is to assist husbands (particularly in their homebase in political careers); to groom promising heirs with the right educational and character credentials; to create networks with other powerful families at national and regional level; to keep the family in good social standing; and to arrange for proper marriages in due course. It is a very disciplined, long-term but yet vital role for the type of dynastic power acquisition which appears to be a major objective of most members of the power elite. Given their husbands' relentless full-time schedules, the wives' support plays irreplaceable (short-term) logistical and (long-term) dynastical roles. This division of labour leaves the male decision-makers (who for decades have lived thoroughly sheltered lives, divorced from the everyday concerns of shopping, child-rearing and family finance) pretty ill-equipped to deal with the daily concerns of average Japanese citizens. Rather, they seem to have a fairly alienated upper-class approach to life (which might explain some of the flagrant *faux-pas* when a VAT system was introduced in Japan in 1989).

LIFE-STYLES AND VALUES

All members of the Japanese power elite are ethnically 'pure' Japanese nationals. Almost all have gone through 13 years of schooling and tertiary education in Japan. Hence they are thoroughly inbued with the conformist value system and social discipline prevalent in the Japanese mainstream. These socialising influences have been strongest in the elite members recruited through achievement, who successfully managed successive promotions and survived the periodical selection procedures arranged by personnel departments. Social pressures to conform to salaried middle-class standards have been less intensive on the members of the heriditary 'new aristocracy'. They could often pay their way through private universities, with quick promotions later being a foregone decision. Often only outright incompetence or social deviance would stop them.

Once in office as a more or less acknowledged member of Japan's power elite, social constraints are much reduced. A power holder no longer needs to be liked by his personnel department, nor to be popular with his subordinates. While overt arrogance and vanity may not be helpful and certainly does not correspond to Japanese ideals of leadership behaviour, in Japan a fair share of its elite enjoys this vice that appears so irresistible to weak characters who have tasted power.

Yet there are checks and balances in the Japanese power system: we have already covered the mutual checks in the ministry–LDP–*Zaikai* triangle. Within each system constraints on abuse of individual power apply: the vice-ministers and directors general are being watched by their peers (and can quickly be retired). Senior politicians may be safe for re-election (but none the less they still cannot afford to neglect their constituency work), but need to remain popular and/or feared amongst fellow MPs – particularly in their own faction. Presidents of *keiretsu* companies are more safely positioned (and particularly well-protected from shareholders), subject to eviction by peer pressure only when 'scandals' are uncovered or companies suffer heavy losses due to mismanagement. Owner-presidents enjoy the most job security and can exercise near-absolute managerial power in their company and indulge most of their ideosyncracies (to be fair, many continue to live lives of exemplary frugality and modesty, remaining respected but still accessible to their employees), subject only to the checks of their clan's code of conduct (if one exists). Tales of despotism and conspicuous waste abound about some of them, which often disqualifies them from the highest *zaikai* positions usually reserved for well-disciplined and well-adjusted *keiretsu* career executives. Most members of the national elite (except perhaps for a few hereditary owner presidents) are, like most Japanese, convinced that they work very hard. Very long hours are dedicated to official duties, including unavoidable social obligations covering attendance at funerals/marriages, membership of government panels, PR presentations, perfunctory board meetings, the reception of visitors and of petitions by unions and clientele groups, briefings to the press, attendance at inaugurations, ceremonial blessings, political and corporate parties, extensive visits to bars, the usual weekend golf outings and numerous periods of domestic and foreign business travel – in addition to the regular executive management work.

Normal family life is sacrificed, as with most white-collar employees in the Japanese metropolises, delegating child-rearing, education, family finance and other family duties to their wives who, in the case of the national elite, also have to do human networking tasks to support their husbands' careers (for achievers) or to work hard on clan cohesion (for inheritors), with the utmost importance being placed on grooming a successor son and doing the right *omiai* matchmaking for him.

Wealth is distributed unequally among the Japanese elite. Administrative vice-ministers may still have to pay mortgages for their modest suburban homes, politicians may be deeply in debt and barely able to meet their assistants' monthly payroll, while some of the tycoons, such as Yoshiaki Tsutsumi, probably have difficulties knowing precisely at how many billions of US$ their current net worth stands.

For the salaried elite members, the use of ministerial and corporate executive privileges, the generous use of the perks of office and of symbols of power and affluence is closely linked to incumbency. The wealth of the *keiretsu* is to their presidents like the riches of the Catholic Church to their cardinals – once an incumbent leaves the organisation, there is very little individual material gain left with him. If there is no dynastic succession, or if an *amukudari* career does not succeed, this means blending back into the (upper) middle-class mainstream.

For Japan's super-rich the truism holds that the newer the money, the stronger the craving for old-elite acceptance and for non-monetary status symbols: honours (both foreign and domestic), medals, cultural attributes (collections of paintings, of historical artefacts, of theatres), the ownership of baseball clubs and well-publicised sponsorship of the arts and sciences. The ready availability of cash for symbols of vanity among the Japanese moneyed upper classes has led to various forms of fire sales of foreign honours (the cheapest to come by seem to be honorary consulates, medals on national days and honorary doctorates).

Values professed by members of elite abound, from liberal references to the love of mankind, peace, progress and the environment. If these were only partially true, Japan would be by far the kindest nation on earth. But, in fact, the national policy and the national elite appear *grosso modo* no better and no worse than that of any other developed country. The supreme objective of all elite members is power maintenance (or else they would be quickly down and out), a purpose for which they employ varying degrees of sublety similar to the means of 'higher amorality' which C. Wright Mills in the 1950s observed in the US power elite. The structural corruption endemic in Japan's upper crust results from the wide discretionary power these gentlemen enjoy over entrusted money and capital (corporate funds, credit allocations, public budgets, political donations, expense accounts, favours in kind and so on), and are helped by the discouragement of ethical convictions and the absence of effective legal auditing and enforcement in Japan. It is the media which serves as a final check on elite transgressions against commonly accepted behaviour. Sustained media campaigns producing sequences of 'scandalous' misbehaviour at regular intervals lead to elite careers being ended in public humilation facing the public prosecutors (who, in the glare of television lights, sometimes feel enboldened to bring to book representatives of the prominent crooks).

More prudent, lucky and/or resilient operators in the power elite, advanced in years, have dynastic ambitions which may reflect a wish to achieve immortality by procreation. Given the frequency and relative success of this practice, notably in the political domain (and – though to a lesser extent – in the field of big business, especially but not solely in family owned enterprises), Japan's contemporary power elite in large measure appears as a new aristocracy in the making. As such, the right of birth severely curtails elite recruitment by merit and achievement. The current and future power elite will hence be short of both talent and legitimacy in a country which, by and large, for most of its ranks is socially mobile with achievement based on merit.

So far Japan's current semi-aristocratic power elite seems to have managed well with its periodic crises of legitimacy (following its irresistible tendency to view the country and its resources as its self-service shop) to the extent that its hold on power has always been defended successfully (though requiring occasionally public humiliations and symbolic sacrifices). Yet in the long run – which may well be the *very* long run: some 15–20 years ahead – a Japanese-style *perestroika* may overtake the next generation of Japan's ever more ossified power elite and trigger a wholesome regime change. This, however, requires not only the current elite and its successors to continue past policies and mistakes (which is easy and likely), but (which is more difficult and less likely) for an alternative elite to offer plausibly more attractive options for the country's administration, its public policies and for running its economy. So far, such options have not reached public knowledge in Japan and, almost by default, Japan's power elite is allowed to continue its generally benevolent, if somewhat self-serving and frequently corrupt, rule of Japan's political economy.

DESIGNS FOR JAPAN AND FOR THE WORLD

For foreign politicians and business executives on short-term visits to Japan, the world-view of their Japanese counterparts must be enigmatic at best. Even when asking the right probing questions, Japanese replies will almost inevitably consist of trivial commonplaces (focusing on 'peace', 'co-operation', 'harmony', 'consensus', 'understanding') and conflicts played down as unfortunate misunderstandings (the Pacific war is usually addressed as an 'unfortunate incident', presumably because Japan lost it). Murray Sayle, for instance, has come to the conclusion:

> As operator of the system, the LDP has produced by Darwinian selection a breed of politician unique in the profession. These men (the nationalist element of the party, left over from the war, has little use for women) cannot make a persuasive speech or present a clear policy, because they have never had to, but they are masters of back-handed fund-raising, closed-door intrigue and impenetrable double-talk.[7]

Although usually more celebral and articulate, many administrative and corporate executives will often find it more advisable to stick to convenient *tatemae* declarations in public encounters, which represent commonly accepted, strongly idealised versions of real intentions and events (*honne*). Meaningful top-level communication in a Western sense should certainly be based on versions of the latter.

Written documentation and presentations (ranging from corporate reports to government policy descriptions and analyses) are equally in mild and mellow self-congratulatory futurist language, with slogans (of the 'For a green high-tech Japan of the 21st century' sort) effectively substituting for substance. Stripped of PR glitter and false sloganeering, an analysis of *actual* policies pursued and of repeated off-the-record utterances by key power players to a domestic audience, however, reveals a certain consistent elite view of Japan and of the world and on desirable strategies for the country and its people.

Having grown up in a strictly hierarchical society (which ranks not only persons, but also companies, parties, prefectures, universities, the world with its nation states is also a hierarchical place, where Japan's position should be close to the top. Definitions on how Japan's top ranking is to be achieved varies between the three power centres. The clearest strategic vision is that of Japan's corporate sector (which internationally is the most resourceful and effective of the three): it projects to a global scale its past domestic economic strategy of market conquest by rapid product innovation, predatory pricing, mass production, and cost squeezes of captive suppliers.

Driven by keen inter-*keiretsu* and intra-sectoral competition as well as by their internal dynamics urging ever more corporate growth (to expand the social standing of the executives and to supply additional management posts for ageing white-collar officers), Japan's corporate empires aim at the global dominance of their respective sectors. The electronics and the car industry – as well as a series of smaller sectors, ranging from motorcycles to zip-fasteners and vegetables seeds – demonstrate well-designed, resourceful and long-term Japanese strategies to this end. Sectoral world domination is not the objective of an evil design plotted in dark conspiracies on Japan's golf courses and teahouses. It is rather the logical external extension of domestic competition (if your domestic competitor is about to conquer a foreign market you must do likewise in order not to be left behind and allow him undisputed cost and revenue advantages), and a product of the bureaucratic outlook in Japan's corporate headquarters: the deep-seated wish to ensure corporate growth and survival by reducing external uncertainties *ad minimis*.

What better means is there to achieve maximum sectoral control than to subjugate inherently unpredictable foreign competition, either by destruction, absorption or by establishing clientele relations through suffocating joint ventures and subcontracting? While there is little wrong in principle with the world domination of industrial sectors by companies headquartered in a particular country (such as US computer and aircraft manufacturers throughout the 1960s and 1970s), the nationalist, centralist orientation of Japan's corporate system will not allow the promotion of foreigners into positions of senior decision-making in headquarters, nor will headquarters allow any meaningful autonomy to overseas affiliates and subsidiaries. The bureaucratic instinct for HQ control and domination overrules economic rationality which would favour decentralisation and local profit centres. Most meaningful and sensitive R&D work will also remain limited to Japanese nationals and to research facilities at home. Not playing by the rule-book of liberal economics will make corporate Japan's overseas conquest politically unacceptable in most developed host countries before long.

Japan and the Japanese don't seem to fare much better in corporate planning either. The people are welcome as a diligent, hard-working, well-trained and disciplined workforce ready to put in long hours (with *Nikkeiren* making sure that there are no effective cuts in annual work-time) and to undertake any sacrifice (including death from overwork) required by the hierarchy for the corporate good. They are also welcome as a mass of captive consumers to pay for overpriced goods and services which, due to corporate Japan's domestic preference for non-price competition, helps to fill corporate coffers for investment, ever-quicker product cycles and finance for overseas expansion.

Japan's central administration has regularly been accused of haughtiness towards ordinary people, and in many ways contacts between the population at large and officialdom (ranging from municipal administration to national customs and taxation offices) may often be unpleasant and unequal, given the authorities' wide discretionary powers that allow a degree of arbitrariness against which legal recourse (in the absence of administrative courts) is usually not a realistic option for an individual citizen. Seen from their way of life, senior ministry officers are the sector of the national elite which has lived middle-class metropolitan lives for most of their careers and hence should sympathise with Japanese people's most pressing worries about housing, education, commuting and environmental degradation. Ministry visions for a futurist Japan hence inevitably envisage the high-tech, capital–intensive resolution of all these problems, with affluent computer operators in wooded, semi-rural settings strolling about leisurely in clean, light, spacious office landscapes: Japan as a magnified Switzerland. There is again nothing wrong with this vision. It is only that past and current government policies do precisely the opposite. They do everything to contribute to the further concentration of service industries and corporate headquarters in Tokyo and further depopulation of the regional rural areas.

The world-view of Japan's fractious ministries is relatively more timid than that of big business. The foreign ministry for the time being sticks to traditional notions of a junior role in the alliance with the US. MITI, being in charge of foreign trade, has to worry about continued access to Japan's export markets and occasionally about essential raw material/energy supplies from volatile producer areas. MOF, sitting on a pile of surplus cash, is rather more self-assured in its role in international finance and in funding the IMF, various development banks and the US budget deficit. The other ministries with their smallish international departments are too domestic in focus to offer any international track careers or any meaningful international outlook for its senior administrators. As a world design, MITI favours a corporate HQ and clean R&D functions as the main occupation for the Japanese islands. MOF is probably content to live on interest earned from foreign bonds. For MFA it is presumably most essential that Japanese delegates should sit (and sleep) in the front seats of all major international conferences. To enhance Japan's world status the ministries are ready to throw around quite a lot of money for purposes presumed to aid development and for a more expensive military arm which (so far) has been fairly useless. On aggregate, the ministerial vision of foreign affairs rather adds up to a regional power position for Japan: dominating East Asia (that is, East of Burma minus mainland China, plus Oceania and Hawaii) by virtue of its economic power and the military power vacuum created by the gradual disengagement undertaken by Russia and the US, and as such to preside over the world's emerging Pacific economic power house and talk shop to the US and to Europe.

As in most big and in insular countries, politics in Japan is local politics. Politicians make their career and secure their revenues through constitutuency work and local issues. Foreign policy expertise and extensive international contacts are useful only to MPs who have already reached a fairly senior level and entertain ambitions to be foreign, MITI, finance or eventually prime minister.

The foreign expertise required from potential prime ministers may none the less not amount to much. From the days of PM Yoshida until the arrival of PM Miyazawa in 1991, very few (if any) PMs were able to utter one coherent sentence in English or in any other foreign tongue. With the innate insularity both of their personal careers and of their constitutuency interests, the international ambitions of Japan's political class are very limited. For most office-holders it means to being treated with respect and with due honours when travelling abroad and to return with photographs of themselves shaking hands with the world's mighty and famous. They also probably agree that a Japanese prime minister when attending world summits should be in a position to deliver the right promises expected from him by fellow summetiers and by the international media. Except for handful of prominent right-wingers, most LDP MPs share civic visions of Japanese grandeur and influence not dissimilar to the corporate or administrative elites. This does not add up to any grand foreign policy design. Based on its economic strength and on its regional primacy almost by default (until China democratises and modernises successfully), Japan's global role is bound to increase, although its administrative and, particularly its political elites are ill-equipped for the job. While its corporate global conquest has begun to send shivers down the spines of their overseas competitors and their economic administrations, Japan's current and likely future political role appears as decidedly less frightening.

The domestic view of Japan's political elite appears to consist of a curious amalgam of the value of progress-orientated patriotism and of the cynical principles of 'machine politics'. Most will readily agree on all major public concerns: that quality of life, housing, work situations and the urban environment need to be enhanced, that Japan should keep up its educational, R&D and investment levels to stay ahead. This is not mere rhetoric. Under Nakasone's rule serious efforts were undertaken to modernise Japan's educational, fiscal and administrative system. Under Kaifu 'political reform' was attempted (and aborted) which had the objective of ridding Japan's political class of its proneness to paralysing corruption scandals.

Yet in actual policies, policy-makers opt clearly for massive public works projects, for discretionary licensing systems and import protection, in order to ingratiate themselves with vested interests at the expense of the general public. With regard to high land prices, the lack of city planning and inner-city parks, and on Japan's metropolitan concentration in general, effective policies on these issues that are vital for the Japanese people's quality of life are not taken, for fear of the reactions of powerful land-owning interest groups (many of which are *zaikai*-affiliated). In fact, Japan's power elite seems remarkably relaxed about the fact that Japan's surplus wealth is largely either squandered in conspicuous consumption or recycled in the corporate sector, with the last ten-year growth-cycle having brought only minimal additional benefits in terms of quality of life to Japan's non-elitist population at large.

Housing, commuting and work situations (except for a handful of show-case industrial plants) have remained as bad as they ever were since the country in per capita income levels reached those of leading OECD countries in the mid 1970s. LDP MPs perceive their voters and supporters as a greedy and selfish lot (which appears to be a mirror image of the public's perception of them), continuously requesting special favours and handouts. During the Recruit scandal, many LDP MPs would agree with Michio Watanabe that Japanese voters had the politicians they deserved. If they expected fewer gifts in cash and in kind, conservative Dietmen's fund-raising requirements would be correspondingly reduced and so would Japan's structural corruption. For regional voters, however, these handouts and other public subsidies represent only a – in their view legitimate – compensation for the relative economic and cultural deprivation they face in view of the vast regional imbalances in Japan's metropolitan central state. It would appear, then, that political corruption is only a poor substitute for effective decentralisation policies.

ELITE ACCEPTANCE

Elite rule in a parliamentary democracy such as Japan depends on public acceptance. The Japanese learn to live with hierarchies from early child-hood socialisation: families are stratified, as are play-groups in kindergartens and peer groups of primary-school children. Ascribed dominances rule unquestioned according to seniority (age) and gender. There is hardly a society among other developed countries which is more rigidly hierarchical than Japan's, a country to which Robert Michel's 'iron law of obligarchisation' surely applies.

Looking at current alternatives, the only option available for elite change is to vote an opposition coalition into power (displacing the LDP oligarchy), which would subsequently have to enact legislation dismantling the *keiretsu*, taxing the wealth of the super-rich, permitting corporate co-determination by trade unions and employees (thus breaking *zaikai*'s exclusive power hold) and decentralising administrative power to Japan's regions, so as disperse the bureaucratic primacy of Tokyo's central ministries. There is, however, little indication that Japan's opposition parties have any unified concept aiming at this sort of comprehensive elite change, nor does the Japanese population (judging by their voting behaviour, by declining rates of unionisation and by the absence of any public debate on the subject) seem to have much confidence in the superior abilities of such an alternative elite. This is in spite of the regular reoccurrence of scandals revealing the wholesale corruption of Japan's political and corporate sector, which in their public relevation equally regularly trigger short-lived erosions in public trust and hence of elite legitimacy. When all the televised sound and fury has settled, the Japanese seem to prefer the devil they know. Each of the three elite sectors has merits of its own:

- the ministries' top-track officials have had to pass two of the world's most competitive examinations, work undisputably hard for long hours and for little direct remuneration;
- *zaikai*'s corporate executives managed the build-up of the world's most powerful export machine, pushing Japan to the forefront of global technological progress, and created the industrial foundation of the country's continued material prosperity;
- the LDP politicians have finally acquired presentable merit in their constituencies. They provided jobs for the boys, public favours for their friends and retainers, and in general are approachable powerful intermediaries for those citizens who are normally deprived of access to power or of redress against administrative decisions. Japan's dynastic tradition allows for the transfer of merits from (political) fathers to their legitimate successors in the perception of many traditional voters.

THE OUTLOOK

Restricting recruitment and thus frustrating the best and the brightest among the ambitious of a nation's young men often spells the beginning of the end of a power elite's prolonged rule. In Japan since its postwar consolidation this exclusionist tendency is undeniable. LDP politics has become a family trade. The founder-generation of the larger interwar and postwar corporate successes has given way to a second generation whose principal merit was the right birth. A new aristocracy with its complement of *keibatsu* (strategic marriages) is also seen to be spreading to the executive ranks of the *keiretsu* and the central ministries. The Todai Law entry ticket has increasingly become restricted to the sons of upper-class families who can afford the costs now needed for supplementary tuition, as well as providing the strength of motivation needed to persist.

With a narrowing recruitment base the power elite's legitimacy is threatened on two fronts: an unending stream of scandals, publicly detailing an ever more extensive degree of corruption, of tax evasion and of gangland links with its corporate and political elite, as well as of the manifest failure of this very same elite to address effectively the Japanese middle classes most pressing issues: the sorry states of housing, commuting, leisure, working conditions and the environment. While basic social needs are well taken care of, the justifiable demands for a more adequate quality of life, which would be in line with Japan's GNP per capita, are neglected for the average 'salarymen' and their families who, in the light of their relative deprivation *vis à vis* the owners of corporate shares and of land in the metropolises, have begun to question their middle-class status. With the incompetence of Japan's unions and opposition parties, the widespread latent discontent has led to political apathy and to a grumbling depoliticisation. Yet, as was evident during the 1989 Upper House elections, Japan's voters are ready to switch sides once the opposition is able to present fresh faces and a unified strategy that challenges the LDP's outworn and corrupt rule. But this honeymoon turned out to be shortlived, as the opposition and the unions quickly returned to their favourite pastime: internal doctrinal squabbles while competing to sell out to the LDP for the lowest bid. Due to the lack of alternatives, Japan's power elite is by default bound to continue its rule. Their conservative hegemony is not a reactionary one (like China's octogenerian Stalinists). In due course there will be cautious modernising reforms in public administration and in corporate management, with gradual repercussions on the power elite's composition. *Zaikai* will open its doors to new sectors, particularly to conglomerates operating in services, with a corresponding decline of the old heavy industries. The rapidly declining number of applicants to the ministries' class I examinations will force reforms to make work and careers in the public civil service more attractive and accessible before long.

Finally, the LDP (or some of its major factions)[8] may chose or be forced to enter into formal coalition rule with the centrist parties (DSP and *Komeito*) or with the JSP's centre-right mainstream. In either case fresh blood of different social origin would be co-opted into the power elite. It is with this cautiously modernising and pragmatic co-option strategy that Japan's new aristocracy will continue its elite rule well into the twenty-first century.

Notes

Chapter 1: Society and Power in Japan

1. Chi Nakane, *Japanese Society* (Harmondsworth, Middx: Penguin Books, 1973) p. 24.

Chapter 2: The Liberal Democratic Party

1. Norman Macrae, 'Must Japan Slow?', *Economist*, 23 Feb. 1980.
2. *Liberal Star*, 10 March 1987.
3. Haruhiro Fukui, *Party in Power* (Berkeley, Cal.: University of California Press, 1970) p. 74.
4. *Asahi Shimbun*, 17 Jan. 1990.
5. *Mainichi Daily News*, 7 Jan. 1989.
6. *Süddeutsche Zeitung*, 17 Dec. 1983; *Der Spiegel*, 26 Dec. 1983.
7. *Economist*, 24 Oct. 1987.
8. *Asahi Evening News*, 1 Oct. 1987.

Chapter 3: Political Careers

1. Gerald L. Curtis, *Election Campaigning Japanese Style* (New York: Columbia University Press, 1971).
2. *Daily Yomiuri*, 8 Nov. 1989.
3. *The Financial Times*, 14 Feb. 1990.
4. *Far Eastern Economic Review*, 9 March 1989.
5. Ibid.
6. *Asahi Evening News*, 20 April 1989.
7. *Mainichi Shimbun*, 26 Nov. 1989.
8. *The Japan Times*, 13 July 1989 (figures provided by the Secretariat of the House of Representatives).
9. *Asahi Evening News*, 20 April 1989 and 21 April 1989.
10. *Asahi Evening News*, 2 June 1989.
11. *Mainichi Daily News*, 17 Feb.–22 March 1989.
12. At Japan Political Studies Seminar, Tokyo, 19 April 1990.
13. *Mainichi Daily News*, 17 Feb. 1989.
14. *Mainichi Daily News*, 18 Feb. 1989.
15. *Japan Times*, 20 Dec. 1990.
16. *Mainichi Daily News*, 20 Feb. 1989.
17. *Mainichi Daily News*, 21 Feb. 1989.
18. *AERA Magazine*, 6 Sept. 1988.
19. At Japan Political Studies Seminar, Tokyo, 19 April 1990.
20. *Asahi Evening News*, 21 April 1989.
21. At Japan Political Studies Seminar, Tokyo, 5 Sep. 1989.
22. Cornelia Meyer, in *Nagatacho Focus* (UBS Philips & Drew) no. 2, 21 April 1991.

23. Helmut Schmidt, however, appears convinced that Takeo Fukuda belongs to the peaceloving left wing of the LDP: Helmut Schmidt, *Menschen und Mächte* (Berlin: Siedler Verlag, 1987) pp. 423 and 432.
24. *The Deai* of March 1989 and January 1989.
25. *Mainichi Daily News*, 8 June 1989.
26. Provided by Mr Hori's parliamentary office, 1990.
27. Provided by Mr Ozawa's parliamentary office, 1990.
28. Provided by Mr Kato's parliamentary office, 1990.
29. The biographical data are mostly taken from: Seizaburo Sato, Kenichi Koyama and Shumpei Kumon, *Postwar Politician: The Life of Former Prime Minister Masayoshi Ohira* (Tokyo: Kodansha, 1990).
30. Ibid., p. 400.
31. Ibid., p. 524
32. *Japan Times*, 22 Feb. 1979.
33. *Financial Times*, 8 July 1986.
34. Ministry of Foreign Affairs, *Yasuhiro Nakasone*, Official Government Bulletin, May 1986, pp. 9–10.
35. *The Economist*, 5 April 1986.
36. *Japan Times*, 21 Feb. 1984.
37. *Japan Times*, 2 June 1987.
38. *Japan Times*, 3 June 1987.

Chapter 4: Legitimacy Crises

1. At Japan Political Studies Seminar, Tokyo, 26 Oct. 1988.
2. See also Bernd Reddies, *Der Recruit Skandal in Japan* (Tokyo: OAG Aktuell, 1989).
3. *Asahi Evening News*, 24 May 1989.
4. David E. Kaplan and Alec Dubro, *Yakuza: The Explosive Account of Japan's Criminal Underworld* (London: Macdonald, 1987).
5. *Mainichi Daily News*, 18 Sept. 1991.
6. *Japan Times*, 26 Feb. 1988.
7. *Asahi Shimbun*, 10 April 1990.
8. At Japan Political Studies Seminar, Tokyo, 3 July 1991.

Chapter 5: The Civil Service System

1. Jinjiin (National Personnel Authority), *Komuinhakusho* (White Paper on Civil Servants) (Tokyo: Ogurasho Ensatsu Kyoku, 1988) pp. 157–8.
2. B. C. Koh, *Japan's Administrative Elite* (Berkeley, Cal.: University of California Press, 1989) p. 92.
3. *Nihon Keizai Shimbun*, 7 Aug. 1990.
4. Koh, *Japan's Administrative Elite*, p. 223.
5. National Personnel Authority, *Outline of National Personnel Authority and Civil Service System* (Tokyo, 1988) p. 30.
6. For the first four persons: *Japan Economic Journal*, 15 April 1989; for the rest: my own data collection.
7. *The Economist*, 23 June 1990.
8. Koh, *Japan's Administrative Elite*, p. 241.

Chapter 6: Government Operations

1. *The Financial Times*, 19 June 1985.
2. *Japan Foundation Newsletter*, October 1989, p. 6.
3. In Kiyoaki Tsuji, *Public Administration in Japan* (Tokyo: University of Tokyo Press, 1984), p. 33.
4. Chalmers Johnson, *MITI and the Japanese Miracle* (Stanford, Cal.: University of Stanford Press, 1982) p. 29.
5. See Albrecht Rothacher, 'The Difficulties of Donor Aid Co-operation: the Case of Japan and the European Community', in United Nations University (ed.), *Development and ODA: Japan–ASEAN Forum, November 1990* (Tokyo: UNU, 1991) pp. 170–2.
6. See also Yung H. Park, *Bureaucrats and Ministries in Contemporary Japanese Government* (Berkeley, Cal.: University of California Press, 1986).
7. Albrecht Rothacher, *Japan's Agro Food Sector* (London: Macmillan, 1989) p. 108.
8. See Management and Co-ordination Agency, *Organization of the Government of Japan* (Tokyo, 1986) p. 28.
9. Data taken from *Seikai, Kancho, Jinjiroku* (Personal Records of the Political World and Government Administration) (Tokyo: Toyo Keizai Shimposha, 1989 Handbook).
10. AMA, '*Administrative Inspection*', in Kiyoaki Tsuji (ed.), *Public Administration in Japan* (Tokyo: University of Tokyo Press 1984) pp. 173–83, esp. p. 176.
11. Yasuo Maeda, 'The State Audit System', in Tsuji (ed.) *Public Administration in Japan*, pp. 185–202, esp. p. 186.
12. For an example, see Albrecht Rothacher, *Economic Diplomacy between the European Community and Japan, 1959–1981* (Aldershot: Gower, 1983) p. 293.
13. *Japan Economic Journal*, 16 Feb. 1991.

Chapter 7: Elite Civil Servants

1. *Tsusan Journal*, August 1988, pp. 6–9.
2. Provided by the Ministry of Foreign Affairs, 1991.
3. Ibid., 1990.
4. *MITI Handbook* (Tokyo, 1990).
5. Provided by the Ministry of Finance, 1989.
6. Provided by the Ministry of Labor, 1991.
7. Provided by Suntory Ltd, 1988.

Chapter 8: The *Keiretsu* Business Conglomerates

1. Source: Toyo Keizai
2. John G. Roberts, *Mitsui: Three Centuries of Japanese Business*, 2nd edn (New York/Tokyo: Weatherhill, 1989) p. 3.
3. See Yasuo Mishima, *The Mitsubishi: Its Challenge and Strategy* (Greenwich, Conn./London: JAI Press, 1989).
4. Roberts, *Mitsui*, p. 384.
5. Ibid., pp. 311–15.

6. Kazuo Shibagaki, 'Dissolution of Zaibatsu and Deconcentration of Economic Power', *Annals of the Institute of Social Science*, University of Tokyo, no. 20, 1979, pp. 1–60, esp. p. 53.
7. Ibid., p. 44.
8. Ibid., p. 50.
9. Dodwell Marketing Consultants, *Industrial Groupings in Japan* (Tokyo: Dodwell, 1984–5) p. 6.
10. Source: *Japan Company Handbook*, Section 1 (Tokyo: 1991).
11. *The Financial Times*, 22 May 1990.
12. Dodwell, *Industrial Groupings*, p. 11.
13. *Oriental Economist*, December 1980, p. 10.
14. *Nihon Keizai Shimbun*, 13 April 1990.
15. *Oriental Economist*, May 1981, p. 20.
17. Ibid.
18. *Far Eastern Economic Review*, 14 Sept. 1989.
19. *Oriental Economist*, October 1981, p. 19.
20. Ibid., p. 19.
21. *Oriental Economist*, February 1982, p. 24.
22. *Oriental Economist*, April 1982, p. 14.
23. Ibid., p. 19.
24. *Oriental Economist*, September 1982, p. 14.
25. Ibid., p. 16.
26. Tokyu Corporation, *Annual Report 1990*, p. 14.
27. *Japan Times*, 5 June 1991.
28. Keidanren, 'The Significance of the SII Talks and Directions for the Future', 14 May 1991, Typescript.
29. Robert Lawrence, *Efficient or Exclusionist? The Import Behaviour of Japanese Corporate Groups*, Brookings Papers, 1991, vol. I.
30. James C. Abegglen, and George Stalk, *Kaisha: The Japanese Corporation* (Tokyo: Charles E. Tuttle, 1987) pp. 185–6.
31. *Oriental Economist*, October 1981, pp. 18–19.
32. See Kiyoshi Kojima and Terutomo Ozawa, *Japan's General Trading Companies: Merchants of Economic Development* (Paris: OECD Development Center Studies, 1984) pp. 28 and 48–50.
33. *The Financial Times*, 12 May 1986.
34. *The Financial Times*, 29 May 1985.

Chapter 9: *Zaikai* – the Organisation of Big Business Interests

1. Chitoshi Yanaga, *Big Business in Japanese Politics* (New Haven, Conn.: Yale University Press, 1968) p. 32.
2. Yonosuke Tanaka, 'The World of the Zaikai', in H. Murakami and J. Hirshmeier (eds), *Politics and Economics in Contemporary Japan* (Tokyo: Japan Culture Institute, 1979) pp. 64–78, esp. p. 68.
3. *Daily Yomiuri*, 30 May 1988 and 19 March 1990.
4. *Nihon Keizai Shimbun*, 26 Sept. 1990.
5. *Economic Eye*, Spring 1990, p. 20.
6. *Keidanren Review*, no. 125, 1990, p. 4.
7. *Journal of Japanese Trade and Industry*, no. 1, 1985, pp. 56–8.

8. *Daily Yomiuri*, 4 June 1990.
9. *Daily Yomiuri*, 28 April 1991.
10. See Keizai Koho Center, *KKC Brief*, no. 59, Aug. 1990.
11. *Japan Times*, 4 April 1991.
12. Keizai Koho Center, *KKC Brief*, no. 55, June 1990.
13. *Japan Times*, 15 May 1991.
14. Eiji Suzuki, in Nikkeiren, *Toward Sound Growth: Report of the Committee for the Study of Labour Questions* (Tokyo, 1990) p. 1.
15. Nikkeiren, *Japan's Federation of Employers' Associations* (Tokyo, 1982) p. 3.
16. Ibid.
17. Nikkeiren, *Current Labour Economy in Japan* (Tokyo, 1990) p. 10.
18. Ibid.
19. Ibid., p. 12.
20. Nikkeiren, *Toward Sound Growth*, p. 12.
21. *Sankei Shimbun*, 15 May 1991.
22. *Japan Times*, 21 Dec. 1987.
23. *Japan Times*, 1 July 1991.
24. *Asahi Shimbun*, 20 March 1991.
25. *Japan Times*, 1 July 1991.
26. *Asahi Shimbun*, 13 May 1991.
27. *Daily Yomiuri*, 25 May 1991.

Chapter 10: Executive Careers

1. *Mainichi Daily News*, 20 Oct. 1988.
2. For Toyota's case, see *Far Eastern Economic Review*, 17 Aug. 1989.
3. Karin Bogart, 'Employment Practices in Japan: the Social and Industrial Background', in EC Commission (ed.), *Working the Japanese Way: Japanese Employment Practices at Home and in Europe* (Brussels, 1989) pp. 5–25, esp p. 8.
4. JETRO, *Japanese Corporate Decision Making*, Business Information Series 9 (Tokyo, 1982) p. 10.
5. *Japan Times*, 11–16 April 1979.
6. Ken Moroi, 'Designing a Management System for the Next Century', *Economic Eye*, Spring 1991, pp. 29–31.
7. Provided by Mitsui Bussan, 1990.
8. Provided by Nissan Motor Co., 1990.
9. Provided by Tokyo Electric Power Co., 1990.
10. Provided by Keidanren, 1990.
11. Provided by Nikkeiren, 1990.
12. Source: *Nikkei Who's Who*.
13. Source: Teikoku Data Bank.
14. Moroi, 'Designing a Management System', p. 30.
15. *Nihon Keizai Shimbun*, 5 July 1987.
16. *Forbes*, 22 July 1991.
17. Nikkei Venture Survey, quoted in *Japan Economic Journal*, 20 Oct. 1988.
18. *Japan Times*, 30 Nov. 1989.
19. *Mainichi Shimbun*, 1 May 1991.
20. *Wall Street Journal*, 21 May 1990.

21. Matthews Masayuki Hamabata, *Crested Kimono: Power and Love in the Japanese Business Family* (Ithaca: Cornell University Press, 1990).
22. Text supplied by Toyota Motor Corporation, 1991.
23. Jon Woronoff, 'Fading Role of Entrepreneurs', *Oriental Economist*, June 1985, pp. 35–7, esp. p. 36.
24. See, for instance, Konosuke Matsushita, *Quest for Prosperity* (Tokyo: PHP Institute, 1989); Akio Morita, *Made in Japan* (London: Fontana/Collins, 1989).
25. *The Economist*, 16 Jan. 1988.
26. *Asahi Evening News*, 6 July 1991.
27. *Asahi Shimbun*, 3 Jan. 1991.

Chapter 11: Elite Mobility and Elite Rule

1. Robert D. Putnam, *The Comparative Study of Political Elites* (Englewood Cliffs, N.J.: Prentice-Hall, 1976) pp. 3–4.
2. *International Herald Tribune*, 11 April 1988.
3. John A. Cicco Jr, 'Japan's Administrative Elite: Criteria for Membership', *International Review of Administrative Sciences*, vol. 41 (1975) pp. 179–84, esp. p. 383.
4. Haru Matsukata Reischauer, *Samurai and Silk* (Tokyo: Charles E. Tuttle, 1986) p. 263.
5. Karl F. Zahl, 'The Social Structure of the Political Elite in Postwar Japan', *Transactions of the Asiatic Society of Japan*, vol. 11 (1973) pp. 128–44.
6. Peter P. Cheng, 'Japanese Cabinets, 1885–1973: an Elite Analysis', *Asian Survey*, vol. 14 (1974) pp. 1055–71.
7. *Far Eastern Economic Review*, 10 Aug. 1989, p. 22.
8. *Mainichi Shimbun*, 2 April 1990.

Bibliography

Abegglen, James C. and George Stalk Jr, *Kaisha: The Japanese Corporation* (Tokyo: Charles E. Tuttle, 1988).

Alletzhauser, Al, *The House of Nomura* (London: Bloomsbury, 1990).

Allinson, Gary D., 'Public Servants and Public Interests in Contemporary Japan', *Asian Survey*, vol. 20 (1980) pp. 1048–68.

Altuzarra, Philippe, 'A First-hand Inside View of Japan's Civil Service', *The Financial Times*, 11 July 1988.

Baldwin, Frank, 'The Kokumin Kyokai', *Japan Interpreter*, vol. 10 (1975) pp. 66–78.

Bärwald, Hans H., *Japan's Parliament* (London: Cambridge University Press, 1974).

Beasley, W. G., *The Meiji Restauration* (Stanford, Cal.: Stanford University Press, 1971).

Campbell, John Creighton, *Contemporary Japanese Budget Politics* (Berkeley, Cal.: University of California Press, 1977).

Castles, F. G., D. J. Murray and D. C. Potter (eds), *Decisions, Organizations and Society* (Harmondsworth, Middx: Penguin, 1975).

Cheng, Peter P., 'Japanese Cabinets, 1885–1973: an Elite Analysis', *Asian Survey*, vol. 14 (1974) pp. 1055–71.

Cicco, John A. Jr, 'Japan's Administrative Elite: Criteria for Membership', *International Review of Administrative Sciences*, vol. 41 (1975) pp. 379–84.

Commission of the European Communities, *Working the Japanese Way: Japanese Employment Practices at Home and in Europe* (Brussels: European Service Network, 1989).

Curtis, Gerald L., *Election Campaigning, Japanese Style* (New York: Columbia University Press, 1971).

Deutsche Industrie- und Handelskammer (ed.), *Personalwesen in Japan* (Tokyo: DIHK, 1991).

Dodwell Marketing Consultants, *Industrial Groupings in Japan*, rev. edn (Tokyo: Dodwell, 1984).

Dower, John W., *Empire and Afterwards: Yoshida Shigeru and the Japanese Experience, 1878–1954* (Cambridge, Mass.: Harvard University Press, 1979).

Economic Planning Agency, *An Affluent Society Amenable to All People*, Annual Report on the National Life for Fiscal 1990 (Tokyo: Government Publications Service Center, 1990).

Eli, Max, *Japans Wirtschaft im Griff der Konglomerate – Verbandsgruppen, Banken, Universalhandelshäuser* (Frankfurt am Main: Frankfurter Allgemeine, 1988).

Eto, Shinkichi, 'Foreign Policy Formation in Japan', *Japan Interpreter*, vol. 10 (1976) pp. 251–66.

Foreign Press Center, *The Diet, Elections and Political Parties* (Tokyo: Foreign Press Center, 1990).

Frank, Isaiah (ed.), *The Japanese Economy in International Perspective* (Baltimore, Md: Johns Hopkins University Press, 1975).

Fruin, Mark W., *Kikkoman: Company, Clan and Community* (Cambridge, Mass.: Harvard University Press, 1983).

Fukui, Haruhiro, *Party in Power* (Berkeley, Cal.: University of California Press, 1970).

Futatsugi, Yusaku, 'What Share Crossholdings Mean for Corporate Management', *Economic Eye*, Spring 1990, pp. 17–19.

Hamabata, Matthews M., *Crested Kimono: Power and Love in the Japanese Business Family* (Ithaca, N. Y.: Cornell University Press, 1990).

Hellmann, Donald C., *Japanese Foreign Policy and Domestic Politics* (Berkeley, Cal.: University of California Press, 1969).

Herold, Renate (ed.), *Das Industrieunternehmen in Japan* (Berlin: Erich Schmidt Verlag, 1986).

Imai, Kenichi, 'The Legitimacy of Japan's Corporate Groups', *Economic Eye*, Autumn 1990, pp. 16–21.

Institute of Administrative Management, *The Administrative Management and Reform in Japan* (Tokyo: Institute of Administrative Management, 1987).

Ishii, Ryosuke, *A History of Political Institutions in Japan* (Tokyo: University of Tokyo Press, 1980).

Ito, Masaya, *Jiminto: Senkokushi* (The LDP: Postwar National History) (Tokyo: Asahi Shimbunsha, 1985).

Iyasu, Tadashi, *Jiminto* (The LDP) (Tokyo: Kodansha, 1984).

Japan Company Handbook, First Section/Second Section (Tokyo: Toyo Keizai Inc., 1991).

Japan Foreign Trade Council, *The Sogo Shosha: What They Are and How They Can Work for You* (Tokyo: JFTC, undated).

JETRO, *Japanese Corporate Decision Making*, Business Information Series no. 9 (Tokyo: JETRO, 1982).

JETRO, *Japanese Corporate Personnel Management*, Business Information Series no. 10 (Tokyo: JETRO, 1982).

Jinjiin (National Personnel Authority), *Komuin Hakusho* (White Paper on Civil Servants) (Tokyo: Ogurasho Ensatsukyoko, 1988).

Johnson, Chalmers, *MITI and the Japanese Miracle* (Stanford, Cal.: Stanford University Press, 1982).

Kan, Ori, *Political Parties and Elections in Postwar Japan* (Tokyo: Japan Foundation, 1982).

Kaplan, David E. and Alec Dubro, *Yakuza: The Explosive Account of Japan's Criminal Underworld* (London: Macdonald, 1987).

Kaplan, Eugene J., *Japan: The Government–Business Relationship* (Washington, D.C.: US Department of Commerce, 1972).

Kawakita, Takao, *Okurasho* (MOF) (Tokyo: Kodansha, 1989).

Keizai Koho Center (ed.), *Economic Views from Japan* (Tokyo: KKC, 1986).

Kishimoto, Koichi, *Politics in Modern Japan* (Tokyo: Japan Echo Inc., 1982).

Koh, B. C., *Japan's Administrative Elite* (Berkeley, Cal.: University of California Press, 1989).

Kojima, Kiyushi and Terutomo Ozawa, *Japan's General Trading Companies* (Paris: OECD Development Center Studies, 1984).

Lawrence, Robert Z., 'Efficient or Exclusionist?: the Import Behavior of Japan's Corporate Groups', *Brookings Paper on Economic Activity* no. 1 (1991).

Management and Co-ordination Agency, *Organization of the Government of Japan* (Tokyo: Prime Minister's Office, 1990).

Marubeni, *The Unique World of the Sogo Shosha* (Tokyo: Marubeni Corporation, 1978).

Masumi, Junnosuke, *Gendai Seiji. 1955nen Igo* (Contemporary Politics: After 1955) (Tokyo: Tokyo Daigaku Shuppankai, 1987).

Matsukata Reischauer, Haru, *Samurai and Silk* (Tokyo: Charles E. Tuttle, 1988).

Mills, C. Wright, *The Power Elite* (New York: Oxford University Press, 1956).

Mills, C. Wright, *The Sociological Imagination* (1959; London: Oxford University Press, 1977).

Ministry of Foreign Affairs, *Yasuhiro Nakasone* (Tokyo: Official Government Bulletin, 1986).

Mishima, Yasuo, *The Mitsubishi* (Greenwich, Conn.: JAI Press, 1989).

MITI Handbook 1990 (Tokyo: Japan Trade and Industry Publicity Inc., 1990).

Moore, Gwen and Richard D. Alba, *Class and Prestige Origins in the American Elite*, EUI Working Paper no. 40 (San Domenico di Fiesole (FI): European University Institute, 1982).

Moroi, Ken, 'Designing a Management System for the Next Century', *Economic Eye*, Spring 1991, pp. 29–31.

Murakami, Hyoe and Johannes Hirschmeier (eds), *Politics and Economics in Contemporary Japan* (Tokyo: Japan Culture Institute, 1979).

Murobushi, Tetsuro, *Kokyukanryo* (Elite Civil Servants) (Tokyo: Kodansha, 1987).

Nakamura, Takefusa, *Economic Development of Modern Japan* (Tokyo: Ministry of Foreign Affairs, 1985).

Nakane, Chie, *Japanese Society* (Harmondsworth, Middx: Penguin, 1973).

Nakazawa, Momoko, *Who's Who in Japanese Government* (Tokyo: International Culture Association, 1990).

National Personnel Authority, *Outline of National Personnel Authority and Civil Service System* (Tokyo,1988).

Nikkeiren, *Current Labour Economy in Japan* (Tokyo: Nikkeiren, 1990).

Nikkeiren, *Towards South Growth*, Report of the Committee for the Study of Labour Questions (Tokyo: Nikkeiren, 1990).

Nukuzawa, Kazuo, *Implications of Japan's Emerging Service Economy*, Keidanren Paper no. 8, 1980.

Okazawa, Norio, *Seito* (Parties) (Tokyo: Tokyo Daigaku Shuppankai, 1988).

Okimoto, Daniel I. and Thomas P. Rohlen (eds), *Inside the Japanese System* (Stanford, Cal.: Stanford University Press, 1988).

Oyama, Yoichi (ed.), *Kyodai Kigyo to Rodosha: Toyota no Jirei* (Labour and the Large Enterprise: A Study of the Toyota Motor Company) (Tokyo: Ochanomizu Shobo, 1985).

Ozawa, Terumoto, *Multinationalism, Japanese Style* (Princeton, N. J.: Princeton University Press, 1979).

Pape, Wolfgang, *Gyoseishido und das Anti-Monopol-Gesetz in Japan* (Cologne: Carl Heymanns Verlag, 1980).

Park, Yung H., *Bureaucrats and Ministers in Contemporary Japanese Government* (Berkeley, Cal.: University of California Press, 1986).

Putnam, Robert D., *The Comparative Study of Political Elites* (Englewood Cliffs, N. J.: Prentice-Hall, 1976).

Reddies, Bernd, *Der Recruit Skandal in Japan* (Tokyo: OAG Aktuell, 1989).

Roberts, John G., *Mitsui: Three Centuries of Japanese Business*, 2nd edn (New York: Weatherhill, 1989).

Roster of Members of the Japanese National Diet (Tokyo: Japan Times, 1990).

Rothacher, Albrecht, 'On Effects and Noneffects of Military Socialization', *Armed Forces and Society*, vol. 6 (1980) pp. 332–4.

Rothacher, Albrecht, 'Der Trilateralismus als internationales Politikmanagement', *Aus Politik und Zeitgeschichte*, B6/1981, pp. 25–30.

Rothacher, Albrecht, *Economic Diplomacy between the European Community and Japan, 1959–1981* (Aldershot, Hants.: Gower, 1983).

Rothacher, Albrecht, 'Das japanische Unternehmen', in Sepp Linhart (ed.), *40 Jahre Modernes Japan* (Vienna: Literas Universitätsverlag, 1986) pp. 93–103.

Rothacher, Albrecht, *Japan's Agro-food Sector: The Politics and Economics of Excess Protection* (London: Macmillan, 1989).

Rothacher, Albrecht, 'The Difficulties of Donor Aid Cooperation: the Case of Japan and the European Community', in United Nations University (ed.), *Development and ODA*, Japan–ASEAN Forum, November 1990 (Tokyo: UNU, 1991) pp. 170–2.

Rothacher, Albrecht and Malcolm Colling, 'The Community's Top Management: a Meritocracy in the Making', *Courrier du personnel* (EC Commission), no. 489, October 1987, pp. 10–25.

Sasago, Katuya, *Sejishigin* (Political Money) (Tokyo: Shakai Shisosha, 1988).

Sato, Seizaburo, *et al.*, *Postwar Politician: The Life of Former Prime Minister Masayoshi Ohira* (Tokyo: Kodansha, 1990).

Scalapino, Robert A. (ed.), *The Foreign Policy of Modern Japan* (Berkeley Cal.: University of California Press, 1977).

Schmidt, Helmut, *Menschen und Mächte* (Berlin: Siedler Verlag, 1987).

Seikai, Kancho, Jinjiroku (Personal Records of the Political World and Government Administration) (Tokyo: Toyo Keizai Shimposha, 1989).

Seikan Yoran (Handbook on Public Officials) (Tokyo: Seisakujiyosha, 1990).

Shibagaki, Kazuo, 'Dissolution of *Zaibatsu* and Deconcentration of Economic Power', *Annals of the Institute of Social Science* (University of Tokyo), vol. 20 (1979) pp. 1–60.

Shibata, Tokue (ed.), *Public Finance in Japan* (Tokyo: University of Tokyo Press, 1986).

Small and Medium Enterprise Agency, MITI, *White Paper on Small and Medium Enterprises in Japan* (Tokyo: MITI, 1990).

Stockman, Frans N., Rolf Ziegler and John Scott (eds), *Networks of Corporate Power: A Comparative Analysis of Ten Countries* (Cambridge: Polity Press, 1985).

Thayer, Nathaniel, *How the Conservatives Rule Japan* (Princeton, N. J.: Princeton University Press, 1973).

Tsuji, Kiyoaki (ed.), *Public Administration in Japan* (Tokyo: Tokyo University Press, 1984).

Van Wolferen, Karel, *The Enigma of Japanese Power* (London: Macmillan, 1989).

Vogel, Ezra F. (ed.), *Modern Japanese Organization and Decision Making* (Tokyo: Charles E. Tuttle, 1979).

Watanuki, Joji, *Politics in Postwar Japanese Society* (Tokyo: University of Tokyo Press, 1977).

Who's Who in Japan (Tokyo: International Cultural Center, 1987).

Woronoff, Jon, 'Fading Role of Entrepreneurs', *Oriental Economist*, June 1985, pp. 35–7.

Yanaga, Chitoshi, *Big Business in Japanese Politics* (New Haven, Conn.: Yale University Press, 1968).

Yomiuri Chosa Kenkyuhonbusho, *Nihon no Kokkai* (Japan's Parliament) (Tokyo: Yomiuri Shimbun-sha, 1988).

Zahl, Karl F., 'The Social Structure of the Political Elite in Postwar Japan', *Transactions of the Asiatic Society of Japan*, vol. 11 (1973) pp. 128–46.

Index

293